I0155687

Printed in the USA

# Macedonian Language:

## 101 Macedonian Verbs

By Kalina Nikolov

## Contents

# Introduction to Macedonian verbs

The Macedonian verb is different from the other parts of speech in the Macedonian language both in form and meaning. The Macedonian verbs indicate action, condition or state and they are connected with the person that is doing the action.

The verb is the most complicated structure of the Macedonian language.

The verbs of the Macedonian language can be divided in different groups.

1. **Division of the verbs according to person, gender and number**
    a. *Person* - indicates a participant in the conversation
    Verbs agree with personal pronouns. There are three persons in singular and plural.
    1st person specifies the person who is talking;
    2nd person specifies the person who is addressed;
    3rd person specifies person in general, usually neither speaker nor addressee.
    b. *Number* - verbs have singular and plural.
    c. *Gender* - Macedonian verbs do not have gender, except for some impersonal verb forms.

2. **Division of the verbs according to their ending**
    Verbs can be divided into groups according to which vowel they end in 3rd person singular in present tense:
    a. *-a group*
    E.g. чит**а** - reads; игр**а** - plays; глед**а**- sees
    b. *-i group*
    E.g. од**и** - walks; нос**и** - carries; сто**и**- stands
    c. *-e group*
    E.g. спи**е** - sleeps; пи**е** - drinks; ми**е**- washes

**3. Division of the verbs according to transitivity**

a. *Transitive verbs* - their action "passes onto" the object, i.e. it completely encloses it

E.g. Тој носи***вода***. - He is carrying***water***.

b. *Intransitive verbs* - their action does not "pass onto" anything

E.g. Тој оди. - He is walking.

c. *Reflexive verbs* - their action "passes onto" the person doing the action, but not always because there are a lot of verbs that are part of the group of verbs which are preceded by the short form of the reflective pronoun „себе си".

E.g. Тој **се**смее. - He is laughing.

**4. Division of the verbs according to aspect**

Verbs are used to express an action that can last longer or end at the same moment. According to this we differentiate:

a. *Progressiveverbs* - these verbs denote an action which still lasts, which has not finished yet.

i. *Progressiveverbs* - these denote an action which lasts without being interrupted (we don't know when the action started or when it finished)

E.g. Тој **чита**. - He is **reading**.

ii. *Reflexiveverbs* - these denote a series of several progressive actions which are done one after another

E.g. Тој **прелистува** една книга. - He is **turning** the pages of a book.

b. *Perfective verbs* - these verbs denote a completed action that is viewed as a whole. The action might have happened

*i. For a moment*

E.g. Тој **чукна** на вратата. - He **knocked** on the door.

They can also denote:

*ii. The beginning of the action*

E.g. Тој **заигра**. - He **starteddancing**.

*iii. The end of the action*

E.g. Тој ја **прочита** книгата. - He **finishedreading** the book.

5. **Division of the verbs according to voice**

Voice describes the relationship between the action that the verb expresses and the subject.

a. *Active voice* - the subject is the one that performs the action

E.g. **Петре** чита книга. - **Pete** is reading a book.

b. *Passive voice* - the subject does not perform the action, but the object does or the person who is affected by this action. Respectively, the subject becomes the object, and the object becomes the subject.

E.g. **Книгата** беше читана од Петре. - **The book** was being read by Pete.

* In Macedonian the passive voice is rarely used.

6. **Division of the verbs according to mood**

Mood allows us to express our attitude toward what we are speaking

a. *Declarative mood* - this mood expresses a real attitude

E.g. Петре чита книга. - Pete is reading a book.

b. *Imperative mood* - this mood expresses imperative attitude.

E.g. Петре, донеси ми ја книгата! - Pete, go get me the book!

c. *Potential mood* - this mood expresses the possibility of an action to happen due to a given condition

E.g. Кога би имал време, Петре би ја прочитај книгата. - If he had the time, Pete would read the book.

7. **Division of the verbs according to tense**

Tense expresses the time relationships between the performance of the verb action to the moment of speaking: present, past or future.

In Macedonian we differentiate between the following tenses:

a. *Present Tense (Сегашно време)*

b. *Past (simple and continuous) (Минато определено свршено и несвршено време)*

c. *Present perfect (simple and continuous) (Минато неопределено свршено и несвршено време)*

d. *Past perfect (Предминато време)*
e. *Future simple (Идно време)*
f. *Used to + infinitive, would + infinitive (Минато-идно време)*
g. *Future perfect-in-the-past tense (Идно прекажано време)*

8. **Division of the verbs according to verb forms**

Depending on whether we change only the verb (with suffixes) or there is some other word included in the verb form apart from the base verb we differentiate:

a. *Simple verb forms*
b. *Complex verb forms*

## Introduction to Macedonian tenses

Macedonian tenses are included in the 7th division of the verbs, namely the division of the verbs according to verb forms. So that is why the Macedonian tenses can be divided into simple verb forms and complex verb forms.

1. **Simple Verb Forms**

a. *Present Simple Tense*

The present tense in Macedonian indicates a verb action that is happening at the moment of speaking. It can be formed with progressive verbs.

It is used to denote:

1. Proverbially use

E.g. Железото се кове дури е жешко. - Iron is forged while it is hot.

1. Description or qualification

E.g. Марко е добар учител. - Marco is a good teacher.

2. Past

E.g. Првата светска војна трае од 1914-1918. - The first world war lasts from 1914-1918.

3. Future

E.g. Утре летам за Америка. - Tomorrow I fly to America.

4. Simultaneousness

E.g. Почнува да станува жешко. - It is starting to become hot.

| Personal endings for Present Tense | | |
|---|---|---|
| *Person* | *Singular* | *Plural* |
| 1st person | - м | - ме |
| 2nd person | -ш | - те |
| 3rd person | - | -ат |

Examples:

| | **Оди (to walk)** | | **Гледа (to see)** | |
|---|---|---|---|---|
| *Person* | *Singular* | *Plural* | *Singular* | *Plural* |
| 1st person | Од-а-**м** | Од-и-**ме** | Глед-а-**м** | Глед-а-**ме** |
| 2nd person | Од-и-**ш** | Од-и-**те** | Глед-а-**ш** | Глед-а-**те** |
| 3rd person | Од-и | Од-**ат** | Глед-а | Глед-а-**ат** |

b. *Past Simple Tense*

The past simple tense indicates a verb action that has been completed in the past in the presence of the person talking. It is formed with perfective verbs.

It can be used to denote:

1. Timelessness

E.g. Се наполнија бочвите, дојдоа гостите. - The bundles are filled, the guests came.

2. Condition

E.g. Ги напишав ли сите домашни порано, ќе ме пуштат да излезам. - If I were to do all my homework earlier, I will have the permission to go out.

3. Future

E.g. Дојдете да јадеме нешто оти умревме од глад. - Let's eat something because we died of hunger.

| **Personal endings for Past Simple Tense** | | |
|---|---|---|
| *Person* | *Singular* | *Plural* |
| 1st person | - в | - вме |
| 2nd person | - | - вте |
| 3rd person | - | - а |

Examples:

| | **тропне(to knock)** | | **дознае(to find out)** | |
|---|---|---|---|---|
| *Person* | *Singular* | *Plural* | *Singular* | *Plural* |
| 1st person | Тропн-а-**в** | Тропн-а-**вме** | Дозн-а-**в** | Дозн-а-**вме** |
| 2nd person | Тропн-а | Тропн-а-**вте** | Дозн-а | Дозн-а-**вте** |
| 3rd person | Тропн-а | Тропн-а-**а** | Дозн-а | Дозн-а-**а** |

c. *Past Continuous Tense*

The past continuous tense indicates a verb action which has been executed in the past in the presence of the person speaking. It is formed with progressive verbs.

It used to denote:

1. Mild demand

E.g. Да ми донесеше една чаша вода, не ќе беше лошо. - If you were bringing me a glass of water, that would be nice.

2. Condition

E.g. Ако останеше со мене, немаше да чекаш на студот сама. - If you had stayed with me, you wouldn't have waited in the cold alone.

3. Readiness

E.g. Сигурно ќе дојдев да знаев. - I would have come for sure if I knew.

| **Personal endings for Past Continuous Tense** | | |
|---|---|---|
| *Person* | *Singular* | *Plural* |
| 1st person | - в | - вме |
| 2nd person | - ше | - вте |
| 3rd person | - ше | - а |

Examples:

| | **вика(to yell)** | | **носи(to carry)** | |
|---|---|---|---|---|
| *Person* | *Singular* | *Plural* | *Singular* | *Plural* |
| 1st person | Вик-а-**в** | Вик-а-**вме** | Нос-е-**в** | Нос-е-**вме** |
| 2nd person | Вик-а-**ше** | Вик-а-**вте** | Нос-е-**ше** | Нос-е-**вте** |
| 3rd person | Вик-а-**ше** | Вик-а-**а** | Нос-е-**ше** | Нос-е-**а** |

2. **Complex verb forms**
    a. *Present Perfect Simple Tense*

The present perfect simple tense indicates a verb action which is completing or has been completed in the past, without knowing the exact time of completion. It is formed with perfective verbs.

It is used to denote:

1. Demand

E.g. Немој да си пиел акохол вечерва. - Do not dare drink alcohol tonight.

2. Future

E.g. Да излеземе дури не се вратил тој. - Let's go out before he has returned back.

3. Observation, remark

E.g. Многу си се здебелила. - You have gained so much weight.

4. Assumption

E.g. Тој веќе сигурно се вратил дома. - He must have returned home by now.

| Personal endings for Present Perfect Simple Tense | | |
|---|---|---|
| *Person* | *Singular* | *Plural* |
| 1st person | Сум + -л(а) | Сме + -ле |
| 2nd person | Си + -л(а) | Сте + -ле |
| 3rd person | -л(а)(о) | -ле |

Examples:

| | **пие (to drink)** | | **Расте (to grow)** | |
|---|---|---|---|---|
| *Person* | *Singular* | *Plural* | *Singular* | *Plural* |
| 1st person | Сум пие-**л(а)** | Сме пие-**ле** | Сум расте-**л** | Сме расте-**ле** |
| 2nd person | Си пие-**л(а)** | Сте пие-**ле** | Си расте-**л** | Сте расте-**ле** |
| 3rd person | пие-**л(а)** | пие-**ле** | расте-**л(а)** | расте-**ле** |

*b. Present Perfect Continuous Tense*

This tense indicates the same thing as present perfect simple tense. The only difference is that it is formed with progressive verbs. It has the same personal endings as well.

E.g. Никогаш не изгледал повесел. - He has never looked so cheerful.

Example:

| | **порасна(grew up)** | | **прочита (read)** | |
|---|---|---|---|---|
| *Person* | *Singular* | *Plural* | *Singular* | *Plural* |
| 1st person | Сум порасна-**л(а)** | Сме порасна-**ле** | Сум прочита-**л** | Сме прочита-**ле** |
| 2nd person | Си порасна-**л(а)** | Сте порасна-**ле** | Си прочита-**л** | Сте прочита-**ле** |

| | | | | |
|---|---|---|---|---|
| 3rd person | порасна-**л(а)** | порасна-**ле** | прочита-**л(а)** | прочита-**ле** |

*b. Past Perfect Simple Tense*

The past perfect simple tense indicates an action that had been completed before another past action. It is usually formed with perfective verbs.

E.g. Кога стигнав филмот веќе беше почнат. - When I arrived the movie had already started.

| **Personal endings for Past Perfect Simple Tense** | | |
|---|---|---|
| *Person* | *Singular* | *Plural* |
| 1st person | Бев + -л(а) | Бевме + -ле |
| 2nd person | Беше + -л(а) | Бевте + -ле |
| 3rd person | Беше + -л(а)(о) | Беа + -ле |

Example:

| | **носи(to carry)** | | **гледа (to watch)** | |
|---|---|---|---|---|
| *Person* | *Singular* | *Plural* | *Singular* | *Plural* |
| 1st person | Бев носе-**л(а)** | Бевме носе-**ле** | Бев гледа-**л** | Бевме гледа-**ле** |
| 2nd person | Беше носе-**л(а)** | Бевте носе-**ле** | Беше гледа-**л** | Бевте гледа-**ле** |
| 3rd person | Беше носе-**л(а)** | Беа носе-**ле** | Беше гледа-**л(а)** | Беа гледа-**ле** |

*d. Future Simple Tense*

The future simple tense indicates an action which will be completing or will be completed in the future. It is formed with progressive and perfective verbs.

It is used to denote:

a. Demand

E.g. Ќе ми донесеш вода сакал или не. - You will bring me water no matter what.

b. Timelessness

E.g. Кој чита, тој ќе знае. - Who read, he will know.

c. Possibility

E.g. Ќе кажам нешто што не треба. - I will say something I am not supposed to.

d. Assumption

E.g. Колку гола ќе дадат на натпреварот? - Може ќе има само еден. - How many goal will there be in the match? - It is possible there will be only one.

e. Repetitiveness

E.g. Ќе дојде, ќе ме бакне и ќе си отиде. - He will come, he will kiss me and he will leave.

| **Personal endings for Future Simple Tense** | | |
|---|---|---|
| *Person* | *Singular* | *Plural* |
| 1st person | Ќе + -м | Ќе + -ме |
| 2nd person | Ќе + -ш | Ќе + -те |
| 3rd person | Ќе + - | Ќе + -ат |

Example:

| | **игра(toplay)** | | **пее (to sing)** | |
|---|---|---|---|---|
| *Person* | *Singular* | *Plural* | *Singular* | *Plural* |
| 1st person | Ќе игра-**м** | Ќе игра-**ме** | Ќе пеа-**м** | Ќе пее-**ме** |
| 2nd person | Ќе игра-**ш** | Ќе игра-**те** | Ќе пее-**ш** | Ќе пее-**те** |
| 3rd person | Ќе игра | Ќе игра-**ат** | Ќе пее | Ќе пе-**ат** |

c. Used to + infinitive or would + infinitive

This construction forms a tense in Macedonian that is used to indicate a verb action which is future when regarded to some other past event. It is formed with progressive and perfective verbs.

E.g. Ќе го гледав филмот да не заспиев. - I would see the movie if I didn't fall asleep.

| Personal endings for used to + infinitive or would + infinitive | | |
|---|---|---|
| *Person* | *Singular* | *Plural* |
| 1st person | Ќе + -в | Ќе + -вме |
| 2nd person | Ќе + -ше | Ќе + -вте |
| 3rd person | Ќе + -ше | Ќе + -аа |

Example:

| | **вика(toyell)** | |
|---|---|---|
| *Person* | *Singular* | *Plural* |
| 1st person | Ќе вика-**в** | Ќе вика-**вме** |
| 2nd person | Ќе вика-**ше** | Ќе вика-**вте** |
| 3rd person | Ќе вика-**ше** | Ќе вика-**аа** |

d. Future perfect-in-the-past tense

This tense indicates future or future-in-the-past action that we can vouch for ourselves. It is formed with progressive and perfective verbs.

E.g. Ќе го гледал филмот да не заспал. - He would have seen the movie if he hadn't fallen asleep.

| Personal endings for future perfect-in-the-past tense | | |
|---|---|---|
| *Person* | *Singular* | *Plural* |
| 1st person | Ќе + сум + -л(а) | Ќе + сме + -ле |
| 2nd person | Ќе + си + -л(а) | Ќе + сте + -ле |

| | | |
|---|---|---|
| 3rd person | Ќе + -л(а)(о) | Ќе + -ле |

Example:

| | **чита(toread)** | |
|---|---|---|
| *Person* | *Singular* | *Plural* |
| 1st person | Ќе сум чита-**л(а)** | Ќе сме чита-**ле** |
| 2nd person | Ќе си чита-**л(а)** | Ќе сте чита-**ле** |
| 3rd person | Ќе чита-**л(а)** | Ќе чита-**ле** |

- Keep in mind that the Macedonian tenses do not correspond with only one tense in the English language. They can correspond with different tenses, as you can see from the examples, but we have tried to write the ones that correspond the most.

### *To accept - Прифаќа/Прифати*

| | | |
|---|---|---|
| *Infinitive* | To accept | Прифаќа<br>Prifakja |

| Present Simple Tense | | |
|---|---|---|
| *Person* | *Singular* | *Plural* |
| 1st person | I accept -<br>Јас прифаќам<br>*Jas prifakjam* | We accept -<br>Ние прифаќаме<br>*Nie prifakjame* |
| 2nd person | You accept -<br>Ти прифаќаш<br>*Ti prifakjash* | You accept -<br>Вие прифаќате<br>*Vie prifakjate* |
| 3rd person | He/She/It accepts -<br>Тој/Таа/Тоа прифаќа<br>*Toj/Taa/Toa prifakja* | They accept -<br>Тие прифаќаат<br>*Tie prifakjaat* |

| Past Simple Tense | | |
|---|---|---|
| *Person* | *Singular* | *Plural* |
| 1st person | I accepted -<br>Јас прифатив<br>*Jas prifativ* | We accepted -<br>Ние прифативме<br>*Nie prifativme* |
| 2nd person | You accepted-<br>Ти прифати<br>*Ti prifati* | You accepted -<br>Вие прифативте<br>*Vie prifativte* |
| 3rd person | He/She/It accepted -<br>Тој/Таа/Тоа прифати<br>*Toj/Taa/Toa prifati* | They accepted -<br>Тие прифатија<br>*Tie prifatija* |

| Past Continuous Tense | | |
|---|---|---|
| *Person* | *Singular* | *Plural* |
| 1st person | I was accepting -<br>Јас прифаќав<br>*Jas prifakjav* | We were accepting -<br>Ние прифаќавме<br>*Nie prifakjavme* |
| 2nd person | You were accepting -<br>Ти прифаќаше<br>*Ti prifakjashe* | You were accepting -<br>Вие прифаќавте<br>*Vie prifakjavte* |
| 3rd person | He/She/It was accepting -<br>Тој/Таа/Тоа прифаќаше<br>*Toj/Taa/Toa prifakjashe* | They were accepting -<br>Тие прифаќаа<br>*Tie prifakjaa* |

| Present Perfect Simple Tense | | |
|---|---|---|
| *Person* | *Singular* | *Plural* |
| 1st person | I have accepted -<br>Јас сум прифатил(а)<br>*Jas sum prifatil(a)* | We have accepted -<br>Ние сме прифатиле<br>*Nie sme prifatile* |
| 2nd person | You have accepted -<br>Ти си прифатил(а) | You have accepted -<br>Вие сте прифатиле |

| | | |
|---|---|---|
| | *Ti si prifatil(a)* | *Vie ste prifatile* |
| 3rd person | He/She/It has accepted -<br>Тој/Таа/Тоа прифатил(а)(о)<br>*Toj/Taa/Toa prifatil(a)(o)* | They have accepted -<br>Тие прифатиле<br>*Tie prifatile* |

| Present Perfect Continuous Tense | | |
|---|---|---|
| *Person* | *Singular* | *Plural* |
| 1st person | I have been accepting -<br>Јас сум прифаќал(а)<br>Jas sum prifakjal(a) | We have been accepting -<br>Ние сме прифаќале<br>Niesme prifakjale |
| 2nd person | You have been accepting -<br>Ти си прифаќал(а)<br>Ti si prifakajl(a) | You have been accepting -<br>Вие сте прифаќале<br>Vie steprifakjale |
| 3rd person | He/She/It has been accepting-<br>Тој/Таа/Тоа прифаќал(а)(о)<br>*Toj/Taa/Toa prifakjal(a)(o)* | They have accepting -<br>Тие прифаќале<br>*Tie prifakjale* |

| Past Perfect Simple Tense | | |
|---|---|---|
| *Person* | *Singular* | *Plural* |
| 1st person | I had accepted -<br>Јас бев прифатил(а)<br>*Jas bev prifatil(a)* | We had accepted -<br>Ние бевме прифатиле<br>*Nie bevme prifatile* |
| 2nd person | You had accepted -<br>Ти беше прифатил(а)<br>*Ti beshe prifatil(a)* | You had accepted -<br>Вие бевте прифатиле<br>*Vie bevte prifatile* |
| 3rd person | He/She/It had accepted -<br>Тој/Таа/Тоа беше прифатил(а)(о)<br>*Toj/Taa/Toa beshe prifatil(a)(o)* | They had accepted -<br>Тие беа прифатиле<br>*Tie bea prifatile* |

| Future Simple Tense | | |
|---|---|---|
| *Person* | *Singular* | *Plural* |
| 1st person | I will accept -<br>Јас ќе прифаќам/прифатам<br>*Jas kje prifakjam/prifatam* | We will accept -<br>Ние ќе прифаќаме/ прифатиме<br>*Nie kje prifakjame/prifatime* |
| 2nd person | You will accept -<br>Ти ќе прифаќаш/прифатиш<br>*Ti kje prifakjash/prifatish* | You will accept -<br>Вие ќеприфаќате/прифатите<br>*Vie kjeprifakjate/prifatite* |
| 3rd person | He/She/It will accept -<br>Тој/Таа/Тоа ќе прифаќа/прифати<br>*Toj/Taa/Toa kje prifakja/prifati* | They will accept -<br>Тие ќе прифаќаат/прифатат<br>*Tie kje prifakjaat/prifatat* |

| **used to + infinitive or would + infinitive** | | |
|---|---|---|
| *Person* | *Singular* | *Plural* |
| 1st person | I would accept -<br>Јас ќе пр**и**фаќав/пр**и**фатев<br>*Jas kje pr**i**fakjav/pr**i**fatev* | We would accept -<br>Ние ќе приф**а**ќавме/ приф**а**тевме<br>*Nie kje prif**a**kjavme/ prif**a**tevme* |
| 2nd person | You would accept -<br>Ти ќе приф**а**ќаше/приф**а**теше<br>*Ti kje prif**a**kjashe/prif**a**teshe* | You would accept -<br>Вие ќе приф**а**ќавте/приф**а**тевте<br>*Vie kjeprif**a**kjavte/prif**a**tevte* |
| 3rd person | He/She/It would accept -<br>Тој/Таа/Тоа ќе приф**а**ќаше/<br>приф**а**теше<br>*Toj/Taa/Toa kje prif**a**kjashe/<br>prif**a**teshe* | They would accept -<br>Тие ќе приф**а**ќаа/приф**а**теа<br>*Tie kje prif**a**kjaa/prif**a**tea* |

| **Personal endings for future perfect-in-the-past tense** | | |
|---|---|---|
| *Person* | *Singular* | *Plural* |
| 1st person | I would have accepted -<br>Јас ќе сум пр**и**фаќал/<br>пр**и**фатил(а)<br>*Jas kje sumpr**i**fakjal/pr**i**fatil(a)* | We would have accepted -<br>Ние ќе сме приф**а**ќале/<br>приф**а**тиле<br>*Nie kje smeprif**a**kjale/prif**a**tile* |
| 2nd person | You would have accepted -<br>Ти ќе сипр**и**фаќал/<br>пр**и**фатил(а)<br>*Ti kje sipr**i**fakjal/pr**i**fatil(a)* | You would have accepted -<br>Вие ќе степриф**а**ќале/<br>приф**а**тиле<br>*Vie kje steprif**a**kjale/prif**a**tile* |
| 3rd person | He/She/It would have accepted -<br>Тој/Таа/Тоа ќе пр**и**фаќал/<br>пр**и**фатил(а)(о)<br>*Toj/Taa/Toa kje pr**i**fakjal/<br>pr**i**fatil(a)(o)* | They would have accepted - Тие<br>ќе приф**а**ќале/приф**а**тиле<br>*Tie kje prif**a**kjale/prif**a**tile* |

**To admit - Признава/Призна**

| | | |
|---|---|---|
| *Infinitive* | To admit | Признава<br>Priznava |

| Present Simple Tense | | |
|---|---|---|
| *Person* | *Singular* | *Plural* |
| 1st person | I admit -<br>Јас признавам<br>*Jas priznavam* | We admit -<br>Ние признаваме<br>*Nie priznavame* |
| 2nd person | You admit -<br>Ти признаваш<br>*Ti priznavash* | You admit -<br>Вие признавате<br>*Vie priznavate* |
| 3rd person | He/She/It admits - Тој/Таа/Тоа признава<br>*Toj/Taa/Toa priznava* | They admit -<br>Тие признаваат<br>*Tie priznavaat* |

| Past Simple Tense | | |
|---|---|---|
| *Person* | *Singular* | *Plural* |
| 1st person | I admitted -<br>Јас признав<br>*Jas priznav* | We admitted -<br>Ние признавме<br>*Nie priznavme* |
| 2nd person | You admitted -<br>Ти призна<br>*Ti prizna* | You admitted -<br>Вие признавте<br>*Vie priznavte* |
| 3rd person | He/She/It admitted -<br>Тој/Таа/Тоа призна<br>*Toj/Taa/Toa prizna* | They admitted -<br>Тие признаа<br>*Tie priznaa* |

| Past Continuous Tense | | |
|---|---|---|
| *Person* | *Singular* | *Plural* |
| 1st person | I was admitting -<br>Јас признавав<br>*Jas priznavav* | We were admitting -<br>Ние признававме<br>*Nie priznavavme* |
| 2nd person | You were admitting-<br>Ти признаваше<br>*Ti priznavashe* | You were admitting -<br>Вие признававте<br>*Vie priznavavte* |
| 3rd person | He/She/It was admitting -<br>Тој/Таа/Тоа признаваше<br>*Toj/Taa/Toa priznavashe* | They were admitting -<br>Тие признаваа<br>*Tie priznavaa* |

| Present Perfect Simple Tense | | |
|---|---|---|
| *Person* | *Singular* | *Plural* |
| 1st person | I have admitted -<br>Јас сум признал(а)<br>*Jas sum priznal(a)* | We have admitted -<br>Ние сме признале<br>*Nie sme priznale* |
| 2nd person | You have admitted -<br>Ти си признал(а)<br>*Ti si priznal(a)* | You have admitted -<br>Вие сте признале<br>*Vie ste priznale* |

| | | |
|---|---|---|
| 3rd person | He/She/It has admitted -<br>Тој/Таа/Тоа пр**и**знал(а)(о)<br>*Toj/Taa/Toa pr**i**znal(a)(o)* | They have admitted -<br>Тие пр**и**знале<br>*Tie pr**i**znale* |

| Present Perfect Continuous Tense | | |
|---|---|---|
| *Person* | *Singular* | *Plural* |
| 1st person | I have been admitting -<br>Јас сум пр**и**знавал(а)<br>*Jas sum pr**i**znaval(a)* | We have been admitting -<br>Ние сме призн**а**вале<br>*Niesme prizn**a**vale* |
| 2nd person | You have been admitting -<br>Ти си пр**и**знавал(а)<br>*Ti si pr**i**znaval(a)* | You have been admitting -<br>Вие сте призн**а**вале<br>*Vie stepriz**n**avale* |
| 3rd person | He/She/It has been admitting -<br>Тој/Таа/Тоа пр**и**знавал(а)(о)<br>*Toj/Taa/Toa pr**i**znaval(a)(o)* | They have been admitting -<br>Тие призн**а**вале<br>*Tie prizn**a**vale* |

| Past Perfect Simple Tense | | |
|---|---|---|
| *Person* | *Singular* | *Plural* |
| 1st person | I had admitted -<br>Јас бев пр**и**знал(а)<br>*Jas bev pr**i**znal(a)* | We had admitted -<br>Ние бевме пр**и**знале<br>*Nie bevme pr**i**znale* |
| 2nd person | You had admitted -<br>Ти беше пр**и**знал(а)<br>*Ti beshe pr**i**znal(a)* | You had admitted -<br>Вие бевте пр**и**знале<br>*Vie bevte pr**i**znale* |
| 3rd person | He/She/It had admitted -<br>Тој/Таа/Тоа беше пр**и**знал(а)(о)<br>*Toj/Taa/Toa beshe pr**i**znal* | They had admitted<br>Тие беа пр**и**знале<br>*Tie bea pr**i**znale* |

| Future Simple Tense | | |
|---|---|---|
| *Person* | *Singular* | *Plural* |
| 1st person | I will admit -<br>Јас ќе пр**и**знавам/пр**и**знаам<br>*Jas kjepr**i**znavam/pr**i**znaam* | We will admit -<br>Ние ќе призн**а**ваме/призн**а**еме<br>*Nie kje prizn**a**vame/prizn**a**eme* |
| 2nd person | You will admit -<br>Ти ќе пр**и**знаваш/пр**и**знаеш<br>*Ti kje pr**i**znavash/pr**i**znaesh* | You will admit -<br>Вие ќе призн**а**вате/призн**а**ете<br>*Vie kje prizn**a**vate/prizn**a**ete* |
| 3rd person | He/She/It will admit -<br>Тој/Таа/Тоа ќе<br>пр**и**знава/пр**и**знае<br>*Toj/Taa/Toa kje pr**i**znava/pr**i**znae* | They will admit -<br>Тие ќе призн**а**ваат/пр**и**знаат<br>*Tie kje prizn**a**vaat/pr**i**znaat* |

| **used to + infinitive or would + infinitive** | | |
|---|---|---|
| *Person* | *Singular* | *Plural* |
| 1st person | I would admit - Јас ќепр**и**знавав/пр**и**знаев *Jas kjepr**i**znavav/pr**i**znaev* | We would admit - Ние ќе призн**а**вавме/призн**а**евме *Nie kje prizn**a**vavme/prizn**a**evme* |
| 2nd person | You would admit - Ти ќе призн**а**ваше/призн**а**еше *Ti kje prizn**a**vashe/prizn**a**eshe* | You would admit- Вие ќе призн**а**вавте/призн**а**евте *Vie kje prizn**a**vavte/prizn**a**evte* |
| 3rd person | He/She/It would admit - Тој/Таа/Тоа ќе призн**а**ваше/призн**а**еше *Toj/Taa/Toa kje prizn**a**vashe/prizn**a**eshe* | They would admit - Тие ќе призн**а**ваа/призн**а**еа *Tie kje prizn**a**vaa/prizn**a**ea* |

| **Personal endings for future perfect-in-the-past tense** | | |
|---|---|---|
| *Person* | *Singular* | *Plural* |
| 1st person | I would have admitted - Јас ќе сум пр**и**знавал/пр**и**знаел(а) *Jas kje sum pr**i**znaval/pr**i**znael(a)* | We would have admitted - Ние ќе сме призн**а**вале/призн**а**еле *Nie kje sme prizn**a**vale/prizn**a**ele* |
| 2nd person | You would have admitted - Ти ќе си пр**и**знавал/пр**и**знаел(а) *Tie kje si pr**i**znaval/pr**i**znael(a)* | You would have admitted - Вие ќе сте призн**а**вале/призн**а**еле *Vie kje ste prizn**a**vale/prizn**a**ele* |
| 3rd person | He/She/It would have admitted - Тој/Таа/Тоа ќе пр**и**знавал/пр**и**знаел(а)(о) *Toj/Taa/Toa kje pr**i**znaval/ pr**i**znael(a)(o)* | They would have admitted - Тие ќе призн**а**вале/призн**а**еа *Tie kje prizn**a**vale/prizn**a**ea* |

### *To answer - Одговара/Одговори*

| | | |
|---|---|---|
| *Infinitive* | To answer | Одг**о**вара<br>Odg**o**vara |

| Present Simple Tense | | |
|---|---|---|
| *Person* | *Singular* | *Plural* |
| 1st person | I answer -<br>Јас одг**о**варам<br>*Jas odg**o**varam* | We answer -<br>Ние одгов**а**раме<br>*Nie odgov**a**rame* |
| 2nd person | You answer -<br>Ти одг**о**вараш<br>*Ti odg**o**varash* | You answer -<br>Вие одгов**а**рате<br>*Vie odgov**a**rate* |
| 3rd person | He/She/It answers -<br>Тој/Таа/Тоа одг**о**вара<br>*Toj/Taa/Toa odg**o**vara* | They answer -<br>Тие одгов**а**раат<br>*Tie odgov**a**raat* |

| Past Simple Tense | | |
|---|---|---|
| *Person* | *Singular* | *Plural* |
| 1st person | I answered -<br>Јас одг**о**ворив<br>*Jas odg**o**voriv* | We answered -<br>Ние одгов**о**ривме<br>*Nie odgov**o**rivme* |
| 2nd person | You answered -<br>-Ти одг**о**вори<br>*Ti odg**o**vori* | You answered -<br>Вие одгов**о**ривте<br>*Vie odgov**o**rivte* |
| 3rd person | He/She/It answered -<br>- Тој/Таа/Тоа одг**о**вори<br>*Toj/Taa/Toa odg**o**vori* | They answered -<br>Тие одгов**о**рија<br>*Tie odgov**o**rija* |

| Past Continuous Tense | | |
|---|---|---|
| *Person* | *Singular* | *Plural* |
| 1st person | I was answering -<br>Јас одг**о**варав<br>*Jas odg**o**varav* | We were answering -<br>Ние одгов**а**равме<br>*Nie odgov**a**ravme* |
| 2nd person | You were answering -<br>Ти одгов**а**раше<br>*Ti odgov**a**rashe* | You were answering -<br>Вие одгов**а**равте<br>*Vie odgov**a**ravte* |
| 3rd person | He/She/It was answering -<br>Тој/Таа/Тоа одгов**а**раше<br>*Toj/Taa/Toa odgov**a**rashe* | They were answering -<br>Тие одгов**а**раа<br>*Tie odgov**a**raa* |

| Present Perfect Simple Tense | | |
|---|---|---|
| *Person* | *Singular* | *Plural* |
| 1st person | I have answered -<br>Јас сум одг**о**ворил(а)<br>*Jas sum odg**o**voril(a)* | We have answered -<br>Ние сме одгов**о**риле<br>*Nie sme odgov**o**rile* |
| 2nd person | You have answered -<br>Ти си одг**о**ворил(а)<br>*Ti si odg**o**voril(a)* | You have answered -<br>Вие сте одгов**о**риле<br>*Vie ste odgov**o**rile* |

| | | |
|---|---|---|
| 3rd person | He/She/It has answered - Тој/Таа/Тоа одг**о**ворил(а)(о) *Toj/Taa/Toa odg**o**voril(a)(o)* | They have answered - Тие одгов**о**риле *Tie odgov**o**rile* |

| Present Perfect Continuous Tense | | |
|---|---|---|
| *Person* | *Singular* | *Plural* |
| 1st person | I have been answering - Јас сум одг**о**варал(а) *Jas sum odg**o**varal(a)* | We have been answering - Ние сме одгов**а**рале *Nie sme odgov**a**rale* |
| 2nd person | You have been answering - Ти си одг**о**варал(а) Ti si *odg**o**voral(a)* | You have been answering - Вие сте одгов**а**рале *Vie ste odgov**a**rale* |
| 3rd person | He/She/It has been answering Тој/Таа/Тоа одг**о**варал(а)(о) *Toj/Taa/Toa odg**o**voral(a)(o)* | They have been answering - Тие одгов**а**рале *Tie odgov**a**rale* |

| Past Perfect Simple Tense | | |
|---|---|---|
| *Person* | *Singular* | *Plural* |
| 1st person | I had answered - Јас бев одг**о**ворил(а) *Jas bev odg**o**voril(a)* | We had answered - Ние бевме одгов**о**риле *Nie bevme odgov**o**rile* |
| 2nd person | You had answered - Ти беше одг**о**ворил(а) *Ti beshe odg**o**voril(a)* | You had answered - Вие бевте одгов**о**риле *Vie bevte odgov**o**rile* |
| 3rd person | He/She/It had answered - Тој/Таа/Тоа беше одг**о**ворил(а)(о) *Toj/Taa/Toa beshe odg**o**voril(a)(o)* | They had answered - Тие беа одгов**о**риле *Tie bea odgov**o**rile* |

| Future Simple Tense | | |
|---|---|---|
| *Person* | *Singular* | *Plural* |
| 1st person | I will answer - Јас ќе одг**о**варам/одг**о**ворам *Jas kje odg**o**varam/odg**o**voram* | We will answer - Ние ќе одгов**а**раме/одгов**о**риме *Nie kje odgov**a**rame/odgov**o**rime* |
| 2nd person | You will answer - Ти ќе одг**о**вараш/одг**о**вориш *-Ti kje odg**o**varash/odg**o**vorish* | You will answer - Вие ќе одгов**а**рате/одгов**о**рите *Vie kje odgov**a**rate/odgov**o**rite* |
| 3rd person | He/She/It will answer - Тој/Таа/Тоа ќе одг**о**вара/одг**о**вори *Toj/Taa/Toa kje odg**o**vara/odg**o**vori* | They will answer - Тие ќе одгов**а**раат/одг**о**ворат *Tie kje odgov**a**raat/odg**o**vorat* |

| **used to + infinitive or would + infinitive** | | |
|---|---|---|
| *Person* | *Singular* | *Plural* |
| 1st person | I would answer -<br>Јас ќе одг**о**варав<br>*Jas kje odg**o**varav* | We would answer -<br>Ние ќе одгов**а**равме<br>*Nie kje odgov**a**ravme* |
| 2nd person | You would answer -<br>Ти ќе одгов**а**раше<br>*Ti kje odgov**a**rashe* | You would answer -<br>Вие ќе одгов**а**равте<br>*Vie kje odgov**a**ravte* |
| 3rd person | He/She/It would answer -<br>Тој/Таа/Тоа ќе одгов**а**раше<br>*Toj/Taa/Toa kje odgov**a**rashe* | They would answer -<br>Тие ќе одгов**а**раа<br>*Tie kje odgov**a**raa* |

| **Personal endings for future perfect-in-the-past tense** | | |
|---|---|---|
| *Person* | *Singular* | *Plural* |
| 1st person | I would have answered -<br>Јас ќе сум<br>одг**о**варал/одг**о**ворил(а)<br>*Jas kje sum*<br>*odg**o**varal/odg**o**voril(a)* | We would have answered -<br>Ние ќе сме<br>одгов**а**рале/одгов**о**риле<br>*Nie kje sme*<br>*odgov**a**rale/odgov**o**rile* |
| 2nd person | You would have answered -<br>Ти ќе си<br>одг**о**варал/одг**о**ворил(а)<br>*Ti kje si*<br>*odg**o**varal(a)/odg**o**voril(a)* | You would have answered -<br>Вие ќе сте<br>одгов**а**рале/одгов**о**риле<br>*Vie kje ste*<br>*odgov**a**rale/odgov**o**rile* |
| 3rd person | He/She/It would have answered -<br>Тој/Таа/Тоа ќе<br>одг**о**варал/одг**о**ворил(а)(о)<br>*Toj/Taa/Toa*<br>*odg**o**varal/odg**o**voril(a)(o)* | They would have answered -<br>Тие ќе одгов**а**рале/одгов**о**риле<br>*Tie kje odgov**a**rale/odgov**o**rile* |

**To appear – Се појавува/Се појави**

| | | |
|---|---|---|
| *Infinitive* | To appear | Се поj**а**вува<br>Se poj**a**vuva |

| Present Simple Tense | | |
|---|---|---|
| *Person* | *Singular* | *Plural* |
| 1st person | I appear -<br>Јас се пој**а**вувам<br>*Jas se poj**a**vuvam* | We appear -<br>Ние се појав**у**ваме<br>*Nie se pojavu**v**ame* |
| 2nd person | You appear -<br>Ти се по**ја**вуваш<br>*Ti se poj**a**vuvash* | You appear -<br>Вие се појав**у**вате<br>*Vie se pojav**u**vate* |
| 3rd person | He/She/It appears -<br>Тој/Таа/Тоасе пој**а**вува<br>*Toj/Taa/Toa se poj**a**vuva* | They appear -<br>Тие се појав**у**ваат<br>*Tie se pojav**u**vaat* |

| Past Simple Tense | | |
|---|---|---|
| *Person* | *Singular* | *Plural* |
| 1st person | I appeared -<br>Јас се п**о**јавив<br>*Jas se p**o**javiv* | We appeared -<br>Ние се пој**а**вивме<br>*Nie se poj**a**vivme* |
| 2nd person | You appeared -<br>Ти се п**о**јави<br>*Ti se p**o**javi* | You appeared -<br>Вие се пој**а**вивте<br>*Vie se poj**a**vivte* |
| 3rd person | He/She/It appeared -<br>Тој/Таа/Тоа се п**о**јави<br>*Toj/Taa/Toa se p**o**javi* | They appeared -<br>Тие се пој**а**вија<br>*Tie se poj**a**vija* |

| Past Continuous Tense | | |
|---|---|---|
| *Person* | *Singular* | *Plural* |
| 1st person | I was appearing -<br>Јас се пој**а**вував<br>*Jas se poj**a**vuvav* | We were appearing -<br>Ние се појав**у**вавме<br>*Nie se pojav**u**vavme* |
| 2nd person | You were appearing -<br>Ти се појав**у**ваше<br>*Ti se pojav**u**vashe* | You were appearing -<br>Вие се појав**у**вавте<br>*Vie se pojav**u**vavte* |
| 3rd person | He/She/It was appearing -<br>Тој/Таа/Тоа се појав**у**ваше<br>*Toj/Taa/Toa se pojav**u**vashe* | They were appearing -<br>Тие се појав**у**ваа<br>*Tie se pojav**u**vaa* |

| Present Perfect Simple Tense | | |
|---|---|---|
| *Person* | *Singular* | *Plural* |
| 1st person | I have appeared -<br>Јас сум се п**о**јавил(а)<br>*Jas sum se p**o**javil(a)* | We have appeared -<br>Ние сме се пој**а**виле<br>*Nie sme se poj**a**vile* |
| 2nd person | You have appeared -<br>Ти си се п**о**јавил(а)<br>*Ti si se p**o**javil(a)* | You have appeared -<br>Вие сте се пој**а**виле<br>*Vie ste se poj**a**vile* |

| | | |
|---|---|---|
| 3rd person | He/She/It has appeared -<br>Тој/Таа/Тоа се п**о**јавил(а)(о)<br>*Toj/Taa/Toa se p**o**javil(a)(o)* | They have appeared -<br>Тие се поја**в**иле<br>*Tie se poj**a**vile* |

| **Present Perfect Continuous Tense** | | |
|---|---|---|
| *Person* | *Singular* | *Plural* |
| 1st person | I have been appearing -<br>Јас сум се поја**в**увал(а)<br>*Jas sum se poj**a**vuval(a)* | We have been appearing -<br>Ние сме се појав**у**вале<br>*Nie sme se pojav**u**vale* |
| 2nd person | You have been appearing -<br>Ти си се поја**в**увал(а)<br>*Ti si se poj**a**vuval(a)* | You have been appearing -<br>Вие сте се појав**у**вале<br>*Vie ste se pojav**u**vale* |
| 3rd person | He/She/It has been appearing<br>Тој/Таа/Тоа се поја**в**увал(а)(о)<br>*Toj/Taa/Toa se poj**a**vuval(a)(o)* | They have been appearing -<br>Тие се појав**у**вале<br>*Tie se pojav**u**vale* |

| **Past Perfect Simple Tense** | | |
|---|---|---|
| *Person* | *Singular* | *Plural* |
| 1st person | I had appeared -<br>Јас бев се п**о**јавил(а)<br>*Jas bev se p**o**javil(a)* | We had appeared -<br>Ние бевме се поја**в**иле<br>*Nie bevme se poj**a**vile* |
| 2nd person | You had appeared -<br>Ти беше се п**о**јавил(а)<br>*Ti beshe se p**o**javil(a)* | You had appeared -<br>Вие бевте се поја**в**иле<br>*Vie bevte se poj**a**vile* |
| 3rd person | He/She/It had appeared -<br>Тој/Таа/Тоа беше се<br>п**о**јавил(а)(о)<br>*Toj/Taa/Toa beshe se*<br>*p**o**javil(a)(o)* | They had appeared -<br>Тие беа се поја**в**иле<br>*Tie bea se poj**a**vile* |

| **Future Simple Tense** | | |
|---|---|---|
| *Person* | *Singular* | *Plural* |
| 1st person | I will appear -<br>Јас ќе се поја**в**увам/ се п**о**јавам<br>*Jas kje se poj**a**vuvam/se*<br>*p**o**javam* | We will appear -<br>Ние ќе се појав**у**ваме/ се<br>поја**в**име<br>*Nie kje se pojav**u**vame/se*<br>*poj**a**vime* |
| 2nd person | You will appear -<br>Ти ќе се поја**в**уваш/се п**о**јавиш<br>*Ti kje se poj**a**vuvash/se p**o**javish* | You will appear -<br>Вие ќе се појав**у**вате/ се<br>поја**в**ите<br>*Vi kje se pojav**u**vate/se poj**a**vite* |
| 3rd person | He/She/It will appear -<br>Тој/Таа/Тоа ќе се поја**в**ува/ се<br>п**о**јави<br>*Toj/Taa/Toa kje se poj**a**vuva/se*<br>*p**o**javi* | They will appear -<br>Тие ќе се појав**у**ваат/ се<br>п**о**јават<br>*Tie kje se pojav**u**vaat/se p**o**javat* |

| **used to + infinitive or would + infinitive** | | |
|---|---|---|
| *Person* | *Singular* | *Plural* |
| 1st person | I would appear -<br>Јас ќе се пој**а**вував/се п**о**јавев<br>*Jas kje se poj**a**vuvav/se p**o**javev* | We would appear -<br>Ние ќе се појав**у**вавме/се пој**а**вевме<br>*Nie kje se pojav**u**vavme/se poj**a**vevme* |
| 2nd person | You would appear -<br>Ти ќе се појав**у**ваше/се пој**а**веше<br>*Ti kje se pojav**u**vashe/se poj**a**veshe* | You would appear -<br>Вие ќе се појав**у**вавте/се пој**а**вевте<br>*Vie kje se pojav**u**vate/sepoj**a**vevte* |
| 3rd person | He/She/It would appear -<br>Тој/Таа/Тоа ќе се појав**у**ваше/се пој**а**веше<br>*Toj/Taa/Toa kje se pojav**u**vashe/se poj**a**veshe* | They would appear -<br>Тие ќе се појав**у**ваа/се пој**а**веа<br>*Tie kje se pojav**u**vaa/se poj**a**vea* |

| **Personal endings for future perfect-in-the-past tense** | | |
|---|---|---|
| *Person* | *Singular* | *Plural* |
| 1st person | I would have appeared -<br>Јас ќе сум се пој**а**вувал/се п**о**јавил(а)<br>*Jas kje sum se poj**a**vuval/se p**o**javil(a)* | We would have appeared -<br>Ние ќе сме се појав**у**вале/се пој**а**виле<br>*Nie kje sme se pojav**u**vale/se poj**a**vile* |
| 2nd person | You would have appeared -<br>Ти ќе си се пој**а**вувал/се п**о**јавил(а)<br>*Ti kje si se poj**a**vuval/p**o**javil(a)* | You would have appeared -<br>Вие ќе сте се појав**у**вале/се пој**а**виле<br>*Vie kje ste se pojav**u**vale/se poj**a**vile* |
| 3rd person | He/She/It would have appeared -<br>Тој/Таа/Тоа ќе се пој**а**вувал/се п**о**јавил(а)(о)<br>*Toj/Taa/Toa kje se poj**a**vuval/se p**o**javil(a)(o)* | They would have appeared -<br>Тие ќе се појав**у**вале/се пој**а**виле<br>*Tie kje se pojav**u**vale/se poj**a**vile* |

**To ask - Прашува/Праша**

| | | |
|---|---|---|
| *Infinitive* | To ask | Пр**а**шува<br>Pr**a**shuva |

| Present Simple Tense | | |
|---|---|---|
| *Person* | *Singular* | *Plural* |
| 1st person | I ask -<br>Јас пр**а**шувам<br>*Jas pr**a**shuvam* | We ask -<br>Ние прашу**в**аме<br>*Nie prash**u**vame* |
| 2nd person | You ask -<br>Ти пр**а**шуваш<br>*Ti pr**a**shuvash* | You ask -<br>Вие прашу**в**ате<br>*Vie prash**u**vate* |
| 3rd person | He/She/It asks -<br>Тој/Таа/Тоа<br>пр**а**шува<br>*Toj/Taa/Toa*<br>*pr**a**shuva* | They ask -<br>Тие прашу**в**аат<br>Tie prash**u**vaat |

| Past Simple Tense | | |
|---|---|---|
| *Person* | *Singular* | *Plural* |
| 1st person | I asked -<br>Јас пр**а**шав<br>*Jas pr**a**shav* | We asked -<br>Ние пр**а**шавме<br>*Nie pr**a**shavme* |
| 2nd person | You asked -<br>Ти пр**а**ша<br>*Ti pr**a**sha* | You asked -<br>Вие пр**а**шавте<br>*Vie pr**a**shavte* |
| 3rd person | He/She/It asked -<br>Тој/Таа/Тоа пр**а**ша<br>*Toj/Taa/Toa pr**a**sha* | They asked -<br>Тие пр**а**шаа<br>*Tie pr**a**shaa* |

| Past Continuous Tense | | |
|---|---|---|
| *Person* | *Singular* | *Plural* |
| 1st person | I was asking -<br>Јас пр**а**шував<br>*Jas pr**a**shuvav* | We were asking -<br>Ние прaш**у**вавме<br>*Nie prash**u**vavme* |
| 2nd person | You were asking -<br>Ти праш**у**ваше<br>*Ti prash**u**vashe* | You were asking -<br>Вие праш**у**вавте<br>*Vie prash**u**vavte* |
| 3rd person | He/She/It was asking -<br>Тој/Таа/Тоа праш**у**ваше<br>*Toj/Taa/Toa prash**u**vashe* | They were asking -<br>Тие праш**у**ваа<br>*Tie prash**u**vaa* |

| **Present Perfect Simple Tense** | | |
|---|---|---|
| *Person* | *Singular* | *Plural* |
| 1st person | I have asked -<br>Јас сум пр**а**шал(а)<br>*Jas sum pr**a**shal(a)* | We have asked -<br>Ние сме пр**а**шале<br>*Nie sme pr**a**shale* |
| 2nd person | You have asked -<br>Ти си пр**а**шал(а)<br>*Ti si pr**a**shal(a)* | You have asked -<br>Вие сте пр**а**шале<br>*Vie ste pr**a**shale* |
| 3rd person | He/She/It has asked -<br>Тој/Таа/Тоа пр**а**шал(а)(о)<br>*Toj/Taa/Toa pr**a**shal(a)(o)* | They have asked -<br>Тие пр**а**шале<br>*Tie pr**a**shale* |

| **Present Perfect Continuous Tense** | | |
|---|---|---|
| *Person* | *Singular* | *Plural* |
| 1st person | I have been asking -<br>Јас сум пр**а**шувал(а)<br>*Jas sum pr**a**shuval(a)* | We have been asking -<br>Ние сме праш**у**вале<br>*Nie sme prash**u**vale* |
| 2nd person | You have been asking -<br>Ти си пр**а**шувал(а)<br>*Ti si pr**a**shuval(a)* | You have been asking -<br>Вие сте праш**у**вале<br>*Vie ste prash**u**vale* |
| 3rd person | He/She/It has been asking -<br>Тој/Таа/Тоа пр**а**шувал(а)(о)<br>*Toj/Taa/Toa pr**a**shuval(a)(o)* | They have been asking -<br>Тие праш**у**вале<br>*Tie prash**u**vale* |

| ***Past Perfect Simple Tense*** | | |
|---|---|---|
| *Person* | *Singular* | *Plural* |
| 1st person | I had asked -<br>Јас бев пр**а**шал(а)<br>*Jas bev pr**a**shal(a)* | We had asked -<br>Ние бевме пр**а**шале<br>*Nie bevme pr**a**shale* |
| 2nd person | You had asked -<br>Ти беше пр**а**шал(а)<br>*Ti beshe pr**a**shal(a)* | You had asked -<br>Вие бевте пр**а**шале<br>*Vie bevte pr**a**shale* |
| 3rd person | He/She/It had asked -<br>Тој/Таа/Тоа беше пр**а**шал(а)(о)<br>*Toj/Taa/toa beshe pr**a**shal(a)(o)* | They had asked -<br>Тие беа пр**а**шале<br>*Tie bea pr**a**shale* |

| **Future Simple Tense** | | |
|---|---|---|
| *Person* | *Singular* | *Plural* |
| 1st person | I will ask -<br>Јас ќе пр**а**шувам/пр**а**шам<br>*Jas kje pr**a**shuvam/pr**a**sham* | We will ask -<br>Ние ќе праш**у**ваме/пр**а**шаме<br>*Ni kje prash**u**vame/pr**a**shame* |
| 2nd person | You will ask -<br>Ти ќе пр**а**шуваш/пр**а**шаш<br>*Ti kje pr**a**shuvash/pr**a**shash* | You will ask -<br>Вие ќе праш**у**вате/пр**а**шате<br>*Vie kje prash**u**vate/pr**a**shate* |
| 3rd person | He/She/It will ask -<br>Тој/Таа/Тоа ќе пр**а**шува/пр**а**ша<br>*Toj/Taa/Toa kje pr**a**shuva/pr**a**sha* | They will ask -<br>Тие ќе праш**у**ваат/пр**а**шаат<br>*Tie kje prash**u**vaat/pr**a**shaat* |

| used to + infinitive or would + infinitive | | |
|---|---|---|
| *Person* | *Singular* | *Plural* |
| 1st person | I would ask -<br>Јас ќе пр**а**шував/пр**а**шав<br>*Jas kjepr**a**shuvav/pr**a**shav* | We would ask -<br>Ние ќе прашу**в**авме/пр**а**шавме<br>*Nie kje prash**u**vavme/pr**a**shavme* |
| 2nd person | You would ask -<br>Ти ќе прашу**в**аше/пр**а**шаше<br>*Ti kje prash**u**vashe/pr**a**shashe* | You would ask -<br>Вие ќе прашу**в**авте/пр**а**шавте<br>*Vie kje prash**u**vavte/pr**a**shavte* |
| 3rd person | He/She/It would ask -<br>Тој/Таа/Тоа ќе<br>прашу**в**аше/пр**а**шаше<br>*Toj/Taa/Toa kje*<br>*prash**u**vashe/pr**a**shashe* | They would ask -<br>Тие ќе прашу**в**аа/ пр**а**шаа<br>*Tie kje prash**u**vaa/pr**a**shaa* |

| Personal endings for future perfect-in-the-past tense | | |
|---|---|---|
| *Person* | *Singular* | *Plural* |
| 1st person | I would have asked -<br>Јас ќе сум<br>пр**а**шувал/пр**а**шал(а)<br>*Jas kje sum pr**a**shuval/pr**a**shal(a)* | We would have asked -<br>Ние ќе сме<br>прашу**в**але/пр**а**шале<br>*Nie kje sme prash**u**vale/pr**a**shale* |
| 2nd person | You would have asked -<br>Ти ќе си прашувал/прашал<br>*Ti kje si pr**a**shuval/pr**a**shal* | You would have asked -<br>Вие ќе сте<br>прашу**в**але/пр**а**шале<br>*Vie kje ste prash**u**vale/ prashale* |
| 3rd person | He/She/It would have asked -<br>Тој/Таа/Тоа ќе<br>пр**а**шувал/пр**а**шал(а),(о)<br>*Toj/Taa/Toa kje*<br>*pr**a**shuval/pr**a**shal(a),(o)* | They would have asked -<br>Тие ќе прашу**в**але/ пр**а**шале<br>*Tie kje prash**u**vale/pr**a**shale* |

***To be – Е/Беше***

| | | |
|---|---|---|
| *Infinitive* | To be | Сум<br>Sum |

| Present Simple Tense | | |
|---|---|---|
| *Person* | *Singular* | *Plural* |
| 1st person | I am -<br>Јас сум<br>Jas sum | We are -<br>Ние сме<br>Nie sme |
| 2nd person | You are -<br>Ти си<br>Ti si | You are -<br>Вие сте<br>Vie ste |
| 3rd person | He/She/It is -<br>Тој/Таа/Тоа е<br>Toj/Taa/Toa e | They are -<br>Тие се<br>Tie se |

| Past Simple Tense | | |
|---|---|---|
| *Person* | *Singular* | *Plural* |
| 1st person | I was -<br>Јас бев<br>Jas bev | We were -<br>Ние бевме<br>Nie bevme |
| 2nd person | You were -<br>Ти беше<br>Ti beshe | You were -<br>Вие бевте<br>Vie bevte |
| 3rd person | He/She/It was -<br>Тој/Таа/Тоа беше<br>Toj/Taa/Toa beshe | They were -<br>Тие беа<br>Tie bea |

| Past Continuous Tense | | |
|---|---|---|
| *Person* | *Singular* | *Plural* |
| 1st person | I was being -<br>Јас бев<br>Jas bev | We were being -<br>Ние бевме<br>Nie bevme |
| 2nd person | You were being -<br>Ти беше<br>Ti beshe | You were being -<br>Вие бевте<br>Vie bevte |
| 3rd person | He/She/It was being -<br>Тој/Таа/Тоа беше<br>Toj/Taa/Toa beshe | They were being -<br>Тие беа<br>Tie bea |

| Present Perfect Simple Tense | | |
|---|---|---|
| *Person* | *Singular* | *Plural* |
| 1st person | I have been -<br>Јас сум бил<br>Jas sum bil | We have been -<br>Ние сме биле<br>Nie sme bile |
| 2nd person | You have been -<br>Ти си бил<br>Ti si bil | You have been -<br>Вие сте биле<br>Vie ste bile |
| 3rd person | He/She/It has been -<br>Тој/Таа/Тоа бил<br>Toj/Taa/Toa bil | They have been -<br>Тие биле<br>Tie bile |

| Present Perfect Continuous Tense | | |
|---|---|---|
| *Person* | *Singular* | *Plural* |
| 1st person | I have been being -<br>Јас сум бил<br>Jas sum bil | We have been being -<br>Ние сме биле<br>Nie sme bile |
| 2nd person | You have been being -<br>Ти си бил<br>Ti si bil | You have been being -<br>Вие сте биле<br>Vie ste bile |
| 3rd person | He/She/It has been being -<br>Тој/Таа/Тоа бил<br>Toj/Taa/Toa bil | They have been being -<br>Тие биле<br>Tie bile |

| Past Perfect Simple Tense | | |
|---|---|---|
| *Person* | *Singular* | *Plural* |
| 1st person | I had been -<br>Јас бев бил<br>Jas bev bil | We had been -<br>Ние бевме биле<br>Nie bevme bile |
| 2nd person | You had been -<br>Ти беше бил<br>Ti beshe bil | You had been -<br>Вие бевте биле<br>Vie bevte bile |
| 3rd person | He/She/It had been -<br>Тој/Таа/Тоа беше бил<br>Toj/Taa/Toa beshe bil | They had been -<br>Тие беа биле<br>Tie bea bile |

| Future Simple Tense | | |
|---|---|---|
| *Person* | *Singular* | *Plural* |
| 1st person | I will be -<br>Јас ќе сум<br>Jas kje sum | We will be -<br>Ние ќе сме<br>Nie kje sme |
| 2nd person | You will be -<br>Ти ќе си<br>Ти кјe си | You will be -<br>Вие ќе сте<br>Vie kje ste |

| | | |
|---|---|---|
| 3rd person | He/She/It will be -<br>Тој/Таа/Тоа ќе е<br>Toj/Taa/Toa kje e | They will be -<br>Тие ќе се<br>Tie kje se |

| used to + infinitive or would + infinitive | | |
|---|---|---|
| *Person* | *Singular* | *Plural* |
| 1st person | I would be -<br>Јас ќе бев<br>Jas kje bev | We would be -<br>Ние ќе бевме<br>Nie kje bevme |
| 2nd person | You would be -<br>Ти ќе беше<br>Ti kje beshe | You would be -<br>Вие ќе бевте<br>Vie kje bevte |
| 3rd person | He/She/It would be -<br>Тој/Таа/Тоа ќе беше<br>Toj/Taa/Toa kje beshe | They would be -<br>Тие ќе беа<br>Tie kje bea |

| Personal endings for future perfect-in-the-past tense | | |
|---|---|---|
| *Person* | *Singular* | *Plural* |
| 1st person | I would have been -<br>Јас ќе сум бил<br>Jas kje sum bil | We would have been -<br>Ние ќе сме биле<br>Nie kje sme bile |
| 2nd person | You would have been -<br>Ти ќе си бил<br>Ti kje si bil | You would have been -<br>Вие ќе сте биле<br>Vie kje ste bile |
| 3rd person | He/She/It would have been -<br>Тој/Таа/Тоа ќе бил<br>Toj/Taa/Toa kje bil | They would have been -<br>Тие ќе биле<br>Tie kje bile |

**To be able to –Може**

| | | |
|---|---|---|
| *Infinitive* | To be able to | Може<br>Mozhe |

*there is no perfective form of the verb "to be able to" in Macedonian

| Present Simple Tense | | |
|---|---|---|
| *Person* | *Singular* | *Plural* |
| 1st person | I am able to -<br>Јас можам<br>Jas mozham | We are able to -<br>Ние можеме<br>Nie mozheme |
| 2nd person | You are able to -<br>Ти можеш<br>Ti mozhesh | You are able to -<br>Вие можете<br>Vie mozhete |
| 3rd person | He/She/It is able to -<br>Тој/Таа/Тоа може<br>Toj/Taa/Toa mozhe | They are able to -<br>Тие можат<br>Tie mozhat |

| Past Simple Tense | | |
|---|---|---|
| *Person* | *Singular* | *Plural* |
| 1st person | / | / |
| 2nd person | / | / |
| 3rd person | / | / |

| Past Continuous Tense | | |
|---|---|---|
| *Person* | *Singular* | *Plural* |
| 1st person | I was able to -<br>Јас можев<br>Jas mozhev | We were able to -<br>Ние можевме<br>Nie mozhevme |
| 2nd person | You were able to -<br>Ти можеше<br>Ti mozheshe | You were able to -<br>Вие можевте<br>Vie mozhevte |
| 3rd person | He/She/It was able to -<br>Тој/Таа/Тоа можеше<br>Toj/Taa/Toa mozheshe | They were able to -<br>Тие можеа<br>Tie mozhea |

| Present Perfect Simple Tense | | |
|---|---|---|
| *Person* | *Singular* | *Plural* |
| 1st person | / | / |
| 2nd person | / | / |
| 3rd person | / | / |

| Present Perfect Continuous Tense | | |
|---|---|---|
| *Person* | *Singular* | *Plural* |
| 1st person | I have been able to -<br>Јас сум можел<br>Jas sum mozhel | We have been able to -<br>Ние сме можеле<br>Nie sme mozhele |

| | | |
|---|---|---|
| 2nd person | You have been able to -<br>Ти си **мо**жел<br>Ti si m**o**zhel | You have been able to -<br>Вие сте **мо**желе<br>Vie ste m**o**zhele |
| 3rd person | He/She/It has been able to -<br>Тој/Таа/Тоа **мо**жел<br>Toj/Taa/Toa m**o**zhel | They have been able to -<br>Тие **мо**желе<br>Tie m**o**zhele |

| **Past Perfect Simple Tense** | | |
|---|---|---|
| *Person* | *Singular* | *Plural* |
| 1st person | I had been able to -<br>Јас бев **мо**жел<br>Jas bev m**o**zhel | We had been able to -<br>Ние бевме **мо**желе<br>Nie bevme m**o**zhele |
| 2nd person | You had been able to -<br>Ти беше **мо**жел<br>Ti beshe m**o**zhel | You had been able to -<br>Вие бевте **мо**желе<br>Vie bevte m**o**zhele |
| 3rd person | He/She/It had been able to -<br>Тој/Таа/Тоа беше **мо**жел<br>Toj/Taa/Toa beshe m**o**zhel | They had been able to -<br>Тие **мо**желе<br>Tie m**o**zhele |

| **Future Simple Tense** | | |
|---|---|---|
| *Person* | *Singular* | *Plural* |
| 1st person | I will be able to -<br>Јас ќе **мо**жам<br>Jas kje m**o**zham | We will be able to -<br>Ние ќе **мо**жеме<br>Nie kje m**o**zheme |
| 2nd person | You will be able to -<br>Ти ќе **мо**жеш<br>Ti kje m**o**zhesh | You will be able to -<br>Ти ќе **мо**жеш<br>Ti kje m**o**zhesh |
| 3rd person | He/She/It will be able to -<br>Тој/Таа/Тоа ќе **мо**же<br>Toj/Taa/Toa kje m**o**zhe | They will be able to -<br>Тие ќе **мо**жат<br>Tie kje m**o**zhat |

| **used to + infinitive or would + infinitive** | | |
|---|---|---|
| *Person* | *Singular* | *Plural* |
| 1st person | I would be able to -<br>Јас ќе **мо**жев<br>Jas kje m**o**zhev | We would be able to -<br>Ние ќе **мо**жевме<br>Nie kje m**o**zhevme |
| 2nd person | You would be able to -<br>Ти ќе **мо**жеше<br>Ti kje m**o**zheshe | You would be able to -<br>Вие ќе **мо**жевте<br>Vie kje m**o**zhevte |
| 3rd person | He/She/It would be able to -<br>Тој/Таа/Тоа ќе **мо**жеше<br>Toj/Taa/Toa kje m**o**zheshe | They would be able to -<br>Тие ќе **мо**жеа<br>Tie kje m**o**zhea |

| Personal endings for future perfect-in-the-past tense | | |
|---|---|---|
| *Person* | *Singular* | *Plural* |
| 1st person | I would have been able to -<br>Јас ќе сум м**о**жел<br>Jas kje sum m**o**zhel | We would have been able to -<br>Ние ќе сме м**о**желе<br>Nie kje sme m**o**zhele |
| 2nd person | You would have been able to -<br>Ти ќе си м**о**жел<br>Ti kje si m**o**zhel | You would have been able to -<br>Вие ќе сте м**о**желе<br>Vie kje ste m**o**zhele |
| 3rd person | He/She/It would have been able to -<br>Тој/Таа/Тоа ќе м**о**жел(а)(о)<br>Toj/Taa/Toa kje m**o**zhel(a)(o) | They would have been able to<br>Тие ќе м**о**желе<br>Tie kje m**o**zhele |

***To become – Станува/Стана***

| | | |
|---|---|---|
| *Infinitive* | To become | Ст**а**нува<br>St**a**nuva |

| Present Simple Tense | | |
|---|---|---|
| *Person* | *Singular* | *Plural* |
| 1st person | I become -<br>Јас ст**а**нувам<br>Jas st**a**nuvam | We become -<br>Ние стан**у**ваме<br>Nie stan**u**vame |
| 2nd person | You become -<br>Ти ст**а**нуваш<br>Ti st**a**nuvash | You become -<br>Вие стан**у**вате<br>Vie stan**u**vate |
| 3rd person | He/She/It becomes -<br>Тој/Таа/Тоа ст**а**нува<br>Toj/Taa/Toa st**a**nuva | They become -<br>Тие стан**у**ваат<br>Tie stan**u**vaat |

| Past Simple Tense | | |
|---|---|---|
| *Person* | *Singular* | *Plural* |
| 1st person | I became -<br>Јас ст**а**нав<br>Jas st**a**nav | We became -<br>Ние ст**а**навме<br>Nie st**a**navme |
| 2nd person | You became -<br>Ти ст**а**на<br>Ti st**a**na | You became -<br>Вие ст**а**навте<br>Vie st**a**navte |
| 3rd person | He/She/It became –<br>Тој/Таа/Тоа ст**а**на<br>Toj/Taa/Toa st**a**na | They became -<br>Тие ст**а**наа<br>Tie st**a**naa |

| Past Continuous Tense | | |
|---|---|---|
| *Person* | *Singular* | *Plural* |
| 1st person | I was becoming -<br>Јас ст**а**нував<br>Jas st**a**nuvav | We were becoming -<br>Ние стан**у**вавме<br>Nie stan**u**vavme |
| 2nd person | You were becoming -<br>Ти стан**у**ваше<br>Ti stan**u**vashe | You were becoming -<br>Вие стан**у**вавте<br>Vie stan**u**vavte |
| 3rd person | He/She/It was becoming -<br>Тој/Таа/Тоа стан**у**ваше<br>Toj/Taa/Toa stan**u**vashe | They were becoming –<br>Тие стан**у**ваа<br>Tie stan**u**vaa |

| Present Perfect Simple Tense | | |
|---|---|---|
| *Person* | *Singular* | *Plural* |
| 1st person | I have become -<br>Јас сум ст**а**нал(а)<br>Jas sum st**a**nal(a) | We have become -<br>Ние сме ст**а**нале<br>Nie sme st**a**nale |
| 2nd person | You have become -<br>Ти си ст**а**нал(а)<br>Ti si st**a**nal(a) | You have become -<br>Вие сте ст**а**нале<br>Vie ste st**a**nale |

| | | |
|---|---|---|
| 3rd person | He/She/It has become -<br>Тој/Таа/Тоа ст**а**нал(а)(о)<br>Toj/Taa/Toa st**a**nal(a)(o) | They have become -<br>Тие ст**а**нале<br>Tie st**a**nale |

| **Present Perfect Continuous Tense** | | |
|---|---|---|
| *Person* | *Singular* | *Plural* |
| 1st person | I have been becoming -<br>Јас сум ст**а**нувал(а)<br>Jas sum st**a**nuval(a) | We have been becoming -<br>Ние сме стан**у**вале<br>Nie sme stan**u**vale |
| 2nd person | You have been becoming -<br>Ти си ст**а**нувал(а)<br>Ti si st**a**nuval(a) | You have been becoming -<br>Вие сте стан**у**вале<br>Vie ste stan**u**vale |
| 3rd person | He/She/It has been becoming-<br>Тој/Таа/Тоа ст**а**нувал(а)(о)<br>Toj/Taa/Toa st**a**nuval(a)(o) | They have been becoming -<br>Тие стан**у**вале<br>Tie stan**u**vale |

| **Past Perfect Simple Tense** | | |
|---|---|---|
| *Person* | *Singular* | *Plural* |
| 1st person | I had become -<br>Јас бев ст**а**нал(а)<br>Jas bev st**a**nal(a) | We had become -<br>Ние бевме ст**а**нале<br>Nie bevme st**a**nale |
| 2nd person | You had become -<br>Ти беше ст**а**нал(а)<br>Ti beshe st**a**nal(a) | You had become -<br>Вие бевте ст**а**нале<br>Vie bevte st**a**nale |
| 3rd person | He/She/It had become -<br>Тој/Таа/Тоа беше ст**а**нал(а)(о)<br>Toj/Taa/Toa beshe st**a**nal(a)(o) | They had become -<br>Тие беа ст**а**нале<br>Tie bea st**a**nale |

| **Future Simple Tense** | | |
|---|---|---|
| *Person* | *Singular* | *Plural* |
| 1st person | I will become -<br>Јас ќе ст**а**нувам/ст**а**нам<br>Jas kje st**a**nuvam/st**a**nam | We will become -<br>Ние ќе стан**у**ваме/ст**а**неме<br>Nie kje stan**u**vame/st**a**neme |
| 2nd person | You will become -<br>Ти ќе ст**а**нуваш/ст**а**неш<br>Ti kje st**a**nuvash/st**a**nesh | You will become -<br>Вие ќе стан**у**вате/ст**а**нете<br>Vie kje stan**u**vate/st**a**nete |
| 3rd person | He/She/It will become -<br>Тој/Таа/Тоа ќе ст**а**нува/ст**а**не<br>Toj/Taa/Toa kje st**a**nuva/st**a**ne | They will become -<br>Тие ќе стан**у**ваат/ст**а**нат<br>Tie kje stan**u**vaat/st**a**nat |

| **used to + infinitive or would + infinitive** | | |
|---|---|---|
| *Person* | *Singular* | *Plural* |
| 1st person | I would become -<br>Јас ќе ст**а**нував/ст**а**нев<br>Jas kje st**a**nuvav/st**a**nev | We would become -<br>Ние ќе стан**у**вавме/ст**а**невме<br>Nie kje stan**u**vavme/st**a**nevme |
| 2nd person | You would become -<br>Ти ќе стан**у**ваше/ст**а**неше<br>Ti kje stan**u**vashe/st**a**neshe | You would become -<br>Вие ќе стан**у**вавте/ст**а**невте<br>Vie kje stan**u**vavte/st**a**nevte |

| | | |
|---|---|---|
| 3rd person | He/She/It would become - Тој/Таа/Тоа ќе стан**у**ваше/ст**а**неше Toj/Taa/Toa kje stan**u**vashe/st**a**neshe | They would become - Тие ќе стан**у**ваа/ст**а**неа Tie kje stan**u**vaa/st**a**nea |

| **Personal endings for future perfect-in-the-past tense** | | |
|---|---|---|
| *Person* | *Singular* | *Plural* |
| 1st person | I would have become - Јас ќе сум ст**а**нувал/ст**а**нал(а) Jas kje sum st**a**nuval/st**a**nal(a) | We would have become - Ние ќе сме стан**у**вале/ст**а**неле Nie kje sme stan**u**vale/st**a**nele |
| 2nd person | You would have become - Ти ќе си ст**а**нувал/ст**а**нал(а) Ti kje si st**a**nuval/st**a**nal(a) | You would have become - Вие ќе сте стан**у**вале/ст**а**неле Vie kje ste stan**u**vale/st**a**nele |
| 3rd person | He/She/It would have become Тој/Таа/Тоа ќе ст**а**нувал/ст**а**нал(а)(о) Toj/Taa/Toa kje st**a**nuval/st**a**nal(a)(o) | They would have become - Тие ќе стан**у**вале/ст**а**неле Tie kje stan**u**vale/st**a**nele |

***To begin - Почнува/Почна***

| | | |
|---|---|---|
| *Infinitive* | To begin | П**о**чнува<br>P**o**chnuva |

| Present Simple Tense | | |
|---|---|---|
| *Person* | *Singular* | *Plural* |
| 1st person | I begin -<br>Јас п**о**чнувам<br>*Jas p**o**chuvnam* | We begin -<br>Ние почн**у**ваме<br>*Nie pochn**u**vame* |
| 2nd person | You begin -<br>Ти п**о**чнуваш<br>*Ti p**o**chnuvash* | You begin -<br>Вие почн**у**вате<br>*Vie pochn**u**vate* |
| 3rd person | He/She/It begins -<br>Тој/Таа/Тоа п**о**чнува<br>*Toj/Taa/Toa p**o**chnuva* | They begin -<br>Тие почн**у**ваат<br>*Tie pochn**u**vaat* |

| Past Simple Tense | | |
|---|---|---|
| *Person* | *Singular* | *Plural* |
| 1st person | I began -<br>Јас п**о**чнав<br>*Jas p**o**chnav* | We began -<br>Ние п**о**чнавме<br>*Nie p**o**chnavme* |
| 2nd person | You began -<br>Ти п**о**чна<br>*Ti p**o**chna* | You began -<br>Вие п**о**чнавте<br>*Vie p**o**chnavte* |
| 3rd person | He/She/It began -<br>Тој/Таа/Тоа п**о**чна<br>*Toj/Taa/Toa p**o**chna* | They began -<br>Тие п**о**чнаа<br>*Tie p**o**chnaa* |

| Past Continuous Tense | | |
|---|---|---|
| *Person* | *Singular* | *Plural* |
| 1st person | I was beginning -<br>Јас п**о**чнував<br>*Jas p**o**chnuvav* | We were beginning -<br>Ние почн**у**вавме<br>*Nie pochn**u**vavme* |
| 2nd person | You were beginning -<br>Ти почн**у**ваше<br>*Ti pochn**u**vashe* | You were beginning -<br>Вие почн**у**вавте<br>*Vie pochn**u**vavte* |
| 3rd person | He/She/It was beginning -<br>Тој/Таа/Тоа почн**у**ваше<br>*Toj/Taa/Toa pochn**u**vashe* | They were beginning -<br>Тие почн**у**ваа<br>*Tie pochn**u**vaa* |

| Present Perfect Simple Tense | | |
|---|---|---|
| *Person* | *Singular* | *Plural* |
| 1st person | I have begun -<br>Јас сум п**о**чнал(а)<br>*Jas sum p**o**chnal(a)* | We have begun -<br>Ние сме п**о**чнале<br>*Nie sme p**o**chnale* |
| 2nd person | You have begun -<br>Ти си п**о**чнал(а)<br>Ti si p**o**chnal(a) | You have begun -<br>Вие сте п**о**чнале<br>*Vie ste p**o**chnale* |

| | | |
|---|---|---|
| 3rd person | He/She/It has begun -<br>Тој/Таа/Тоап**о**чнал(а)(о)<br>*Toj/Taa/Toa p**o**chnal(a)(o)* | They have begun -<br>Тие п**о**чнале<br>*Tie p**o**chnale* |

| Present Perfect Continuous Tense | | |
|---|---|---|
| *Person* | *Singular* | *Plural* |
| 1st person | I have been beginning -<br>Јас сум п**о**чнувал(а)<br>*Jas sum p**o**chnuval(a)* | We have been beginning -<br>Ние сме почн**у**вале<br>*Nie sme pochn**u**vale* |
| 2nd person | You have been beginning -<br>Ти сип**о**чнувал(а)<br>*Ti si p**o**chnuval(a)* | You have been beginning -<br>Вие сте почн**у**вале<br>*Vie ste pochn**u**vale* |
| 3rd person | He/She/It has been beginning-<br>Тој/Таа/Тоа п**о**чнувал(а)(о)<br>*Toj/Taa/Toa p**o**chnuval(a)(o)* | They have been beginning -<br>Тие почн**у**вале<br>*Tie pochn**u**vale* |

| Past Perfect Simple Tense | | |
|---|---|---|
| *Person* | *Singular* | *Plural* |
| 1st person | I had begun -<br>Јас бев п**о**чнал(а)<br>*Jas bev p**o**chnal(a)* | We had begun -<br>Ние бевме п**о**чнале<br>*Nie bevme p**o**chnale* |
| 2nd person | You had begun -<br>-Ти беше п**о**чнал(а)<br>*Ti beshe p**o**chnal(a)* | You had begun -<br>Вие бевте п**о**чнале<br>*Vie bevte  p**o**chnale* |
| 3rd person | He/She/It had begun -<br>Тој/Таа/Тоа беше п**о**чнал(а)(о)<br>*Toj/Taa/Toa p**o**chnal(a)(o)* | They had begun -<br>Тие беа п**о**чнале<br>*Tie bea p**o**chnale* |

| Future Simple Tense | | |
|---|---|---|
| *Person* | *Singular* | *Plural* |
| 1st person | I will begin<br>Јас ќе п**о**чнувам/п**о**чнам<br>*Jas kje p**o**chnuvam/p**o**chnam* | We will begin<br>Ние ќе почн**у**ваме/п**о**чнеме<br>*Nie kje pochn**u**vame/p**o**chneme* |
| 2nd person | You will begin<br>Ти ќе п**о**чнуваш/п**о**чнеш<br>*Ti kje p**o**chnuvash/p**o**chnesh* | You will begin<br>Вие ќе почн**у**вате/п**о**чнете<br>*Vie kje pochn**u**vate/p**o**chnete* |
| 3rd person | He/She/It will begin<br>Тој/Таа/Тоаќе п**о**чнува/п**о**чне<br>*Toj/Taa/Toa p**o**chnuva/p**o**chne* | They will begin<br>Тие ќе почнуваат/почнат<br>*Tie kje pocn**u**vaat/p**o**chnat* |

| used to + infinitive or would + infinitive | | |
|---|---|---|
| *Person* | *Singular* | *Plural* |
| 1st person | I would begin<br>Јас ќе п**о**чнував/п**о**чнев<br>*Jas kje p**o**chnuvav/p**o**chnev* | We would begin<br>Ние ќе почн**у**вавме/п**о**чневме<br>*Nie kje pochn**u**vavme/p**o**chneme* |
| 2nd person | You would begin<br>Ти ќе почн**у**ваше/п**о**чнеше<br>*Ti kje pochn**u**vashe/p**o**chneshe* | You would begin<br>Вие ќе почн**у**вавте/п**о**чневте<br>*Vie kje  pochn**u**vavate/p**o**chnete* |

| | | |
|---|---|---|
| 3rd person | He/She/It would begin<br>Тој/Таа/Тоа ќе<br>почн**у**ваше/п**о**чнеше<br>*Toj/Taa/Toa*<br>*pochn**u**vashe/p**o**chneshe* | They would begin<br>Тие ќе почн**у**ваа/п**о**чнаа<br>*Tie kje pochn**u**vaa/p**o**chnaa* |

| **Personal endings for future perfect-in-the-past tense** | | |
|---|---|---|
| *Person* | *Singular* | *Plural* |
| 1st person | I would have begun<br>Јас ќе сум п**о**чнувал/п**о**чнал(а)<br>*Jas kje sum*<br>*p**o**chnuval/p**o**chnal(a)* | We would have begun<br>Ние ќе сме почн**у**вале/п**о**чнале<br>*Nie kje sme*<br>*pochn**u**vale/p**o**chnale* |
| 2nd person | You would have begun<br>Ти ќе сип**о**чнувал/п**о**чнал(а)<br>*Ti kje si p**o**chnuval/p**o**chnal(a)* | You would have begun<br>Вие ќе сте почн**у**вале/п**о**чнале<br>*Vie kje ste pochn**u**vale/p**o**chnale* |
| 3rd person | He/She/It would have begun<br>Тој/Таа/Тоаќе<br>п**о**чнувал/п**о**чнал(а)(о)<br>*Toj/Taa/Toa kje*<br>*p**o**chnuval/p**o**chnal(a)(o)* | They would have begun<br>Тие ќе почн**у**вале/п**о**чнале<br>*Tie kje pochn**u**vale/p**o**chnale* |

**_To break – Крши/Скрши_**

| | | |
|---|---|---|
| *Infinitive* | To break | Крши<br>Krsi |

| Present Simple Tense | | |
|---|---|---|
| *Person* | *Singular* | *Plural* |
| 1st person | I break -<br>Јас кршам<br>*Jas krsham* | We break -<br>Ние кршиме<br>*Nie krshime* |
| 2nd person | You break -<br>Ти кршиш<br>*Ti krshish* | You break -<br>Вие кршите<br>*Vie krshite* |
| 3rd person | He/She/It breaks -<br>Тој/Таа/Тоакрши<br>*Toj/Taa/Toa krshi* | They break -<br>Тие кршат<br>*Tie krshat* |

| Past Simple Tense | | |
|---|---|---|
| *Person* | *Singular* | *Plural* |
| 1st person | I broke -<br>Јас скршив<br>*Jas skrshiv* | We broke -<br>Ние скршивме<br>*Nie skrshivme* |
| 2nd person | You broke -<br>Ти скрши<br>*Ti skrshi* | You broke -<br>Вие скршивте<br>*Vie skrshivte* |
| 3rd person | He/She/It broke -<br>Тој/Таа/Тоа скрши<br>*Toj/Taa/Toa skrshi* | They broke -<br>Тие скршија<br>*Tie skrshija* |

| Past Continuous Tense | | |
|---|---|---|
| *Person* | *Singular* | *Plural* |
| 1st person | I was breaking -<br>Јас кршев<br>*Jas krshev* | We were breaking -<br>Ние кршевме<br>*Nie krshevme* |
| 2nd person | You were breaking -<br>Ти кршеше<br>*Ti krsheshe* | You were breaking -<br>Вие кршевте<br>*Vie krshevte* |
| 3rd person | He/She/It was breaking -<br>Тој/Таа/Тоа кршеше<br>*Toj/Taa/Toa krsheshe* | They were breaking -<br>Тие кршеа<br>*Tie krshea* |

| Present Perfect Simple Tense | | |
|---|---|---|
| *Person* | *Singular* | *Plural* |
| 1st person | I have broken -<br>Јас сум скршил(а)<br>*Jas sum skrshil(a)* | We have broken -<br>Ние сме скршиле<br>*Nie sme skrshile* |
| 2nd person | You have broken -<br>Ти си скршил(а)<br>*Ti si skrshil(a)* | You have broken -<br>Вие сте скршиле<br>*Vie ste skrshile* |

| | | |
|---|---|---|
| 3rd person | He/She/It has broken -<br>Тој/Таа/Тоа ск**р**шил(а)(о)<br>*Toj/Taa/Toa sk**r**shil(a)(o)* | They have broken -<br>Тие ск**р**шиле<br>*Tie sk**r**shile* |

| **Present Perfect Continuous Tense** | | |
|---|---|---|
| *Person* | *Singular* | *Plural* |
| 1st person | I have been breaking -<br>Јас сум к**р**шел(а)<br>*Jas sum k**r**shel(a)* | We have been breaking -<br>Ние сме к**р**шеле<br>*Nie sme k**r**shele* |
| 2nd person | You have been breaking -<br>Ти си к**р**шел(а)<br>Ti si k**r**shel(a) | You have been breaking -<br>Ве сте к**р**шеле<br>Vie ste k**r**shele |
| 3rd person | He/She/It has been breaking -<br>Тој/Таа/Тоа к**р**шел(а)(о)<br>Toj/Taa/Toa k**r**shel(a)(o) | They have been breaking -<br>Тие к**р**шеле<br>Tie k**r**shele |

| **Past Perfect Simple Tense** | | |
|---|---|---|
| *Person* | *Singular* | *Plural* |
| 1st person | I had broken -<br>Јас бев ск**р**шил(а)<br>*Jas bev sk**r**shil(a)* | We had broken -<br>Ние бевме ск**р**шиле<br>Nie bevme sk**r**shile |
| 2nd person | You had broken -<br>Ти беше ск**р**шил(а)<br>*Ti beshe sk**r**shil(a)* | You had broken -<br>Вие бевте ск**р**шиле<br>*Vie bevte sk**r**shile* |
| 3rd person | He/She/It had broken -<br>Тој/Таа/Тоа беше ск**р**шил(а)(о)<br>*Toj/Taa/Toa beshe sk**r**shil(a)(o)* | They had broken -<br>Тие беа ск**р**шиле<br>*Tie bea sk**r**shile* |

| **Future Simple Tense** | | |
|---|---|---|
| *Person* | *Singular* | *Plural* |
| 1st person | I will break -<br>Јас ќе к**р**шам/ск**р**шам<br>*Jas kje k**r**sham/sk**r**sham* | We will break -<br>Ние ќе к**р**шиме/ск**р**шиме<br>*Nie kje k**r**shime/sk**r**shime* |
| 2nd person | You will break -<br>Ти ќе к**р**шиш/ск**р**шиш<br>*Ti kje k**r**shish/sk**r**shish* | You will break -<br>Вие ќе к**р**шите/ск**р**шите<br>*Vie kje k**r**shite/sk**r**shite* |
| 3rd person | He/She/It will break -<br>Тој/Таа/Тоа ќе к**р**ши/ск**р**ши<br>*Toj/Taa/Toa kje k**r**shi/sk**r**shi* | They will break -<br>Тие ќе к**р**шат/ск**р**шат<br>*Tie kje k**r**shat/sk**r**shat* |

| **used to + infinitive or would + infinitive** | | |
|---|---|---|
| *Person* | *Singular* | *Plural* |
| 1st person | I would break -<br>Јас ќе к**р**шев/ск**р**шев<br>*Jas kje k**r**shev/sk**r**shev* | We would break -<br>Ние ќе к**р**шевме/ск**р**шевме<br>*Nie kje k**r**shevme/sk**r**shesvme* |
| 2nd person | You would break -<br>Ти ќе к**р**шеше/ск**р**шеше<br>*Ti kje k**r**sheshe/sk**r**sheshe* | You would break -<br>Вие ќе к**р**шевте/ск**р**шевте<br>*Vie kje k**r**shevte/sk**r**shevte* |
| 3rd person | He/She/It would break -<br>Тој/Таа/Тоа ќе<br>к**р**шеше/ск**р**шеше<br>*Toj/Taa/Toa k**r**sheshe/sk**r**sheshe* | They would break -<br>Тие ќе к**р**шеа/ск**р**шеја<br>*Tie kje k**r**shea/sk**r**sheja* |

| **Personal endings for future perfect-in-the-past tense** | | |
|---|---|---|
| *Person* | *Singular* | *Plural* |
| 1st person | I would have broken -<br>Јас ќе сум к**р**шел/ск**р**шел(а)<br>*Jas kje sum k**r**shel/sk**r**shel(a)* | We would have broken -<br>Ние ќе сме к**р**шеле/ск**р**шеле<br>*Nie kje sme k**r**shele/sk**r**shele* |
| 2nd person | You would have broken -<br>Ти ќе си к**р**шел/ск**р**шел(а)<br>*Ti kje si k**r**shel/sk**r**shel(a)* | You would have broken -<br>Вие ќе сте кршеле/скршеле<br>*Vie kje ste k**r**shele/sk**r**shele* |
| 3rd person | He/She/It would have broken -<br>Тој/Таа/Тоа ќе<br>к**р**шел/ск**р**шел(а)(о)<br>Тој/Таа/Тоа*kje*<br>*k**r**shel/sk**r**shel(a)(o)* | They would have broken -<br>Тие ќе к**р**шеле/ск**р**шеле<br>*Tie kje k**r**hele/sk**r**shele* |

**To breathe - Дише/Издиша**

| | | |
|---|---|---|
| *Infinitive* | To breathe | Дише<br>Dishe |

| Present Simple Tense | | |
|---|---|---|
| *Person* | *Singular* | *Plural* |
| 1st person | I breathe -<br>Јас дишам<br>*Jas disham* | We breathe -<br>Ние дишеме<br>*Nie dishime* |
| 2nd person | You breathe -<br>Ти дишеш<br>*Ti dishesh* | You breathe -<br>Вие дишете<br>*Vie dishite* |
| 3rd person | He/She/It breathes -<br>Тој/Таа/Тоа дише<br>*Toj/Taa/Toa dishe* | They breathe -<br>Тие дишат<br>*Tie dishat* |

| Past Simple Tense | | |
|---|---|---|
| *Person* | *Singular* | *Plural* |
| 1st person | I breathed -<br>Јас издишав<br>*Jas izdishav* | We breathed -<br>Ние издишавме<br>*Nie izdishavme* |
| 2nd person | You breathed -<br>Ти издиша<br>*Ti izdisha* | You breathed -<br>Вие издишавте<br>*Vie izdishavte* |
| 3rd person | He/She/It breathed -<br>Тој/Таа/Тоа издиша<br>*Toj/Taa/Toa izdisha* | They breathed -<br>Тие издишаа<br>*Tie izdishaa* |

| Past Continuous Tense | | |
|---|---|---|
| *Person* | *Singular* | *Plural* |
| 1st person | I was breathing -<br>Јас дишев<br>*Jas dishev* | We were breathing -<br>Ние дишевме<br>*Nie dishevme* |
| 2nd person | You were breathing -<br>Ти дишеше<br>*Ti disheshe* | You were breathing -<br>Вие дишевте<br>*Vie dishevte* |
| 3rd person | He/She/It was breathing -<br>Тој/Таа/Тоа дишеше<br>*Toj/Taa/Toa disheshe* | They were breathing -<br>Тие дишеа<br>*Tie dishea* |

| Present Perfect Simple Tense | | |
|---|---|---|
| *Person* | *Singular* | *Plural* |
| 1st person | I have breathed -<br>Јас сум издишал(а)<br>*Jas sum izdishal(a)* | We have breathed -<br>Ние сме издишале<br>*Nie sme izdishale* |

| | | |
|---|---|---|
| 2nd person | You have breathed -<br>Ти си **и**здишал(а)<br>*Ti si **i**zdishal(a)* | You have breathed -<br>Вие сте изд**и**шале<br>*Vie ste izd**i**shale* |
| 3rd person | He/She/It has breathed -<br>Тој/Таа/Тоа**и**здишал(а)(о)<br>*Toj/Taa/Toa **i**zdishal(a)(o)* | They have breathed -<br>Тие изд**и**шале<br>*Tie izd**i**shale* |

| Present Perfect Continuous Tense | | |
|---|---|---|
| *Person* | *Singular* | *Plural* |
| 1st person | I have been breathing -<br>Јас сум д**и**шел(а)<br>*Jas sum d**i**shel(a)* | We have been breathing -<br>Ние сме д**и**шеле<br>*Nie sme d**i**shele* |
| 2nd person | You have been breathing -<br>Ти си д**и**шел(а)<br>*Ti si d**i**shel(a)* | You have been breathing -<br>Вие сте д**и**шеле<br>*Vie ste d**i**shele* |
| 3rd person | He/She/It has been breathing-<br>Тој/Таа/Тоа д**и**шел(а)(о)<br>*Toj/Taa/Toa d**i**shel(a)(o)* | They have been breathing -<br>Тие д**и**шеле<br>*Tie d**i**shele* |

| Past Perfect Simple Tense | | |
|---|---|---|
| *Person* | *Singular* | *Plural* |
| 1st person | I had breathed -<br>Јас бев **и**здишал(а)<br>*Jas bev **i**zdishal* | We had breathed -<br>Ние бевме изд**и**шале<br>*Nie bevme izd**i**shale* |
| 2nd person | You had breathed -<br>Ти беше **и**здишал(а)<br>*Ti beshe **i**zdishal* | You had breathed -<br>Вие бевте изд**и**шале<br>*Vie bevte izd**i**shale* |
| 3rd person | He/She/It had breathed -<br>Тој/Таа/Тоа беше<br>**и**здишал(а)(о)<br>*Toj/Taa/Toa beshe **i**zdishal(a)(o)* | They had breathed -<br>Тие беа изд**и**шале<br>*Tie bea izd**i**shale* |

| Future Simple Tense | | |
|---|---|---|
| *Person* | *Singular* | *Plural* |
| 1st person | I will breathe -<br>Јас ќе д**и**шам/**и**здишам<br>*Jas kje **i**sham/**i**zdisham* | We will breathe -<br>Ние ќе д**и**шеме/изд**и**шеме<br>*Nie kje d**i**sheme/izd**i**sheme* |
| 2nd person | You will breathe -<br>Ти ќе д**и**шеш/**и**здишеш<br>*Ti kje d**i**shesh/**i**zdishesh* | You will breathe -<br>Вие ќе д**и**шете/изд**и**шете<br>Vie kje d**i**shete/izd**i**shete |
| 3rd person | He/She/It will breathe -<br>Тој/Таа/Тоа ќе д**и**ше/**и**здише<br>*Toj/Taa/Toa kje d**i**she/**i**zdishe* | They will breathe -<br>Тие ќе д**и**шат/изд**и**шат<br>*Tie d**i**shat/izd**i**shat* |

| **used to + infinitive or would + infinitive** | | |
|---|---|---|
| *Person* | *Singular* | *Plural* |
| 1st person | I would breathe - Јас ќе **ди**шев/**из**дишев *Jas kje dishev/izdishev* | We would breathe - Ние ќе **ди**шевме/изд**и**шевме *Nie kje dishevme/izdishevme* |
| 2nd person | You would breathe - Ти ќе **ди**шеше/изд**и**шеше *Ti kje disheshe/izdisheshe* | You would breathe - Вие ќе **ди**шевте/изд**и**шевте *Vie kje dishevte/izdishevte* |
| 3rd person | He/She/It would breathe - Тој/Таа/Тоаќе **ди**шеше/изд**и**шеше *Toj/Taa/Toa kje disheshe/izdisheshe* | They would breathe - Тие ќе **ди**шеа/изд**и**шеа *Tie kje dishea/izdishea* |
| **Personal endings for future perfect-in-the-past tense** | | |
| *Person* | *Singular* | *Plural* |
| 1st person | I would have breathed - Јас ќе сум **ди**шел/**из**дишел(а) *Jas kje sum dishel/izdishel(a)* | We would have breathed - Ние ќе сме **ди**шеле/изд**и**шеле *Nie kje sme dishele/izdishele* |
| 2nd person | You would have breathed - Ти ќе си **ди**шел/**из**дишел(а) *Ti kje si dishel/izdishel(a)* | You would have breathed - Вие ќе сте **ди**шеле/изд**и**шеле *Vie kje ste dishele/izdishele* |
| 3rd person | He/She/It would have breathed - Тој/Таа/Тоа **ди**шел/**из**дишел(а),(о) *Toj/Taa/Toa kje dishel/izdishel(a),(o)* | They would have breathed - Тие ќе **ди**шеле/изд**и**шеле *Tie kje dishele/izdishele* |

**_To buy - Купува/Купи_**

| | | |
|---|---|---|
| *Infinitive* | To buy | К**у**пува<br>K**u**puva |

| Present Simple Tense | | |
|---|---|---|
| *Person* | *Singular* | *Plural* |
| 1st person | I buy -<br>Јас к**у**пувам<br>*Jas k**u**puvam* | We buy -<br>Ние куп**у**ваме<br>*Nie kup**u**vame* |
| 2nd person | You buy -<br>Ти к**у**пуваш<br>*Ti k**u**puvash* | You buy -<br>Вие куп**у**вате<br>*Vie kup**u**vate* |
| 3rd person | He/She/It buys -<br>Тој/Таа/тоа к**у**пува<br>*Toj/Taa/Toa k**u**puva* | They buy -<br>Тие куп**у**ваат<br>*Tie kup**u**vaat* |

| Past Simple Tense | | |
|---|---|---|
| *Person* | *Singular* | *Plural* |
| 1st person | I bought -<br>Јас к**у**пив<br>*Jas k**u**piv* | We bought -<br>Ние к**у**пивме<br>*Nie k**u**pivme* |
| 2nd person | You bought -<br>Ти к**у**пи<br>*Ti k**u**pi* | You bought -<br>Вие к**у**пивте<br>*Vie k**u**pivte* |
| 3rd person | He/She/It bought -<br>Тој/Таа/тоа к**у**пи<br>*Toj/Taa/Toa k**u**pi* | They bought -<br>Тие к**у**пија<br>*Tie k**u**pija* |

| Past Continuous Tense | | |
|---|---|---|
| *Person* | *Singular* | *Plural* |
| 1st person | I was buying -<br>Јас куп**у**вав<br>*Jas kup**u**vav* | We were buying -<br>ие куп**у**вавме<br>*Nie kup**u**vavme* |
| 2nd person | You were buying -<br>Ти куп**у**ваше<br>*Ti kup**u**vashe* | You were buying -<br>Вие куп**у**вавте<br>*Vie kup**u**vavte* |
| 3rd person | He/She/It was buying -<br>Тој/Таа/Тоа куп**у**ваше<br>*Toj/Taa/Toa kup**u**vashe* | They were buying -<br>Тие куп**у**ваа<br>*Tie kup**u**vaa* |

| Present Perfect Simple Tense | | |
|---|---|---|
| *Person* | *Singular* | *Plural* |
| 1st person | I have bought -<br>Јас сум к**у**пил<br>*Jas sum k**u**pil* | We have bought -<br>Ние сме к**у**пиле<br>*Nie sme k**u**pile* |
| 2nd person | You have bought -<br>Ти си к**у**пил<br>*Ti si k**u**pil* | You have bought -<br>Вие сте к**у**пиле<br>*Vie ste k**u**pile* |

| | | |
|---|---|---|
| 3rd person | He/She/It has bought -<br>Тој/Таа/Тоа **ку**пил(а)(о)<br>*Toj/Taa/Toa **ku**pil(a)(o)* | They have bought -<br>Тие **ку**пиле<br>*Tie **ku**pile* |

| **Present Perfect Continuous Tense** | | |
|---|---|---|
| *Person* | *Singular* | *Plural* |
| 1st person | I have been buying -<br>Јас сум **ку**пувал<br>*Jas sum **ku**puval* | We have been buying -<br>Ние сме купу**ва**ле<br>*Nie sme kupu**va**le* |
| 2nd person | You have been buying -<br>Ти си **ку**пувал<br>*Ti si **ku**puval* | You have been buying -<br>Вие сте купу**ва**ле<br>*Vie ste kupu**va**le* |
| 3rd person | He/She/It has been buying -<br>Тој/Таа/Тоа **ку**пувал(а)(о)<br>*Toj/Taa/Toa **ku**puval(a)(o)* | They have been buying -<br>Тие купу**ва**ле<br>*Tie kupu**va**le* |

| **Past Perfect Simple Tense** | | |
|---|---|---|
| *Person* | *Singular* | *Plural* |
| 1st person | I had bought -<br>Јас бев **ку**пил<br>*Jas bev **ku**pil* | We had bought -<br>Ние бевме **ку**пиле<br>*Nie bevme **ku**pile* |
| 2nd person | You had bought -<br>Ти беше **ку**пил<br>*Ti beshe **ku**pil* | You had bought -<br>Вие бевте **ку**пиле<br>*Vie bevte **ku**pile* |
| 3rd person | He/She/It had bought -<br>Тој/Таа/Тоа беше **ку**пил(а)(о)<br>*Toj/Taa/Toa beshe **ku**pil(a)(o)* | They had bought -<br>Тие беа **ку**пиле<br>*Tie bea **ku**pile* |

| **Future Simple Tense** | | |
|---|---|---|
| *Person* | *Singular* | *Plural* |
| 1st person | I will buy -<br>Јас ќе **ку**пувам/**ку**пам<br>*Jas kje **ku**puvam/**ku**pam* | We will buy -<br>Ние ќе купу**ва**ме/**ку**пиме<br>*Nie kje kupu**va**me/**ku**pime* |
| 2nd person | You will buy -<br>Ти ќе **ку**пуваш/**ку**пиш<br>*Ti kje **ku**puvash/**ku**pish* | You will buy -<br>Вие ќе купу**ва**те/**ку**пите<br>*Vie kje kupu**va**te/**ku**pite* |
| 3rd person | He/She/It will buy -<br>Тој/Таа/Тоа ќе **ку**пува/**ку**пи<br>*Toj/Taa/Toa kje **ku**puva/**ku**pi* | They will buy -<br>Тие ќе купу**ва**ат/**ку**пат<br>*Tie kje kupu**va**at/**ku**pat* |

| **used to + infinitive or would + infinitive** | | |
|---|---|---|
| *Person* | *Singular* | *Plural* |
| 1st person | I would buy -<br>Јас ќе **ку**пував/**ку**пев<br>*Jas kje **ku**puvav/**ku**pev* | We would buy -<br>Ние ќе купу**ва**вме/**ку**певме<br>*Nie kje kupu**va**vme/**ku**pevme* |
| 2nd person | You would buy -<br>Ти ќе купу**ва**ше/**ку**пеше<br>*Ti kje kupu**va**she/**ku**peshe* | You would buy -<br>Вие ќе купу**ва**вте/**ку**певте<br>*Vie kje kupu**a**vte/**ku**pevte* |

| | | |
|---|---|---|
| 3rd person | He/She/It would buy - Тој/Таа/Тоа ќе куп**у**ваше/**ку**пеше *Toj/Taa/Toa kje kup**u**vashe/**ku**peshe* | They would buy - Тие ќе куп**у**ваа/**ку**пеја *Tie kje kup**u**vaa/**ku**peja* |

| **Personal endings for future perfect-in-the-past tense** | | |
|---|---|---|
| *Person* | *Singular* | *Plural* |
| 1st person | I would have bought Јас ќе сум **ку**пувал/**ку**пил(а) *Jas kje sum **ku**puval/**ku**pil(a)* | We would have bought Ние ќе сме куп**у**вале/**ку**пиле *Nie kje sme kup**u**vale/**ku**pile* |
| 2nd person | You would have bought Ти ќе си **ку**пувал/**ку**пил(а) *Ti kje si **ku**puval/**ku**pil(a)* | You would have bought Вие ќе сте куп**у**вале/**ку**пиле *Vie kje ste kup**u**vale/**ku**pile* |
| 3rd person | He/She/It would have bought Тој/Таа/Тоа ке **ку**пувал/**ку**пил(а)(о) *Toj/Taa/Toa kje **ku**puval/**ku**pil(a)(o)* | They would have bought Тие ќе куп**у**вале/**ку**пиле *Tie kje kup**u**vale/**ku**pile* |

**To call – Се јавува/Се јави**

| | | |
|---|---|---|
| *Infinitive* | To call | Се јавува<br>Se javuva |

| Present Simple Tense | | |
|---|---|---|
| *Person* | *Singular* | *Plural* |
| 1st person | I call -<br>Јас се јавувам<br>*Jas se javuvam* | We call -<br>Ние се јавуваме<br>*Nie se javuvame* |
| 2nd person | You call -<br>Ти се јавуваш<br>*Ti se javuvash* | You call -<br>Вие се јавувате<br>*Vie se javuvate* |
| 3rd person | He/She/It calls -<br>Тој/Таа/Тоа се јавува<br>*Toj/Taa/Toa se javuva* | They call -<br>Тие се јавуваат<br>*Tie se javuvaat* |

| Past Simple Tense | | |
|---|---|---|
| *Person* | *Singular* | *Plural* |
| 1st person | I called -<br>Јас се јавив<br>*Jas se javiv* | We called -<br>Ние се јавивме<br>Nie *se* javivme |
| 2nd person | You called -<br>Ти се јави<br>*Ti se javi* | You called -<br>Вие се јавивте<br>*Vie se javivte* |
| 3rd person | He/She/It called -<br>Тој/Таа/Тоа се јави<br>*Toj/Taa/Toa se javi* | They called-<br>Тие се јавија<br>*Tie se javija* |

| Past Continuous Tense | | |
|---|---|---|
| *Person* | *Singular* | *Plural* |
| 1st person | I was calling -<br>Јас се јавував<br>*Jas se javuvav* | We were calling -<br>Ние се јавувавме<br>*Nie se javuvavme* |
| 2nd person | You were calling -<br>Ти се јавуваше<br>*Ti se javuvashe* | You were calling -<br>Вие се јавувавте<br>*Vie se javuvavte* |
| 3rd person | He/She/It was calling -<br>Тој/Таа/Тоа се јавуваше<br>*Toj/Taa/Toa se javuvashe* | They were calling -<br>Тие се јавуваа<br>*Tie se javuvaa* |

| Present Perfect Simple Tense | | |
|---|---|---|
| *Person* | *Singular* | *Plural* |
| 1st person | I have called<br>Јас сум се јавил(а)<br>*Jas sum javil(a)* | We have called<br>Ние сме сејавиле<br>*Nie sme se javile* |
| 2nd person | You have called<br>Ти си се јавил(а)<br>*Ti si se javil(a)* | You have called<br>Вие сте сејавиле<br>*Vie ste se javile* |

| | | |
|---|---|---|
| 3rd person | He/She/It has called<br>Тој/Таа/Тоа се ј**а**вил(а)(о)<br>*Toj/Taa/Toa se j**a**vil(a)(o)* | They have called<br>Тие сеј**а**виле<br>*Tie se j**a**vile* |

| Present Perfect Continuous Tense | | |
|---|---|---|
| *Person* | *Singular* | *Plural* |
| 1st person | I have been calling -<br>Јас сум се ј**а**вувал(а)<br>*Jas sum se j**a**vuval(a)* | We have been calling -<br>Ние сме се јав**у**вале<br>*Nie sme se jav**u**vale* |
| 2nd person | You have been calling -<br>Ти си се ј**а**вувал(а)<br>*Ti si se j**a**vuval(a)* | You have been calling -<br>Вие сте се јав**у**вале<br>*Vie ste se jav**u**vale* |
| 3rd person | He/She/It has been calling -<br>Тој/Таа/Тоа се ј**а**вувал(а)(о)<br>*Toj/Taa/Toa se j**a**vuval(a)(o)* | They have been calling -<br>Тие се јав**у**вале<br>*Tie se jav**u**vale* |

| Past Perfect Simple Tense | | |
|---|---|---|
| *Person* | *Singular* | *Plural* |
| 1st person | I had called -<br>Јас бев се ј**а**вил(а)<br>*Jas bev se j**a**vil(a)* | We had called -<br>Ние бевме се ј**а**виле<br>*Nie bevme se j**a**vile* |
| 2nd person | You had called -<br>Ти беше се ј**а**вил(а)<br>*Ti beshe se j**a**vil(a)* | You had called -<br>Вие бевте се ј**а**виле<br>*Vie bevte se j**a**vile* |
| 3rd person | He/She/It had called -<br>Тој/Таа/Тоа беше се ј**а**вил(а)<br>(о)<br>*-Toj/Taa/Toa beshe se j**a**vil(a)(o)* | They had called -<br>Тие беа се ј**а**виле<br>*Tie bea se j**a**vile* |

| Future Simple Tense | | |
|---|---|---|
| *Person* | *Singular* | *Plural* |
| 1st person | I will call -<br>Јас ќе се ј**а**вувам/се ј**а**вам<br>*Jas kje se j**a**vuvam/se j**a**vam* | We will call -<br>Ниеќе се јав**у**ваме/се ј**а**виме<br>*Nie kje se jav**u**vame/se j**a**vime* |
| 2nd person | You will call -<br>Тиќе се ј**а**вуваш/се ј**а**виш<br>*Ti kje se j**a**vuvash/se j**a**vish* | You will call -<br>Вие ќе се јав**у**вате/се ј**а**вите<br>*Vie kje se jav**u**vate/se j**a**vite* |
| 3rd person | He/She/It will call -<br>Тој/Таа/Тоа ќе се ј**а**вува/се ј**а**ви<br>*Toj/Taa/Toa kje se j**a**vuva/se j**a**vi* | They will call -<br>Тие ќе се јав**у**ваат/се ј**а**ват<br>*Tie kje se jav**u**vaat/se j**a**vat* |

| **used to + infinitive or would + infinitive** | | |
|---|---|---|
| *Person* | *Singular* | *Plural* |
| 1st person | I would call -<br>Јас ќе се **ја**вував/се **ја**вев<br>*Jas kje se **ja**vuvvav/se **ja**vev* | We would call -<br>Ние ќе се јав**у**вавме/се **ја**вевме<br>*Nie kje se jav**u**vavme/se **ja**vevme* |
| 2nd person | You would call -<br>Ти ќе се јав**у**ваше/се **ја**веше<br>*Ti kje se jav**u**vashe/se **ja**veshe* | You would call -<br>Вие ќе се јав**у**вавте/се **ја**вевте<br>*Vie kje se jav**u**vate/se **ja**vevte* |
| 3rd person | He/She/It would call -<br>Тој/Таа/Тоа се јав**у**ваше/се<br>**ја**веше<br>*Toj/Taa/Toa kje se jav**u**vashe/se*<br>***ja**veshe* | They would call -<br>Тие ќе се јав**у**ваа/се **ја**веја<br>*Tie kje se jav**u**vaa/se **ja**veja* |

| **Personal endings for future perfect-in-the-past tense** | | |
|---|---|---|
| *Person* | *Singular* | *Plural* |
| 1st person | I would have called -<br>Јас ќе сум се **ја**вувал/<br>се **ја**вил(а)<br>*Jas kje sum se **ja**vuval/*<br>*se **ja**vil(a)* | We would have called -<br>Ние ќе сме се јав**у**вале/<br>се **ја**веле<br>*Nie kje sme se jav**u**vale/*<br>*se **ja**vele* |
| 2nd person | You would have called -<br>Ти ќе си се **ја**вувал/<br>се **ја**вил(а)<br>*Ti kje si se **ja**vuval/se **ja**vil* | You would have called -<br>Вие ќе сте се јав**у**вале/<br>се **ја**веле<br>*Vie kje ste se jav**u**vale/*<br>*se **ja**vele* |
| 3rd person | He/She/It would have called -<br>Тој/Таа/Тоа ќе се **ја**вувал/<br>се **ја**вел(а) (о)<br>*Toj/Taa/Toa kje se **ja**vuval/*<br>*se **ja**vel(a)(o)* | They would have called -<br>Тие ќе се јав**у**вале/се **ја**веле<br>*Tie kje se jav**u**vale/se **ja**viele* |

***To can - Може***

| | | |
|---|---|---|
| *Infinitive* | To can | Може<br>Mozhe |

| Present Simple Tense | | |
|---|---|---|
| *Person* | *Singular* | *Plural* |
| 1st person | I can -<br>Јас можам<br>Jas mozham | We can -<br>Ние можеме<br>Nie mozheme |
| 2nd person | You can -<br>Ти можеш<br>Ti mozhesh | You can -<br>Вие можете<br>Vie mozhete |
| 3rd person | He/She/It can -<br>Тој/Таа/Тоа може<br>Toj/Taa/Toa mozhe | They can -<br>Тие можат<br>Tie mozhat |

| Past Simple Tense | | |
|---|---|---|
| *Person* | *Singular* | *Plural* |
| 1st person | I could -<br>Јас можев<br>Jas mozhev | We could -<br>Ние можевме<br>Nie mozhevme |
| 2nd person | You could -<br>Ти можеше<br>Ti mozheshe | You could -<br>Вие можевте<br>Vie mozhevte |
| 3rd person | He/She/It could -<br>Тој/Таа/Тоа можеше<br>Toj/Taa/Toa mozheshe | They could -<br>Тие можеа<br>Tie mozhea |

| Past Continuous Tense | | |
|---|---|---|
| *Person* | *Singular* | *Plural* |
| 1st person | / | / |
| 2nd person | / | / |
| 3rd person | / | / |

| Present Perfect Simple Tense | | |
|---|---|---|
| *Person* | *Singular* | *Plural* |
| 1st person | / | / |
| 2nd person | / | / |
| 3rd person | / | / |

| Present Perfect Continuous Tense | | |
|---|---|---|
| *Person* | *Singular* | *Plural* |
| 1st person | / | / |
| 2nd person | / | / |
| 3rd person | / | / |

| Past Perfect Simple Tense |
|---|

| *Person* | *Singular* | *Plural* |
|---|---|---|
| 1st person | / | / |
| 2nd person | / | / |
| 3rd person | / | / |

| **Future Simple Tense** | | |
|---|---|---|
| *Person* | *Singular* | *Plural* |
| 1st person | I will can -<br>Јас ќе можам<br>Jas kje m**o**zham | We will can -<br>Ние ќе можеме<br>Nie kje m**o**zheme |
| 2nd person | You will can -<br>Ти ќе можеш<br>Ti kje m**o**zhesh | You will can -<br>Ти ќе можеш<br>Ti kje m**o**zhesh |
| 3rd person | He/She/It will can -<br>Тој/Таа/Тоа ќе може<br>Toj/Taa/Toa kje m**o**zhe | They will can -<br>Тие ќе можат<br>Tie kje m**o**zhat |

| **used to + infinitive or would + infinitive** | | |
|---|---|---|
| *Person* | *Singular* | *Plural* |
| 1st person | / | / |
| 2nd person | / | / |
| 3rd person | / | / |

| **Personal endings for future perfect-in-the-past tense** | | |
|---|---|---|
| *Person* | *Singular* | *Plural* |
| 1st person | I would have could -<br>Јас ќе сум можел<br>Jas kje sum m**o**zhel | We would have could -<br>Ние ќе сме можеле<br>Nie kje sme m**o**zhele |
| 2nd person | You would have could -<br>Ти ќе си можел<br>Ti kje si m**o**zhel | You would have could -<br>Вие ќе сте можеле<br>Vie kje ste m**o**zhele |
| 3rd person | He/She/It would have could -<br>Тој/Таа/Тоа ќе можел(а)(о)<br>Toj/Taa/Toa kje m**o**zhel(a)(o) | They would have could -<br>Тие ќе можеле<br>Tie kje m**o**zhele |

**To choose - Одбира/Одбра**

| | | |
|---|---|---|
| Infinitive | To choose | **О**дбира<br>**O**dbira |

| Present Simple Tense | | |
|---|---|---|
| *Person* | *Singular* | *Plural* |
| 1st person | I choose -<br>Јас **о**дбирам<br>*Jas **o**dbiram* | We choose -<br>Ние одб**и**раме<br>*Nie odb**i**rame* |
| 2nd person | You choose -<br>Ти **о**дбираш<br>*Ti **o**dbirash* | You choose -<br>Вие одб**и**рате<br>*Vie odb**i**rate* |
| 3rd person | He/She/It chooses -<br>Тој/Таа/Тоа **о**дбира<br>*Toj/Taa/Toa **o**dbira* | They choose -<br>Тие одб**и**раат<br>*Tie odb**i**raat* |

| Past Simple Tense | | |
|---|---|---|
| *Person* | *Singular* | *Plural* |
| 1st person | I chose -<br>Јас **о**дбрав<br>*Jas **o**dbrav* | We chose -<br>Ние **о**дбравме<br>*Nie **o**dbravme* |
| 2nd person | You chose -<br>Ти **о**дбра<br>*Ti **o**dbra* | You chose -<br>Вие **о**дбравте<br>*Vie **o**dbravte* |
| 3rd person | He/She/It chose -<br>Тој/Таа/Тоа**о**дбра<br>*Toj/Taa/Toa **o**dbra* | They chose -<br>Тие **о**дбраа<br>*Tie **o**dbraa* |

| Past Continuous Tense | | |
|---|---|---|
| *Person* | *Singular* | *Plural* |
| 1st person | I was choosing -<br>Јас **о**дбирав<br>*Jas **o**dbirav* | We were choosing -<br>Ние одб**и**равме<br>*Nie odb**i**ravme* |
| 2nd person | You were choosing -<br>Ти одб**и**раше<br>*Ti odb**i**rashe* | You were choosing -<br>Вие одб**и**равте<br>*Vie odb**i**ravte* |
| 3rd person | He/She/It was choosing -<br>Тој/Таа/Тоаодб**и**раше<br>*Toj/Taa/Toa odb**i**rashe* | They were choosing -<br>Тие одб**и**раа<br>*Tie odb**i**raa* |

| Present Perfect Simple Tense | | |
|---|---|---|
| *Person* | *Singular* | *Plural* |
| 1st person | I have chosen -<br>Јас сум **о**дбрал(а)<br>*Jas sum **o**dbral(a* | We have chosen -<br>Ние сме **о**дбрале<br>*Nie sme **o**dbrale* |
| 2nd person | You have chosen -<br>Ти си **о**дбрал(а)<br>*Ti si **o**dbral(a)* | You have chosen -<br>Вие сте **о**дбрале<br>*Vie ste **o**dbrale* |

| | | |
|---|---|---|
| 3rd person | He/She/It has chosen -<br>Toj/Таа/Тоа **о**дбрал(а)(о)<br>*Toj/Taa/Toa **o**dbral(a)(o)* | They have chosen -<br>Тие **о**дбрале<br>*Tie **o**dbrale* |

| **Present Perfect Continuous Tense** | | |
|---|---|---|
| *Person* | *Singular* | *Plural* |
| 1st person | I have been choosing -<br>Јас сум **о**дбирал(а)<br>*Jas sum **o**dbiral(a)* | We have been choosing -<br>Ние сме одб**и**рале<br>*Nie sme odb**i**rale* |
| 2nd person | You have been choosing -<br>Ти си **о**дбирал(а)<br>*Ti si **o**dbiral(a)* | You have been choosing -<br>Вие сте одб**и**рале<br>*Vie ste odb**i**rale* |
| 3rd person | He/She/It has been choosing -<br>Toj/Таа/Тоа **о**дбирал(а)(о)<br>*Toj/Taa/Toa **o**dbiral(a)(o)* | They have been choosing -<br>Тие одб**и**рале<br>*Tie odb**i**rale* |

| **Past Perfect Simple Tense** | | |
|---|---|---|
| *Person* | *Singular* | *Plural* |
| 1st person | I had chosen -<br>Јас бев **о**дбрал(а)<br>*Jas bev **o**dbral(a)* | We had chosen -<br>Ние бевме **о**дбрале<br>*Nie bevme **o**dbrale* |
| 2nd person | You had chosen -<br>Ти беше **о**дбрал(а)<br>*Ti beshe **o**dbral(a)* | You had chosen -<br>Вие бевте **о**дбрале<br>*Vie bevte **o**dbrale* |
| 3rd person | He/She/It had chosen -<br>Toj/Таа/Тоа беше **о**дбрал(а)(о)<br>*Toj/Taa/Toa beshe **o**dbral(a)(o)* | They had chosen -<br>Тие беа **о**дбрале<br>*Tie bea **o**dbrale* |

| **Future Simple Tense** | | |
|---|---|---|
| *Person* | *Singular* | *Plural* |
| 1st person | I will choose -<br>Јас ќе **о**дбирам/**о**дберам<br>*Jas kje **o**dbiram/**o**dberam* | We will choose -<br>Ние ќе одб**и**раме/одб**е**реме<br>*Nie kje odb**i**rame/odb**e**reme* |
| 2nd person | You will choose -<br>Ти ќе **о**дбираш/**о**дбереш<br>*Ti kje **o**dbirash/**o**dberesh* | You will choose -<br>Вие ќе одб**и**рате/одб**е**рете<br>*Vie kje odb**i**rate/odb**e**rete* |
| 3rd person | He/She/It will choose -<br>Toj/Таа/Тоа ќе **о**дбира/**о**дбере<br>*Toj/Taa/Toa kje **o**dbira/**o**dbere* | They will choose -<br>Тие ќе одб**и**раат/одб**е**рат<br>*Tie kje odb**i**raat/odb**e**rat* |

| **used to + infinitive or would + infinitive** | | |
|---|---|---|
| *Person* | *Singular* | *Plural* |
| 1st person | I would choose -<br>Јас ќе **о**дбирав/**о**дберев<br>*Jas kje **o**dbirav/**o**dberev* | We would choose -<br>Ние ќе одб**и**равме/одб**е**ревме<br>*Nie kje odb**i**ravme/odb**e**revme* |

| | | |
|---|---|---|
| 2nd person | You would choose - Ти ќе одб**и**раше/одб**е**реше *Ti kje odb**i**rashe/odb**e**reshe* | You would choose - Вие ќе одб**и**равте/одб**е**ревте *Vie kje odb**i**ravte/odb**e**revte* |
| 3rd person | He/She/It would choose - Тој/Таа/Тоа ќе одб**и**раше/одб**е**реше *Toj/Taa/Toa kje odb**i**rashe/odb**e**reshe* | They would choose - Тие ќе одб**и**раат/**о**дберат *Tie kje odb**i**raat/**o**dberat* |

| **Personal endings for future perfect-in-the-past tense** | | |
|---|---|---|
| *Person* | *Singular* | *Plural* |
| 1st person | I would have chosen - Јас ќе сум **о**дбирал/**о**дбрал(а) *Jas kje sum **o**dbiral/**o**dbral(a)* | We would have chosen - Ние ќе сме одб**и**рале/**о**дбрале Nie kje sme odb**i**rale/**o**dbrale |
| 2nd person | You would have chosen - Ти ќе си**о**дбирал/**о**дбрал(а) *Ti kje si **o**dbiral/**o**dbral(a)* | You would have chosen - Вие ќе сте одб**и**рале/**о**дбрале *Vie kje ste odb**i**rale/**o**dbrale* |
| 3rd person | He/She/It would have chosen- Тој/Таа/Тоаќе **о**дбирал/**о**дбрал(а)(о) *Toj/Taa/Toa kje **o**dbiral/**o**dbral(a)(o)* | They would have chosen - Тие ќеодб**и**рале/**о**дбрале *Tie kje odb**i**rale/**o**dbrale* |

***To close - Затвара/ Затвори***

| | | |
|---|---|---|
| *Infinitive* | To close | Затвара<br>Zatvara |

| **Present Simple Tense** | | |
|---|---|---|
| *Person* | *Singular* | *Plural* |
| 1st person | I close -<br>Јас затварам<br>*Jas zatvaram* | We close -<br>Ние затвараме<br>*Nie zatvaram* |
| 2nd person | You close -<br>Ти затвараш<br>*Ti zatvarash* | You close -<br>Вие затварате<br>*Vie zatvarate* |
| 3rd person | He/She/It closes -<br>Тој/Таа/Тоазатвара<br>*Toj/Taa/Toa zatvara* | They close -<br>Тие затвараат<br>*Tie zatvaraat* |

| **Past Simple Tense** | | |
|---|---|---|
| *Person* | *Singular* | *Plural* |
| 1st person | I closed -<br>Јас затворив<br>*Jas zatvoriv* | We closed -<br>Ние затворивме<br>*Nie zatvorivme* |
| 2nd person | You closed -<br>Ти затвори<br>*Ti zatvori* | You closed -<br>Вие затворивте<br>*Vie zatvorivte* |
| 3rd person | He/She/It closed -<br>Тој/Таа/Тоа затвори<br>*Toj/Taa/Toa zatvori* | They closed -<br>Тие затворија<br>*Tie zatvorija* |

| **Past Continuous Tense** | | |
|---|---|---|
| *Person* | *Singular* | *Plural* |
| 1st person | I was closing -<br>Јас затварав<br>*Jas zatvarav* | We were closing -<br>Ние затваравме<br>*Nie zatvaravme* |
| 2nd person | You were closing -<br>Ти затвараше<br>*Ti zatvarashe* | You were closing -<br>Вие затваравте<br>*Vie zatvaravte* |
| 3rd person | He/She/It was closing -<br>Тој/Таа/Тоа затвараше<br>*Toj/Taa/Toa zatvarashe* | They were closing -<br>Тие затвараа<br>*Tie zatvaraa* |

| **Present Perfect Simple Tense** | | |
|---|---|---|
| *Person* | *Singular* | *Plural* |
| 1st person | I have closed -<br>Јас сум **за**творил(а)<br>*Jas sum **za**tvoril(a)* | We have closed -<br>Ние сме затв**о**риле<br>*Nie sme zatv**o**rile* |
| 2nd person | You have closed -<br>Ти си **за**творил(а)<br>*Ti si **za**tvoril(a)* | You have closed -<br>Вие сте затв**о**риле<br>*Vie ste zatv**o**rile* |
| 3rd person | He/She/It has closed -<br>Тој/Таа/Тоа **за**творил(а)(о)<br>*Toj/Taa/Toa **za**tvoril(a)(o)* | They have closed -<br>Тие затв**о**риле<br>*Tie zatv**o**rile* |

| **Present Perfect Continuous Tense** | | |
|---|---|---|
| *Person* | *Singular* | *Plural* |
| 1st person | I have been closing -<br>Јас сум **за**тварал(а)<br>*Jas sum **za**tvaral(a)* | We have been closing -<br>Ние сме затв**а**рале<br>*Nie sme zatv**a**rale* |
| 2nd person | You have been closing -<br>Ти си **за**тварал(а)<br>*Ti si **za**tvaral(a)* | You have been closing -<br>Вие сте затв**а**рале<br>*Vie ste zatv**a**rale* |
| 3rd person | He/She/It has been closing -<br>Тој/Таа/Тоа **за**тварал(а)(о)<br>*Toj/Taa/Toa **za**tvaral(a)(o)* | They have been closing -<br>Тие затв**а**рале<br>*Tie zatv**a**rale* |

| **Past Perfect Simple Tense** | | |
|---|---|---|
| *Person* | *Singular* | *Plural* |
| 1st person | I had closed -<br>Јас сум **за**творил(а)<br>*Jas sum **za**tvoril(a)* | We had closed -<br>Ние сме затв**о**риле<br>*Nie sme zatv**o**rile* |
| 2nd person | You had closed -<br>Ти си **за**творил(а)<br>*Ti si **za**tvoril(a)* | You had closed -<br>Вие сте затв**о**риле<br>*Vie ste zatv**o**rile* |
| 3rd person | He/She/It had closed -<br>Тој/Таа/Тоа**за**творил(а)(о)<br>*Toj/Taa/Toa **za**tvoril(a)* | They had closed -<br>Тие затв**о**риле<br>*Tie zatv**o**rile* |

| **Future Simple Tense** | | |
|---|---|---|
| *Person* | *Singular* | *Plural* |
| 1st person | I will close -<br>Јас ќе **за**тварам/**за**творам<br>*Jas kje **za**tvaram/**za**tvoram* | We will close -<br>Ние ќе затв**а**раме/затв**о**риме<br>*Nie kje zatv**a**rame/zatv**o**rime* |
| 2nd person | You will close -<br>Ти ќе **за**твараш/**за**твориш<br>Ti kje **za**tvarash/**za**tvorish | You will close -<br>Вие ќе затв**а**рате/затв**о**рите<br>*Vie kje zatv**a**rate/zatv**o**rite* |
| 3rd person | He/She/It will close -<br>Тој/Таа/Тоа ќе **за**твара/**за**твори<br>*Toj/Taa/Toa kje **za**tvara/**za**tvori* | They will close -<br>Тие ќе затв**а**раат/затв**о**раат<br>*Tie kje zatv**a**raat/zatv**o**raat* |

| **used to + infinitive or would + infinitive** | | |
|---|---|---|
| *Person* | *Singular* | *Plural* |
| 1st person | I would close -<br>Јас ќе з**а**тварав/з**а**творив<br>*Jas kje z**a**tvarav/z**a**tvoriv* | We would close -<br>Ние ќе затв**а**равме/затв**о**ривме<br>*Nie kje zatv**a**rame/zatv**o**rivme* |
| 2nd person | You would close -<br>Ти ќезатв**а**раше/затв**о**реше<br>*Ti kje zatv**a**rashe/zatv**o**reshe* | You would close -<br>Вие ќезатвар**а**вте/затв**о**ривте<br>*Vie kje zatv**a**ravte/zatv**o**rivte* |
| 3rd person | He/She/It would close -<br>Тој/Таа/Тоа<br>ќезатв**а**раше/затв**о**реше<br>*Toj/Taa/Toa<br>zatv**a**rashe/zatv**o**reshe* | They would close -<br>Тие ќезатв**а**раа/затв**о**реа<br>*Tie kje zatv**a**raa/zatv**o**rea* |

| **Personal endings for future perfect-in-the-past tense** | | |
|---|---|---|
| *Person* | *Singular* | *Plural* |
| 1st person | I would have closed -<br>Јас ќе сум<br>з**а**тварал/з**а**творил(а)<br>*Jas kje sum z**a**tvaral/z**a**tvoril(a)* | We would have closed -<br>Ние ќе сме<br>затв**а**рале/затв**о**риле<br>*Nie kje sme zatv**a**rale/zatv**o**rile* |
| 2nd person | You would have closed -<br>Ти ќе си з**а**тварал/з**а**творил(а)<br>*Ti kje si z**a**tvaral/z**a**tvoril(a)* | You would have closed -<br>Вие ќе<br>стезатв**а**рале/затв**о**риле<br>*Vie kje ste zatv**a**rale/zatv**o**rile* |
| 3rd person | He/She/It would have closed -<br>Тој/Таа/Тоаќе<br>з**а**тварал/з**а**творил(а)(о)<br>*Toj/Taa/Toa<br>z**a**tvaral/z**a**tvoril(a)(o)* | They would have closed -<br>Тие ќе затв**а**рале/затв**о**риле<br>*Tie kje zatv**a**rale/zatv**o**rile* |

**To come - Доаѓа/Дојде**

| | | |
|---|---|---|
| *Infinitive* | Tocome | Д**о**аѓа<br>D**o**agja |

| Present Simple Tense | | |
|---|---|---|
| *Person* | *Singular* | *Plural* |
| 1st person | I come -<br>Јас д**о**аѓам<br>*Jas d**o**agjam* | We come -<br>Ние доа**ѓ**аме<br>*Nie doa**g**jame* |
| 2nd person | You come -<br>Ти д**о**аѓаш<br>*Ti d**o**agjash* | You come -<br>Вие доа**ѓ**ате<br>*Vie doa**g**jate* |
| 3rd person | He/She/It comes -<br>Тој/Таа/Тоа д**о**аѓа<br>*Toj/Taa/Toa d**o**agja* | They come -<br>Тие доа**ѓ**аат<br>*Tie doa**g**jaa* |

| Past Simple Tense | | |
|---|---|---|
| *Person* | *Singular* | *Plural* |
| 1st person | I came -<br>Јас д**о**јдов<br>*Jas d**o**jdov* | We came -<br>Ние д**о**јдовме<br>*Nie d**o**jdovme* |
| 2nd person | You came -<br>Ти д**о**јде<br>*Ti d**o**jde* | You came -<br>Вие д**о**јдовте<br>*Vie d**o**jdovte* |
| 3rd person | He/She/It came -<br>Тој/Таа/тоа д**о**јде<br>*Toj/Taa/moa d**o**jde* | They came -<br>Тие д**о**јдоа<br>*Tie d**o**jdoa* |

| Past Continuous Tense | | |
|---|---|---|
| *Person* | *Singular* | *Plural* |
| 1st person | I was coming -<br>Јас д**о**аѓав<br>Jas d**o**agjav | We were coming -<br>Ние доа**ѓ**авме<br>Nie doa**g**javme |
| 2nd person | You were coming -<br>Ти доа**ѓ**аше<br>Ti doa**g**jashe | You were coming -<br>Вие доа**ѓ**авте<br>Vie doa**g**javte |
| 3rd person | He/She/It was coming -<br>Тој/Таа/тоа доа**ѓ**аше<br>Toj/Taa/тоа doa**g**jashe | They were coming -<br>Тие доа**ѓ**аа<br>Tie doa**g**jaa |

| Present Perfect Simple Tense | | |
|---|---|---|
| *Person* | *Singular* | *Plural* |
| 1st person | I have come -<br>Јас сум д**о**шол(а)<br>*Jas sum d**o**shol(a)* | We have come -<br>Ние сме д**о**шле<br>*Nie sme d**o**shle* |
| 2nd person | You have come -<br>Ти си д**о**шол(а)<br>*Ti si d**o**shol(a)* | You have come -<br>Вие стед**о**шле<br>*Vie ste d**o**shle* |

| | | |
|---|---|---|
| 3rd person | He/She/It has come -<br>Тој/Таа/тоа дошол(а)<br>*Toj/Taa/moa doshol(a)* | They have come -<br>Тиедошле<br>*Tie doshle* |

| **Present Perfect Continuous Tense** | | |
|---|---|---|
| *Person* | *Singular* | *Plural* |
| 1st person | I have been coming -<br>Јас сум доаѓал(а)<br>*Jas sum doagjal(a)* | We have been coming -<br>Ние сме доаѓале<br>*Nie sme doagjale* |
| 2nd person | You have been coming -<br>Ти си доаѓал(а)<br>*Ti si doagjal(a)* | You have been coming -<br>Вие сте доаѓале<br>*Vie ste doagjale* |
| 3rd person | He/She/It has been coming -<br>Тој/Таа/тоа доаѓал(а)(о)<br>*Toj/Taa/moa doagjal(a)(o)* | They have been coming -<br>Тие доаѓале<br>*Tie doagjale* |

| **Past Perfect Simple Tense** | | |
|---|---|---|
| *Person* | *Singular* | *Plural* |
| 1st person | I had come -<br>Јас бев дошол(а)<br>*Jas bev doshol(a)* | We had come -<br>Ние бевме дошле<br>*Nie bevme doshle* |
| 2nd person | You had come -<br>Ти беше дошол(а)<br>*Ti beshe doshol(a)* | You had come -<br>Вие бевте дошле<br>*Vie bevte doshle* |
| 3rd person | He/She/It had come -<br>Тој/Таа/тоа беше дошол(а)(о)<br>*Toj/Taa/moa beshe doshol(a)(o)* | They had come -<br>Тие беа дошле<br>*Tie bea doshle* |

| **Future Simple Tense** | | |
|---|---|---|
| Person | Singular | Plural |
| 1st person | I will come -<br>Јас ќе доаѓам/дојдам<br>*Jas kje doagjam/dojdam* | We will come-<br>Ние ќе доаѓаме/дојдеме<br>*Nie kje doagjame/dojdeme* |
| 2nd person | You will come -<br>Ти ќе доаѓаш/дојдеш<br>*ti kje doagjash/dojdesh* | You will come -<br>Вие ќе доаѓате/дојдете<br>*Vie kje doagjate/dojdete* |
| 3rd person | He/She/It will come -<br>Тој/Таа/тоа ќе доаѓа/дојде<br>*Toj/Taa/moa kje doagja/dojde* | They will come -<br>Тие ќе доаѓаат/дојдат<br>*Tie kje doagjaat/dojdat* |

| **used to + infinitive or would + infinitive** | | |
|---|---|---|
| *Person* | *Singular* | *Plural* |
| 1st person | I would come -<br>Јас ќе доаѓав/дојдов<br>*Jas kje doagjav/dojdov* | We would come -<br>Ние ќе доаѓавме/дојдовме<br>*Nie kje doagjavme/dojdovme* |
| 2nd person | You would come -<br>Ти ќе доаѓаше/дојдеше<br>*Ti kje doagjashe/dojdeshe* | You would come -<br>Вие ќе доаѓавте/дојдовте<br>*Vie kje doagjavte/dojdovte* |

| | | |
|---|---|---|
| 3rd person | He/She/It would come - Тој/Таа/тоа ќе доаѓ**а**ше/дојд**е**ше *Toj/Taa/moa kje doagj**a**she/dojd**e**she* | They would come - Тие ќе до**а**ѓаа/д**о**јдоа *Tie kje do**a**gjaa/d**o**jdoa* |

| Personal endings for future perfect-in-the-past tense | | |
|---|---|---|
| *Person* | *Singular* | *Plural* |
| 1st person | I would have come - Јас ќе сум д**о**аѓал/д**о**шол(а) *Jas kje sum d**o**agjal/d**o**shol(a)* | We would have come - Ние ќе сме до**а**ѓале/д**о**шле *Nie kje sme do**a**gjale/d**o**shle* |
| 2nd person | You would have come - Ти ќе си д**о**аѓал/д**о**шол(а) *Ti kje si d**o**agjal/d**o**shol(a)* | You would have come - -Вие ќе сте до**а**ѓале/д**о**шле *Vie kje ste do**a**gjale/d**o**shle* |
| 3rd person | He/She/It would have come - Тој/Таа/Тоа ќе д**о**аѓал/д**о**шол(а)(о) *Toj/Taa/Toa kje doagjal/doshol(a)(o)* | They would have come - Тие ќе до**а**ѓале/д**о**шле *Tie kje do**a**gjale/d**o**shle* |

***To cook - Готви/Изготви***

| *Infinitive* | To cook | Г**о**тви<br>G**o**tvi |
|---|---|---|

| Present Simple Tense | | |
|---|---|---|
| *Person* | *Singular* | *Plural* |
| 1st person | I cook -<br>Јас г**о**твам<br>*Jas g**o**tvam* | We cook -<br>Ние г**о**твиме<br>*Nie g**o**tvime* |
| 2nd person | You cook -<br>Ти г**о**твиш<br>*Ti g**o**tvish* | You cook -<br>Вие г**о**твите<br>*Vie g**o**tvite* |
| 3rd person | He/She/It cooks -<br>Тој/Таа/Тоа г**о**тви<br>*Toj/Taa/Toa g**o**tvi* | They cook -<br>Тие г**о**тват<br>*Tie g**o**tvat* |

| Past Simple Tense | | |
|---|---|---|
| *Person* | *Singular* | *Plural* |
| 1st person | I cooked -<br>Јас **и**зготвив<br>*Jas **i**zgotviv* | We cooked -<br>Ние изг**о**твивме<br>Nie izg**o**tvivme |
| 2nd person | You cooked -<br>Ти **и**зотви<br>*Ti **i**zgotvi* | You cooked -<br>Вие изг**о**твите<br>*Vie izg**o**tvivte* |
| 3rd person | He/She/It cooked -<br>Тој/Таа/Тоа **и**зготви<br>*Toj/Taa/Toa**i**zgotvi* | They cooked -<br>Тие изг**о**твија<br>*Tie izg**o**tvija* |

| Past Continuous Tense | | |
|---|---|---|
| *Person* | *Singular* | *Plural* |
| 1st person | I was cooking -<br>Јас г**о**твев<br>*Jas g**o**tvev* | We were cooking -<br>Ние г**о**твевме<br>*Nie g**o**tvevme* |
| 2nd person | You were cooking -<br>Ти г**о**твеше<br>*Ti g**o**tveshe* | You were cooking -<br>Вие г**о**твевте<br>*Vie g**o**tvevte* |
| 3rd person | He/She/It was cooking -<br>Тој/Таа/Тоа г**о**твеше<br>*Toj/Taa/Toa g**o**tveshe* | They were cooking -<br>Тие г**о**твеја<br>*Tie g**o**tveja* |

| Present Perfect Simple Tense | | |
|---|---|---|
| *Person* | *Singular* | *Plural* |
| 1st person | I have cooked -<br>Јас сум **и**зготвил(а)<br>*Jas sum **i**zgotvil(a)* | We have cooked -<br>Ние сме изг**о**твиле<br>*Nie sme izg**o**tvile* |
| 2nd person | You have cooked -<br>Ти си **и**зготвил(а)<br>*Ti si **i**zgotvil(a)* | You have cooked -<br>Вие сте изг**о**твиле<br>*Vie ste izg**o**tvile* |

| | | |
|---|---|---|
| 3rd person | He/She/It has cooked -<br>Тој/Таа/Тоа **и**зготвил(а)(о)<br>*Toj/Taa/Toa**i**zgotvil(a)(o)* | They have cooked -<br>Тие изг**о**твиле<br>*Tie izg**o**tvile* |

| Present Perfect Continuous Tense | | |
|---|---|---|
| *Person* | *Singular* | *Plural* |
| 1st person | I have been cooking -<br>Јас сум г**о**твел(а)<br>*Jas sum g**o**tvel(a)* | We have been cooking -<br>Ние сме г**о**твеле<br>*Nie sme g**o**tvele* |
| 2nd person | You have been cooking -<br>Ти си г**о**твел(а)<br>*Ti si g**o**tvel(a)* | You have been cooking -<br>Вие сте г**о**твеле<br>*Vie ste g**o**tvele* |
| 3rd person | He/She/It has been cooking -<br>Тој/Таа/Тоа г**о**твел(а)(о)<br>*Toj/Taa/Toa g**o**tvel(a)(o)* | They have been cooking -<br>Тие г**о**твеле<br>*Tie g**o**tvele* |

| Past Perfect Simple Tense | | |
|---|---|---|
| *Person* | *Singular* | *Plural* |
| 1st person | I had cooked -<br>Јас бев **и**зготвил(а)<br>Jas bev **i**zgotvi(a) | We had cooked -<br>Ние бевме изг**о**твиле<br>Nie bevme izg**o**tvile |
| 2nd person | You had cooked -<br>Ти беше **и**зготвил(а)<br>Ti beshe **i**zgotvil(a) | You had cooked -<br>Вие бевте изг**о**твиле<br>Vie bevte izg**o**tvile |
| 3rd person | He/She/It had cooked -<br>Тој/Таа/Тоа беше<br>**и**зготвил(а)(о)<br>Toj/Taa/Toa beshe **i**zgotvil(a)(o) | They had cooked -<br>Тие беа изг**о**твиле<br>Tie bea izg**o**tvile |

| Future Simple Tense | | |
|---|---|---|
| *Person* | *Singular* | *Plural* |
| 1st person | I will cook -<br>Јас ќе г**о**твам/**и**зготвам<br>*Jas kje g**o**tvam/**i**zgotvam* | We will cook -<br>Ние ќе г**о**твиме/изг**о**твиме<br>*Nie kje g**o**tvime/izg**o**tvime* |
| 2nd person | You will cook -<br>Ти ќе г**о**твиш/**и**зготвиш<br>*Ti kje g**o**tvish/**i**zgotvish* | You will cook -<br>Вие ќе г**о**твите/изг**о**твите<br>*Vie kje g**o**tvite/izg**o**tvite* |
| 3rd person | He/She/It will cook -<br>Тој/Таа/Тоа ќе г**о**тви/**и**зготви<br>*Toj/Taa/Toa kje g**o**tvi/**i**zgotvi* | They will cook -<br>Тие ќе г**о**тват/**и**зготват<br>*Tie kje g**o**tvat/**i**zgotvat* |

| used to + infinitive or would + infinitive | | |
|---|---|---|
| *Person* | *Singular* | *Plural* |
| 1st person | I would cook-<br>Јас ќе г**о**твев/**и**зготвев<br>*Jas kje g**o**tvev/**i**zgotvev* | We would cook -<br>Ние ќе г**о**твевме/изг**о**твевме<br>*Nie kje g**o**tvevme/izg**o**tvevme* |

| | | |
|---|---|---|
| 2nd person | You would cook -<br>Ти ќе г**о**твеше/изг**о**твеше<br>*Ti kje g**o**tveshe/izg**o**tveshe* | You would cook -<br>Вие ќе г**о**твевте/изг**о**твевте<br>*Vie kje g**o**tvevte/izg**o**tvevte* |
| 3rd person | He/She/It would cook -<br>Тој/Таа/Тоа ќе<br>г**о**твеше/изг**о**твеше<br>*Toj/Taa/Toa kje*<br>*g**o**tveshe/izg**o**tveshe* | They would cook -<br>Тие ќе г**о**твеа/изг**о**твеја<br>*Tie kj g**o**tvea/izgotveja* |

| **Personal endings for future perfect-in-the-past tense** | | |
|---|---|---|
| *Person* | *Singular* | *Plural* |
| 1st person | I would have cooked<br>Јас ќе сум г**о**твел/**и**зготвил(а)<br>*Jas kje sum g**o**tvel/**i**zgotvil(a)* | We would have cooked<br>Ние ќе сме г**о**твеле/изг**о**твиле<br>*Nie kje sme g**o**tvele/izg**o**tvile* |
| 2nd person | You would have cooked -<br>Ти ќе си г**о**твел/**и**зготвил(а)<br>*Ti kje si g**o**tvel/**i**zgotvil(a)* | You would have cooked<br>Вие ќе сте г**о**твеле/изг**о**твиле<br>Vie kje ste g**o**tvele/izg**o**tvile |
| 3rd person | He/She/It would have cooked<br>Тој/Таа/Тоа ќе<br>г**о**твел/**и**зготвил(а)(о)<br>*Toj/Taa/Toa kje*<br>*g**o**tvel/**i**zgotvil(a)(o)* | They would have cooked<br>Тие ќе г**о**твеле/изг**о**твиле<br>*Tie kje g**o**tvele/izg**o**tvile* |

***To cry - Плаче/Заплаче***

| | | |
|---|---|---|
| Infinitive | To cry | Пл**а**че<br>Pl**a**che |

| Present Simple Tense | | |
|---|---|---|
| *Person* | *Singular* | *Plural* |
| 1st person | I cry -<br>Јас пл**а**чам<br>*Jas pl**a**cham* | We cry -<br>Ние пл**а**чеме<br>*Nie pl**a**cheme* |
| 2nd person | You cry -<br>Ти пл**а**чеш<br>*Ti pl**a**chesh* | You cry -<br>Вие пл**а**чете<br>*Vie pl**a**chete* |
| 3rd person | He/She/It cries -<br>Тој/Таа/Тоа пл**а**че<br>*Toj/Taa/Toa pl**a**che* | They cry -<br>Тие пл**а**чат<br>*Tie pl**a**chat* |

| Past Simple Tense | | |
|---|---|---|
| *Person* | *Singular* | *Plural* |
| 1st person | I cried -<br>Јас з**а**плакав<br>*Jas z**a**plakav* | We cried -<br>Ние запл**а**кавме<br>*Nie zapl**a**kavme* |
| 2nd person | You cried -<br>Ти з**а**плака<br>*Ti z**a**plaka* | You cried -<br>Вие се запл**а**кавте<br>*Vie zapl**a**kavte* |
| 3rd person | He/She/It cried -<br>Тој/Таа/Тоа з**а**плака<br>*Toj/Taa/Toa z**a**plaka* | They cried -<br>Тие се запл**а**каа<br>*Tie zapl**a**kaa* |

| Past Continuous Tense | | |
|---|---|---|
| *Person* | *Singular* | *Plural* |
| 1st person | I was crying -<br>Јас пл**а**чев<br>*Jas pl**a**chev* | We were crying -<br>Ние пл**а**чевме<br>*Nie pl**a**chevme* |
| 2nd person | You were crying -<br>Ти пл**а**чеше<br>*Ti pl**a**cheshe* | You were crying -<br>Вие пл**а**чевте<br>*Vie pl**a**chevte* |
| 3rd person | He/She/It was crying -<br>Тој/Таа/Тоа пл**а**чеше<br>*Toj/Taa/Toa pl**a**cheshe* | They were crying -<br>Тие пл**а**чеа<br>*Tie pl**a**chea* |

| Present Perfect Simple Tense | | |
|---|---|---|
| *Person* | *Singular* | *Plural* |
| 1st person | I have cried -<br>Јас сум пл**а**чел(а)<br>*Jas sum pl**a**chel(a)* | We have cried -<br>Ние сме пл**а**челе<br>*Nie sme pl**a**chele* |
| 2nd person | You have cried -<br>Ти си пл**а**чел(а)<br>*Ti si pl**a**chel(a)* | You have cried -<br>Вие сте пл**а**челе<br>*Vie ste pl**a**chele* |

| | | |
|---|---|---|
| 3rd person | He/She/It has cried -<br>Тој/Таа/Тоа плачел(а)(о)<br>*Toj/Taa/Toa plachel(a)(o)* | They have cried -<br>Тие плачеле<br>*Tie plachele* |

| Present Perfect Continuous Tense | | |
|---|---|---|
| *Person* | *Singular* | *Plural* |
| 1st person | I have been crying -<br>Јас сум заплакал(а)<br>*Jas sum zaplakal(a)* | We have been crying -<br>Ние сме заплакале<br>*Nie sme zaplakale* |
| 2nd person | You have been crying -<br>Ти си заплакал(а)<br>*Ti si zaplakal(a)* | You have been crying -<br>Вие сте заплакале<br>*Vie ste zaplakale* |
| 3rd person | He/She/It has been crying -<br>Тој/Таа/Тоа заплакал(а) (о)<br>*Toj/Taa/Toa zaplakal(a) (o)* | They have been crying -<br>Тие заплакале<br>*Tie zaplakale* |

| Past Perfect Simple Tense | | |
|---|---|---|
| *Person* | *Singular* | *Plural* |
| 1st person | I had cried -<br>Јас бев заплакал(а)<br>*Jas bev zaplakal(a)* | We had cried -<br>Ние бевме заплакале<br>*Nie bevme zaplakale* |
| 2nd person | You had cried -<br>Ти беше заплакал (а)<br>*Ti beshe zaplakal (a)* | You had cried -<br>Вие бевте заплакале<br>*Vie bevte zaplakale* |
| 3rd person | He/She/It had cried -<br>Тој/Таа/Тоа беше заплакал (а)(о)<br>*Toj/Taa/Toa beshe zaplakal (a)(o)* | They had cried -<br>Тие беа заплакале<br>*Tie bea zaplakale* |

| Future Simple Tense | | |
|---|---|---|
| *Person* | *Singular* | *Plural* |
| 1st person | I will cry -<br>Јас ќе плачам/заплакам<br>*Jas kje placham/zaplakam* | We will cry -<br>Ние ќе плачеме/заплакаме<br>*Nie kje placheme/zaplakame* |
| 2nd person | You will cry -<br>Ти ќе плачеш/заплакаш<br>*Ti kje plachesh/zaplakash* | You will cry -<br>Вие ќе плачете/заплакате<br>*Vie kje plachete/zaplakate* |
| 3rd person | He/She/It will cry -<br>Тој/Таа/Тоа ќе плаче/заплака<br>*Toj/Taa/Toakje place/zaplaka(a),(o)* | They will cry -<br>Тие ќе плачат/заплакаат<br>*Tie kje plachat/zaplakaat* |

| used to + infinitive or would + infinitive | | |
|---|---|---|
| *Person* | *Singular* | *Plural* |
| 1st person | I would cry -<br>Јас ќе плачев/заплакав<br>*Jas kje plachev/zaplakav* | We would cry -<br>Ние ќе плачевме/заплакавме<br>*Nie kje plachevme/zaplakavme* |

| | | |
|---|---|---|
| 2nd person | You would cry - Ти ќе пл**а**чеше/запл**а**каше Ti kje placheshe/zaplakashe | You would cry - Вие ќе пл**а**чевте/запл**а**кавте *Vie kje plachevte/zaplakavte* |
| 3rd person | He/She/It would cry - Тој/Таа/Тоа ќе пл**а**чеше/запл**а**каше *Toj/Taa/Toa kje pl**a**cheshe/zapl**a**kashe* | They would cry - Тие ќе пл**а**чеа/запл**а**каа *Tie kje pl**a**chea/zapl**a**kaa* |

| Personal endings for future perfect-in-the-past tense | | |
|---|---|---|
| *Person* | *Singular* | *Plural* |
| 1st person | I would have cried - Јас ќе сум пл**а**чел/з**а**плакал(а) *Jas kje sum pl**a**chel/z**a**plakal(a)* | We would have cried - Ние ќе сме пл**а**челе/запл**а**кале *Nie kje sme pl**a**chele/zapl**a**kale* |
| 2nd person | You would have cried - Ти ќе си пл**а**чел/з**а**плакал(а) *Ti kje si pl**a**chel/z**a**plakal (a)* | You would have cried - Вие ќе сте пл**а**челе/запл**а**кале *Vie kje ste pl**a**chele/zapl**a**kale* |
| 3rd person | He/She/It would have cried - Тој/Таа/Тоа ќе пл**а**чел/ з**а**плакал(а)(о) *Toj/Taa/Toa kje pl**a**chel/z**a**plakal(a)(o)* | They would have cried - Ти ќепл**а**челе/запл**а**кале *Tie kje pl**a**chele/zapl**a**kale* |

***To dance – Танцува/Потанцува***

| | | |
|---|---|---|
| *Infinitive* | To dance | Т**а**нцува<br>Tancuva |

| **Present Simple Tense** | | |
|---|---|---|
| *Person* | *Singular* | *Plural* |
| 1st person | I dance -<br>Јас т**а**нцувам<br>*Jas t**a**ncuvam* | We dance -<br>Ние танц**у**ваме<br>*Nie tanc**u**vame* |
| 2nd person | You dance -<br>Ти т**а**нцуваш<br>*Ti t**a**ncuvash* | You dance -<br>Вие танц**у**вате<br>*Vie tanc**u**vate* |
| 3rd person | He/She/It dances -<br>Тој/Таа/Тоат**а**нцува<br>*Toj/Taa/Toa t**a**ncuva* | They dance -<br>Тие танц**у**ваат<br>*Tie tanc**u**vaat* |

| **Past Simple Tense** | | |
|---|---|---|
| *Person* | *Singular* | *Plural* |
| 1st person | I danced -<br>Јас пот**а**нцував<br>*Jas pot**a**ncuvav* | We danced -<br>Ние потанц**у**вавме<br>*Nie potanc**u**vavme* |
| 2nd person | You danced -<br>Ти пот**а**нцува<br>Ti *pot**a**ncuva* | You danced -<br>Вие потанц**у**вавте<br>*Vie potanc**u**vavte* |
| 3rd person | He/She/It danced -<br>Тој/Таа/Тоа пот**а**нцува<br>*Toj/Taa/Toa pot**a**ncuva* | They danced -<br>Тие потанц**у**ваа<br>*Tie potanc**u**vaa* |

| **Past Continuous Tense** | | |
|---|---|---|
| *Person* | *Singular* | *Plural* |
| 1st person | I was dancing -<br>Јас т**а**нцував<br>*Jas t**a**ncuvav* | We were dancing -<br>Ние танц**у**вавме<br>*Nietanc**u**vavme* |
| 2nd person | You were dancing -<br>Ти танц**у**ваше<br>*Ti tanc**u**vashe* | You were dancing -<br>Вие танц**у**вавте<br>*Vie tanc**u**vavte* |
| 3rd person | He/She/It was dancing -<br>Тој/Таа/Тоа танц**у**ваше<br>*Toj/Taa/Toa tanc**u**vashe* | They were dancing -<br>Тие танц**у**ваа<br>*Tie tanc**u**vaa* |

| **Present Perfect Simple Tense** | | |
|---|---|---|
| *Person* | *Singular* | *Plural* |
| 1st person | I have danced -<br>Јас сум пот**а**нцувал(а)<br>*Jas sum pot**a**ncuval(a)* | We have danced -<br>Ние сме потанц**у**вале<br>*Nie sme potanc**u**vale* |
| 2nd person | You have danced -<br>Ти си пот**а**нцувал(а)<br>*Ti si pot**a**ncuval(a)* | You have danced -<br>Вие сте потанц**у**вале<br>*Vie ste potanc**u**vale* |

| | | |
|---|---|---|
| 3rd person | He/She/It has danced -<br>Тој/Таа/Тоапот**а**нцувал(а)(о)<br>*Toj/Taa/Toapot**a**ncuval(a)(o)* | They have danced -<br>Тие потанц**у**вале<br>*Tie potanc**u**vale* |

| **Present Perfect Continuous Tense** | | |
|---|---|---|
| Person | Singular | Plural |
| 1st person | I have been dancing -<br>Јас сум т**а**нцувал(а)<br>*Jas sum t**a**ncuval(a)* | We have been dancing -<br>Ние сме танц**у**вале<br>Nie sme *tanc**u**vale* |
| 2nd person | You have been dancing -<br>Ти си т**а**нцувал(а)<br>*Ti si t**a**ncuval(a)* | You have been dancing -<br>Вие сте танц**у**вале<br>Vie ste *tanc**u**vale* |
| 3rd person | He/She/It has been dancing -<br>Тој/Таа/Тоа т**а**нцувал(а)(о)<br>*Toj/Taa/Toa t**a**ncuval(a)(o)* | They have been dancing -<br>Тие танц**у**вале<br>*Tie tanc**u**vale* |

| **Past Perfect Simple Tense** | | |
|---|---|---|
| *Person* | *Singular* | *Plural* |
| 1st person | I had danced -<br>Јас бев пот**а**нцувал(а)<br>*Jas bev pot**a**ncuval(a)* | We had danced -<br>Ние бевме потанц**у**вале<br>*Nie bevme potanc**u**vale* |
| 2nd person | You had danced -<br>Ти беше пот**а**нцувал(а)<br>*Ti beshe pot**a**ncuval(a)* | You had danced -<br>Вие бевте потанц**у**вале<br>*Vie bevte potanc**u**vale* |
| 3rd person | He/She/It had danced -<br>Тој/Таа/Тоа беше<br>пот**а**нцувал(а),(о)<br>*Toj/Taa/Toa beshe pot**a**ncuval(a)* | They had danced -<br>Тие беа потанц**у**вале<br>*Tie bea potanc**u**vale* |

| **Future Simple Tense** | | |
|---|---|---|
| *Person* | *Singular* | *Plural* |
| 1st person | I will dance -<br>Јас ќе т**а**нцувам/пот**а**нцувам<br>*Jas kje t**a**ncuvam/pot**a**ncuvam* | We will dance -<br>Ние ќе танц**у**ваме/потанц**у**ваме<br>Nie kje tanc**u**vame/potanc**u**vame |
| 2nd person | You will dance -<br>Ти ќе т**а**нцуваш/пот**а**нцуваш<br>*Ti kje t**a**ncuvash/pot**a**ncuvash* | You will dance -<br>Вие ќе танц**у**вате/потанц**у**вате<br>Vie kje tanc**u**vate/potanc**u**vate |
| 3rd person | He/She/It will dance -<br>Тој/Таа/Тоа т**а**нцува/пот**а**нцува<br>*Toj/Taa/Toa kje*<br>*t**a**ncuva/pot**a**ncuva* | They will dance -<br>Тие ќе танц**у**ваат/потанц**у**ваат<br>*Tie kje tanc**u**vaat/potanc**u**vaat* |

| **used to + infinitive or would + infinitive** | | |
|---|---|---|
| *Person* | *Singular* | *Plural* |
| 1st person | I would dance - Јас ќе т**а**нцував/пот**а**нцував *Jas kje t**a**ncuvav/pot**a**ncuvav* | We would dance - Ние ќе танц**у**вавме/потанц**у**вавме *Nie kje tanc**u**vavme/potanc**u**vavme* |
| 2nd person | You would dance - Ти ќе танц**у**ваше/потанц**у**ваше *Ti kje tanc**u**vashe/potanc**u**vashe* | You would dance - Вие ќе танц**у**вавте/потанц**у**вавте *Vie kje tanc**u**vavte/potanc**u**vavte* |
| 3rd person | He/She/It would dance - Тој/Таа/Тоа ќе танц**у**ваше/потанц**у**ваше *Toj/Taa/Toa kje tanc**u**vashe/potanc**u**vashe* | They would dance - Тие ќе танц**у**ваа/потанц**у**ваа *Tie kje tanc**u**vaa/potanc**u**vaa* |

| **Personal endings for future perfect-in-the-past tense** | | |
|---|---|---|
| *Person* | *Singular* | *Plural* |
| 1st person | I would have danced - Јас ќе сум т**а**нцувал/пот**а**нцувал(а) *Jas kje sum t**a**ncuval/pot**a**ncuval(a)* | We would have danced Ние ќе сме танц**у**вале/потанц**у**вале *Nie kje sme tanc**u**vale/potanc**u**vale* |
| 2nd person | You would have danced Ти ќе си т**а**нцувал/пот**а**нцувал(а) *Ti kje si tancuval/potancuval(a)* | You would have danced Вие ќе сте танц**у**вале/потанц**у**вале *Vie kje ste tanc**u**vale/potanc**u**vale* |
| 3rd person | He/She/It would have danced Тој/Таа/Тоаќе т**а**нцувал/пот**а**нцувал(а),(о) *Toj/Taa/Toa kje tancuval/potancuval(a)* | They would have danced Тие танц**у**вале/потанц**у**вале *Tie kje tanc**u**vale/potanc**u**vale* |

***To decide - Одлучува/Одлучи***

| | | |
|---|---|---|
| *Infinitive* | To decide | Одл**у**чува<br>Odl**u**chuva |

| **Present Simple Tense** | | |
|---|---|---|
| *Person* | *Singular* | *Plural* |
| 1st person | I decide -<br>Јас одл**у**чувам<br>*Jas odl**u**chuvam* | We decide -<br>Ние одлуч**у**ваме<br>*Nie odluch**u**vame* |
| 2nd person | You decide -<br>Ти одл**у**чуваш<br>*Ti odl**u**chuvash* | You decide -<br>Вие одлуч**у**вате<br>*Vie odluch**u**vate* |
| 3rd person | He/She/It decides -<br>Тој/Таа/Тоа одл**у**чува<br>*Toj/Taa/Toa odl**u**chuva* | They decide -<br>Тие одлуч**у**ваат<br>*Tie odluch**u**vaat* |

| **Past Simple Tense** | | |
|---|---|---|
| *Person* | *Singular* | *Plural* |
| 1st person | I decided -<br>Јас **о**длучив<br>*Jas **o**dluchiv* | We decided -<br>Ние одл**у**чивме<br>*Nie odl**u**chivme* |
| 2nd person | You decided -<br>Ти **о**длучи<br>*Ti **o**dluchi* | You decided -<br>Вие одл**у**чивте<br>*Vie odl**u**chivte* |
| 3rd person | He/She/It decided -<br>Тој/Таа/Тоа **о**длучи<br>*Toj/Taa/Toa **o**dluchi* | They decided -<br>Тие одл**у**чија<br>*Tie odl**u**chija* |

| **Past Continuous Tense** | | |
|---|---|---|
| *Person* | *Singular* | *Plural* |
| 1st person | I was deciding -<br>Јас одл**у**чував<br>*Jas odl**u**chuvav* | We were deciding-<br>Ние одлуч**у**вавме<br>*Nie odluch**u**vavme* |
| 2nd person | You were deciding -<br>Ти одлуч**у**ваше<br>*Ti odluch**u**vashe* | You were deciding -<br>Вие одлуч**у**вавте<br>*Vie odluch**u**vate* |
| 3rd person | He/She/It was deciding -<br>Тој/Таа/Тоа одлуч**у**ваше<br>*Toj/Taa/Toa odluch**u**vashe* | They were deciding -<br>Тие одлуч**у**ваа<br>*Tie odluch**u**vaa* |

| **Present Perfect Simple Tense** | | |
|---|---|---|
| *Person* | *Singular* | *Plural* |
| 1st person | I have decided -<br>Јас сум **о**длучил(а)<br>*Jas sum **o**dluchil(a)* | We have decided -<br>Ние сме одл**у**чиле<br>*Nie sme odl**u**chile* |
| 2nd person | You have decided -<br>Ти си **о**длучил(а)<br>*Ti si **o**dluchil (a)* | You have decided -<br>Вие сте одл**у**чиле<br>*Vie ste odl**u**chile* |

| | | |
|---|---|---|
| 3rd person | He/She/It has decided -<br>Тој/Таа/Тоа **о**длучил(а)(о)<br>*Toj/Taa/Toa **o**dluchil (a)(o)* | They have decided -<br>Тие одл**у**чиле<br>*Tie odl**u**chile* |

| **Present Perfect Continuous Tense** | | |
|---|---|---|
| *Person* | *Singular* | *Plural* |
| 1st person | I have been deciding -<br>Јас сум одл**у**чувал(а)<br>*Jas sum odl**u**chuval(a)* | We have been deciding -<br>Ние сме одлуч**у**вале<br>*Nie sme odluch**u**vale* |
| 2nd person | You have been deciding -<br>Ти си одл**у**чувал(а)<br>*Ti si odl**u**chuval(a)* | You have been deciding -<br>Вие сте одлуч**у**вале<br>*Vie ste odluch**u**vale* |
| 3rd person | He/She/It has been deciding -<br>Тој/Таа/Тоа одл**у**чувал(а)(о)<br>*Toj/Taa/Toa odl**u**chuval(a)(o)* | They have been deciding -<br>Тие одлуч**у**вале<br>*Tie odluch**u**vale* |

| **Past Perfect Simple Tense** | | |
|---|---|---|
| *Person* | *Singular* | *Plural* |
| 1st person | I had decided -<br>Јас бев **о**длучил(а)<br>*Jas bev **o**dluchil(a)* | We had decided -<br>Ние бевме одл**у**чиле<br>*Nie bevme odl**u**chile* |
| 2nd person | You had decided -<br>Ти беше **о**длучил(а)<br>*Ti beshe **o**dluchil (a)* | You had decided -<br>Вие бевте одл**у**чиле<br>*Vie bevte odl**u**chile* |
| 3rd person | He/She/It had decided -<br>Тој/Таа/Тоа беше<br>**о**длучил(а)(о)<br>*Toj/Taa/Toa beshe **o**dluchil(a)(o)* | They had decided -<br>Тие беа одл**у**чиле<br>*Tie bea odl**u**chile* |

| **Future Simple Tense** | | |
|---|---|---|
| *Person* | *Singular* | *Plural* |
| 1st person | I will decide<br>Јас ќе одл**у**чувам/**о**длучам<br>*Jas kje odl**u**chuvam/**o**dlucham* | We will decide<br>Ние ќе одлуч**у**ваме/одл**у**чиме<br>*Nie kje odluch**u**vame/odl**u**chime* |
| 2nd person | You will decide<br>Ти ќе одл**у**чуваш/**о**длучиш<br>Ti kje odl**u**chuvash/**o**dluchish | You will decide<br>Вие ќе одлуч**у**вате/одл**у**чите<br>Vie kje odluch**u**vate/odl**u**chite |
| 3rd person | He/She/It will decide<br>Тој/Таа/Тоа ќе<br>одл**у**чува/**о**длучи<br>*Toj/Taa/Toa kje*<br>*odl**u**chuva/**o**dluchi* | They will decide<br>Тие ќе одлуч**у**ваат/**о**длучат<br>*Tie kje odluch**u**vaat/**o**dluchat* |

| **used to + infinitive or would + infinitive** | | |
|---|---|---|
| *Person* | *Singular* | *Plural* |
| 1st person | I would decide - Јас ќе одлу**у**чував/**о**длучев *Jas kje odl**u**chuvav/**o**dluchev* | We would decide - Ние ќе одлучу**у**вавме/одл**у**чевме *Nie kjeodluch**u**vavme/odl**u**chevme* |
| 2nd person | You would decide - Ти ќе одлучу**у**ваше/одл**у**чеше *Ti kje odluch**u**vashe/odl**u**cheshe* | You would decide - Vie kje одлучу**у**вавте/одл**у**чевте *Vie kjeodluch**u**vavte/odl**u**chevte* |
| 3rd person | He/She/It would decide - Тој/Таа/Тоа ќе одлучу**у**ваше/одл**у**чеше Toj/Taa/Toa odluch**u**vashe/odl**u**cheshe | They would decide - Тие ќе одлучу**у**ваа/одл**у**чеа *Tie кje odluch**u**vaa/odl**u**chea* |

| **Personal endings for future perfect-in-the-past tense** | | |
|---|---|---|
| *Person* | *Singular* | *Plural* |
| 1st person | I would have decided - Јас ќе сум одл**у**чувал/**о**длучил(а) *Jas kje sum odl**u**chuval/**o**dluchil(a)* | We would have decided - Ние ќе сме одлуч**у**вале/одл**у**чиле *Nie kje sme odluch**u**vale/odl**u**chile* |
| 2nd person | You would have decided - Ти ќе си одл**у**чувал/**о**длучил(а) *Ti kje si odl**u**chuval/**o**dluchil(a)* | You would have decided - Вие ќе сте одлуч**у**вале/одл**у**чиле *Vie kje ste odluch**u**vale/odl**u**chile* |
| 3rd person | He/She/It would have decided Тој/Таа/Тоа ќе одл**у**чувал/**о**длучил(а) *Toj/Taa/Toa kje odl**u**chuval/**o**dluchil(a),(o)* | They would have decided - Тие ќе одлуч**у**вале/одл**у**чиле *Tie kje odluch**u**vale/odl**u**chile* |

***To decrease - Намалува/Намали***

| | | |
|---|---|---|
| *Infinitive* | To decrease | Нам**а**лува<br>Nam**a**luva |

| **Present Simple Tense** | | |
|---|---|---|
| *Person* | *Singular* | *Plural* |
| 1st person | I decrease -<br>Јас нам**а**лувам<br>*Jas nam**a**luvam* | We decrease -<br>Ние намал**у**ваме<br>*Nie namal**u**vame* |
| 2nd person | You decrease -<br>Ти нам**а**луваш<br>*Ti nam**a**luvash* | You decrease -<br>Вие намал**у**вате<br>*Vie namal**u**vate* |
| 3rd person | He/She/It decreases -<br>Тој/Таа/Тоа нам**а**лува<br>*Toj/Taa/Toa nam**a**luva* | They decrease -<br>Тие намал**у**ваат<br>*Tie namal**u**vaat* |

| **Past Simple Tense** | | |
|---|---|---|
| *Person* | *Singular* | *Plural* |
| 1st person | I decreased -<br>Јас н**а**малив<br>*Jas n**a**maliv* | We decreased -<br>Ние нам**а**ливме<br>*Nie nam**a**livme* |
| 2nd person | You decreased -<br>Ти н**а**мали<br>*Ti n**a**mali* | You decreased -<br>Вие нам**а**ливте<br>*Vie nam**a**livte* |
| 3rd person | He/She/It decreased -<br>Тој/Таа/Тоа н**а**мали<br>*Toj/Taa/Toa n**a**mali* | They decreased -<br>Тие нам**а**лија<br>*Tie nam**a**lija* |

| **Past Continuous Tense** | | |
|---|---|---|
| *Person* | *Singular* | *Plural* |
| 1st person | I was decreasing -<br>Јас нам**а**лував<br>*Jas nam**a**luvav* | We were decreasing -<br>Ние намал**у**вавме<br>*Nie namal**u**vavme* |
| 2nd person | You were decreasing -<br>Ти намал**у**ваше<br>*Ti namal**u**vashe* | You were decreasing -<br>Вие намал**у**вавте<br>*Vie namal**u**vavte* |
| 3rd person | He/She/It was decreasing -<br>Тој/Таа/Тоа намал**у**ваше<br>*Toj/Taa/Toa namal**u**vashe* | They were decreasing -<br>Тие намал**у**ваа<br>*Tie namal**u**vaa* |

| **Present Perfect Simple Tense** | | |
|---|---|---|
| *Person* | *Singular* | *Plural* |
| 1st person | I have decreased -<br>Јас сум н**а**малил(а)<br>*Jas sum n**a**malil(a)* | We have decreased -<br>Ние сме нам**а**лиле<br>*Nie sme nam**a**lile* |

| | | |
|---|---|---|
| 2nd person | You have decreased - Ти си н**а**малил(а) *Ti si n**a**malil(a)* | You have decreased - Вие сте нам**а**лиле *Vie ste nam**a**lile* |
| 3rd person | He/She/It has decreased - Тој/Таа/Тоа н**а**малил(а)(о) *Toj/Taa/Toa n**a**malil(a)(o)* | They have decreased - Тие нам**а**лиле *Tie nam**a**lile* |

| **Present Perfect Continuous Tense** | | |
|---|---|---|
| *Person* | *Singular* | *Plural* |
| 1st person | I have been decreasing - Јас сум нам**а**лувал(а) *Jas sum nam**a**luval(a)* | We have been decreasing - Ние сме намал**у**вале *Nie sme namal**u**vale* |
| 2nd person | You have been decreasing - Ти си нам**а**лувал(а) *Ti si nam**a**luval(a)* | You have been decreasing - Вие сте намал**у**вале *Vie ste namal**u**vale* |
| 3rd person | He/She/It has been decreasing - Тој/Таа/Тоа нам**а**лувал(а)(о) *Toj/Taa/Toa nam**a**luval(a)(o)* | They have been decreasing - Тие намал**у**вале *Tie namal**u**vale* |

| **Past Perfect Simple Tense** | | |
|---|---|---|
| *Person* | *Singular* | *Plural* |
| 1st person | I had decreased - Јас бев н**а**малил(а) *Jas bev n**a**malil(a)* | We had decreased - Ние бевме нам**а**лиле *Nie bevme nam**a**lile* |
| 2nd person | You had decreased - Ти беше н**а**малил(а) *Ti beshe n**a**malil(a)* | You had decreased - Вие бевте нам**а**лиле *Vie bevte nam**a**lile* |
| 3rd person | He/She/It had decreased - Тој/Таа/Тоа беше н**а**малил(а)(о) *Toj/Taa/Toa beshe n**a**malil(a)(o)* | They had decreased - Тие беа нам**а**лиле *Tie bea nam**a**lile* |

| **Future Simple Tense** | | |
|---|---|---|
| *Person* | *Singular* | *Plural* |
| 1st person | I will decrease Јас ќе нам**а**лувам/н**а**малам *Jas kje nam**a**luvam/n**a**malam* | We will decrease Ние ќе намал**у**ваме/нам**а**лиме *Nie kje namal**u**vame/nam**a**lime* |
| 2nd person | You will decrease Ти ќе нам**а**луваш/н**а**малиш *Ti kje nam**a**luvash/n**a**malish* | You will decrease Вие ќе намал**у**вате/нам**а**лите *Vie kje namal**u**vate/nam**a**lite* |
| 3rd person | He/She/It will decrease Тој/Таа/Тоа ќе нам**а**лува/н**а**мали *Toj/Taa/Toa kje nam**a**luva/n**a**mali* | They will decrease Тие ќе намал**у**ваат/н**а**малат *Tie kje namal**u**vaat/n**a**malat* |

| used to + infinitive or would + infinitive | | |
|---|---|---|
| *Person* | *Singular* | *Plural* |
| 1st person | I would decrease<br>Јас ќе нам**а**лував/н**а**малев<br>*Jas kje nam**a**luvav/n**a**malev* | We would decrease<br>Ние ќе<br>намал**у**вавме/нам**а**левме<br>*Nie kje*<br>*namal**u**vavme/nam**a**levme* |
| 2nd person | You would decrease<br>Ти ќе намал**у**ваше/нам**а**леше<br>*Ti kje namal**u**vashe/nam**a**leshe* | You would decrease<br>Вие ќе намал**у**вавте/нам**а**левте<br>*Vie kje namal**u**vavte/nam**a**levte* |
| 3rd person | He/She/It would decrease<br>Тој/Таа/Тоа ќе<br>намал**у**ваше/нам**а**леше<br>*Тој/Таа/Тоа kje*<br>*namal**u**vashe/nam**a**leshe* | They would decrease<br>Тие ќе намал**у**ваа/нам**а**леа<br>*Tie kje namal**u**vaa/nam**a**lea* |

| Personal endings for future perfect-in-the-past tense | | |
|---|---|---|
| *Person* | *Singular* | *Plural* |
| 1st person | I would have decreased -<br>Јас ќе сум<br>нам**а**лувал/н**а**малил(а)<br>*Jas kje sum*<br>*nam**a**luval/n**a**malil(a)* | We would have decreased -<br>Ние ќе сме<br>намал**у**вале/нам**а**лиле<br>*Nie kje sme*<br>*namal**u**vale/nam**a**lile* |
| 2nd person | You would have decreased -<br>Ти ќе си<br>намал**у**вал/нам**а**лил(а)<br>*Ti kje si namaluval/namalil(a)* | You would have decreased -<br>Вие ќе сте<br>намал**у**вале/нам**а**лиле<br>*Vie kje ste namal**u**vale/nam**a**lile* |
| 3rd person | He/She/It would have decreased<br>-<br>Тој/Таа/Тоа ќе<br>намал**у**вал/нам**а**лил(а)(о)<br>*Тој/Таа/Тоа*<br>*namaluval/namalil(a)(o)* | They would have decreased -<br>Тие ќе намал**у**вале/нам**а**лиле<br>*Tie kje namal**u**vale/nam**a**lile* |

**To die - Умира/Умре**

| | | |
|---|---|---|
| *Infinitive* | To die | **Умира**<br>**U**mira |

| **Present Simple Tense** | | |
|---|---|---|
| *Person* | *Singular* | *Plural* |
| 1st person | I die -<br>Јас **умирам**<br>*Jas **umiram*** | We die -<br>Ние ум**и**раме<br>*Nie umi**r**ame* |
| 2nd person | You die -<br>Ти **умираш**<br>*Ti **umirash*** | You die -<br>Вие ум**и**рате<br>Vie umi**r**ate |
| 3rd person | He/She/It dies -<br>Тој/Таа/Тоа **умира**<br>*Toj/Taa/Toa **umira*** | They die -<br>Тие ум**и**раат<br>*Tie umi**r**aat* |

| **Past Simple Tense** | | |
|---|---|---|
| *Person* | *Singular* | *Plural* |
| 1st person | I died -<br>Јас **умрев**<br>*Jas **umrev*** | We died -<br>Ние **умревме**<br>*Nie **umrevme*** |
| 2nd person | You died -<br>Ти **умре**<br>*Ti **umre*** | You died -<br>Вие **умревте**<br>*Vie **umrevte*** |
| 3rd person | He/She/It died -<br>Тој/Таа/Тоа **умре**<br>*Toj/Taa/Toa **umre*** | They died -<br>Тие **умреа**<br>*Tie **umrea*** |

| **Past Continuous Tense** | | |
|---|---|---|
| *Person* | *Singular* | *Plural* |
| 1st person | I was dying -<br>Јас **умирав**<br>*Jas **umirav*** | We were dying -<br>Ние ум**и**равме<br>*Nie umiravme* |
| 2nd person | You were dying -<br>Ти ум**и**раше<br>*Ti umi**r**ashe* | You were dying -<br>Вие ум**и**равте<br>*Vie umiravte* |
| 3rd person | He/She/It was dying -<br>Тој/Таа/Тоа ум**и**раше<br>*Toj/Taa/Toa umi**r**ashe* | They were dying -<br>Тие ум**и**раа<br>*Tie umi**r**aa* |

| **Present Perfect Simple Tense** | | |
|---|---|---|
| *Person* | *Singular* | *Plural* |
| 1st person | I have died -<br>Јас сум **у**мрел<br>*Jas sum **umrel*** | We have died -<br>Ние сме **у**мреле<br>*Nie sme **umrele*** |
| 2nd person | You have died -<br>Ти си **у**мрел<br>*Ti si **umrel*** | You have died -<br>Вие сте **у**мреле<br>*Toj/Taa/Toa **umrele*** |

| | | |
|---|---|---|
| 3rd person | He/She/It has died -<br>Тој/Таа/Тоа **у**мрел(а)(о)<br>*Toj/Taa/Toa **u**mrel(a)(o)* | They have died -<br>Тие **у**мреле<br>*Tie **u**mrele* |

| Present Perfect Continuous Tense | | |
|---|---|---|
| *Person* | *Singular* | *Plural* |
| 1st person | I have been dying -<br>Јас сум **у**мирал<br>*Jas sum **u**miral* | We have been dying -<br>Ние сме уми**р**але<br>*Nie sme umi**r**ale* |
| 2nd person | You have been dying -<br>Ти си **у**мирал<br>*Ti si **u**miral* | You have been dying -<br>Вие сте уми**р**але<br>*Vie ste umi**r**ale* |
| 3rd person | He/She/It has been dying -<br>Тој/Таа/Тоа **у**мирал(а)(о)<br>*Toj/Taa/Toa **u**miral(a)(o)* | They have been dying -<br>Тие уми**р**але<br>*Tie umi**r**ale* |

| Past Perfect Simple Tense | | |
|---|---|---|
| *Person* | *Singular* | *Plural* |
| 1st person | I had died -<br>Јас бев **у**мрел<br>*Jas bev **u**mrel* | We had died -<br>Ние бевме **у**мреле<br>*Nie bevme **u**mrele* |
| 2nd person | You had died -<br>Ти беше **у**мрел<br>*Ti beshe **u**mrel* | You had died -<br>Вие бевте **у**мреле<br>*Vie bevte **u**mrele* |
| 3rd person | He/She/It had died -<br>Тој/Таа/Тоа беше **у**мрел(а)(о)<br>*Toj/Taa/Toa beshe **u**mrel* | They had died -<br>Тие беа **у**мреле<br>*Tie bea **u**mrele* |

| Future Simple Tense | | |
|---|---|---|
| *Person* | *Singular* | *Plural* |
| 1st person | I will die -<br>Јас ќе **у**мирам/**у**мрам<br>*Jas kje **u**miram/**u**mram* | We will die -<br>Ние ќе уми**р**аме/**у**мреме<br>*Nie kje umi**r**ame/**u**mreme* |
| 2nd person | You will die -<br>Ти ќе **у**мираш/**у**мреш<br>*Ti kje **u**mirash/**u**mresh* | You will die -<br>Вие ќе уми**р**ате/**у**мрете<br>*Vie kje umi**r**ate/**u**mrete* |
| 3rd person | He/She/It will die -<br>Тој/Таа/Тоа ќе **у**мира/**у**мре<br>*Toj/Taa/Toa kje **u**mira/**u**mre* | They will die -<br>Тие ќе уми**р**аат/**у**мрат<br>*Tie kje umi**r**aat/**u**mrat* |

| used to + infinitive or would + infinitive | | |
|---|---|---|
| *Person* | *Singular* | *Plural* |
| 1st person | I would die -<br>Јас ќе **у**мирав/**у**мрев<br>*Jas kje **u**mirav/**u**mrev* | We would die -<br>Ние ќе уми**р**авме/**у**мревме<br>*Nie kje umi**r**avme/**u**mrevme* |
| 2nd person | You would die -<br>Ти ќе уми**р**аше/**у**мреше<br>*Ti kje umi**r**ashe/**u**mreshe* | You would die -<br>Вие ќе уми**р**авте/**у**мревте<br>*Vie kje umi**r**avte/**u**mrevte* |

| | | |
|---|---|---|
| 3rd person | He/She/It would die -<br>Тој/Таа/Тоа ќе ум**и**раше/**у**мреше<br>*Toj/Taa/Toa kje um**i**rashe/**u**mreshe* | They would die -<br>Тие ќе ум**и**раа/**у**мреа<br>*Tie kje um**i**raa/**u**mrea* |

| Personal endings for future perfect-in-the-past tense | | |
|---|---|---|
| *Person* | *Singular* | *Plural* |
| 1st person | I would have died -<br>Јас ќе сум **у**мирал/**у**мрел<br>*Jas kje sum **u**miral/**u**mrel* | We would have died -<br>Ние ќе сме ум**и**рале/**у**мреле<br>*Nie kje sme um**i**rale/**u**mrele* |
| 2nd person | You would have died -<br>Ти ќе си **у**мирал/**у**мрел<br>*Ti kje si **u**miral/**u**mrel* | You would have died -<br>Вие ќе сте ум**и**рале/**у**мреле<br>*Vie kje ste um**i**rale/**u**mrele* |
| 3rd person | He/She/It would have died -<br>Тој/Таа/Тоа ќе **у**мирал/**у**мрел<br>*Toj/Taa/Toa kje **u**miral/**u**mrel* | They would have died -<br>Тие ќе ум**и**рале/**у**мреле<br>*Tie kje um**i**rale/**u**mrele* |

***To do - Прави/Направи***

| | | |
|---|---|---|
| *Infinitive* | To do | Пр**а**ви<br>Pr**a**vi |

| **Present Simple Tense** | | |
|---|---|---|
| *Person* | *Singular* | *Plural* |
| 1st person | I do -<br>Јас пр**а**вам<br>*Jas pr**a**vam* | We do -<br>Ние пр**а**виме<br>*Nie pr**a**vime* |
| 2nd person | You do -<br>Ти пр**а**виш<br>*Ti pr**a**vish* | You do -<br>Вие пр**а**вите<br>*Vie pr**a**vite* |
| 3rd person | He/She/It does -<br>Тој/Таа/Тоа пр**а**ви<br>*Toj/Taa/Toa pr**a**vi* | They do -<br>Тие пр**а**ват<br>*Tie pr**a**vat* |

| **Past Simple Tense** | | |
|---|---|---|
| *Person* | *Singular* | *Plural* |
| 1st person | I did -<br>Јас н**а**правив<br>*Jas n**a**praviv* | We did -<br>Ние напр**а**вивме<br>*Nie napr**a**vivme* |
| 2nd person | You did -<br>Ти н**а**прави<br>*Ti n**a**pravi* | You did -<br>Вие напар**а**вивте<br>*Vie napr**a**vivte* |
| 3rd person | He/She/It did -<br>Тој/Таа/Тоа н**а**прави<br>*Toj/Taa/Toa n**a**pravi* | They did -<br>Тие напр**а**вија<br>*Tie napr**a**vija* |

| **Past Continuous Tense** | | |
|---|---|---|
| *Person* | *Singular* | *Plural* |
| 1st person | I was doing -<br>Јас пр**а**вев<br>*Jas pr**a**vev* | We were doing -<br>Ние пр**а**вевме<br>*Nie pr**a**vevme* |
| 2nd person | You were doing -<br>Ти пр**а**веше<br>*Ti pr**a**veshe* | You were doing -<br>Вие пр**а**вевте<br>*Vie pr**a**vevte* |
| 3rd person | He/She/It was doing -<br>Тој/Таа/Тоа пр**а**веше<br>*Toj/Taa/Toa pr**a**veshe* | They were doing -<br>Тие пр**а**вea<br>*Tie pr**a**vea* |

| **Present Perfect Simple Tense** | | |
|---|---|---|
| *Person* | *Singular* | *Plural* |
| 1st person | I have done -<br>Јас сум н**а**правил(а)<br>*Jas sum n**a**pravil(a)* | We have done -<br>Ние сме напр**а**виле<br>*Nie sme napr**a**vile* |
| 2nd person | You have done -<br>Ти си н**а**правил(а)<br>*Ti si n**a**pravil(a)* | You have done -<br>Вие сте напр**а**виле<br>*Vie ste napr**a**vile* |

| | | |
|---|---|---|
| 3rd person | He/She/It has done - Тој/Таа/Тоа направил(а)(о) *Toj/Taa/Toa napravil(a)(o)* | They have done - Тие направиле *Tie napravile* |

| Present Perfect Continuous Tense | | |
|---|---|---|
| *Person* | *Singular* | *Plural* |
| 1st person | I have been doing - Јас сум правел(а) *Jas sum pravel(a)* | We have been doing - Ние сме правеле *Nie sme pravele* |
| 2nd person | You have been doing - Ти си правел(а) *Ti si pravel(a)* | You have been doing - Вие сте правеле *Vie ste pravele* |
| 3rd person | He/She/It has been doing - Тој/Таа/Тоа правел(а)(о) *Toj/Taa/Toa pravel(a)(o)* | They have been doing - Тие правеле *Tie pravele* |

| Past Perfect Simple Tense | | |
|---|---|---|
| *Person* | *Singular* | *Plural* |
| 1st person | I had done - Јас бев направил(а) *Jas bev napravil(a)* | We had done - Ние бевме направиле *Nie bevme napravile* |
| 2nd person | You had done - Ти беше направил(а) *Ti beshe napravil(a)* | You had done - Вие бевте направиле *Vie bevte napravile* |
| 3rd person | He/She/It had done - Тој/Таа/Тоа беше направил(а)(о) *Toj/Taa/Toa beshe napravil(a)(o)* | They had done - Тие беа направиле *Tie bea napravile* |

| Future Simple Tense | | |
|---|---|---|
| *Person* | *Singular* | *Plural* |
| 1st person | I will do - Јас ќе правам/направам *Jas kje pravam/napravam* | We will do - Ние ќе правиме/направиме *Nie kje pravime/napravime* |
| 2nd person | You will do - Ти ќе правиш/направиш *Ti kje pravish/napravish* | You will do - Вие ќе правите/направите *Vie kje pravite/napravite* |
| 3rd person | He/She/It will do - Тој/Таа/Тоа ќе прави/направи *Toj/Taa/Toa kje pravi/napravi* | They will do - Тие ќе прават/направат *Tie kje pravat/napravat* |

| used to + infinitive or would + infinitive | | |
|---|---|---|
| *Person* | *Singular* | *Plural* |
| 1st person | I would do - Јас ќе правев/направев *jas kje pravev/napravev* | We would do - Ние ќе правевме/направевме *Nie kje pravevme/napravevme* |

| | | |
|---|---|---|
| 2nd person | You would do -<br>Ти ќе правеше/направеше<br>*Ti kje pr**a**veshe/napr**a**veshe* | You would do -<br>Вие ќе пр**а**вевте/напр**а**вевте<br>*Vie kje pr**a**vevte/napr**a**vevte* |
| 3rd person | He/She/It would do -<br>Тој/Таа/Тоа<br>пр**а**веше/напр**а**веше<br>*Toj/Taa/Toa kje<br>paveshe/napraveshe* | They would do -<br>Тие ќе пр**а**веа/напр**а**веа<br>*Tie kje pr**a**vea/napr**a**vea* |

| **Personal endings for future perfect-in-the-past tense** | | |
|---|---|---|
| *Person* | *Singular* | *Plural* |
| 1st person | I would have done -<br>Јас ќе сум пр**а**вел/н**а**правел(а)<br>*Jas kje sum pr**a**vel/n**a**pravel(a)* | We would have done -<br>Ние ќе сме пр**а**веле/напр**а**веле<br>*Nie kje sme pr**a**vele/napr**a**vele* |
| 2nd person | You would have done -<br>Ти ќе си пр**а**вел/н**а**правел(а)<br>*Ti kje si pr**a**vel/n**a**pravel(a)* | You would have done -<br>Вие ќе сте пр**а**веле/напр**а**веле<br>*Vie kje ste pr**a**vele/napr**a**vele* |
| 3rd person | He/She/It would have done -<br>Тој/Таа/Тоа ќе<br>пр**а**вел/н**а**правел(а)(о)<br>*Toj/Taa/Toa kje<br>pr**a**vel/n**a**pravel(a)(o)* | They would have done -<br>Тие ќе пр**а**веле/напр**а**веле<br>*Tie kje pr**a**vele/napr**a**vele* |

**To drink - Пие/Испие**

| | | |
|---|---|---|
| *Infinitive* | To drink | Пие<br>Pie |

| Present Simple Tense | | |
|---|---|---|
| *Person* | *Singular* | *Plural* |
| 1st person | I drink -<br>Јас пијам<br>*Jas pijam* | We drink -<br>Ние пиеме<br>*Nie pirme* |
| 2nd person | You drink -<br>Ти пиеш<br>*Ti piesh* | You drink -<br>Вие пиете<br>*Vie piete* |
| 3rd person | He/She/It drinks -<br>Тој/Таа/Тоа пие<br>*Toj/Taa/Toa pie* | They drink -<br>Тие пијат<br>*Tie pijat* |

| Past Simple Tense | | |
|---|---|---|
| *Person* | *Singular* | *Plural* |
| 1st person | I drank -<br>Јас испив<br>*Jas ispiv* | We drank -<br>Ние испивме<br>*Nie ispivme* |
| 2nd person | You drank -<br>Ти испи<br>*Ti ispi* | You drank -<br>Вие испивте<br>*Vie ispivte* |
| 3rd person | He/She/It drank -<br>Тој/Таа/Тоа испи<br>*Toj/Taa/Toa ispi* | They drank -<br>Тие испија<br>*Tie ispija* |

| Past Continuous Tense | | |
|---|---|---|
| *Person* | *Singular* | *Plural* |
| 1st person | I was drinking -<br>Јас пиев<br>*Jas piev* | We were drinking -<br>Ние пиевме<br>*Nie pievme* |
| 2nd person | You were drinking -<br>Ти пиеше<br>*Ti pieshe* | You were drinking -<br>Вие пиевте<br>*Vie pievte* |
| 3rd person | He/She/It was drinking -<br>Тој/Таа/Тоа пиеше<br>*Toj/Taa/Toa pieshe* | They were drinking -<br>Тие пиеја<br>*Tie pieja* |

| Present Perfect Simple Tense | | |
|---|---|---|
| *Person* | *Singular* | *Plural* |
| 1st person | I have drunk -<br>Јас сум испил(а)<br>*Jas sum ispil(a)* | We have drunk -<br>Ние сме испиле<br>*Nie sme ispile* |
| 2nd person | You have drunk -<br>Ти си испил(а)<br>*Ti si ispil(a)* | You have drunk -<br>Вие сте испиле<br>*Vie ste ispile* |

| | | |
|---|---|---|
| 3rd person | He/She/It has drunk -<br>Тој/Таа/Тоа испил(а)(о)<br>*Toj/Taa/Toa ispil(a)(o)* | They have drunk -<br>Тие испија<br>*Tie ispija* |

| **Present Perfect Continuous Tense** | | |
|---|---|---|
| *Person* | *Singular* | *Plural* |
| 1st person | I have been drinking -<br>Јас сум пиел(а)<br>*Jas sum piel(a)* | We have been drinking -<br>Ние сме пиеле<br>*Nie sme piele* |
| 2nd person | You have been drinking -<br>Ти си пиел(а)<br>*Ti si piel(a)* | You have been drinking -<br>Вие сте пиеле<br>*Vie ste piele* |
| 3rd person | He/She/It has been drinking -<br>Тој/Таа/Тоа пиел(а)(о)<br>*Toj/Taa/Toa piel(a)(o)* | They have been drinking -<br>Тие пиеле<br>*Tie piele* |

| **Past Perfect Simple Tense** | | |
|---|---|---|
| *Person* | *Singular* | *Plural* |
| 1st person | I had drunk -<br>Јас бев испил(а)<br>*Jas bev ispil(a)* | We had drunk -<br>Ние беве испиле<br>*Nie bevme ispile* |
| 2nd person | You had drunk -<br>Ти беше испил(а)<br>*Ti beshe ispil(a)* | You had drunk -<br>Вие бевте испиле<br>*Vie bevte ispile* |
| 3rd person | He/She/It had drunk -<br>Тој/Таа/Тоа беше испил(а)(о)<br>*Toj/Taa/Toa beshe ispil(a)(o)* | They had drunk -<br>Тие беа испиле<br>*Tie bea ispile* |

| **Future Simple Tense** | | |
|---|---|---|
| *Person* | *Singular* | *Plural* |
| 1st person | I will drink -<br>Јас ќе пијам/испијам<br>*Jas kje pijam/ispijam* | We will drink -<br>Ниеќе пиеме/испиеме<br>*Nie kje pieme/ispieme* |
| 2nd person | You will drink -<br>Ти ќе пиеш/испиеш<br>*Ti kje piesh/ispiesh* | You will drink -<br>Вие ќе пиете/испиете<br>*Vie kje piete/ispiete* |
| 3rd person | He/She/It will drink -<br>Тој/Таа/Тоа ќе пие/испие<br>*Toj/Taa/Toa kje pie/ispie* | They will drink -<br>Тие ќе пијат/испијат<br>*Tie kje pijat/ispijat* |

| **used to + infinitive or would + infinitive** | | |
|---|---|---|
| *Person* | *Singular* | *Plural* |
| 1st person | I would drink -<br>Јас ќе пиев/испиев<br>*Jas kje piev/ispiev* | We would drink -<br>Ние ќе пиевме/испиевме<br>*Nie kje pievme/ispievme* |
| 2nd person | You would drink -<br>Ти ќе пиеше/испиеше<br>*Ti kje pieshe/ispieshe* | You would drink -<br>Вие ќе пиевте/испиевте<br>*Vie kje pievte/ispievte* |

| | | |
|---|---|---|
| 3rd person | He/She/It would drink -<br>Тој/Таа/Тоа ќе п**и**еше/исп**и**еше<br>*Toj/Taa/Toa pieshe/ispieshe* | They would drink -<br>Тие ќе п**и**еја/исп**и**еја<br>*Tie kje pieja/ispieja* |

| **Personal endings for future perfect-in-the-past tense** | | |
|---|---|---|
| *Person* | *Singular* | *Plural* |
| 1st person | I would have drunk -<br>Јас ќе сум п**и**ел/**и**спиел(а)<br>*Jas kje sum piel/ispiel(a)* | We would have drunk -<br>Ние ќе сме п**и**еле/исп**и**еле<br>*Nie kje sme piele/ispiele* |
| 2nd person | You would have drunk -<br>Ти ќе си п**и**ел/**и**спиел(а)<br>*Ti kje si piel/ispiel(a)* | You would have drunk -<br>Вие ќе сте п**и**еле/исп**и**еле<br>*Vie kje ste piele/ispiele* |
| 3rd person | He/She/It would have drunk -<br>Тој/Таа/Тоа ќе<br>п**и**ел/**и**спиел(а),(о)<br>*Toj/Taa/Toa kje piel/ispiel(a)* | They would have drunk -<br>Тие ќе п**и**еле/исп**и**еле<br>*Tie kje piele/ispiele* |

***To drive - Вози/Извоза***

| | | |
|---|---|---|
| *Infinitive* | To drive | Вози<br>Vozi |

| Present Simple Tense | | |
|---|---|---|
| *Person* | *Singular* | *Plural* |
| 1st person | I drive -<br>Јас возам<br>*Jas vozam* | We drive -<br>Ние возиме<br>*Nie vozime* |
| 2nd person | You drive -<br>Ти возиш<br>*Ti vozish* | You drive -<br>Вие возите<br>*Vie vozite* |
| 3rd person | He/She/It drives -<br>Тој/Таа/Тоа вози<br>*Toj/Taa/Toa vozi* | They drive -<br>Тие возат<br>*Tie vozat* |

| Past Simple Tense | | |
|---|---|---|
| *Person* | *Singular* | *Plural* |
| 1st person | I drove -<br>Јас **и**звозав<br>*Jas **i**zvozav* | We drove -<br>Ние извозавме<br>*Nie izvozavme* |
| 2nd person | You drove -<br>Ти **и**звоза<br>*Ti **i**zvoza* | You drove -<br>Вие извозавте<br>*Vie izvozavte* |
| 3rd person | He/She/It drove -<br>Тој/Таа/Тоа **и**звоза<br>*Toj/Taa/Toa **i**zvoza* | They drove -<br>Тие извозаа<br>*Tie izvozaa* |

| Past Continuous Tense | | |
|---|---|---|
| *Person* | *Singular* | *Plural* |
| 1st person | I was driving -<br>Јас возев<br>*Jas vozev* | We were driving -<br>Ние возевме<br>*Nie vozevme* |
| 2nd person | You were driving -<br>Ти возеше<br>*Ti vozeshe* | You were driving -<br>Вие возевте<br>*Vie vozevte* |
| 3rd person | He/She/It was driving -<br>Тој/Таа/Тоа возеше<br>*oj/Taa/Toa vozeshe* | They were driving -<br>Тие возеа<br>*Tie vozea* |

| Present Perfect Simple Tense | | |
|---|---|---|
| *Person* | *Singular* | *Plural* |
| 1st person | I have driven<br>Јас сум **и**звозал(а)<br>*Jas sum **i**zvozal(a)* | We have driven<br>Ние сме извозале<br>*Nie sme izvozale* |
| 2nd person | You have driven<br>Ти си **и**звозал(а)<br>*Ti si **i**zvozal(a)* | You have driven<br>Вие сте извозале<br>*Vie ste izvozale* |

| | | |
|---|---|---|
| 3rd person | He/She/It has driven<br>Тој/Таа/Тоа **и**звозал(а),(о)<br>*Toj/Taa/Toa **i**zvozal(a)* | They have driven<br>Тие изв**о**зале<br>*Tie izv**o**zale* |

| Present Perfect Continuous Tense | | |
|---|---|---|
| *Person* | *Singular* | *Plural* |
| 1st person | I have been driving -<br>Јас сум в**о**зел(а)<br>*Jas sum v**o**zel(a)* | We have been driving -<br>Ние сме в**о**зеле<br>*Nie sme v**o**zele* |
| 2nd person | You have been driving -<br>Ти си в**о**зел(а)<br>*Ti si v**o**zel(a)* | You have been driving -<br>Вие сте в**о**зеле<br>*Vie ste v**o**zele* |
| 3rd person | He/She/It has been driving -<br>Тој/Таа/Тоа в**о**зел(а)(о)<br>*Toj/Taa/Toa v**o**zel(a)(o)* | They have been driving -<br>Тие в**о**зеле<br>*Tie v**o**zele* |

| Past Perfect Simple Tense | | |
|---|---|---|
| *Person* | *Singular* | *Plural* |
| 1st person | I had driven -<br>Јас бев **и**звозал(а)<br>*Jas bev **i**zvozal(a)* | We had driven -<br>Ние бевме изв**о**зале<br>*Nie bevme izv**o**zale* |
| 2nd person | You had driven -<br>Ти беше **и**звозал(а)<br>*Ti beshe **i**zvozal(a)* | You had driven -<br>Вие бевте изв**о**зале<br>*Vie bevte izv**o**zale* |
| 3rd person | He/She/It had driven -<br>Тој/Таа/Тоа беше **и**звозал(а)(о)<br>*Toj/Taa/Toa beshe **i**zvozal(a,(o)* | They had driven -<br>Тие беа изв**о**зале<br>*Tie bea izv**o**zale* |

| Future Simple Tense | | |
|---|---|---|
| *Person* | *Singular* | *Plural* |
| 1st person | I will drive -<br>Јас ќе в**о**зам/**и**звозам<br>*Jas kje v**o**zam/**i**zvozam* | We will drive -<br>Ние ќе в**о**зиме/изв**о**зиме<br>Nie kje v**o**zime/izv**o**zime |
| 2nd person | You will drive -<br>Ти ќе в**о**зиш/**и**звозиш<br>*Ti kje v**o**zish/**i**zvozish* | You will drive -<br>Вие ќе в**о**зите/изв**о**зите<br>*Vie kje v**o**zite/izv**o**zite* |
| 3rd person | He/She/It will drive -<br>Тој/Таа/Тоа ќе в**о**зи/**и**звози<br>*Toj/Taa/Toa kje v**o**zi/**i**zvozi* | They will drive -<br>Тие ќе в**о**зат/изв**о**зат<br>*Tiekje v**o**zat/izv**o**zat* |

| used to + infinitive or would + infinitive | | |
|---|---|---|
| *Person* | *Singular* | *Plural* |
| 1st person | I would drive -<br>Јас ќе в**о**зев/**и**звозев<br>*Jas kje v**o**zev/**i**zvozev* | We would drive -<br>Ние ќе в**о**зевме/изв**о**зевме<br>*Nie kje v**o**zevme/izv**o**zevme* |
| 2nd person | You would drive -<br>Ти ќе в**о**зеше/изв**о**зеше<br>*Ti kje v**o**zeshe/izv**o**zeshe* | You would drive -<br>Вие ќе в**о**зевте/изв**о**зевте<br>*Vie kje v**o**zevte/izv**o**zevte* |
| 3rd person | He/She/It would drive -<br>Тој/Таа/Тоа ќе<br>в**о**зеше/изв**о**зеше<br>*Toj/Taa/Toa v**o**zeshe/izv**o**zeshe* | They would drive -<br>Тие ќе в**о**зат/**и**звозат<br>*Tie kje v**o**zat/**i**zvozat* |

| Personal endings for future perfect-in-the-past tense | | |
|---|---|---|
| *Person* | *Singular* | *Plural* |
| 1st person | I would have driven<br>Јас ќе сум в**о**зел/**и**звозел(а)<br>*Jas kje sum v**o**zel/**i**zvozel(a)* | We would have driven<br>Ние ќе сме в**о**зеле/изв**о**зеле<br>*Nie kje sme v**o**zele/izv**o**zele* |
| 2nd person | You would have driven<br>Ти ќе си в**о**зел/**и**звозел(а)<br>*Ti kje si v**o**zel/**i**zvozel(a)* | You would have driven<br>Вие ќе сте в**о**зеле/изв**о**зеле<br>*Vie kje ste v**o**zele/izv**o**zele* |
| 3rd person | He/She/It would have driven<br>Тој/Таа/Тоа ќе<br>в**о**зел/**и**звозел(а)(о)<br>*Toj/Taa/Toa kje*<br>*v**o**zel/**i**zvozel(a)(o)* | They would have driven<br>Ти ќе в**о**зеле/изв**о**зеле<br>*Tie kje v**o**zele/izv**o**zele* |

***To eat - Јаде/Изеде***

| | | |
|---|---|---|
| *Infinitive* | Toeat | Ј**а**де<br>J**a**de |

| Present Simple Tense | | |
|---|---|---|
| *Person* | *Singular* | *Plural* |
| 1st person | I eat -<br>Јас ј**а**дам<br>*Jas j**a**dam* | We eat -<br>Ние ј**а**деме<br>*Nie j**a**deme* |
| 2nd person | You eat -<br>Ти ј**а**деш<br>*Ti j**a**desh* | You eat -<br>Вие ј**а**дете<br>*Vie j**a**dete* |
| 3rd person | He/She/It eats -<br>Тој/Таа/Тоа ј**а**де<br>*Toj/Taa/Toa j**a**de* | They eat -<br>Тие ј**а**дат<br>*Tie j**a**dat* |

| Past Simple Tense | | |
|---|---|---|
| *Person* | *Singular* | *Plural* |
| 1st person | I ate -<br>Јас **и**зедов<br>*Jas **i**zedov* | We ate -<br>Ние из**е**довме<br>*Nie iz**e**dovme* |
| 2nd person | You ate -<br>Ти **и**зеде<br>*Ti **i**zede* | You ate -<br>Вие из**е**довте<br>*Vie iz**e**dovte* |
| 3rd person | He/She/It ate -<br>Тој/Таа/Тоа **и**зеде<br>*Toj/Taa/Toa **i**zede* | They ate -<br>Тие из**е**доа<br>*Tie iz**e**doa* |

| Past Continuous Tense | | |
|---|---|---|
| *Person* | *Singular* | *Plural* |
| 1st person | I was eating -<br>Јас ј**а**дев<br>*Jas j**a**dev* | We were eating -<br>Ние ј**а**девме<br>*Nie j**a**devme* |
| 2nd person | You were eating -<br>Ти ј**а**деше<br>*Ti j**a**deshe* | You were eating -<br>Вие ј**а**девте<br>*Vie j**a**devte* |
| 3rd person | He/She/It was eating -<br>Тој/Таа/Тоа ј**а**деше<br>*Toj/Taa/Toa j**a**deshe* | They were eating -<br>Тие ј**а**деа<br>*Tie j**a**dea* |

| Present Perfect Simple Tense | | |
|---|---|---|
| *Person* | *Singular* | *Plural* |
| 1st person | I have eaten<br>Јас сум **и**зел<br>*Jas sum **i**zel(a)* | We have eaten<br>Ние сме **и**зеле<br>*Nie sme **i**zele* |

| | | |
|---|---|---|
| 2nd person | You have eaten<br>Ти си **изел**<br>*Ti si **izel**(a)* | You have eaten<br>Вие сте **изеле**<br>*Vie ste **izele*** |
| 3rd person | He/She/It has eaten<br>Тој/Таа/Тоа **изел**(а)(о)<br>*Toj/Taa/Toa **izel**(a)(o)* | They have eaten<br>Тие **изеле**<br>*Tie **izele*** |

| **Present Perfect Continuous Tense** | | |
|---|---|---|
| *Person* | *Singular* | *Plural* |
| 1st person | I have been eating -<br>Јас сум ј**а**дел(а)<br>*Jas sum j**a**del(a)* | We have been eating -<br>Ние сме ј**а**деле<br>*Nie sme j**a**dele* |
| 2nd person | You have been eating -<br>Ти си ј**а**дел(а)<br>*Ti si j**a**del(a)* | You have been eating -<br>Вие сте ј**а**деле<br>*Vie ste j**a**dele* |
| 3rd person | He/She/It has been eating -<br>Тој/Таа/Тоа ј**а**дел(а),ж(о)<br>*Toj/Taa/Toa j**a**del(a)(o)* | They have been eating -<br>Тие ј**а**деле<br>*Tie j**a**dele* |

| **Past Perfect Simple Tense** | | |
|---|---|---|
| *Person* | *Singular* | *Plural* |
| 1st person | I had eaten -<br>Јас бев **изел**<br>*Jas bev **izel**(a)* | We had eaten -<br>Ние бевме **изеле**<br>*Nie bevme **izele*** |
| 2nd person | You had eaten -<br>Ти беше **изел**(а)<br>*Ti beshe **izel**(a)* | You had eaten -<br>Вие бевте **изеле**<br>*Vie bevte **izele*** |
| 3rd person | He/She/It had eaten -<br>Тој/Таа/Тоа беше **изел**(а)(о)<br>*Toj/Taa/Toa beshe **izel**(a)(o)* | They had eaten -<br>Тие беа **изеле**<br>*Tie bea **izele*** |

| **Future Simple Tense** | | |
|---|---|---|
| *Person* | *Singular* | *Plural* |
| 1st person | I will eat -<br>Јас ќе ј**а**дам/**и**зедам<br>*Jas kje j**a**dam/**i**zedam* | We will eat -<br>Ние ќе ј**а**деме/из**е**деме<br>*Nie kje j**a**deme/iz**e**deme* |
| 2nd person | You will eat -<br>Ти ќе ј**а**деш/**и**зедеш<br>Ti kje j**a**desh/**i**zedesh | You will eat -<br>Вие ќе ј**а**дете/из**е**дете<br>Vie kje j**a**dete/iz**e**dete |
| 3rd person | He/She/It will eat -<br>Тој/Таа/Тоа ќе ј**а**де/**и**зеде<br>*Toj/Taa/Toa kje j**a**de/**i**zede* | They will eat -<br>Тие ќе ј**а**дат/из**е**дат<br>*Tie kje j**a**dat/iz**e**dat* |

| **used to + infinitive or would + infinitive** | | |
|---|---|---|
| *Person* | *Singular* | *Plural* |
| 1st person | I would eat -<br>Јас ќе ј**а**дев/**и**зедов<br>*Jas kje j**a**dev/**i**zedov* | We would eat -<br>Ние ќе јад**е**вме/изед**е**вме<br>*-Nie kje jadevme/izedevme* |

| | | |
|---|---|---|
| 2nd person | You would eat -<br>Ти ќе j**а**деше/из**е**деше<br>*Ti kje j**a**deshe/iz**e**deshe* | You would eat -<br>Вие ќе јад**е**вте/изед**е**вте<br>*Vie kje jad**e**vte/ized**e**vte* |
| 3rd person | He/She/It would eat -<br>Тој/Таа/Тоа ќе j**а**деше/из**е**деше<br>*Toj/Taa/Toa kje jadeshe/izedehe* | They would eat -<br>Тие ќе j**а**деа/из**е**деа<br>*Tie kje j**a**dea/iz**e**dea* |

| **Personal endings for future perfect-in-the-past tense** | | |
|---|---|---|
| *Person* | *Singular* | *Plural* |
| 1st person | I would have eaten<br>Јас ќе сум ј**а**дел/**и**зел(а)<br>*Jas kje sum j**a**del/**i**zel(a)* | We would have eaten<br>Ние ќе сме ј**а**деле/**и**зеле<br>*Nie kje sme j**a**dele/**i**zele* |
| 2nd person | You would have eaten<br>Ти ќе си ј**а**дел/**и**зел(а)<br>*Ti kje si j**a**del/**i**zel(a)* | You would have eaten<br>Вие ќе сте ј**а**деле/**и**зеле<br>*Vie kje ste j**a**dele/**i**zele* |
| 3rd person | He/She/It would have eaten<br>Тој/Таа/Тоа ќе ј**а**дел/**и**зел(а)(о)<br>*Toj/Taa/Toa kje j**a**del/**i**zel(a)(o)* | They would have eaten<br>Тие ќе ј**а**деле/**и**зеле<br>*Tie kje j**a**dele/**i**zele* |

***To enter - Влегува/Влезе***

| | | |
|---|---|---|
| *Infinitive* | To enter | Вл**е**гува<br>Vl**e**guva |

| **Present Simple Tense** | | |
|---|---|---|
| *Person* | *Singular* | *Plural* |
| 1st person | I enter -<br>Јас вл**е**гувам<br>*Jas vl**e**guvam* | We enter -<br>Ние влег**у**ваме<br>*Nie vleg**u**vame* |
| 2nd person | You enter -<br>Ти вл**е**гуваш<br>*Ti vl**e**guvash* | You enter -<br>Вие влег**у**вате<br>*Vie vleg**u**vate* |
| 3rd person | He/She/It enters -<br>Тој/Таа/Тоа вл**е**гува<br>*Toj/Taa/Toa vl**e**guva* | They enter -<br>Тие влег**у**ваат<br>*Tie vleg**u**vaat* |

| **Past Simple Tense** | | |
|---|---|---|
| *Person* | *Singular* | *Plural* |
| 1st person | I entered -<br>Јас вл**е**гов<br>*Jas vl**e**gov* | We entered -<br>Ние вл**е**говме<br>*Nie vl**e**govme* |
| 2nd person | You entered -<br>Ти вл**е**зе<br>*Ti vl**e**ze* | You entered -<br>Вие вл**е**говте<br>*Vie vl**e**govte* |
| 3rd person | He/She/It entered -<br>Тој/Таа/Тоа вл**е**зе<br>*Toj/Taa/Toa vl**e**ze* | They entered -<br>Тие вл**е**гоа<br>*Tie vl**e**goa* |

| **Past Continuous Tense** | | |
|---|---|---|
| *Person* | *Singular* | *Plural* |
| 1st person | I was entering -<br>Јас вл**е**гував<br>*Jas vl**e**guvav* | We were entering -<br>Ние влег**у**вавме<br>*Nie vleg**u**vavme* |
| 2nd person | You were entering -<br>Ти влег**у**ваше<br>*Ti vleg**u**vashe* | You were entering -<br>Вие влег**у**вавте<br>*Vie vleg**u**vavte* |
| 3rd person | He/She/It was entering -<br>Тој/Таа/Тоа влег**у**ваше<br>*Toj/Taa/Toa vleg**u**vashe* | They were entering -<br>Тие влег**у**ваа<br>*Tie vleg**u**vaa* |

| **Present Perfect Simple Tense** | | |
|---|---|---|
| *Person* | *Singular* | *Plural* |
| 1st person | I have entered -<br>Јас сум вл**е**гол(а)<br>*Jas sum vl**e**gol(a)* | We have entered -<br>Ние сме вл**е**гле<br>*Nie sme vl**e**gele* |

| | | |
|---|---|---|
| 2nd person | You have entered -<br>Ти си влегол(а)<br>*Ti si vlegol(a)* | You have entered -<br>Вие сте влегле<br>*Vie ste vlegele* |
| 3rd person | He/She/It has entered -<br>Тој/Таа/Тоа влегол(а)(о)<br>*Toj/Taa/Toa vlegol(a)(o)* | They have entered -<br>Тие влегле<br>*Tie vlegele* |

| **Present Perfect Continuous Tense** | | |
|---|---|---|
| *Person* | *Singular* | *Plural* |
| 1st person | I have been entering -<br>Јас сум влегувал(а)<br>*Jas sum vleguval(a)* | We have been entering -<br>Ние сме влегувале<br>*Nie sme vleguvale* |
| 2nd person | You have been entering -<br>Ти си влегувал(а)<br>*Ti si vleguval(a)* | You have been entering -<br>Вие сте влегувале<br>*Vie ste vleguvale* |
| 3rd person | He/She/It has been entering -<br>Тој/Таа/Тоа влегувал(а)(о)<br>*Toj/Taa/Toa vleguval(a)(o)* | They have been entering -<br>Тие влегувале<br>*Tie vleguvale* |

| **Past Perfect Simple Tense** | | |
|---|---|---|
| *Person* | *Singular* | *Plural* |
| 1st person | I had entered -<br>Јас бев влегол(а)<br>*Jas bev vlegol(a)* | We had entered -<br>Ние бевме влегле<br>*Nie bevme vlegle* |
| 2nd person | You had entered -<br>Ти беше влегол(а)<br>*Ti beshe vlegol(a)* | You had entered -<br>Вие бевте влегле<br>*Vie bete vlegle* |
| 3rd person | He/She/It had entered -<br>Тој/Таа/Тоа беше влегол(а)(о)<br>*Toj/Taa/Toa beshe vlegol(a)(o)* | They had entered -<br>Тие беа влегле<br>*Tie bea vlegle* |

| **Future Simple Tense** | | |
|---|---|---|
| *Person* | *Singular* | *Plural* |
| 1st person | I will enter -<br>Јас ќе влегувам/влезам<br>*Jas kje vleguvam/vlezam* | We will enter -<br>Ние ќе влегуваме/влеземе<br>*Nie kje vleguvame/vlezeme* |
| 2nd person | You will enter -<br>Ти ќе влегуваш/влезеш<br>*Ti kje vleguvash/vlezesh* | You will enter -<br>Вие ќе влегувате/влезете<br>*Vie kje vleguvate/vlezete* |
| 3rd person | He/She/It will enter -<br>Тој/Таа/Тоа ќе влегува/влезе<br>*Toj/Taa/Toa kje vleguva/vleze* | They will enter -<br>Тие ќе влегуваат/влезат<br>*Tie kje vleguvaat/vlezat* |

| used to + infinitive or would + infinitive | | |
|---|---|---|
| *Person* | *Singular* | *Plural* |
| 1st person | I would enter -<br>Јас ќе влегував/влезев<br>*Jas kje vleguvav/vlezev* | We would enter -<br>Ние ќе влегувавме/влезевме<br>*Nie kje vleguvame/vlezeme* |
| 2nd person | You would enter -<br>Ти ќе влегуваше/влезеше<br>*Ti kje vleguvashe/vlezeshe* | You would enter -<br>Вие ќе влегувавте/влезевте<br>*Vie kje vleguvavte/vlezete* |
| 3rd person | He/She/It would enter -<br>Тој/Таа/Тоа ќе влегуваше/влезеше<br>*Toj/Taa/Toa kje vleguvashe/vlezeshe* | They would enter -<br>Тие ќе влегуваат/влезат<br>*Tie kje vleguvaat/vlezat* |

| Personal endings for future perfect-in-the-past tense | | |
|---|---|---|
| *Person* | *Singular* | *Plural* |
| 1st person | I would have entered -<br>Јас ќе сум влегувал/влегол(а)<br>*Jas kje sum vleguval/vlegol(a)* | We would have entered -<br>Ние ќе сме влегувале/влегле<br>*Nie kje sme vleguvale/vlegle* |
| 2nd person | You would have entered -<br>Ти ќе си влегувал/влегол(а)<br>*Ti kje si vleguval/vlegol(a)* | You would have entered -<br>Вие ќе сте влегувале/влегле<br>*Vie kje ste vleguvale/vlegle* |
| 3rd person | He/She/It would have entered-<br>Тој/Таа/Тоа ќе влегувал/влегол(а)(о)<br>*Toj/Taa/Toa kje vleguval/vlegol(a)(o)* | They would have entered -<br>Тие ќе влегувале/влегле<br>*Tie kje vleguvale/vlegle* |

**To exit - Излегува/Излезе**

| | | |
|---|---|---|
| *Infinitive* | To exit | Изл**е**гува<br>Izl**e**guva |

| **Present Simple Tense** | | |
|---|---|---|
| *Person* | *Singular* | *Plural* |
| 1st person | I exit -<br>Јас изл**е**гувам<br>*Jas izl**e**guvam* | We exit -<br>Ние излег**у**ваме<br>*Nie izleg**u**vame* |
| 2nd person | You exit -<br>Ти изл**е**гуваш<br>*Ti izl**e**guvash* | You exit -<br>Вие излег**у**вате<br>*Vie izleg**u**vate* |
| 3rd person | He/She/It exits -<br>Тој/Таа/Тоа изл**е**гува<br>*Toj/Taa/Toa izl**e**guva* | They exit -<br>Тие излег**у**ваат<br>*Tie izleg**u**vaat* |

| **Past Simple Tense** | | |
|---|---|---|
| *Person* | *Singular* | *Plural* |
| 1st person | I exited -<br>Јас **и**злегов<br>*Jas **i**zlegov* | We exited -<br>Ние изл**е**говме<br>*Nie izl**e**govme* |
| 2nd person | You exited -<br>Ти **и**злезе<br>*Ti **i**zleze* | You exited -<br>Вие изл**е**говте<br>*Vie izl**e**govte* |
| 3rd person | He/She/It exited -<br>Тој/Таа/Тоа **и**злезе<br>*Toj/Taa/Toa **i**zleze* | They exited -<br>Тие изл**е**гоа<br>*Tie izl**e**goa* |

| **Past Continuous Tense** | | |
|---|---|---|
| *Person* | *Singular* | *Plural* |
| 1st person | I was exiting -<br>Јас изл**е**гував<br>*Jas izl**e**guvav* | We were exiting -<br>Ние излег**у**вавме<br>*Nie izleg**u**vavme* |
| 2nd person | You were exiting -<br>Ти излег**у**ваше<br>*Ti izleg**u**vashe* | You were exiting -<br>Вие излег**у**вавте<br>*Vie izleg**u**vavte* |
| 3rd person | He/She/It was exiting -<br>Тој/Таа/Тоа излег**у**ваше<br>*Toj/Taa/Toa izleg**u**vashe* | They were exiting -<br>Тие излег**у**ваа<br>*Tie izleg**u**vaa* |

| **Present Perfect Simple Tense** | | |
|---|---|---|
| *Person* | *Singular* | *Plural* |
| 1st person | I have exited<br>Јас сум **и**злегол(а)<br>*Jas sum **i**zlegol(a)* | We have exited<br>Ние сме **и**злегле<br>*Nie sme **i**zlegle* |
| 2nd person | You have exited<br>Ти си **и**злегол(а)<br>*Ti si **i**zlegol(a)* | You have exited<br>Вие сте **и**злегле<br>*Vie ste **i**zlegle* |

| | | |
|---|---|---|
| 3rd person | He/She/It has exited<br>Тој/Таа/Тоа **и**злегол(а)(о)<br>*Toj/Taa/Toa **i**zlegol(a) (o)* | They have exited<br>Тие **и**злегле<br>*Tie **i**zlegle* |

| Present Perfect Continuous Tense | | |
|---|---|---|
| *Person* | *Singular* | *Plural* |
| 1st person | I have been exiting -<br>Јас сум изл**е**гувал(а)<br>*Jas sum izl**e**guval(a)* | We have been exiting -<br>Ние сме излег**у**вале<br>*Nie sme izleg**u**vale* |
| 2nd person | You have been exiting -<br>Ти си изл**е**гувал(а)<br>*Ti si izl**e**guval(a)* | You have been exiting -<br>Вие сте излег**у**вале<br>*Vie ste izleg**u**vale* |
| 3rd person | He/She/It has been exiting -<br>Тој/Таа/Тоа изл**е**гувал(а)(о)<br>*Toj/Taa/Toa izl**e**guval(a)(o)* | They have been exiting -<br>Тие излег**у**вале<br>*Tie izleg**u**vale* |

| Past Perfect Simple Tense | | |
|---|---|---|
| *Person* | *Singular* | *Plural* |
| 1st person | I had exited -<br>Јас бев **и**злегол(а)<br>*Jas bev **i**zlegol(a)* | We had exited -<br>Ние бевме **и**злегле<br>*Nie bevme **i**zlegle* |
| 2nd person | You had exited -<br>Ти беше **и**злегол(а)<br>*Ti beshe **i**zlegol(a)* | You had exited -<br>Вие бевте **и**злегле<br>*Vie bevte **i**zlegle* |
| 3rd person | He/She/It had exited -<br>Тој/Таа/Тоа беше **и**злегол(а)(о)<br>*Toj/Taa/Toa beshe **i**zlegol(a)(o)* | They had exited -<br>Тие беа **и**злегле<br>*Tie bea **i**zlegle* |

| Future Simple Tense | | |
|---|---|---|
| *Person* | *Singular* | *Plural* |
| 1st person | I will exit -<br>Јас ќе изл**е**гувам/**и**злезам<br>*Jas kje izl**e**guvam/**i**zlezam* | We will exit -<br>Ние ќе излег**у**ваме/изл**е**земе<br>*Nie kje izleg**u**vame/izl**e**zeme* |
| 2nd person | You will exit -<br>Ти ќе изл**е**гуваш/**и**злезеш<br>*Ti kje izl**e**guvash/**i**zlezesh* | You will exit -<br>Вие ќе излег**у**вате/изл**е**зете<br>*Vie kje izleg**u**vate/izl**e**zete* |
| 3rd person | He/She/It will exit -<br>Тој/Таа/Тоа ќе изл**е**гува/**и**злезе<br>*Toj/Taa/Toa kje izl**e**guva/**i**zleze* | They will exit -<br>Тие ќе излег**у**ваат/**и**злезат<br>*Tie kje izleg**u**vaat/**i**zlezat* |

| **used to + infinitive or would + infinitive** | | |
|---|---|---|
| *Person* | *Singular* | *Plural* |
| 1st person | I would exit -<br>Јас ќе изл**е**гував/**и**злегов<br>*Jas kje izl**e**guvav/**i**zlegov* | We would exit -<br>Ние ќе излег**у**вавме/изл**е**зевме<br>*Nie kje izleg**u**vavme/izl**e**zeme* |
| 2nd person | You would exit -<br>Ти ќе излег**у**ваше/изл**е**зеше<br>*Ti kje izleg**u**vashe/izl**e**zeshe* | You would exit -<br>Вие ќе излег**у**вавте/изл**е**зевте<br>*Vie kje izleg**u**vavte/izl**e**zete* |
| 3rd person | He/She/It would exit -<br>Тој/Таа/Тоа ќе<br>излег**у**ваше/изл**е**зеше<br>*Toj/Taa/Toa kje*<br>*izleg**u**vashe/izlez**e**she* | They would exit -<br>Тие ќе излег**у**ваа/изл**е**зеа<br>*Tie kje izleg**u**vaa/izl**e**zea* |

| **Personal endings for future perfect-in-the-past tense** | | |
|---|---|---|
| *Person* | *Singular* | *Plural* |
| 1st person | I would have exited -<br>Јас ќе сум<br>изл**е**гувал/**и**злегол(а)<br>*Jas kje sum izl**e**guval/**i**zlegol(a)* | We would have exited -<br>Ние ќе сме<br>излег**у**вале/**и**злегле<br>*Nie kje sme izleg**u**vale/**i**zlegle* |
| 2nd person | You would have exited -<br>Ти ќе си изл**е**гувал/**и**злегол(а)<br>*Ti kje izl**e**guval/**i**zlegol(a)* | You would have exited -<br>Вие ќе сте излег**у**вале/**и**злегле<br>*Vie kje ste izleg**u**vale/**i**zlegle* |
| 3rd person | He/She/It would have exited -<br>Тој/Таа/Тоа ќе<br>изл**е**гувал/**и**злегол(а)(о)<br>*Toj/Taa/Toa kje*<br>*izl**e**guval/**i**zlegol(a)(o)* | They would have exited -<br>Тие ќе излег**у**вале/**и**злегле<br>*Tie kje izleg**u**vale/**i**zlegle* |

***To explain - Објаснува/Објасни***

| | | |
|---|---|---|
| *Infinitive* | Toexplain | Обј**а**снува<br>Obj**a**snuva |

| **Present Simple Tense** | | |
|---|---|---|
| *Person* | *Singular* | *Plural* |
| 1st person | I explain -<br>Јас обј**а**снувам<br>*Jas obj**a**snuvam* | We explain -<br>Ние објасн**у**ваме<br>*Nie objasn**u**vame* |
| 2nd person | You explain -<br>Ти обј**а**снуваш<br>*Ti obj**a**snuvash* | You explain -<br>Вие објасн**у**вате<br>*Vie objasn**u**vate* |
| 3rd person | He/She/It explains -<br>Тој/Таа/Тоа обј**а**снува<br>*Toj/Taa/Toa obj**a**snuva* | They explain -<br>Тие објасн**у**ваат<br>*Tie objasn**u**vat* |

| **Past Simple Tense** | | |
|---|---|---|
| *Person* | *Singular* | *Plural* |
| 1st person | I explained -<br>Јас **о**бјаснив<br>*Jas **o**bjasniv* | We explained -<br>Ние обј**а**снивме<br>*Nie obj**a**snuvame* |
| 2nd person | You explained -<br>Ти **о**бјасни<br>*Ti **o**bjasni* | You explained -<br>Вие обј**а**снивате<br>*Vie obj**a**snuvate* |
| 3rd person | He/She/It explained -<br>Тој/Таа/Тоа **о**бјасни<br>*Toj/Taa/Toa **o**bjasni* | They explained -<br>Тие обј**а**снија<br>*Tie obj**a**snija* |

| **Past Continuous Tense** | | |
|---|---|---|
| *Person* | *Singular* | *Plural* |
| 1st person | I was explaining -<br>Јас обј**а**снував<br>*Jas obj**a**snuvav* | We were explaining -<br>Ние објасн**у**вавме<br>*Nie objasnuvavme* |
| 2nd person | You were explaining -<br>Ти објасн**у**ваше<br>*Ti objasn**u**vashe* | You were explaining -<br>Вие објасн**у**вавте<br>*Vie objasnuvavte* |
| 3rd person | He/She/It was explaining -<br>Тој/Таа/Тоа објасн**у**ваше<br>*Toj/Taa/Toa objasn**u**vashe* | They were explaining -<br>Тие објасн**у**ваа<br>*Tie objasn**u**vaa* |

| **Present Perfect Simple Tense** | | |
|---|---|---|
| *Person* | *Singular* | *Plural* |
| 1st person | I have explained<br>Јас сум **о**бјаснил(а)<br>*Jas sum **o**bjasnil(a)* | We have explained<br>Ние сме обј**а**сниле<br>*Nie sme obj**a**snile* |
| 2nd person | You have explained<br>Ти си **о**бјаснил(а)<br>*Ti si **o**bjasnil(a)* | You have explained<br>Вие сте обј**а**сниле<br>*Vie ste obj**a**snile* |

| | | |
|---|---|---|
| 3rd person | He/She/It has explained<br>Тој/Таа/Тоа **о**бјаснил(а)(о)<br>*Toj/Taa/Toa* ***o****bjasnil(a)(o)* | They have explained<br>Тие обј**а**сниле<br>*Tie obj****a****snile* |

| Present Perfect Continuous Tense | | |
|---|---|---|
| *Person* | *Singular* | *Plural* |
| 1st person | I have been explaining -<br>Јас сум обј**а**снувал(а)<br>*Jas sum obj****a****snuval(a)* | We have been explaining -<br>Ние сме објасн**у**вале<br>*Nie sme objasn****u****vale* |
| 2nd person | You have been explaining -<br>Ти си обј**а**снувал(а)<br>*Ti si obj****a****snuval(a)* | You have been explaining -<br>Вие сте објасн**у**вале<br>*Vie ste objasn****u****vale* |
| 3rd person | He/She/It has been explaining<br>Тој/Таа/Тоа обј**а**снувал(а)(о)<br>*Toj/Taa/Toa obj****a****snuval(a)(o)* | They have been explaining -<br>Тие објасн**у**вале<br>*Tie objasn****u****vale* |

| Past Perfect Simple Tense | | |
|---|---|---|
| *Person* | *Singular* | *Plural* |
| 1st person | I had explained -<br>Јас бев **о**бјаснил(а)<br>*Jas bev* ***o****bjasnil(a)* | We had explained -<br>Ние бевме обј**а**сниле<br>*Nie bevme obj****a****snile* |
| 2nd person | You had explained -<br>Ти беше **о**бјаснил(а)<br>*Ti beshe****o****bjasnil(a)* | You had explained -<br>Вие бевте обј**а**сниле<br>*Vie bevteobj****a****snile* |
| 3rd person | He/She/It had explained -<br>Тој/Таа/Тоа беше<br>**о**бјаснил(а)(о)<br>*Toj/Taa/Toa beshe* ***o****bjasnil(a)(o)* | They had explained -<br>Тие беа обј**а**сниле<br>*Tie bea obj****a****snile* |

| Future Simple Tense | | |
|---|---|---|
| *Person* | *Singular* | *Plural* |
| 1st person | I will explain<br>Јас ќе обј**а**снувам/**о**бјаснам<br>*Jas kje obj****a****snuvam/****o****bjasnam* | We will explain<br>Ние ќе објасн**у**ваме/обј**а**сниме<br>*Nie kje objasn****u****vame/obj****a****snime* |
| 2nd person | You will explain<br>Ти ќе обј**а**снуваш/**о**бјаниш<br>*Ti kje obj****a****snuvash/****o****bjasnish* | You will explain<br>Вие ќе објасн**у**вате/обј**а**сните<br>*Vie kje objasn****u****vate/obj****a****snite* |
| 3rd person | He/She/It will explain<br>Тој/Таа/Тоа ќе<br>обј**а**снува/**о**бјасни<br>*Toj/Taa/Toa kje*<br>*obj****a****snuva/****o****bjasni* | They will explain<br>Тие ќе објасн**у**ваат/**о**бјаснат<br>*Tie kje objasn****u****vaat/****o****bjasnat* |

| used to + infinitive or would + infinitive | | |
|---|---|---|
| *Person* | *Singular* | *Plural* |
| 1st person | I would explain - Јас ќе об**ја**снував/**о**бјаснев *Jas kje obj**a**snuvav/**o**bjasnev* | We would explain - Ние ќе објасн**у**вавме/об**ја**сневме *Nie kje objasn**u**vavme/obj**a**snevme* |
| 2nd person | You would explain - Ти ќе објасн**у**ваше/обј**а**снеше *Ti kje objasn**u**vashe/obj**a**sneshe* | You would explain - Вие ќе објасн**у**вавте/обј**а**сневте *Vie kje objasn**u**vavte/obj**a**snevte* |
| 3rd person | He/She/It would explain - Тој/Таа/Тоа ќе објасн**у**ваше/обј**а**снеше *Тој/Таа/Тоа kje objasn**u**vashe/obj**a**sneshe* | They would explain - Тие ќе објасн**у**ваа/обј**а**снеа *Tie kje objasn**u**vaa/obj**a**snea* |

| Personal endings for future perfect-in-the-past tense | | |
|---|---|---|
| *Person* | *Singular* | *Plural* |
| 1st person | I would have explained Јас ќе сум обј**а**снувал/**о**бјаснил(а) *Jas kje sum obj**a**snuval/**o**bjasnil(a)* | We would have explained Ние ќе сме објасн**у**вале/обј**а**сниле *Nie kje sme objasn**u**vale/obj**a**snile* |
| 2nd person | You would have explained Ти ќе си обј**а**снувал/**о**бјаснил(а) *Ti kje si obj**a**snuval/**o**bjasnil(a)* | You would have explained Вие ќе сте објасн**у**вале/обј**а**сниле *Vie kje ste objasn**u**vale/obj**a**snile* |
| 3rd person | He/She/It would have explained Тој/Таа/Тоа ќе обј**а**снувал/**о**бјаснил(а)(о) *Тој/Таа/Тоakje obj**a**snuval/**o**bjasnil(a)(o)* | They would have explained Тие ќе објасн**у**вале/обј**а**сниле *Tie kje objasn**u**vale/obj**a**snile* |

***To fall - Паѓа/Падна***

| *Infinitive* | To fall | Па**ѓ**а<br>P**a**gja |
|---|---|---|

| **Present Simple Tense** | | |
|---|---|---|
| *Person* | *Singular* | *Plural* |
| 1st person | I fall -<br>Јас па**ѓ**ам<br>*Jas p**a**gjam* | We fall -<br>Ние па**ѓ**аме<br>*Nie p**a**gjame* |
| 2nd person | You fall -<br>Ти па**ѓ**аш<br>*Ti p**a**gjash* | You fall -<br>Вие па**ѓ**ате<br>*Vie p**a**gjate* |
| 3rd person | He/She/It falls -<br>Тој/Таа/Тоа па**ѓ**а<br>*Toj/Taa/Toa p**a**gja* | They fall -<br>Тие па**ѓ**аат<br>*Tie p**a**gjaat* |

| **Past Simple Tense** | | |
|---|---|---|
| *Person* | *Singular* | *Plural* |
| 1st person | I fell -<br>Јас п**а**днав<br>*Jas p**a**dnav* | We fell -<br>Ние п**а**днавме<br>*Nie p**a**dnavme* |
| 2nd person | You fell -<br>Ти п**а**дна<br>*Ti p**a**dna* | You fell -<br>Вие п**а**днавте<br>*Vie p**a**dnavte* |
| 3rd person | He/She/It fell -<br>Тој/Таа/Тоа п**а**дна<br>*Toj/Taa/Toa p**a**dna* | They fell -<br>Тие п**а**днаа<br>*Tie p**a**dnaa* |

| **Past Continuous Tense** | | |
|---|---|---|
| *Person* | *Singular* | *Plural* |
| 1st person | I was falling -<br>Јас па**ѓ**ав<br>*Jas p**a**gjav* | We were falling -<br>Ние па**ѓ**авме<br>*Nie p**a**gjavme* |
| 2nd person | You were falling -<br>Ти па**ѓ**аше<br>*Ti p**a**gjashe* | You were falling -<br>Вие па**ѓ**авте<br>*Vie p**a**gjavte* |
| 3rd person | He/She/It was falling -<br>Тој/Таа/Тоа па**ѓ**аше<br>*Toj/Taa/Toa p**a**gjashe* | They were falling -<br>Тие па**ѓ**аа<br>*Tie p**a**gjaa* |

| **Present Perfect Simple Tense** | | |
|---|---|---|
| *Person* | *Singular* | *Plural* |
| 1st person | I have fallen -<br>Јас сум п**а**днал(а)<br>*Jas sum p**a**dnal(a)* | We have fallen -<br>Ние сме п**а**днале<br>*Nie sme p**a**dnale* |

| | | |
|---|---|---|
| 2nd person | You have fallen -<br>Ти си паднал(а)<br>*-Ti si padnal(a)* | You have fallen -<br>Вие сте паднале<br>*Tie ste padnale* |
| 3rd person | He/She/It has fallen -<br>Тој/Таа/Тоа паднал(а)(о)<br>*Toj/Taa/Toa padnal(a)(o)* | They have fallen -<br>Тие паднале<br>*Tie padnale* |

| **Present Perfect Continuous Tense** | | |
|---|---|---|
| *Person* | *Singular* | *Plural* |
| 1st person | I have been falling -<br>Јас сум паѓал(а)<br>*Jas sum pagjal(a)* | We have been falling -<br>Ние сме паѓале<br>*Nie sme pagjale* |
| 2nd person | You have been falling -<br>Ти сипаѓал(а)<br>*Ti si pagjal(a)* | You have been falling -<br>Вие сте паѓале<br>*Vie ste pagjale* |
| 3rd person | He/She/It has been falling -<br>Тој/Таа/Тоа паѓал(а)(о)<br>*Toj/Taa/Toa pagjal (a)(o)* | They have been falling -<br>Тие паѓале<br>*Tie pagjale* |

| **Past Perfect Simple Tense** | | |
|---|---|---|
| *Person* | *Singular* | *Plural* |
| 1st person | I had fallen -<br>Јас бев паднал(а)<br>*Jas bev padnal(a)* | We had fallen -<br>Ние бевме паднале<br>*Nie bevme padnale* |
| 2nd person | You had fallen -<br>Ти беше паднал(а)<br>*Ti beshe padnal(a)* | You had fallen -<br>Вие бевте паднале<br>*Vie bevte padnale* |
| 3rd person | He/She/It had fallen -<br>Тој/Таа/Тоа беше паднал(а)(о)<br>*Toj/Taa/Toa beshe padnal(a)(o)* | They had fallen -<br>Тие беа паднале<br>*Tie bea padnale* |

| **Future Simple Tense** | | |
|---|---|---|
| *Person* | *Singular* | *Plural* |
| 1st person | I will fall -<br>Јас ќе паѓам/паднам<br>*Jas kje pagjam/padnam* | We will fall -<br>Ние ќе паѓаме/паднеме<br>*Nie kje pagjame/padneme* |
| 2nd person | You will fall -<br>Ти ќе паѓаш/паднеш<br>*Ti kje pagjash/padnesh* | You will fall -<br>Вие ќе паѓате/паднете<br>*Vie kje pagjate/padneme* |
| 3rd person | He/She/It will fall -<br>Тој/Таа/Тоа ќе паѓа/падне<br>*Toj/Taa/Toa kje pagja/padne* | They will fall -<br>Тие ќе паѓаат/паднат<br>*Tie kje pagjaat/padnat* |

| **used to + infinitive or would + infinitive** | | |
|---|---|---|
| *Person* | *Singular* | *Plural* |
| 1st person | I would fall -<br>Јас ќе паѓав/паднев<br>*Jas kje pagjav/padnev* | We would fall -<br>Ние ќе паѓавме/падневме<br>*Nie kje pagjavme/padnevme* |

| | | |
|---|---|---|
| 2nd person | You would fall -<br>Ти ќе п**а**ѓаше/п**а**днеше<br>*Ti kje p**a**gjashe/p**a**dneshe* | You would fall -<br>Вие ќе п**а**ѓавте/п**а**дневте<br>*Vie kje p**a**gjavte/p**a**dnevte* |
| 3rd person | He/She/It would fall -<br>Тој/Таа/Тоа ќе п**а**ѓаше/п**а**днеше<br>*Toj/Taa/Toa kje p**a**gjashe/p**a**dneshe* | They would fall -<br>Тие ќе п**а**ѓаат/п**а**днеа<br>*Tie kje p**a**gjaat/p**a**dnea* |

| **Personal endings for future perfect-in-the-past tense** | | |
|---|---|---|
| *Person* | *Singular* | *Plural* |
| 1st person | I would have fallen -<br>Јас ќе сум п**а**ѓал/п**а**днал(а)<br>*Jas kje sum p**a**gjal/p**a**dnal(a)* | We would have fallen -<br>Ние ќе сме п**а**ѓале/п**а**днале<br>*Nie kje sme p**a**gjale/p**a**dnale* |
| 2nd person | You would have fallen -<br>Ти ќе си п**а**ѓал/п**а**днал(а)<br>*Ti kje si p**a**gjal/p**a**dnal(a)* | You would have fallen -<br>Вие ќе сте п**а**ѓале/п**а**днале<br>*Vie kje ste p**a**gjale/p**a**dnale* |
| 3rd person | He/She/It would have fallen -<br>Тој/Таа/Тоа ќе п**а**ѓал/п**а**днал(а)(о)<br>*Toj/Taa/Toa kje p**a**gjal/p**a**dnal(a)(o)* | They would have fallen -<br>Тие ќе п**а**ѓале/п**а**днале<br>*Tie kje p**a**gjale/p**a**dnale* |

### *To feel – Чувствува/Почувствува*

| | | |
|---|---|---|
| *Infinitive* | To feel | Ч**у**вствува<br>Ch**u**vstvuva |

| Present Simple Tense | | |
|---|---|---|
| *Person* | *Singular* | *Plural* |
| 1st person | I feel -<br>Јас ч**у**вствувам<br>*Jas ch**u**vstvuvam* | We feel -<br>Ние чувств**у**ваме<br>*Nie chuvstv**u**vame* |
| 2nd person | You feel -<br>Ти ч**у**вствуваш<br>*Ti ch**u**vstvuvash* | You feel -<br>Вие чувств**у**вате<br>*Vie chuvstv**u**vate* |
| 3rd person | He/She/It feels -<br>Тоа/Таа/Тоа ч**у**вствува<br>*Toj/Taa/Toa ch**u**vstvuva* | They feel -<br>Тие чувств**у**ваат<br>*Tie chuvstv**u**vaat* |

| Past Simple Tense | | |
|---|---|---|
| *Person* | *Singular* | *Plural* |
| 1st person | I felt -<br>Јас поч**у**вствував<br>*Jas poch**u**vstvuvav* | We felt -<br>Ние почувств**у**вавме<br>*Nie pochuvstv**u**vavme* |
| 2nd person | You felt -<br>Ти поч**у**вствува<br>*Ti poch**u**vstvuva* | You felt -<br>Вие почувств**у**вавте<br>*Vie pochuvstv**u**vavte* |
| 3rd person | He/She/It felt -<br>Тоа/Таа/Тоа поч**у**вствува<br>*Toj/Taa/Toa poch**u**vstvuva* | They felt -<br>Тие почувств**у**ваа<br>*Tie pochuvstv**u**vaa* |

| Past Continuous Tense | | |
|---|---|---|
| *Person* | *Singular* | *Plural* |
| 1st person | I was feeling -<br>Јас ч**у**вствував<br>*Jas ch**u**vstvuvav* | We were feeling -<br>Ние чувств**у**вавме<br>*Nie chuvstv**u**vavme* |
| 2nd person | You were feeling -<br>Ти чувств**у**ваше<br>*Ti chuvstv**u**vashe* | You were feeling -<br>Вие чувств**у**вавте<br>*Vie chuvstv**u**vavte* |
| 3rd person | He/She/It was feeling -<br>Тоа/Таа/Тоа чувств**у**ваше<br>*Toj/Taa/Toa chuvstv**u**vashe* | They were feeling -<br>Тие чувств**у**ваа<br>*Tie chuvstv**u**vaa* |

| Present Perfect Simple Tense | | |
|---|---|---|
| *Person* | *Singular* | *Plural* |
| 1st person | I have felt -<br>Јас сум поч**у**вствувал(а)<br>*Jas sum poch**u**vstvuval(a)* | We have felt -<br>Ние сме почувств**у**вале<br>*Nie sme pochuvstv**u**vale* |

| | | |
|---|---|---|
| 2nd person | You have felt -<br>Ти си почувствувал(а)<br>*Ti si poch**u**vstvuval(a)* | You have felt -<br>Вие сте почувствувале<br>*Vie ste pochuvstv**u**vale* |
| 3rd person | He/She/It has felt -<br>Тоа/Таа/Тоа почувствувал(а)(о)<br>*Toj/Taa/Toa poch**u**vstvuval(a)(o)* | They have felt -<br>Тие почувствувале<br>*Tie pochuvstv**u**vale* |

| **Present Perfect Continuous Tense** | | |
|---|---|---|
| *Person* | *Singular* | *Plural* |
| 1st person | I have been feeling -<br>Јас сум чувствувал(а)<br>*Jas sum ch**u**vstvuval(a)* | We have been feeling -<br>Ние смечувствувале<br>*Nie sme chustv**u**vale* |
| 2nd person | You have been feeling -<br>Ти си чувствувал(а)<br>*Ti si ch**u**vstvuval(a)* | You have been feeling -<br>Вие сте чувствувале<br>*Vie ste chustv**u**vale* |
| 3rd person | He/She/It has been feeling -<br>Тоа/Таа/Тоа чувствувал(а)(о)<br>*Toj/Taa/Toa ch**u**vstvuval(a)(o)* | They have been feeling -<br>Тие чувствувале<br>*Tie chustv**u**vale* |

| **Past Perfect Simple Tense** | | |
|---|---|---|
| *Person* | *Singular* | *Plural* |
| 1st person | I had felt -<br>Јас бев почувствувал(а)<br>*Jas bev poch**u**vstvuval(a)* | We had felt -<br>Ние бевме почувствувале<br>*Nie bevme pocuvstv**u**vale* |
| 2nd person | You had felt -<br>Ти беше почувствувал(а)<br>*Ti beshe poch**u**vstvuval(a)* | You had felt -<br>Вие бевте почувствувале<br>*Vie bevte pocuvstv**u**vale* |
| 3rd person | He/She/It had felt -<br>Тоа/Таа/Тоа беше почувствувал(а)(о)<br>*Toj/Taa/Toa beshe poch**u**vstvuval(a)(o)* | They had felt -<br>Тие беа почувствувале<br>*Tie bea pocuvstv**u**vale* |

| **Future Simple Tense** | | |
|---|---|---|
| *Person* | *Singular* | *Plural* |
| 1st person | I will feel -<br>Јас ќе чувствувам/почувствувам<br>*Jas kje ch**u**vstvuvam/poch**u**vstvuvam* | We will feel -<br>Ние ќе чувствуваме/почувствуваме<br>*Nie kje chuvstv**u**vame/pocuvstv**u**vame* |
| 2nd person | You will feel -<br>Ти ќе чувствуваш/почувствуваш<br>*Ti kje ch**u**vstvuvash/poch**u**vstvuvash* | You will feel -<br>Вие ќе чувствувате/почувствувате<br>*Vie kje chuvstv**u**vate/pochuvstv**u**vate* |

| | | |
|---|---|---|
| 3rd person | He/She/It will feel -<br>Тоа/Таа/Тоа ќе<br>ч**у**вствува/поч**у**вствува<br>*Toj/Taa/Toa kje*<br>*ch**u**vstvuva/poch**u**vstvuva* | They will feel -<br>Тие ќе<br>чувств**у**ваат/почувств**у**ваат<br>*Tie kje*<br>*chuvstv**u**vaat/pochuvstv**u**vaat* |

| **used to + infinitive or would + infinitive** | | |
|---|---|---|
| *Person* | *Singular* | *Plural* |
| 1st person | I would feel -<br>Јас ќе<br>ч**у**вствував/поч**у**вствував<br>*Jas kje*<br>*ch**u**vstvuvav/poch**u**vstvuvav* | We would feel -<br>Ние ќе чувств**у**вавме/<br>почувств**у**вавме<br>*Nie kje chuvstv**u**vavme/*<br>*pochuvstv**u**vavme* |
| 2nd person | You would feel -<br>Ти ќе ч**у**вствуваше/<br>почувств**у**ваше<br>*Ti kje ch**u**vstvuvashe/*<br>*pochuvstv**u**vashe* | You would feel -<br>Вие ќе чувств**у**вавте/<br>почувств**у**вавте<br>*Vie kje chuvstv**u**vavte/*<br>*pochuvstv**u**vavte* |
| 3rd person | He/She/It would feel -<br>Тоа/Таа/Тоа ние ќе<br>ч**у**вствуваше/<br>почувств**у**ваше<br>*Toj/Taa/Toa kje chuvstv**u**vashe/*<br>*pochuvstv**u**vashe* | They would feel -<br>Тие ќе чувств**у**ваа/почувств**у**ваа<br>*Tie kje*<br>*chuvstv**u**vaa/pochuvstv**u**vaa* |

| **Personal endings for future perfect-in-the-past tense** | | |
|---|---|---|
| *Person* | *Singular* | *Plural* |
| 1st person | I would have felt<br>Јас ќе сум<br>ч**у**вствувал/поч**у**вствувал(а)<br>*Jas kje sum*<br>*ch**u**vstvuval/poch**u**vstvuval(a)* | We would have felt<br>Не ќе сме<br>чувств**у**вале/почувств**у**вале<br>*Nie kje sme*<br>*chuvstv**u**vale/pochuvstv**u**vale* |
| 2nd person | You would have felt<br>Ти ќе си<br>ч**у**вствувал/поч**у**вствувал(а)<br>*Ti kje si*<br>*ch**u**vstvuval/poch**u**vstvuval(a)* | You would have felt<br>Вие ќе сте<br>чувств**у**вале/почувств**у**вале<br>*Vie kje ste*<br>*chuvstv**u**vale/pochuvstv**u**vale* |
| 3rd person | He/She/It would have felt<br>Тоа/Таа/Тоа ќе ч**у**вствувал/<br>поч**у**вствувал(а)(о)<br>*Toj/Taa/Toa kje ch**u**vstvuval/*<br>*poch**u**vstvuval(a)(o)* | They would have felt<br>Тие ќе<br>чувств**у**вале/почувств**у**вале<br>*Tie kje*<br>*chuvstv**u**vale/pochuvstv**u**vale* |

***To fight - Тепа/Истепа***

| | | |
|---|---|---|
| *Infinitive* | To fight | Тепа<br>Tepa |

| **Present Simple Tense** | | |
|---|---|---|
| *Person* | *Singular* | *Plural* |
| 1st person | I fight -<br>Jас тепам<br>*Jas tepam* | We fight -<br>Ние тепаме<br>*Nie tepame* |
| 2nd person | You fight -<br>Ти тепаш<br>*Ti tepash* | You fight -<br>Вие тепате<br>*Vie tepate* |
| 3rd person | He/She/It fights -<br>Тoj/Таа/Тоа тепа<br>*Toj/Taa/Toa tepa* | They fight -<br>Тие тепаат<br>*Tie tepaat* |

| **Past Simple Tense** | | |
|---|---|---|
| *Person* | *Singular* | *Plural* |
| 1st person | I fought -<br>Jас истепав<br>*Jas istepav* | We fought -<br>Ние истепавме<br>*Nie istepavme* |
| 2nd person | You fought -<br>Ти истепа<br>*Ti istepa* | You fought -<br>Вие истепавте<br>*Vie istepavte* |
| 3rd person | He/She/It fought -<br>Тoj/Таа/Тоа истепа<br>*Toj/Taa/Toa istepa* | They fought -<br>Тие истепаа<br>*Tie istepaa* |

| **Past Continuous Tense** | | |
|---|---|---|
| *Person* | *Singular* | *Plural* |
| 1st person | I was fighting -<br>Jас тепав<br>*Jas tepav* | We were fighting -<br>Ние тепавме<br>*Nie tepavme* |
| 2nd person | You were fighting -<br>Ти тепаше<br>*Ti tepashe* | You were fighting -<br>Вие тепавте<br>*Vie tepavte* |
| 3rd person | He/She/It was fighting -<br>Тoj/Таа/Тоа тепаше<br>*Toj/Taa/Toa tepashe* | They were fighting -<br>Тие тепаа<br>*Tie tepaa* |

| **Present Perfect Simple Tense** | | |
|---|---|---|
| *Person* | *Singular* | *Plural* |
| 1st person | I have fought -<br>Jас сум истепал(а)<br>*Jas sum istepal(a)* | We have fought -<br>Ние сме истепале<br>*Nie sme istepale* |

| | | |
|---|---|---|
| 2nd person | You have fought -<br>Ти си **и**степал(а)<br>*Ti si **i**stepal(a)* | You have fought<br>Вие сте ист**е**пале<br>*Vie ste ist**e**pale* |
| 3rd person | He/She/It has fought -<br>Тој/Таа/Тоа **и**степал(а)(о)<br>*Toj/Taa/Toa istep **i**stepalal(a)(o)* | They have fought -<br>Тие ист**е**пале<br>*Tie ist**e**pale* |

| **Present Perfect Continuous Tense** | | |
|---|---|---|
| *Person* | *Singular* | *Plural* |
| 1st person | I have been fighting -<br>Јас сум т**е**пал(а)<br>*Jas sum t**e**pal(a)* | We have been fighting -<br>Ние сме т**е**пале<br>*Nie sme t**e**pale* |
| 2nd person | You have been fighting -<br>Ти си т**е**пал(а)<br>*Ti si t**e**pal(a)* | You have been fighting -<br>Вие сте т**е**пале<br>*Vie ste t**e**pale* |
| 3rd person | He/She/It has been fighting -<br>Тој/Таа/Тоа т**е**пал(а)(о)<br>*Toj/Taa/Toa t**e**pal(a)(o)* | They have been fighting -<br>Тие т**е**пале<br>*Tie t**e**pale* |

| **Past Perfect Simple Tense** | | |
|---|---|---|
| *Person* | *Singular* | *Plural* |
| 1st person | I had fought -<br>Јас бев **и**степал(а)<br>*Jas bev **i**stepal(a)* | We had fought -<br>Ние бевме ист**е**пале<br>Nie bevme ist**e**pale |
| 2nd person | You had fought -<br>Ти беше **и**степал(а)<br>*Ti beshe **i**stepal(a)* | You had fought -<br>Вие бевте ист**е**пале<br>*Vie bevte* ist**e**pale |
| 3rd person | He/She/It had fought -<br>Тој/Таа/Тоа беше **и**степал(а)(о)<br>*Toj/Taa/Toa beshe **i**stepal(a)(o)* | They had fought -<br>Тие беа ист**е**пале<br>*Tie bea* ist**e**pale |

| **Future Simple Tense** | | |
|---|---|---|
| *Person* | *Singular* | *Plural* |
| 1st person | I will fight -<br>Јас ќе т**е**пам/**и**степам<br>*Jas kje t**e**pam/**i**stepam* | We will fight -<br>Ние ќе т**е**паме/ист**е**паме<br>*Nie kje t**e**pame/ist**e**pame* |
| 2nd person | You will fight -<br>Ти ќе т**е**паш/**и**степаш<br>*Ti kje t**e**pash/**i**stepash* | You will fight -<br>Вие ќе т**е**пате/ист**е**пате<br>*Vie kje t**e**pate/ist**e**pate* |
| 3rd person | He/She/It will fight -<br>Тој/Таа/Тоа ќе т**е**па/**и**степа<br>*Toj/Taa/Toa kje t**e**pa/**i**stepa* | They will fight -<br>Тие ќе т**е**паат/ист**е**паат<br>*Tie kje t**e**paat/ist**e**paat* |

| **used to + infinitive or would + infinitive** | | |
|---|---|---|
| *Person* | *Singular* | *Plural* |
| 1st person | I would fight -<br>Јас ќе т**е**пав/**и**степав<br>*Jas kje t**e**pav/**i**stepav* | We would fight -<br>Ние ќе т**е**павме/ист**е**павме<br>*Nie kje t**e**pavme/ist**e**pavte* |

| | | |
|---|---|---|
| 2nd person | You would fight -<br>Ти ќе т**е**паше/ист**е**паше<br>*Ti kje t**e**pashe/ist**e**pashe* | You would fight -<br>Вие ќе т**е**павте/ист**е**павте<br>*Vie kje t**e**pavte/ist**e**pavte* |
| 3rd person | He/She/It would fight -<br>Тој/Таа/Тоа т**е**паше/ист**е**паше<br>*Toj/Taa/Toa kje t**e**pashe/ist**e**pashe* | They would fight -<br>Тие ќе т**е**паа/ист**е**паа<br>*Tie kje t**e**paa/ist**e**paa* |

| **Personal endings for future perfect-in-the-past tense** | | |
|---|---|---|
| *Person* | *Singular* | *Plural* |
| 1st person | I would have fought<br>Јас ќе сум т**е**пал/**и**степал(а)<br>*Jas kje sum t**e**pal/**i**stepal(a)* | We would have fought<br>Ние ќе сме т**е**пале/ист**е**пале<br>*Nie kje sme t**e**pale/ist**e**pale* |
| 2nd person | You would have fought<br>Ти ќе си т**е**пал/**и**степал(а)<br>*Ti kje si t**e**pal/**i**stepal(a)* | You would have fought<br>Вие ќе сте т**е**пале/ист**е**пале<br>*Vie kje ste t**e**pale/ist**e**pale* |
| 3rd person | He/She/It would have fought<br>Тој/Таа/Тоа ќе т**е**пал/**и**степал(а)(о)<br>*Toj/Taa/Toa kje t**e**pal/**i**stepal(a)(o)* | They would have fought<br>Тие ќе т**е**пале/ист**е**пале<br>*Tie kje t**e**pale/ist**e**pale* |

***To find - Haoѓa/Најде***

| | | |
|---|---|---|
| *Infinitive* | To find | Н**а**оѓа<br>N**a**ogja |

| Present Simple Tense | | |
|---|---|---|
| *Person* | *Singular* | *Plural* |
| 1st person | I find -<br>Јас н**а**оѓам<br>*Jas n**a**ogjam* | We find -<br>Ние на**о**ѓаме<br>*Nie na**o**gjame* |
| 2nd person | You find -<br>Ти н**а**оѓаш<br>*Ti n**a**ogjash* | You find -<br>Вие на**о**ѓате<br>*Vie na**o**gjate* |
| 3rd person | He/She/It finds -<br>Тој/Таа/Тоа н**а**оѓа<br>*Toj/Taa/Toa n**a**ogja* | They find -<br>Тие на**о**ѓаат<br>*Tie na**o**gjaat* |

| Past Simple Tense | | |
|---|---|---|
| *Person* | *Singular* | *Plural* |
| 1st person | I found -<br>Јас н**а**јдов<br>*Jas n**a**jdov* | We found -<br>Ние н**а**јдовме<br>*Nie n**a**jdovme* |
| 2nd person | You found -<br>Ти н**а**јде<br>*Ti n**a**jde* | You found -<br>Вие н**а**јдовте<br>*Vie n**a**jdovte* |
| 3rd person | He/She/It found -<br>Тој/Таа/Тоа н**а**јде<br>*Toj/Taa/Toa n**a**jde* | They found -<br>Тие н**а**јдоа<br>*tie n**a**jdoa* |

| Past Continuous Tense | | |
|---|---|---|
| *Person* | *Singular* | *Plural* |
| 1st person | I was finding -<br>Јас н**а**оѓав<br>*Jas n**a**ogjav* | We were finding -<br>Ние на**о**ѓавме<br>*Nie na**o**gjavme* |
| 2nd person | You were finding -<br>Ти на**о**ѓаше<br>*Ti na**o**gjashe* | You were finding -<br>Вие на**о**ѓавте<br>*Vie na**o**gjavte* |
| 3rd person | He/She/It was finding -<br>Тој/Таа/Тоа на**о**ѓаше<br>*Toj/Taa/Toa na**o**gjashe* | They were finding -<br>Тие на**о**ѓаа<br>*Tie na**o**gjaa* |

| Present Perfect Simple Tense | | |
|---|---|---|
| *Person* | *Singular* | *Plural* |
| 1st person | I have found -<br>Јас сум н**а**шол(а)<br>*Jas sum n**a**shol(a)* | We have found -<br>Ние сме н**а**шле<br>*Ne sme n**a**shle* |

| | | |
|---|---|---|
| 2nd person | You have found -<br>Ти си нашол(а)<br>*Ti si nashol(a)* | You have found -<br>Вие сте нашле<br>*Vie ste nashle* |
| 3rd person | He/She/It has found -<br>Тој/Таа/Тоа нашол(а)(о)<br>*Toj/Taa/Toa nashol(a)(o)* | They have found -<br>Тие нашле<br>*Tie nashle* |

| **Present Perfect Continuous Tense** | | |
|---|---|---|
| *Person* | *Singular* | *Plural* |
| 1st person | I have been finding -<br>Јас сум наоѓал(а)<br>*Jas sum naogjal(a)* | We have been finding -<br>Ние сме наоѓале<br>*Nie sme naogjale* |
| 2nd person | You have been finding -<br>Ти си наоѓал(а)<br>*Ti si naogjal(a)* | You have been finding -<br>Вие сте наоѓале<br>*Vie ste naogjale* |
| 3rd person | He/She/It has been finding -<br>Тој/Таа/Тоа наоѓал(а)(о)<br>*Toj/Taa/Toa naogjal(a)(o)* | They have been finding -<br>Тие наоѓале<br>*Tie naogjale* |

| **Past Perfect Simple Tense** | | |
|---|---|---|
| *Person* | *Singular* | *Plural* |
| 1st person | I had found -<br>Јас бев нашол(а)<br>*Jas bev nashol(a)* | We had found -<br>Ние бевме нашле<br>*Nie bevme nashle* |
| 2nd person | You had found -<br>Ти беше нашол(а)<br>*Ti beshe nashol(a)* | You had found -<br>Вие бевте нашле<br>*Vie bevte nashle* |
| 3rd person | He/She/It had found -<br>Тој/Таа/Тоа беше нашол(а)(о)<br>*Toj/Taa/Toa beshe nashol(a)(o)* | They had found -<br>Тие беа нашле<br>*Tie bea nashle* |

| **Future Simple Tense** | | |
|---|---|---|
| *Person* | *Singular* | *Plural* |
| 1st person | I will find -<br>Јас ќе наоѓам/најдам<br>*Jas kje naogjam/najdam* | We will find -<br>Ние ќе наоѓаме/најдеме<br>*Nie kje naogjame/najdeme* |
| 2nd person | You will find -<br>Ти ќе наоѓаш/најдеш<br>*Ti kje naogjash/najdesh* | You will find -<br>Вие ќе наоѓате/најдете<br>*Vie kje naogjate/najdete* |
| 3rd person | He/She/It will find -<br>Тој/Таа/Тоа ќе наоѓа/најде<br>*Toj/Taa/Toa naogja/najde* | They will find -<br>Тие ќе наоѓаат/најдат<br>*Tie kje naogjaat/najdat* |

| **used to + infinitive or would + infinitive** | | |
|---|---|---|
| *Person* | *Singular* | *Plural* |
| 1st person | I would find -<br>Јас ќе наоѓав/најдев<br>*Jas kje naogjav/najdev* | We would find -<br>Ние ќе наоѓавме/најдевме<br>*Nie kje naogjavme/najdevme* |

| | | |
|---|---|---|
| 2nd person | You would find -<br>Ти ќе наоѓаше/најдеше<br>*Ti kje naogjashe/najdeshe* | You would find -<br>Вие ќе наоѓавте/најдевте<br>*Vie kje naojavte/najdevte* |
| 3rd person | He/She/It would find -<br>Тој/Таа/Тоа ќе<br>наоѓаше/најдеше<br>*Toj/Taa/Toa kje*<br>*naogjashe/najdeshe* | They would find -<br>Тие ќе наоѓаа/најдеа<br>*Tie kje naogjaa/najdea* |

| **Personal endings for future perfect-in-the-past tense** | | |
|---|---|---|
| *Person* | *Singular* | *Plural* |
| 1st person | I would have found -<br>Јас ќе сум наоѓал/нашол(а)<br>*Jas kje sum naogjal/nashol(a)* | We would have found -<br>Ние ќе сме наоѓале/нашле<br>*Nie sme naogjale/nashle* |
| 2nd person | You would have found -<br>Ти ќе си наоѓал/нашол(а)<br>*Ti kje si naogjal/nashol(a)* | You would have found -<br>Вие ќе сте наоѓале/нашле<br>*Vie kje ste naogjale/nashle* |
| 3rd person | He/She/It would have found -<br>Тој/Таа/Тоа ќе<br>наоѓал/нашол(а)(о)<br>*Toj/Taa/Toa ke*<br>*naogjal/nashol(a)(o)* | They would have found -<br>Тие ќе наоѓале/нашле<br>*Tie kje naogjale/nashle* |

**To finish - Завршува/Заврши**

| | | |
|---|---|---|
| *Infinitive* | To finish | За**в**ршува<br>Zav**r**shuva |

| Present Simple Tense | | |
|---|---|---|
| *Person* | *Singular* | *Plural* |
| 1st person | I finish -<br>Јас завр**ш**увам<br>*Jas zavrshuvam* | We finish -<br>Ние завршу**в**аме<br>*Nie zavrsh**u**vame* |
| 2nd person | You finish -<br>Ти завр**ш**уваш<br>*Ti zavrshuvash* | You finish -<br>Вие завршу**в**ате<br>*Vie zavrsh**u**vate* |
| 3rd person | He/She/It finishes -<br>Тој/Таа/Тоа завр**ш**ува<br>*Тој/Таа/Тоа zavrshuva* | They finish -<br>Тие завршу**в**аат<br>*Tie zavrsh**u**vaat* |

| Past Simple Tense | | |
|---|---|---|
| *Person* | *Singular* | *Plural* |
| 1st person | I finished -<br>Јас зав**р**шив<br>*Jas zav**r**shiv* | We finished -<br>Ние зав**р**шивме<br>*Nie zav**r**shivme* |
| 2nd person | You finished -<br>Ти зав**р**ши<br>*Ti zav**r**shi* | You finished -<br>Вие зав**р**шивте<br>*Vie zav**r**shivte* |
| 3rd person | He/She/It finished -<br>Тој/Таа/Тоа зав**р**ши<br>*Тој/Таа/Тоа zav**r**shi* | They finished -<br>Тие зав**р**шија<br>*Tie zav**r**shija* |

| Past Continuous Tense | | |
|---|---|---|
| *Person* | *Singular* | *Plural* |
| 1st person | I was finishing -<br>Јас зав**р**шував<br>*Jas zav**r**shuvav* | We were finishing -<br>Ние завршу**в**авме<br>*Nie zavrsh**u**vavme* |
| 2nd person | You were finishing -<br>Ти завршу**в**аше<br>*Ti zavrsh**u**vashe* | You were finishing -<br>Вие завршу**в**авте<br>*Vie zavrsh**u**vavte* |
| 3rd person | He/She/It was finishing -<br>Тој/Таа/Тоа завршу**в**аше<br>*Тој/Таа/Тоа zavrsh**u**vashe* | They were finishing -<br>Тие завршу**в**аа<br>*Tie zavrsh**u**vaa* |

| Present Perfect Simple Tense | | |
|---|---|---|
| *Person* | *Singular* | *Plural* |
| 1st person | I have finished -<br>Јас сум **за**вршил(а)<br>*Jas sum **za**vrshil(a)* | We have finished -<br>Ние сме зав**р**шиле<br>*Nie sme zav**r**shile* |
| 2nd person | You have finished -<br>Ти си **за**вршил(а)<br>*Ti si **za**vrshil(a)* | You have finished -<br>Вие сте зав**р**шиле<br>*Vie ste zav**r**shile* |

| | | |
|---|---|---|
| 3rd person | He/She/It has finished -<br>Тој/Таа/Тоа завршил(а)(о)<br>*Toj/Taa/Toa zavrshil(a)(o)* | They have finished -<br>Тие завршиле<br>*Tie zavrshile* |

| **Present Perfect Continuous Tense** | | |
|---|---|---|
| *Person* | *Singular* | *Plural* |
| 1st person | I have been finishing -<br>Јас сум завршувал(а)<br>*Jas sum zavrshuval(a)* | We have been finishing -<br>Ние сме завршувале<br>*Nie sme zavrshuvale* |
| 2nd person | You have been finishing -<br>Ти си завршувал(а)<br>*Ti si zavrshuval(a)* | You have been finishing -<br>Вие сте завршувале<br>*Vie ste zavrshuvale* |
| 3rd person | He/She/It has been finishing -<br>Тој/Таа/Тоа завршувал(а)(о)<br>*Toj/Taa/Toa zavrshuval(a)(o)* | They have been finishing -<br>Тие завршувале<br>*Tie zavrshuvale* |

| **Past Perfect Simple Tense** | | |
|---|---|---|
| *Person* | *Singular* | *Plural* |
| 1st person | I had finished -<br>Јас бев завршил(а)<br>*Jas bev zavrshil(a)* | We had finished -<br>Ние бевме завршиле<br>*Nie bevme zavrshile* |
| 2nd person | You had finished -<br>Ти беше завршил(а)<br>*Ti beshe zavrshil(a)* | You had finished -<br>Вие евте завршиле<br>*Vie bevte zavrshile* |
| 3rd person | He/She/It had finished -<br>Тој/Таа/Тоа беше завршил(а)(о)<br>*Toj/Taa/Toa beshe zavrshil(a)(o)* | They had finished -<br>Тие беа завршиле<br>*Tie bea zavrshile* |

| **Future Simple Tense** | | |
|---|---|---|
| *Person* | *Singular* | *Plural* |
| 1st person | I will finish<br>Јас ќе завршувам/завршам<br>*Jas kje zavrshuvam/zavrsham* | We will finish<br>Ние ќе завршуваме/завршиме<br>*Nie kje zavrshuvame/zavrshime* |
| 2nd person | You will finish<br>Ти ќе завршуваш/завршиш<br>*Ti kje zavrshuvash/zavrshish* | You will finish<br>Вие ќе завршувате/завршите<br>*Vie kje zavrshuvate/zavrshite* |
| 3rd person | He/She/It will finish<br>Тој/Таа/Тоа ќе завршува/заврши<br>*Toj/Taa/Toa kje zavrshuva/zavrshi* | They will finish<br>Тие ќе завршуваат/завршат<br>*Tie kje zavrshuvaat/zavrshat* |

| used to + infinitive or would + infinitive | | |
|---|---|---|
| *Person* | *Singular* | *Plural* |
| 1st person | I would finish - Јас ќе зав**р**шував/з**а**вршев *Jas kje zav**r**shuvav/z**a**vrshev* | We would finish - Ние ќе завршувавме/зав**р**шевме *Nie kje zavrsh**u**vavme/zav**r**shevme* |
| 2nd person | You would finish - Ти ќе завршуваше/зав**р**шеше *Ti kje zavrsh**u**vashe/zav**r**sheshe* | You would finish - Вие ќе завршувавте/зав**р**шевте *Vie kje zavrsh**u**vavte/zav**r**shevte* |
| 3rd person | He/She/It would finish - Тој/Таа/Тоа ќе заврш**у**ваше/зав**р**шеше *Toj/Taa/Toa kje zavrsh**u**vashe/zav**r**sheshe* | They would finish - Тие ќе заврш**у**ваа/зав**р**шеа *Tie kje zavrsh**u**vaa/zav**r**shea* |

| Personal endings for future perfect-in-the-past tense | | |
|---|---|---|
| *Person* | *Singular* | *Plural* |
| 1st person | I would have finished - Јас ќе сум зав**р**шувал/з**а**вршил(а) *Jas kje sum zav**r**shuval/z**a**vrshil(a)* | We would have finished - Ние ќе сме заврш**у**вале/зав**р**шиле *Nie kje sme zavrsh**u**vale/zavrshile* |
| 2nd person | You would have finished - Ти ќе си зав**р**шувал/з**а**вршил(а) *Ti kje si zav**r**shuval/z**a**vrshil(a)* | You would have finished - Вие ќе сте заврш**у**вале/зав**р**шиле *Vie kje ste zavrsh**u**vale/zavrshile* |
| 3rd person | He/She/It would have finished Тој/Таа/Тоа ќе зав**р**шувал/з**а**вршил(а)(о) *Toj/Taa/Toa zav**r**shuval/z**a**vrshil(a)(o)* | They would have finished - Тие ќе завршувале/зав**р**шиле *Tie kje zavrsh**u**vale/zavrshile* |

### *To fly - Лета/Прелета*

| | | |
|---|---|---|
| *Infinitive* | To fly | Л**е**та<br>L**e**ta |

| Present Simple Tense | | |
|---|---|---|
| *Person* | *Singular* | *Plural* |
| 1st person | I fly -<br>Јас л**е**там<br>*Jas l**e**tam* | We fly -<br>Ние л**е**таме<br>*Nie l**e**tame* |
| 2nd person | You fly -<br>Ти л**е**таш<br>*Ti l**e**tash* | You fly -<br>Вие л**е**тате<br>*Vie l**e**tate* |
| 3rd person | He/She/It flies -<br>Тој/Таа/Тоа л**е**та<br>*Toj/Taa/Toa l**e**ta* | They fly -<br>Тие л**е**таат<br>*Tie l**e**taat* |

| Past Simple Tense | | |
|---|---|---|
| *Person* | *Singular* | *Plural* |
| 1st person | I flew -<br>Јас пр**е**летав<br>*Jas pr**e**letav* | We flew -<br>Ние прел**е**тавме<br>*Nie prel**e**tavme* |
| 2nd person | You flew -<br>Ти пр**е**лета<br>*Ti pr**e**leta* | You flew -<br>Вие прел**е**тавте<br>*Vie prel**e**tavte* |
| 3rd person | He/She/It flew -<br>Тој/Таа/Тоа пр**е**лета<br>*Toj/Taa/Toa pr**e**leta* | They flew -<br>Тие прел**е**таа<br>*Tie prel**e**taa* |

| Past Continuous Tense | | |
|---|---|---|
| *Person* | *Singular* | *Plural* |
| 1st person | I was flying -<br>Јас л**е**тав<br>*Jas l**e**tav* | We were flying -<br>Ние л**е**тавме<br>*Nie l**e**tavme* |
| 2nd person | You were flying -<br>Тие л**е**таше<br>*Ti l**e**tashe* | You were flying -<br>Вие л**е**тавте<br>*Vie l**e**tavte* |
| 3rd person | He/She/It was flying -<br>Тој/Таа/Тоа л**е**таше<br>*Toj/Taa/Toa l**e**tashe* | They were flying -<br>Тие л**е**таа<br>*Tie l**e**taa* |

| Present Perfect Simple Tense | | |
|---|---|---|
| *Person* | *Singular* | *Plural* |
| 1st person | I have flown -<br>Јас сум л**е**тал(а)<br>*Jas sum l**e**tal(a)* | We have flown -<br>Ние сме л**е**тале<br>*Nie sme l**e**tale* |

| | | |
|---|---|---|
| 2nd person | You have flown -<br>Ти си летал(а)<br>*Ti si letal(a)* | You have flown -<br>Вие сте летале<br>*Vie ste letale* |
| 3rd person | He/She/It has flown -<br>Тој/Таа/Тоа<br>летал(а)(о)<br>*Toj/Taa/Toa letal(a)*(o) | They have flown -<br>Тие летале<br>*Tie letale* |

| Present Perfect Continuous Tense | | |
|---|---|---|
| *Person* | *Singular* | *Plural* |
| 1st person | I have been flying -<br>Јас сум прелетал(а)<br>*Jas sum preletal(a)* | We have been flying -<br>Ние сме прелетале<br>*Nie sme preletale* |
| 2nd person | You have been flying -<br>Ти си прелетал(а)<br>*Ti si preletal(a)* | You have been flying -<br>Вие сте прелетале<br>*Vie ste preletale* |
| 3rd person | He/She/It has been flying -<br>Тој/Таа/Тоа прелетал(а)(о)<br>*Toj/Taa/Toa preletal(a)(o)* | They have been flying -<br>Тие прелетале<br>*Tie preletale* |

| Past Perfect Simple Tense | | |
|---|---|---|
| *Person* | *Singular* | *Plural* |
| 1st person | I had flown -<br>Јас бев прелетал(а)<br>*Jas bev preletal(a)* | We had flown -<br>Ние бевме прелетале<br>*Nie bevme preletale* |
| 2nd person | You had flown -<br>Ти беше прелетал(а)<br>*Ti beshe preletal (a)* | You had flown -<br>Вие бевте прелетале<br>*Vie bevte preletale* |
| 3rd person | He/She/It had flown -<br>Тој/Таа/Тоа беше<br>прелетал(а)(о)<br>*Toj/Taa/Toa beshe preletal(a)(o)* | They had flown -<br>Тие беа прелетале<br>*Tie bea preletale* |

| Future Simple Tense | | |
|---|---|---|
| *Person* | *Singular* | *Plural* |
| 1st person | I will fly-<br>Јас ќе летам/прелетам<br>*Jas kje letam/preletam* | We will fly -<br>Ние ќе летаме/прелетаме<br>*Nie kje letame/preletame* |
| 2nd person | You will fly -<br>Ти ќе леташ/прелеташ<br>*Ti kje letash/preletash* | You will fly -<br>Вие ќе летате/прелетате<br>*Vie kje letate/preletate* |
| 3rd person | He/She/It will fly -<br>Тој/Таа/Тоа<br>Тој ќе лета/прелета<br>*Toj/Taa/Toakje leta/preleta* | They will fly -<br>Тие ќе летаат/прелетаат<br>*Tie kje letaat/preletaat* |

| used to + infinitive or would + infinitive | | |
|---|---|---|
| *Person* | *Singular* | *Plural* |
| 1st person | I would fly -<br>Јас ќе летав/прелетав<br>*Jas kje letav/preletav* | We would fly -<br>Ние ќе летавме/прелетавме<br>*Nie kje letavme/preletavme* |
| 2nd person | You would fly -<br>Ти ќе леташе/прелеташе<br>*Ti kje letashe/preletashe* | You would fly -<br>Вие ќе летавте/прелетавте<br>*Vie kje letavte/preletavte* |
| 3rd person | He/She/It would fly -<br>Тој/Таа/Тоа ќе<br>леташе/пелеташе<br>*Toj/Taa/Toa kje<br>letashe/preletashe* | They would fly -<br>Тие ќе летаа/прелетаа<br>*Tie kje letaa/preletaa* |

| Personal endings for future perfect-in-the-past tense | | |
|---|---|---|
| *Person* | *Singular* | *Plural* |
| 1st person | I would have flown -<br>Јас ќе сум летал/прелетал(а)<br>*Jas kje sum letal/preletal(a)* | We would have flown -<br>Ние ќе сме летале/прелетале<br>*Nie kje sme letale/preletale* |
| 2nd person | You would have flown -<br>Ти ќе си летал/прелетал(а)<br>*Ti kje si letal/preletal(a)* | You would have flown -<br>Вие ќе сте летале/прелетале<br>*Vie kje ste letale/preletale* |
| 3rd person | He/She/It would have flown -<br>Тој/Таа/Тоа ќе<br>летал/прелетал(а)(о)<br>*Toj/Taa/Toa kje<br>letal/preletal(a)(o)* | They would have flown -<br>Тие ќе летале/прелетале<br>*Tie kje letale/preletale* |

***To forget - Заборава/Испозаборави***

| | | |
|---|---|---|
| *Infinitive* | Toforget | Заб**о**рава<br>Zab**o**rava |

| **Present Simple Tense** | | |
|---|---|---|
| *Person* | *Singular* | *Plural* |
| 1st person | I forget -<br>Јас заб**о**равам<br>*Jas zab**o**ravam* | We forget -<br>Ние забор**а**ваме<br>*Nie zabor**a**vame* |
| 2nd person | You forget -<br>Ти заб**о**раваш<br>*Ti zab**o**ravash* | You forget -<br>Вие забор**а**вате<br>*Vie zabor**a**vate* |
| 3rd person | He/She/It forgets -<br>Тој/Таа/Тоа заб**о**рава<br>*Toj/Taa/Toa zab**o**rava* | They forget -<br>Тие забор**а**ваат<br>*Tie zabor**a**vaat* |

| **Past Simple Tense** | | |
|---|---|---|
| *Person* | *Singular* | *Plural* |
| 1st person | I forgot -<br>Јас испозаб**о**равив<br>*Jas ispozab**o**raviv* | We forgot -<br>Ние испозабор**а**вивме<br>*Nie ispozabor**a**vivme* |
| 2nd person | You forgot -<br>Ти испозаб**о**рави<br>*Ti ispozab**o**ravi* | You forgot -<br>Вие испозабор**а**вивте<br>*Vie ispozabor**a**vivte* |
| 3rd person | He/She/It forgot -<br>Тој/Таа/Тоа испозаб**о**рави<br>*Toj/Taa/Toa ispozab**o**ravi* | They forgot -<br>Тие испозабор**а**вија<br>*Tie ispozabor**a**vija* |

| **Past Continuous Tense** | | |
|---|---|---|
| *Person* | *Singular* | *Plural* |
| 1st person | I was forgetting -<br>Јас заб**о**равав<br>*Jas zab**o**ravav* | We were forgetting -<br>Ние забор**а**вавме<br>*Nie zabor**a**vavme* |
| 2nd person | You were forgetting -<br>Ти забор**а**ваше<br>*Ti zabor**a**vashe* | You were forgetting -<br>Вие забор**а**вавте<br>*Vie zabor**a**vavte* |
| 3rd person | He/She/It was forgetting -<br>Тој/Таа/Тоа забор**а**ваше<br>*Toj/Taa/Toa zabor**a**vashe* | They were forgetting -<br>Тие забор**а**ваа<br>*Tie zabor**a**vaa* |

| **Present Perfect Simple Tense** | | |
|---|---|---|
| *Person* | *Singular* | *Plural* |
| 1st person | I have forgotten -<br>Јас сум испозаб**о**равил<br>*Jas sum ispozab**o**ravil* | We have forgotten -<br>Ние сме испозабор**а**виле<br>*Nie sme ispozabor**a**vile* |
| 2nd person | You have forgotten -<br>Ти си испозаб**о**равил<br>*Ti si ispozab**o**ravil* | You have forgotten -<br>Вие сте испозабор**а**виле<br>*Vie ste ispozabor**a**vile* |

| | | |
|---|---|---|
| 3rd person | He/She/It has forgotten -<br>Тој/Таа/Тоа испозаб**о**равил<br>*Toj/Taa/Toa ispozab**o**ravil* | They have forgotten -<br>Тие испозабор**а**виле<br>*Tie ispozabor**a**vile* |

| Present Perfect Continuous Tense | | |
|---|---|---|
| *Person* | *Singular* | *Plural* |
| 1st person | I have been forgetting -<br>Јас сум заб**о**равал<br>*Jas sum zab**o**raval* | We have been forgetting -<br>Ние сме забор**а**вале<br>*Nie sme zabor**a**vale* |
| 2nd person | You have been forgetting -<br>Ти си заб**о**равал<br>*Ti si zab**o**raval* | You have been forgetting -<br>Вие сте забор**а**вале<br>*Vie ste zabor**a**vale* |
| 3rd person | He/She/It has been forgetting-<br>Тој/Таа/Тоа заб**о**равал<br>*Toj/Taa/Toa zab**o**raval* | They have been forgetting -<br>Тие забор**а**вале<br>*Tie zabor**a**vale* |

| Past Perfect Simple Tense | | |
|---|---|---|
| *Person* | *Singular* | *Plural* |
| 1st person | I had forgotten -<br>Јас бев испозаб**о**равил(а)<br>*Jas bev ispozab**o**ravil(a)* | We had forgotten -<br>Ние бевме испозабор**а**виле<br>*Nie bevme ispozabor**a**vile* |
| 2nd person | You had forgotten -<br>Ти беше испозаб**о**равил(а)<br>*Ti beshe ispozab**o**ravil(a)* | You had forgotten -<br>Вие бевте испозабор**а**виле<br>*Vie bevte ispozabor**a**vile* |
| 3rd person | He/She/It had forgotten -<br>Тој/Таа/Тоа беше<br>испозаб**о**равил(а)(о)<br>*Toj/Taa/Toa ispozab**o**ravil(a)(o)* | They had forgotten -<br>Тие беа испозабор**а**виле<br>*Tie bea ispozabor**a**vile* |

| Future Simple Tense | | |
|---|---|---|
| *Person* | *Singular* | *Plural* |
| 1st person | I will forget -<br>Јас ќе<br>заб**о**равам/испозаб**о**равам<br>*Jas kje*<br>*zab**o**ravam/ispozab**o**ravam* | We will forget -<br>Ние ќе<br>забор**а**виме/испозабор**а**виме<br>*Nie kje*<br>*zabor**a**vime/ispozabor**a**vime* |
| 2nd person | You will forget -<br>Ти ќе<br>заб**о**равиш/испозаб**о**равиш<br>*Ti kje zab**o**ravish/ispozab**o**ravish* | You will forget -<br>Вие ќе<br>забор**а**вите/испозабор**а**вите<br>*Vie kje zabor**a**vite/ispozabor**a**vite* |
| 3rd person | He/She/It will forget -<br>Тој/Таа/Тоа ќе<br>заб**о**рави/испозаб**о**рави<br>*Toj/Taa/Toa kje*<br>*zab**o**ravi/ispozab**o**ravi* | They will forget -<br>Тие ќе<br>забор**а**ват/испозабор**а**ват<br>*Tie kje zabor**a**vat/ispozabor**a**vat* |

| **used to + infinitive or would + infinitive** | | |
|---|---|---|
| *Person* | *Singular* | *Plural* |
| 1st person | I would forget - Јас ќе заб**о**равев/испозаб**о**равев *Jas kje zab**o**ravev/ispozab**o**ravev* | We would forget - Ние ќе забор**а**вевме/ испозабор**а**вевме *Nie kje zabor**a**vevme/ ispozabor**a**vevme* |
| 2nd person | You would forget - Ти ќе забор**а**веше/испозабор**а**веше *Ti kje zabor**a**veshe/ispozabor**a**veshe* | You would forget - Вие ќе забор**а**вевте/ испозабор**а**вевте *Vie kje zabor**a**vevte/ ispozabor**a**vevte* |
| 3rd person | He/She/It would forget - Тој/Таа/Тоа ќе забор**а**веше/испозабор**а**веше *Toj/Taa/Toa kje zabor**a**veshe/ispozabor**a**veshe* | They would forget - Тие ќе забор**а**веа/испозабор**а**веа *Tie kje zabor**a**vea/ispozabor**a**vea* |

| **Personal endings for future perfect-in-the-past tense** | | |
|---|---|---|
| *Person* | *Singular* | *Plural* |
| 1st person | I would have forgotten - Јас ќе сум заб**о**равел/испозаб**о**равел(а) *Jas kje sum zab**o**ravel/ispozab**o**ravel(a)* | We would have forgotten - Ние ќе сме забор**а**веле/испозабор**а**веле *Nie kje sme zabor**a**vele/ispozabor**a**vele* |
| 2nd person | You would have forgotten - Ти ќе си заб**о**равел/испозаб**о**равел(а) *Ti kje si zab**o**ravel/ispozab**o**ravel(a)* | You would have forgotten - Вие ќе сте забор**а**веле/испозабор**а**веле *Vie kje ste zabor**a**vele/ispozabor**a**vele* |
| 3rd person | He/She/It would have forgotten - Тој/Таа/Тоа ќе заб**о**равел/ испозаб**о**равел(а)(о) *Toj/Taa/Toa kje zab**o**ravel/ispozab**o**ravel(a)(o)* | They would have forgotten - Тие ќе се забор**а**веле/испозабор**а**веле *Tie kje zabor**a**vele/ispozabor**a**vele* |

***To get up - Станува/Стана***

| | | |
|---|---|---|
| *Infinitive* | To get up | Ст**а**нува<br>St**a**nuva |

| **Present Simple Tense** | | |
|---|---|---|
| *Person* | *Singular* | *Plural* |
| 1st person | I get up -<br>Јас ст**а**нувам<br>*Jas st**a**nuvam* | We get up -<br>Ние стан**у**ваме<br>*Nie stan**u**vame* |
| 2nd person | You get up -<br>Ти ст**а**нуваш<br>*Ti st**a**nuvash* | You get up -<br>Вие стан**у**вате<br>*Vie stan**u**vate* |
| 3rd person | He/She/It gets up -<br>Тој/Таа/Тоа ст**а**нува<br>*Toj/Taa/Toa st**a**nuva* | They get up -<br>Тие стан**у**ваат<br>*Tie stan**u**vaat* |

| **Past Simple Tense** | | |
|---|---|---|
| *Person* | *Singular* | *Plural* |
| 1st person | I got up -<br>Јас ст**а**нав<br>*Jas st**a**nav* | We got up -<br>Ние ст**а**навме<br>*Nie st**a**navme* |
| 2nd person | You got up -<br>Ти ст**а**на<br>*Ti st**a**na* | You got up -<br>Вие ст**а**навте<br>*Vie st**a**navte* |
| 3rd person | He/She/It got up -<br>Тој/Таа/Тоа ст**а**на<br>*Toj/Taa/Toa st**a**na* | They got up -<br>Тие ст**а**наа<br>*Tie st**a**naa* |

| **Past Continuous Tense** | | |
|---|---|---|
| *Person* | *Singular* | *Plural* |
| 1st person | I was getting up -<br>Јас ст**а**нував<br>*Jas st**a**nuvav* | We were getting up -<br>Ние стан**у**вавме<br>*Nie stan**u**vavme* |
| 2nd person | You were getting up -<br>Ти стан**у**ваше<br>*Ti stan**u**vashe* | You were getting up -<br>Вие стан**у**вавте<br>*Vie stan**u**vavte* |
| 3rd person | He/She/It was getting up -<br>Тој/Таа/Тоа стан**у**ваше<br>*Toj/Taa/Toa stan**u**vashe* | They were getting up -<br>Тие стан**у**ваа<br>*Tie stan**u**vaa* |

| **Present Perfect Simple Tense** | | |
|---|---|---|
| *Person* | *Singular* | *Plural* |
| 1st person | I have gotten up -<br>Јас сум ст**а**нал(а)<br>*Jas sum st**a**nal(a)* | We have gotten up -<br>Ние сме ст**а**нале<br>*Nie sme st**a**nale* |

| | | |
|---|---|---|
| 2nd person | You have gotten up - Ти си ст**а**нал(а) *Ti si st**a**nal(a)* | You have gotten up - Вие сте ст**а**нале *Vie ste st**a**nale* |
| 3rd person | He/She/It has gotten up - Тој/Таа/Тоа ст**а**нал(а)(о) *Toj/Taa/Toa st**a**nal(a)(o)* | They have gotten up - Тие ст**а**нале *Tie st**a**nale* |

| **Present Perfect Continuous Tense** | | |
|---|---|---|
| *Person* | *Singular* | *Plural* |
| 1st person | I have been getting up - Јас сум ст**а**нувал(а) *Jas sum st**a**nuval(a)* | We have been getting up - Ние сме стан**у**вале *Nie sme stan**u**vale* |
| 2nd person | You have been getting up - Ти си ст**а**нувал(а) *Ti si st**a**nuval(a)* | You have been getting up - Вие сте стан**у**вале *Vie ste stan**u**vale* |
| 3rd person | He/She/It has been getting up Тој/Таа/Тоаст**а**нувал(а)(о) *Toj/Taa/Toa st**a**nuval(a)(o)* | They have been getting up - Тие стан**у**вале *Tie stan**u**vale* |

| **Past Perfect Simple Tense** | | |
|---|---|---|
| *Person* | *Singular* | *Plural* |
| 1st person | I had gotten up - Јас бев ст**а**нал(а) *Jas bev st**a**nal(a)* | We had gotten up - Ние бевме ст**а**нале *Nie bevme st**a**nale* |
| 2nd person | You had gotten up - Ти беше ст**а**нал(а) *Ti beshe st**a**nal(a)* | You had gotten up - Вие бевте ст**а**нале *Vie bevte st**a**nale* |
| 3rd person | He/She/It had gotten up - Тој/Таа/Тоа беше ст**а**нал(а)(о) *Toj/Taa/Toa beshe st**a**nal(a)(o)* | They had gotten up - Тие беа ст**а**нале *Tie bea st**a**nale* |

| **Future Simple Tense** | | |
|---|---|---|
| *Person* | *Singular* | *Plural* |
| 1st person | I will get up - Јас ќе ст**а**нувам/ст**а**нам *Jas kje st**a**nuvam/st**a**nam* | We will get up - Ние ќе стан**у**ваме/ст**а**неме *Nie kje stan**u**vame/st**a**neme* |
| 2nd person | You will get up - Ти ќе ст**а**нуваш/ст**а**неш *Ti kje st**a**nuvash/st**a**nesh* | You will get up - Вие ќе стан**у**вате/ст**а**нете *Vie kje stan**u**vate/st**a**nete* |
| 3rd person | He/She/It will get up - Тој/Таа/Тоа ќе ст**а**нува/ст**а**не *Toj/Taa/Toa kje st**a**nuva/st**a**ne* | They will get up - Тие ќе стан**у**ваат/ст**а**нат *Tie kje stanuvaat/stanat* |

| **used to + infinitive or would + infinitive** | | |
|---|---|---|
| *Person* | *Singular* | *Plural* |
| 1st person | I would get up - Јас ќе ст**а**нував/ст**а**нев *Jas kje st**a**nuvav/st**a**nev* | We would get up - Ние ќе стан**у**вавме/ст**а**невме *Nie kje stan**u**vavme/st**a**nevme* |
| 2nd person | You would get up - Ти ќе стан**у**ваше/ст**а**неше *Ti kje stan**u**vashe/st**a**neshe* | You would get up - Вие ќе стан**у**вавте/ст**а**невте *Vie kje stan**u**vavte/st**a**nevte* |
| 3rd person | He/She/It would get up - Тој/Таа/Тоа ќе стан**у**ваше/ст**а**неше *Toj/Taa/Toa kje stan**u**vashe/st**a**neshe* | They would get up - Тие ќе стан**у**ваа/ст**а**неа *Tie kje stan**u**vaa/st**a**nea* |

| **Personal endings for future perfect-in-the-past tense** | | |
|---|---|---|
| *Person* | *Singular* | *Plural* |
| 1st person | I would have gotten up - Јас ќе сум ст**а**нувал/ст**а**нал(а) *Jas kje sum st**a**nuval/st**a**nal(a)* | We would have gotten up - Ние ќе сме стан**у**вале/ст**а**нале *Nie kje sme stan**u**vale/st**a**nale* |
| 2nd person | You would have gotten up - Ти ќе си ст**а**нувал/ст**а**нал(а) *Ti kje si st**a**nuval/st**a**nal(a)* | You would have gotten up - Вие ќе сте стан**у**вале/ст**а**нале *Vie kje ste stan**u**vale/st**a**nale* |
| 3rd person | He/She/It would have gotten up - Тој/Таа/Тоа ќе ст**а**нувал/ст**а**нал(а)(о) *Toj/Taa/Toa kje st**a**nuval/st**a**nal(a)(o)* | They would have gotten up - Тие ќе стан**у**вале/ст**а**нале *Tie kje stan**u**vale/st**a**nale* |

**To give - Дава/Даде**

| | | |
|---|---|---|
| *Infinitive* | To give | Дава<br>Dava |

| Present Simple Tense | | |
|---|---|---|
| *Person* | *Singular* | *Plural* |
| 1st person | I give -<br>Јас давам<br>*Jas davam* | We give -<br>Ние даваме<br>*Nie davame* |
| 2nd person | You give -<br>Ти даваш<br>*Ti davash* | You give -<br>Вие давате<br>*Vie davate* |
| 3rd person | He/She/It gives -<br>Тој/Таа/Тоа дава<br>*Toj/Taa/Toa dava* | They give -<br>Тие даваат<br>*Tie davaat* |

| Past Simple Tense | | |
|---|---|---|
| *Person* | *Singular* | *Plural* |
| 1st person | I gave -<br>Јас дадов<br>*Jas dadov* | We gave -<br>Ние дадовме<br>*Nie dadovme* |
| 2nd person | You gave -<br>Ти даде<br>*Ti dade* | You gave -<br>Вие дадовте<br>*Vie dadovte* |
| 3rd person | He/She/It gave -<br>Тој/Таа/Тоа даде<br>*Toj/Taa/Toa dade* | They gave -<br>Тие дадоа<br>*Tie dadoa* |

| Past Continuous Tense | | |
|---|---|---|
| *Person* | *Singular* | *Plural* |
| 1st person | I was giving -<br>Јас давав<br>*Jas davav* | We were giving -<br>Ние дававме<br>*Nie davavme* |
| 2nd person | You were giving -<br>Ти даваше<br>*Ti davashe* | You were giving -<br>Вие дававте<br>*Vie davavte* |
| 3rd person | He/She/It was giving -<br>Тој/Таа/Тоа даваше<br>*Toj/Taa/Toa davashe* | They were giving -<br>Тие даваа<br>*Tie davaa* |

| Present Perfect Simple Tense | | |
|---|---|---|
| *Person* | *Singular* | *Plural* |
| 1st person | I have given -<br>Јас сум дал(а)<br>*Jas sum dal(a)* | We have given -<br>Ние сме дале<br>*Nie sme dale* |

| | | |
|---|---|---|
| 2nd person | You have given -<br>Ти си **да**л(а)<br>*Ti si **da**l(a)* | You have given -<br>Вие сте **да**ле<br>*Vie ste **da**le* |
| 3rd person | He/She/It has given -<br>Тој/Таа/Тоа **да**л(а)(о)<br>*Toj/Taa/Toa **da**l(a)(o)* | They have given -<br>Тие **да**ле<br>*Tie **da**le* |

| **Present Perfect Continuous Tense** | | |
|---|---|---|
| *Person* | *Singular* | *Plural* |
| 1st person | I have been giving -<br>Јас сум **да**вал(а)<br>*Jas sum **da**val(a)* | We have been giving -<br>Ние сме **да**вале<br>*Nie sme **da**vale* |
| 2nd person | You have been giving -<br>Ти сида**ва**л(а)<br>*Ti si **da**val(a)* | You have been giving -<br>Вие сте **да**вале<br>*Vie ste **da**vale* |
| 3rd person | He/She/It has been giving -<br>Тој/Таа/Тоа **да**вал(а)(о)<br>*Toj/Taa/Toa **da**val(a)(o)* | They have been giving -<br>Тие **да**вале<br>*Tie **da**vale* |

| **Past Perfect Simple Tense** | | |
|---|---|---|
| *Person* | *Singular* | *Plural* |
| 1st person | I had given -<br>Јас бев **да**л(а)<br>*Jas bev **da**l(a)* | We had given -<br>Ние бевме **да**ле<br>*Nie bevme **da**le* |
| 2nd person | You had given -<br>Ти беше **да**л(а)<br>*Ti beshe **da**l(a)* | You had given -<br>Вие бевте **да**ле<br>*Vie bevte **da**le* |
| 3rd person | He/She/It had given -<br>Тој/Таа/Тоа беше **да**л(а)(о)<br>*Toj/Taa/Toa beshe **da**l(a)(o)* | They had given -<br>Тие беа **да**ле<br>*Tie bea **da**le* |

| **Future Simple Tense** | | |
|---|---|---|
| *Person* | *Singular* | *Plural* |
| 1st person | I will give -<br>Јас ќе **да**вам/**да**дам<br>*Jas kje **da**vam/**da**dam* | We will give -<br>Ние ќе **да**ваме/**да**деме<br>*Nie kje **da**vame/**da**deme* |
| 2nd person | You will give -<br>Ти ќе **да**ваш/**да**деш<br>*Ti kje **da**vash/**da**desh* | You will give -<br>Ви ќе **да**вате/**да**дете<br>*Vie kje **da**vate/**da**dete* |
| 3rd person | He/She/It will give -<br>Тој/Таа/Тоа ќе **да**ва/**да**де<br>*Toj/Taa/Toakje **da**va/**da**de* | They will give -<br>Тие ќе **да**ваат/**да**дат<br>*Tie kje **da**vaat/**da**dat* |

| **used to + infinitive or would + infinitive** | | |
|---|---|---|
| *Person* | *Singular* | *Plural* |
| 1st person | I would give -<br>Јас ќе **да**вав/**да**дев<br>*Jas kje **da**vav/**da**dev* | We would give -<br>Ние ќе **да**вавме/**да**девме<br>*Nie kje **da**vavme/**da**devme* |

| | | |
|---|---|---|
| 2nd person | You would give -<br>Ти ќе д**а**ваше/д**а**деше<br>*Ti kje d**a**vashe/d**a**deshe* | You would give -<br>Вие ќе д**а**вавте/д**а**девте<br>*Vie kje d**a**vatve/d**a**devt* |
| 3rd person | He/She/It would give -<br>Тој/Таа/Тоа ќе д**а**ваше/д**а**деше<br>*Toj/Taa/Toa kje d**a**vashe/d**a**deshe* | They would give -<br>Тие ќе д**а**ваа/д**а**деа<br>*Tie kje d**a**vaa/d**a**dea* |

| **Personal endings for future perfect-in-the-past tense** | | |
|---|---|---|
| *Person* | *Singular* | *Plural* |
| 1st person | I would have given -<br>Јас ќе сум д**а**вал/д**а**л(а)<br>*Jas kje sum d**a**val/d**a**l(a)* | We would have given -<br>Ние ќе сме д**а**вале/д**а**ле<br>*Nie kje sme d**a**vale/d**a**le* |
| 2nd person | You would have given -<br>Ти ќе си д**а**вал/д**а**л(а)<br>*Ti kje si d**a**val/d**a**l(a)* | You would have given -<br>Вие ќе сте д**а**вале/д**а**ле<br>*Vie kje ste d**a**vale/d**a**le* |
| 3rd person | He/She/It would have given -<br>Тој/Таа/Тоа ќе д**а**вал/д**а**л(а)(о)<br>*Toj/Taa/Toa kje d**a**val/d**a**l(a)(o)* | They would have given -<br>Тие ќе д**а**вале/д**а**ле<br>*Tie kje d**a**vale/d**a**le* |

***To go - Оди/Отиде***

| Infinitive | To go | **О**ди<br>**O**di |
|---|---|---|

| Present Simple Tense | | |
|---|---|---|
| *Person* | *Singular* | *Plural* |
| 1st person | I go -<br>Јас **одам**<br>*Jas **odam*** | We go -<br>Ние **одиме**<br>*Nie **odime*** |
| 2nd person | You go -<br>Ти **одиш**<br>*Ti **odish*** | You go -<br>Вие **одите**<br>*Vie **odite*** |
| 3rd person | He/She/It goes -<br>Тој/Таа/Тоа **оди**<br>*Toj/Taa/Toa **odi*** | They go -<br>Тие **одат**<br>*Tie **odat*** |

| Past Simple Tense | | |
|---|---|---|
| *Person* | *Singular* | *Plural* |
| 1st person | I went -<br>Јас **отидов**<br>*Jas **otidov*** | We went -<br>Ние от**и**довме<br>*Nie ot**i**dovme* |
| 2nd person | You went -<br>Ти **отиде**<br>*Ti **otide*** | You went -<br>Вие от**и**довте<br>*Vie ot**i**dovte* |
| 3rd person | He/She/It went -<br>Тој/Таа/Тоа **отиде**<br>*Toj/Taa/Toa **otide*** | They went -<br>Тие от**и**доа<br>*Tie ot**i**doa* |

| Past Continuous Tense | | |
|---|---|---|
| *Person* | *Singular* | *Plural* |
| 1st person | I was going -<br>Јас **одев**<br>*Jas **odev*** | We were going -<br>Ние **одевме**<br>*Nie **odevme*** |
| 2nd person | You were going -<br>Ти **одеше**<br>*Ti **odeshe*** | You were going -<br>Вие **одевте**<br>*Vie **odevte*** |
| 3rd person | He/She/It was going -<br>Тој/Таа/Тоа **одеше**<br>*Toj/Taa/Toa **odeshe*** | They were going -<br>Тие **одеа**<br>*Tie **odea*** |

| Present Perfect Simple Tense | | |
|---|---|---|
| *Person* | *Singular* | *Plural* |
| 1st person | I have gone -<br>Јас сум **отишол**(а)<br>*Jas sum **otishol**(a)* | We have gone -<br>Ние сме **отишле**<br>*Nie sme **otishle*** |

| | | |
|---|---|---|
| 2nd person | You have gone - Ти си **о**тишол(а) *Ti si **o**tishol(a)* | You have gone - Вие сте **о**тишле *Vie ste **o**tishle* |
| 3rd person | He/She/It has gone - Тој/Таа/Тоа **о**тишол(а)(о) *Toj/Taa/Toa **o**tishol(a)(o)* | They have gone - Тие **о**тишле *Tie **o**tishle* |

| **Present Perfect Continuous Tense** | | |
|---|---|---|
| *Person* | *Singular* | *Plural* |
| 1st person | I have been going - Јас сум **о**дел(а) *Jas sum **o**del(a)* | We have been going - Ние сме **о**деле *Nie sme **o**dele* |
| 2nd person | You have been going - Ти си **о**дел(а) *Ti si **o**del(a)* | You have been going - Вие сте **о**деле *Vie ste **o**dele* |
| 3rd person | He/She/It has been going - Тој/Таа/Тоа **о**дел(а)(о) *Toj/Taa/Toa **o**del(a)(o)* | They have been going - Тие **о**деле *Tie **o**dele* |

| **Past Perfect Simple Tense** | | |
|---|---|---|
| *Person* | *Singular* | *Plural* |
| 1st person | I had gone - Јас бев **о**тишол(а) *Jas bev **o**tishol(a)* | We had gone - Ние бевме **о**тишле *Nie bevme **o**tishle* |
| 2nd person | You had gone - Ти беше **о**тишол(а) *Ti beshe **o**tishol(a)* | You had gone - Вие бевте **о**тишле *Vie bevte **o**tishle* |
| 3rd person | He/She/It had gone - Тој/Таа/Тоа беше **о**тишол(а)(о) *Toj/Taa/Toa beshe **o**tishol(a)(o)* | They had gone - Тие беа **о**тишле *Tie bea **o**tishle* |

| **Future Simple Tense** | | |
|---|---|---|
| *Person* | *Singular* | *Plural* |
| 1st person | I will go - Јас ќе **о**дам/**о**тидам *Jas kje **o**dam/**o**tidam* | We will go - Ние ќе **о**диме/от**и**деме *Nie kje **o**dime/ot**i**deme* |
| 2nd person | You will go - Ти ќе **о**диш/**о**тидеш *Ti kje **o**dish/**o**tidesh* | You will go - Вие ќе **о**дите/от**и**дете *Vie kje **o**dite/ot**i**dete* |
| 3rd person | He/She/It will go - Тој/Таа/Тоа ќе **о**ди/**о**тиде *Toj/Taa/Toa kje **o**di/**o**tide* | They will go - Тие ќе **о**дат/**о**тидат *Tie kje **o**dat/**o**tidat* |

| **used to + infinitive or would + infinitive** | | |
|---|---|---|
| *Person* | *Singular* | *Plural* |
| 1st person | I would go - Јас ќе **о**дев/**о**тидов *Jas kje **o**dev/**o**tidov* | We would go - Ние ќе **о**девме/от**и**довме *Nie kje **o**devme/ot**i**dovme* |

| | | |
|---|---|---|
| 2nd person | You would go -<br>Ти ќе **о**деше/от**и**деше<br>*Ti kje **o**deshe/ot**i**deshe* | You would go -<br>Вие ќе **о**девте/от**и**довте<br>*Vie kje **o**devte/ot**i**dovte* |
| 3rd person | He/She/It would go -<br>Тој/Таа/Тоа ќе **о**деше/от**и**деше<br>*Toj/Taa/Toa kje **o**deshe/ot**i**deshe* | They would go -<br>Тие ќе **о**деа/**о**тидоа<br>*Tie kje **o**dea/**o**tidoa* |

| Personal endings for future perfect-in-the-past tense | | |
|---|---|---|
| *Person* | *Singular* | *Plural* |
| 1st person | I would have gone -<br>Јас ќе сум **о**дел/**о**тишол(а)<br>*Jas kje sum **o**del/**o**tishol(a)* | We would have gone -<br>Ние ќе сме **о**деле/**о**тишле<br>*Nie kje sme **o**dele/**o**tishle* |
| 2nd person | You would have gone -<br>Ти ќе си **о**дел/**о**тишол(а)<br>*Ti kje si **o**del/**o**tishol(a)* | You would have gone -<br>Вие ќе сте **о**деле/**о**тишле<br>*Vie kje ste **o**dele/**o**tishle* |
| 3rd person | He/She/It would have gone -<br>Тој/Таа/Тоа ќе<br>**о**дел/**о**тишол(а)(о)<br>*Toj/Taa/Toa kje **o**del/**o**tishol(a)(o)* | They would have gone -<br>Тие ќе **о**деле/**о**тишле<br>*Tie kje **o**dele/**o**tishle* |

**_To happen– Се случува/Се случи_**

| | | |
|---|---|---|
| *Infinitive* | To happen | Се слу**ч**ува<br>Se sl**u**cuva |

***the usage of this verb in this way in the Macedonian language is not natural and has a philosophical view. The main usage is often with "to be" or "to go" and in this way it is translated as an adverb – случајно.***

| **Present Simple Tense** | | |
|---|---|---|
| *Person* | *Singular* | *Plural* |
| 1st person | I happen -<br>Јас се слу**ч**увам<br>*Jas se sl**u**chuvam* | We happen -<br>Ние се случ**у**ваме<br>*Nie se sluch**u**vame* |
| 2nd person | You happen -<br>Ти се слу**ч**уваш<br>*Ti se sl**u**chuvash* | You happen -<br>Вие се случ**у**вате<br>*Vie se sluch**u**vate* |
| 3rd person | He/She/It happens -<br>Тој/Таа/Тоа се слу**ч**ува<br>*Toj/Taa/Toa se sl**u**chuva* | They happen -<br>Тие се случ**у**ваат<br>*Tie se sluch**u**vaat* |

| **Past Simple Tense** | | |
|---|---|---|
| *Person* | *Singular* | *Plural* |
| 1st person | I happened -<br>Јас се сл**у**чив<br>*Jas se sl**u**chiv* | We happened -<br>Ние се сл**у**чивме<br>*Nie se sl**u**chivme* |
| 2nd person | You happened -<br>Ти се сл**у**чи<br>*Ti se sl**u**chi* | You happened -<br>Вие се сл**у**чивте<br>*Vie se sl**u**chivte* |
| 3rd person | He/She/It happened -<br>Тој/Таа/Тоа се сл**у**чи<br>*Toj/Taa/Toa se sl**u**chi* | They happened -<br>Тие се сл**у**чија<br>*Tie se sl**u**chija* |

| **Past Continuous Tense** | | |
|---|---|---|
| *Person* | *Singular* | *Plural* |
| 1st person | I was happening -<br>Јас се сл**у**чував<br>*Jas se sl**u**chuvav* | We were happening -<br>Ние се случ**у**вавме<br>*Nie se sluch**u**vavme* |
| 2nd person | You were happening -<br>Ти се случ**у**ваше<br>*Ti se sluch**u**vashe* | You were happening -<br>Вие се случ**у**вавте<br>*Vie se sluch**u**vavte* |
| 3rd person | He/She/It was happening -<br>Тој/Таа/Тоа се случ**у**ваше<br>*Toj/Taa/Toa se sluch**u**vashe* | They were happening -<br>Тие се случ**у**ваа<br>*Tie se sluch**u**vaa* |

| **Present Perfect Simple Tense** | | |
|---|---|---|
| *Person* | *Singular* | *Plural* |
| 1st person | I have happened -<br>Јас сум се сл**у**чил(а)<br>*Jas sum se sl**u**chil(a)* | We have happened -<br>Ние сме се сл**у**чиле<br>*Nie sme se sl**u**chile* |

| | | |
|---|---|---|
| 2nd person | You have happened -<br>Ти си се сл**у**чил(а)<br>*Ti si se sl**u**chil(a)* | You have happened -<br>Вие сте се се сл**у**чиле<br>*Vie ste se sl**u**chile* |
| 3rd person | He/She/It has happened -<br>Тој/Таа/Тоа се сл**у**чил(а)(о)<br>*Toj/Taa/Toa se sl**u**chil(a)(o)* | They have happened -<br>Тие се сл**у**чиле<br>*Tie se sl**u**chile* |

| **Present Perfect Continuous Tense** | | |
|---|---|---|
| *Person* | *Singular* | *Plural* |
| 1st person | I have been happening -<br>Јас сум се сл**у**чувал(а)<br>*Jas sum se sl**u**chuval(a)* | We have been happening -<br>Ние сме се сл**у**чувале<br>*Nie sme se sl**u**chuvale* |
| 2nd person | You have been happening -<br>Ти си се се сл**у**чувал(а)<br>*Ti si se sl**u**chuval(a)* | You have been happening -<br>Вие сте се се сл**у**чувале<br>*Vie ste se sl**u**chuvale* |
| 3rd person | He/She/It has been happening<br>Тој/Таа/Тоа се сл**у**чувал(а)(о)<br>*Toj/Taa/Toa se sl**u**chuval(a)(o)* | They have been happening -<br>Тие се сл**у**чувале<br>*Tie se sl**u**chuvale* |

| **Past Perfect Simple Tense** | | |
|---|---|---|
| *Person* | *Singular* | *Plural* |
| 1st person | I had happened -<br>Јас бев се сл**у**чил(а)<br>*Jas bev se sl**u**chil(a)* | We had happened -<br>Ние бевме се сл**у**чиле<br>*Nie bevme se sl**u**chile* |
| 2nd person | You had happened -<br>Ти беше се сл**у**чил(а)<br>*Ti beshe* se sl**u**chil(a) | You had happened -<br>Вие бевте се сл**у**чиле<br>*Vie bevte se sl**u**chile* |
| 3rd person | He/She/It had happened -<br>Тој/Таа/Тоа беше се сл**у**чил(а)(о)<br>*Toj/Taa/Toa beshe* se sl**u**chil(a)(o) | They had happened -<br>Тие беа се сл**у**чиле<br>*Tie bea se sl**u**chile* |

| **Future Simple Tense** | | |
|---|---|---|
| *Person* | *Singular* | *Plural* |
| 1st person | I will happen -<br>Јас ќе се сл**у**чувам/ се сл**у**чам<br>*Jas kje se sl**u**chuvam/ se sl**u**cham* | We will happen -<br>Ние ќе се случ**у**ваме/ се сл**у**чиме<br>*Nie kje se sluch**u**vame/ se sl**u**chime* |
| 2nd person | You will happen -<br>Ти ќе се сл**у**чуваш/ се сл**у**чиш<br>*Ti kje se sl**u**chuvash/ se sl**u**chish* | You will happen -<br>Вие ќе се случ**у**вате/ се сл**у**чите<br>*Vie kje se sluch**u**vate/ se sl**u**chite* |

| | | |
|---|---|---|
| 3rd person | He/She/It will happen -<br>Тој/Таа/Тоа ќе се сл**у**чува/<br>се сл**у**чи<br>*Toj/Taa/Toa kje se sl**u**chuva/ se sl**u**chi* | They will happen -<br>Тие ќе се случ**у**ваат/<br>се сл**у**чат<br>*Tie kje se sluch**u**vaat/ se sl**u**chat* |

| **used to + infinitive or would + infinitive** | | |
|---|---|---|
| *Person* | *Singular* | *Plural* |
| 1st person | I would happen -<br>Јас ќе се случ**у**вав/<br>се сл**у**чев<br>*Jas kje se sl**u**chuvav/*<br>*se sl**u**chev* | We would happen -<br>Ние ќе се случ**у**вавме/<br>се сл**у**чевме<br>*Nie kje se sluch**u**vavme/*<br>*se sl**u**chevme* |
| 2nd person | You would happen -<br>Ти ќе се случ**у**ваше/<br>се сл**у**чеше<br>*Ti kje se sluch**u**vashe/*<br>*se sl**u**chese* | You would happen -<br>Вие ќе се случ**у**вавте/<br>се сл**у**чевте<br>*Vie kje se sluch**u**vavte/*<br>*se sl**u**chevte* |
| 3rd person | He/She/It would happen -<br>Тој/Таа/Тоа ќе<br>се случ**у**ваше/се сл**у**чеше<br>*Toj/Taa/Toa kje*<br>*se sluc**u**vashe/se sl**u**chese* | They would happen -<br>Тие ќе се случ**у**ваа/<br>се сл**у**чеа<br>*Tie kje se sluch**u**vaa/*<br>*se sl**u**chea* |

| **Personal endings for future perfect-in-the-past tense** | | |
|---|---|---|
| *Person* | *Singular* | *Plural* |
| 1st person | I would have happened -<br>Јас ќе сум се случ**у**вал/<br>се сл**у**чел(а)<br>*Jas kje sum se sl**u**chuval/*<br>*se sl**u**chel* | We would have happened -<br>Ние ќе сме се случ**у**вале/<br>се сл**у**челе<br>*Nie kje sme se sluch**u**vale/*<br>*se sl**u**chele* |
| 2nd person | You would have happened -<br>Ти ќе си се случ**у**вал/<br>се сл**у**чел(а)<br>*Ti kje si se sl**u**chuval/*<br>*se sl**u**chel* | You would have happened -<br>Вие ќе сте се случ**у**вале/<br>се сл**у**челе<br>*Vie kje ste se sluch**u**vale/*<br>*se sl**u**chele* |
| 3rd person | He/She/It would have happened -<br>Тој/Таа/Тоа ќе се случ**у**вал/<br>се сл**у**чел(а)<br>*Toj/Taa/Toa kje se sl**u**chuval/*<br>*se sl**u**chel* | They would have happened -<br>Тие ќе се случ**у**вале/<br>се сл**у**челе<br>*Tie kje se sluch**u**vale/*<br>*se sl**u**chele* |

***To have – Има***

| | | |
|---|---|---|
| *Infinitive* | To have | **Им**а<br>**Im**a |

| Present Simple Tense | | |
|---|---|---|
| *Person* | *Singular* | *Plural* |
| 1st person | I have -<br>Јас **имам**<br>*Jas **imam*** | We have -<br>Ние **имаме**<br>*Nie **imame*** |
| 2nd person | You have -<br>Ти **имаш**<br>*Ti **imash*** | You have -<br>Вие **имате**<br>*Vie **imate*** |
| 3rd person | He/She/It goes -<br>Тој/Таа/Тоа **има**<br>*Toj/Taa/Toa **ima*** | They have -<br>Тие **имаат**<br>*Tie **imaat*** |

| Past Simple Tense | | |
|---|---|---|
| *Person* | *Singular* | *Plural* |
| 1st person | / | / |
| 2nd person | / | / |
| 3rd person | / | / |

*there is no perfective form of the verb "to have" in the Macedonian, that is why the progressive form is used to describe the meaning of the tenses that are formed with perfective verbs.

| Past Continuous Tense | | |
|---|---|---|
| *Person* | *Singular* | *Plural* |
| 1st person | I was having -<br>Јас **имав**<br>*Jas **imav*** | We were having -<br>Ние **имавме**<br>*Nie **imavme*** |
| 2nd person | You were having -<br>Ти **имаше**<br>*Ti **imashe*** | You were having -<br>Вие **имавте**<br>*Vie **imavte*** |
| 3rd person | He/She/It was having -<br>Тој/Таа/Тоа **имаше**<br>*Toj/Taa/Toa **imashe*** | They were having -<br>Тие **имаа**<br>*Tie **imaa*** |

| Present Perfect Simple Tense | | |
|---|---|---|
| *Person* | *Singular* | *Plural* |
| 1st person | / | / |
| 2nd person | / | / |
| 3rd person | / | / |

| Present Perfect Continuous Tense | | |
|---|---|---|
| *Person* | *Singular* | *Plural* |
| 1st person | I have been having -<br>Јас сум **имал**(а)<br>*Jas sum **imal**(a)* | We have been having -<br>Ние сме **имале**<br>*Nie sme **imale*** |

| | | |
|---|---|---|
| 2nd person | You have been having - Ти си **имал**(а) *Ti si **i**mal(a)* | You have been having - Вие сте **и**мале *Vie ste **i**male* |
| 3rd person | He/She/It has been having - Тој/Таа/Тоа **имал**(а)(о) *Toj/Taa/Toa **i**mal(a)(o)* | They have been having - Тие **и**мале *Tie **i**male* |

| **Past Perfect Simple Tense** | | |
|---|---|---|
| *Person* | *Singular* | *Plural* |
| 1st person | I had had - Јас бев **имал**(а) *Jas bev **i**mal(a)* | We had had - Ние бевме **и**мале *Nie bevme **i**male* |
| 2nd person | You had had - Ти беше **имал**(а) *Ti beshe **i**mal(a)* | You had had - Вие бевте **и**мале *Vie bevte **i**male* |
| 3rd person | He/She/It had had - Тој/Таа/Тоа беше **имал**(а)(о) *Toj/Taa/Toa beshe **i**mal(a)(o)* | They had had - Тие беа **и**мале *Tie bea **i**male* |

| **Future Simple Tense** | | |
|---|---|---|
| *Person* | *Singular* | *Plural* |
| 1st person | I will have - Јас ќе **имам** *Jas kje **i**mam* | We will have - Ние ќе **имаме** *Nie kje **i**mame* |
| 2nd person | You will have - Ти ќе **имаш** *Ti kje **i**mash* | You will have - Вие ќе **имате** *Vie kje **i**mate* |
| 3rd person | He/She/It will have - Тој/Таа/Тоа ќе **има** *Toj/Taa/Toa kje **i**ma* | They will have - Тие ќе **имаат** *Tie kje **i**maat* |

| **used to + infinitive or would + infinitive** | | |
|---|---|---|
| *Person* | *Singular* | *Plural* |
| 1st person | I would have - Јас ќе **имав** *Jas kje **i**mav* | We would have - Ние ќе **имавме** *Nie kje **i**mavme* |
| 2nd person | You would have - Ти ќе **имаше** *Ti kje **i**mashe* | You would have - Вие ќе **имавте** *Vie kje **i**mavte* |
| 3rd person | He/She/It would have - Тој/Таа/Тоа ќе **имаше** *Toj/Taa/Toa kje **i**mashe* | They would have - Тие ќе **имаа** *Tie kje **i**maa* |

| **Personal endings for future perfect-in-the-past tense** | | |
|---|---|---|
| *Person* | *Singular* | *Plural* |
| 1st person | I would have had - Јас ќе сум **имал**(а) *Jas kje sum **i**mal(a)* | We would have had - Ние ќе сме **имале** *Nie kje sme **i**male* |

| | | |
|---|---|---|
| 2nd person | You would have had -<br>Ти ќе си **имал**(а)<br>*Ti kje si **imal**(a)* | You would have had -<br>Вие ќе сте **имале**<br>*Vie kje ste **imale*** |
| 3rd person | He/She/It would have had -<br>Тој/Таа/Тоа ќе **имал**(а)(о)<br>*Toj/Taa/Toa kje **imal**(a)(o)* | They would have had -<br>Тие ќе **имале**<br>*Tie kje **imale*** |

### *To hear - Слуша/Слушна*

| | | |
|---|---|---|
| *Infinitive* | To hear | Сл**у**ша<br>Sl**u**sha |

| Present Simple Tense | | |
|---|---|---|
| *Person* | *Singular* | *Plural* |
| 1st person | I hear -<br>Јас сл**у**шам<br>*Jas sl**u**sham* | We hear -<br>Ние сл**у**шаме<br>*Nie sl**u**shame* |
| 2nd person | You hear -<br>Ти сл**у**шаш<br>*Ti sl**u**shash* | You hear -<br>Вие сл**у**шате<br>*Vie sl**u**shate* |
| 3rd person | He/She/It hears -<br>Тој/Таа/Тоа сл**у**ша<br>*Toj/Taa/Toa sl**u**sha* | They hear -<br>Тие сл**у**шаат<br>*Tie sl**u**shaat* |

| Past Simple Tense | | |
|---|---|---|
| *Person* | *Singular* | *Plural* |
| 1st person | I heard -<br>Јас сл**у**шнав<br>*Jas sl**u**shnav* | We heard -<br>Ние сл**у**шнавме<br>*Nie sl**u**snavme* |
| 2nd person | You heard -<br>Ти сл**у**шна<br>*Ti sl**u**shna* | You heard -<br>Вие сл**у**шнавте<br>*Vie sl**u**shnavte* |
| 3rd person | He/She/It heard -<br>Тој/Таа/Тоа сл**у**шна<br>*Toj/Taa/Toa sl**u**shna* | They heard -<br>Тие сл**у**шнаа<br>*Tie sl**u**shnaa* |

| Past Continuous Tense | | |
|---|---|---|
| *Person* | *Singular* | *Plural* |
| 1st person | I was hearing -<br>Јас сл**у**шав<br>*Jas sl**u**shav* | We were hearing -<br>Ние сл**у**шавме<br>*Nie sl**u**shavme* |
| 2nd person | You were hearing -<br>Ти сл**у**шаше<br>*Ti sl**u**shashe* | You were hearing -<br>Вие сл**у**шавте<br>*Vie sl**u**shavte* |
| 3rd person | He/She/It was hearing -<br>Тој/Таа/Тоа Тој сл**у**шаше<br>*Toj/Taa/Toa sl**u**shashe* | They were hearing -<br>Тие сл**у**шаа<br>*Tie sl**u**shaa* |

| Present Perfect Simple Tense | | |
|---|---|---|
| *Person* | *Singular* | *Plural* |
| 1st person | I have heard -<br>Јас сум сл**у**шнал(а)<br>*Jas sum sl**u**shnal(a)* | We have heard -<br>Ние сме сл**у**шнале<br>*Nie sme sl**u**shnale* |

| | | |
|---|---|---|
| 2nd person | You have heard -<br>Ти си сл**у**шнал(а)<br>*Ti si sl**u**shnal(a)* | You have heard -<br>Вие сте сл**у**шнале<br>*Vie ste sl**u**shnale* |
| 3rd person | He/She/It has heard -<br>Тој/Таа/Тоа сл**у**шнал(а)(о)<br>*Toj/Taa/Toa sl**u**shnal(a)(o)* | They have heard -<br>Тие сл**у**шнале<br>*Tie sl**u**shnale* |

| **Present Perfect Continuous Tense** | | |
|---|---|---|
| *Person* | *Singular* | *Plural* |
| 1st person | I have been hearing -<br>Јас сум сл**у**шал(а)<br>*Jas sum sl**u**shal(a)* | We have been hearing -<br>Ние сме сл**у**шале<br>*Nie sme sl**u**shale* |
| 2nd person | You have been hearing -<br>Ти си сл**у**шал(а)<br>*Ti si sl**u**shnal(a)* | You have been hearing -<br>Вие сте сл**у**шале<br>*Vie ste sl**u**shale* |
| 3rd person | He/She/It has been hearing -<br>Тој/Таа/Тоа сл**у**шал(а)(о)<br>*Toj/Taa/Toa sl**u**shnal(a)(o)* | They have been hearing -<br>Тие сл**у**шале<br>*Tie sl**u**shale* |

| **Past Perfect Simple Tense** | | |
|---|---|---|
| *Person* | *Singular* | *Plural* |
| 1st person | I had heard -<br>Јас бев сл**у**шнал(а)<br>*Jas bev sl**u**shnal(a)* | We had heard -<br>Ние бевме сл**у**шнале<br>*Nie bevme sl**u**shnale* |
| 2nd person | You had heard -<br>Ти беше сл**у**шнал(а)<br>*Ti beshe sl**u**shnal(a)* | You had heard -<br>Вие бевте сл**у**шнале<br>*Vie bevte sl**u**shnale* |
| 3rd person | He/She/It had heard -<br>Тој/Таа/Тоа беше сл**у**шнал(а)(о)<br>*Toj/Taa/Toa sl**u**shnal(a)(o)* | They had heard -<br>Тие беа сл**у**шнале<br>*Tie bea sl**u**shnale* |

| **Future Simple Tense** | | |
|---|---|---|
| *Person* | *Singular* | *Plural* |
| 1st person | I will hear -<br>Јас ќе сл**у**шам/сл**у**шнам<br>*Jas kje sl**u**sham/sl**u**shnam* | We will hear -<br>Ние ќе сл**у**шаме/сл**у**шнеме<br>*Nie kje sl**u**shame/sl**u**shneme* |
| 2nd person | You will hear -<br>Ти ќе сл**у**шаш/сл**у**шнеш<br>*Ti kje sl**u**shash/sl**u**shnesh* | You will hear -<br>Вие ќе сл**у**шате/сл**у**шнете<br>*Vie kje sl**u**shate/sl**u**shnete* |
| 3rd person | He/She/It will hear -<br>Тој/Таа/Тоа ќе сл**у**ша/сл**у**шне<br>*Toj/Taa/Toa slusha/slushne* | They will hear -<br>Тие ќе сл**у**шат/сл**у**шнат<br>*Tie kje sl**u**shat/sl**u**shnat* |

| **used to + infinitive or would + infinitive** | | |
|---|---|---|
| *Person* | *Singular* | *Plural* |
| 1st person | I would hear -<br>Јас ќе сл**у**шав/сл**у**шнев<br>*Jas kje sl**u**shav/sl**u**shnev* | We would hear -<br>Ние ќе сл**у**шавме/сл**у**шневме<br>*Nie kje sl**u**shavme/sl**u**hnevme* |
| 2nd person | You would hear -<br>Ти ќе сл**у**шаше/сл**у**шнеше<br>*Ti kje sl**u**shashe/sl**u**shneshe* | You would hear -<br>Вие ќе сл**у**шавте/сл**у**шневте<br>*Vie kje sl**u**shavte/sl**u**shnevte* |
| 3rd person | He/She/It would hear -<br>Тој/Таа/Тоа ќе<br>сл**у**шаше/сл**у**шнеше<br>*Toj/Taa/Toa*<br>*sl**u**shashe/sl**u**shneshe* | They would hear -<br>Тие ќе сл**у**шаа/сл**у**шнаа<br>*Tie kje sl**u**shaa/sl**u**shnaa* |

| **Personal endings for future perfect-in-the-past tense** | | |
|---|---|---|
| *Person* | *Singular* | *Plural* |
| 1st person | I would have heard -<br>Јас ќе сум сл**у**шал/сл**у**шнал(а)<br>*Jas kje sum sl**u**shal/sl**u**shnal(a)* | We would have heard -<br>Ние ќе сме сл**у**шале/сл**у**шнале<br>*Nie kje sme sl**u**shale/sl**u**shnale* |
| 2nd person | You would have heard -<br>Ти ќе си сл**у**шал/сл**у**шнал(а)<br>*Ti kje si sl**u**shal/sl**u**shnal(a)* | You would have heard -<br>Вие ќе сте сл**у**шале/сл**у**шнале<br>*Vie kje ste sl**u**shale/sl**u**shnale* |
| 3rd person | He/She/It would have heard -<br>Тој/Таа/Тоа ќе<br>сл**у**шал/сл**у**шнал(а)<br>*Toj/Taa/Toa kje*<br>*sl**u**shal/sl**u**shnal(a)* | They would have heard -<br>Тие ќе сл**у**шале/сл**у**шнале<br>*Tie kje sl**u**shale/sl**u**shnale* |

**To help - Помага/Помогна**

| *Infinitive* | To help | Помага<br>Pomaga |
|---|---|---|

| **Present Simple Tense** | | |
|---|---|---|
| *Person* | *Singular* | *Plural* |
| 1st person | I help -<br>Јас помагам<br>*Jas pomagam* | We help -<br>Ние помагаме<br>*Nie pomagame* |
| 2nd person | You help -<br>Ти помагаш<br>*Ti pomagash* | You help -<br>Вие помагате<br>*Vie pomagate* |
| 3rd person | He/She/It helps -<br>Тој/Таа/Тоа помага<br>*Toj/Taa/Toa pomaga* | They help -<br>Тие помагаат<br>*Tie pomagaat* |

| **Past Simple Tense** | | |
|---|---|---|
| *Person* | *Singular* | *Plural* |
| 1st person | I helped -<br>Јас помогнав<br>*Jas pomognav* | We helped -<br>Ние помогнавме<br>*Nie pomognavme* |
| 2nd person | You helped -<br>Ти помогна<br>*Ti pomogna* | You helped -<br>Вие помогнавте<br>*Vie pomognavte* |
| 3rd person | He/She/It helped -<br>Тој/Таа/Тоа помогна<br>*Toj/Taa/Toa pomogna* | They helped -<br>Тие помогнаа<br>*Tie pomognaa* |

| **Past Continuous Tense** | | |
|---|---|---|
| *Person* | *Singular* | *Plural* |
| 1st person | I was helping -<br>Јас помагав<br>*Jas pomagav* | We were helping -<br>Ние помагавме<br>*Nie pomagavme* |
| 2nd person | You were helping -<br>Ти помагаше<br>*Ti pomagashe* | You were helping -<br>Вие помагавте<br>*Vie pomagavte* |
| 3rd person | He/She/It was helping -<br>Тој/Таа/Тоа помагаше<br>*Toj/Taa/Toa pomagashe* | They were helping -<br>Тие помагаа<br>*Tie pomagaa* |

| **Present Perfect Simple Tense** | | |
|---|---|---|
| *Person* | *Singular* | *Plural* |
| 1st person | I have helped -<br>Јас сум помогнал(а)<br>*Jas sum pomognal(a)* | We have helped -<br>Ние сме помогнале<br>*Nie sme pomognale* |

| | | |
|---|---|---|
| 2nd person | You have helped -<br>Ти си п**о**могнал(а)<br>*Ti si p**o**mognal(a)* | You have helped -<br>Вие сте пом**о**гнале<br>*Vie ste pom**o**gnale* |
| 3rd person | He/She/It has helped -<br>Тој/Таа/Тоа п**о**могнал(а)(о)<br>*Toj/Taa/Toa p**o**mognal(a)(o)* | They have helped -<br>Тие пом**о**гнале<br>*Tie pom**o**gnale* |

| **Present Perfect Continuous Tense** | | |
|---|---|---|
| *Person* | *Singular* | *Plural* |
| 1st person | I have been helping -<br>Јас сум п**о**магал(а)<br>*Jas sum p**o**magal(a)* | We have been helping -<br>Ние сме пом**а**гале<br>*Nie sme pom**a**gale* |
| 2nd person | You have been helping -<br>Ти си п**о**магал(а)<br>*Ti si p**o**magal(a)* | You have been helping -<br>Вие сте пом**а**гале<br>*Vie ste pom**a**gale* |
| 3rd person | He/She/It has been helping -<br>Тој/Таа/Тоа п**о**магал(а)(о)<br>*Toj/Taa/Toa p**o**magal(a)(o)* | They have been helping -<br>Тие пом**а**гале<br>*Tie pom**a**gale* |

| **Past Perfect Simple Tense** | | |
|---|---|---|
| *Person* | *Singular* | *Plural* |
| 1st person | I had helped -<br>Јас бев п**о**могнал(а)<br>*Jas bev p**o**mognal(a)* | We had helped -<br>Ние бевме пом**о**гнале<br>*Nie bevme pom**o**gnale* |
| 2nd person | You had helped -<br>Ти беше п**о**могнал(а)<br>*Ti beshe p**o**mognal(a)* | You had helped -<br>Вие бевте пом**о**гнале<br>*Vie bevte pom**o**gnale* |
| 3rd person | He/She/It had helped -<br>Тој/Таа/Тоа беше<br>п**о**могнал(а)(о)<br>*Toj/Taa/Toa beshe*<br>*p**o**mognal(a)(o)* | They had helped -<br>Тие беа пом**о**гнале<br>*Tie bea pom**o**gnale* |

| **Future Simple Tense** | | |
|---|---|---|
| *Person* | *Singular* | *Plural* |
| 1st person | I will help -<br>Јас ќе п**о**магам/п**о**могнам<br>*Jas kje p**o**magam/p**o**mognam/* | We will help -<br>Ние ќе пом**а**гаме/пом**о**гнеме<br>*Nie kje pom**a**game/pom**o**gneme* |
| 2nd person | You will help -<br>Ти ќе п**о**магаш/п**о**могнеш<br>*Ti kje p**o**magash/p**o**mognesh* | You will help -<br>Вие ќе пом**а**гате/пом**о**гнете<br>*Vie kje pom**a**gate/pom**o**gnete* |
| 3rd person | He/She/It will help -<br>Тој/Таа/Тоа п**о**мага/п**о**могне<br>*Toj/Taa/Toa kje*<br>*pomaga/pomogne* | They will help -<br>Тие ќе пом**о**гнат/пом**а**гаат<br>*Tie kje pom**o**gnat pom**a**gaat* |

| used to + infinitive or would + infinitive | | |
|---|---|---|
| *Person* | *Singular* | *Plural* |
| 1st person | I would help - Јас ќе по**ма**гав/по**мо**гнев *Jas kje p**o**magav/p**o**mognev* | We would help - Ние ќе пома**га**вме/помо**гн**евме *Nie kje poma**g**avme/pom**o**gnevme* |
| 2nd person | You would help - Ти ќе пома**г**аше/помо**г**неше *Ti kje pom**a**gashe/pom**o**gneshe* | You would help - Вие ќе пом**а**гавте/пом**о**гневте *Vie kje pom**a**gavte/pom**o**gnevte* |
| 3rd person | He/She/It would help - Тој/Таа/Тоа ќе пом**а**гаше/пом**о**гнеше *Toj/Taa/Toa kje pom**a**gashe/pom**o**gneshe* | They would help - Тие ќе пом**а**гаат/пом**о**гнат *Tie kje pom**a**gaat/pom**o**gnat* |

| Personal endings for future perfect-in-the-past tense | | |
|---|---|---|
| *Person* | *Singular* | *Plural* |
| 1st person | I would have helped - Јас ќе сум п**о**магал/п**о**могнел(а) *Jas kje sum p**o**magal/p**o**mognel(a)* | We would have helped - Ние ќе сме пом**а**гале/пом**о**гнеле *Nie kje sme pom**a**gale/pom**o**gnele* |
| 2nd person | You would have helped - Ти ќе си п**о**магал/п**о**могнел(а) *Ti kje si p**o**magal/p**o**mognel(a)* | You would have helped - Вие ќе сте пом**а**гале/пом**о**гнеле *Vie kje ste pom**a**gale/pom**o**gnele* |
| 3rd person | He/She/It would have - Тој/Таа/Тоа helped Тој/Таа/Тоа ќе п**о**магал/п**о**могнел(а) *Toj/Taa/Toa kje p**o**magal/p**o**mognel(a)* | They would have helped - Тие ќе пом**а**гале/пом**о**гнеле *Tie kje pom**a**gale/pom**o**gnele* |

### *To hold - Држи/Подржа*

| | | |
|---|---|---|
| *Infinitive* | Tohold | Држи<br>Drzhi |

| Present Simple Tense | | |
|---|---|---|
| *Person* | *Singular* | *Plural* |
| 1st person | I hold -<br>Јас држам<br>*Jas drzham* | We hold -<br>Ние држиме<br>*Nie drzhime* |
| 2nd person | You hold -<br>Ти држиш<br>*Ti drzhish* | You hold -<br>Вие држите<br>*Vie drzhite* |
| 3rd person | He/She/It holds -<br>Тој/Таа/Тоа држи<br>*Toj/Taa/Toa drzhi* | They hold -<br>Тие држат<br>*Tie drzhat* |

| Past Simple Tense | | |
|---|---|---|
| *Person* | *Singular* | *Plural* |
| 1st person | I held -<br>Јас подржав<br>*Jas podrzhav* | We held -<br>Ние подржавме<br>*Nie podrzhavme* |
| 2nd person | You held -<br>Ти подржа<br>*Ti podrzha* | You held -<br>Вие подржавте<br>*Vie podrzhavte* |
| 3rd person | He/She/It held -<br>Тој/Таа/Тоа подржа<br>*Toj/Taa/Toa podrzha* | They held -<br>Тие подржаа<br>*Tie podrzhaa* |

| Past Continuous Tense | | |
|---|---|---|
| *Person* | *Singular* | *Plural* |
| 1st person | I was holding-<br>Јас држев<br>*Jas drzhev* | We were holding -<br>Ние држевме<br>*Nie drzhevme* |
| 2nd person | You were holding -<br>Ти држеше<br>*Ti drzheshe* | You were holding -<br>Вие држевте<br>*Vie drzhevte* |
| 3rd person | He/She/It was holding -<br>Тој/Таа/Тоа држеше<br>*Toj/Taa/Toa drzheshe* | They were holding -<br>Тие држеја<br>*Tie drzheja* |

| Present Perfect Simple Tense | | |
|---|---|---|
| *Person* | *Singular* | *Plural* |
| 1st person | I have held -<br>Јас сум подржал(а)<br>*Jas sum podrzhal(a)* | We have held -<br>Ние сме подржале<br>*Nie sme podrzhale* |

| | | |
|---|---|---|
| 2nd person | You have held - Ти си п**о**држал(а) *Ti si p**o**drzhal(a)* | You have held - Вие сте подр**ж**але *Vie ste pod**r**zhale* |
| 3rd person | *He/She/It has held - Toj/Taa/Toa п**о**држал(а)(о) Toj/Taa/Toa p**o**drzhal(a)(o)* | *They have held -* Тие подр**ж**але *Tie pod**r**zhale* |

| **Present Perfect Continuous Tense** | | |
|---|---|---|
| *Person* | *Singular* | *Plural* |
| 1st person | I have been holding - Јас сум д**р**жел(а) *Jas sum d**r**zhel(a)* | We have been holding - Ние сме д**р**желе *Nie sme d**r**zhele* |
| 2nd person | You have been holding - Ти сид**р**жел(а) *Nie sme d**r**zhel(a)* | You have been holding - Вие сте д**р**желе *Vie ste d**r**zhele* |
| 3rd person | He/She/It has been holding - Тој/Таа/Тоа д**р**жел(а)(о) *Toj/Taa/Toa d**r**zhel(a)(o)* | They have been holding - Тие д**р**желе *Tie d**r**zhele* |

| **Past Perfect Simple Tense** | | |
|---|---|---|
| *Person* | *Singular* | *Plural* |
| 1st person | I had held - Јас бев п**о**држал(а) *Jas bev p**o**drzhal(a)* | We had held - Ние бевме подр**ж**але *Nie bevme pod**r**zhale* |
| 2nd person | You had held - Ти беше п**о**држал(а) *Ti beshe p**o**drzhal(a)* | You had held - Вие бевте подр**ж**але *Vie bevte pod**r**zhale* |
| 3rd person | He/She/It had held - Тој/Таа/Тоа беше п**о**држал(а)(о) *Toj/Taa/Toa beshe p**o**drzhal(a)(o)* | They had held - Тие беа подр**ж**але *Tie bea pod**r**zhale* |

| **Future Simple Tense** | | |
|---|---|---|
| *Person* | *Singular* | *Plural* |
| 1st person | I will hold - Јас ќе д**р**жам/п**о**држам *Jas kje d**r**zham/p**o**drzham* | We will hold - Ние ќед**р**жиме/подр**ж**име *Nie kje d**r**zhime/pod**r**zhime* |
| 2nd person | You will hold - Ти ќе д**р**жиш/п**о**држиш *Ti kje kje d**r**zhish/p**o**drzhish* | You will hold - Вие ќе д**р**жите/подр**ж**ите *Vie kje d**r**zhite/pod**r**zhite* |
| 3rd person | He/She/It will hold - Тој/Таа/Тоа ќе д**р**жи/п**о**држи *Toj/Taa/Toa kje d**r**zhi/p**o**drzhi* | They will hold - Тие ќе д**р**жат/подр**ж**ат *Tie kje d**r**zhat/pod**r**zhat* |

| **used to + infinitive or would + infinitive** | | |
|---|---|---|
| *Person* | *Singular* | *Plural* |
| 1st person | I would hold - Јас ќе **др**жев/п**о**држев *Jas kje d**r**zhev/p**o**drzhev* | We would hold - Ние ќе **др**жевме/под**р**жевме *Nie kje d**r**zhevme/pod**r**zhevme* |
| 2nd person | You would hold - Ти ќе **др**жеше/под**р**жеше *Ti kje d**r**zheshe/pod**r**zheshe* | You would hold - Вие ќе **др**жевте/под**р**жевте *Vie kje d**r**zhevte/pod**r**zhevte* |
| 3rd person | He/She/It would hold - Тој/Таа/Тоа ќе д**р**жеше/под**р**жеше *Toj/Taa/Toa kje drzheshe/podrzheshe* | They would hold - Тие ќе д**р**жеа/под**р**жеа *Tie kje drzhea/podrzhea* |

| **Personal endings for future perfect-in-the-past tense** | | |
|---|---|---|
| *Person* | *Singular* | *Plural* |
| 1st person | I would have held Јас ќе сум д**р**жал/под**р**жал(а) *Jas kje sum d**r**zhal/pod**r**zhal(a)* | We would have held Ние ќе сме д**р**жале/под**р**жале *Nie kje sme d**r**zhale/pod**r**zhale* |
| 2nd person | *You would have held* *Ти ќе си д**р**жал/под**р**жал(а)* *Ti kje si d**r**zhal/pod**r**zhal(a)* | *You would have held* *Вие ќе сте* д**р**жале/под**р**жале Vie kje ste *d**r**zhale/pod**r**zhale* |
| 3rd person | He/She/It would have held Тој/Таа/Тоа ќе д**р**жал/под**р**жал(а)(о) *Toj/Taa/Toa kje d**r**zhal/pod**r**zhal(a)(o)* | They would have held Тие ќе д**р**жале/под**р**жале *Tie kje d**r**zhale/pod**r**zhale* |

### *To increase -Зголемува/Зголеми*

| | | |
|---|---|---|
| *Infinitive* | Toincrease | Згол**е**мува<br>Zgol**e**muva |

| **Present Simple Tense** | | |
|---|---|---|
| *Person* | *Singular* | *Plural* |
| 1st person | I increase -<br>Јас згол**е**мувам<br>*Jas sum zgol**e**muvam* | We increase -<br>Ние зголем**у**ваме<br>*Nie zgolem**u**vame* |
| 2nd person | You increase -<br>Ти згол**е**муваш<br>*Ti zgol**e**muvash* | You increase -<br>Вие зголем**у**вате<br>*Vie zgolem**u**vate* |
| 3rd person | He/She/It increases -<br>Тој/Таа/Тоа згол**е**мува<br>*Toj/Taa/Toa zgol**e**muva* | They increase -<br>Тие зголем**у**ваат<br>*Tie zgolem**u**vaat* |

| **Past Simple Tense** | | |
|---|---|---|
| *Person* | *Singular* | *Plural* |
| 1st person | I increased -<br>Јас зг**о**лемив<br>*Jas zg**o**lemiv* | We increased -<br>Ние згол**е**мивме<br>*Nie zgol**e**mivme* |
| 2nd person | You increased -<br>Ти зг**о**леми<br>*Ti zg**o**lemi* | You increased -<br>Вие згол**е**мивте<br>*Vie zgol**e**mivte* |
| 3rd person | He/She/It increased -<br>Тој/Таа/Тоа тој зг**о**леми<br>*Toj/Taa/Toa zg**o**lemi* | They increased -<br>Тие згол**е**мија<br>*Tie zgol**e**mija* |

| **Past Continuous Tense** | | |
|---|---|---|
| *Person* | *Singular* | *Plural* |
| 1st person | I was increasing -<br>Јас згол**е**мував<br>*Jas zgol**e**muvav* | We were increasing -<br>Ние зголем**у**вавме<br>*Nie zgolem**u**vame* |
| 2nd person | You were increasing -<br>Ти зголем**у**ваше<br>*Ti zgolem**u**vashe* | You were increasing -<br>Вие зголем**у**вавте<br>*Vie zgolem**u**vavte* |
| 3rd person | He/She/It was increasing -<br>Тој/Таа/Тоа зголем**у**ваше<br>*Toj/Taa/Toa zgolem**u**vashe* | They were increasing -<br>Тие зголем**у**ваа<br>*Tie zgolem**u**vaa* |

| **Present Perfect Simple Tense** | | |
|---|---|---|
| *Person* | *Singular* | *Plural* |
| 1st person | I have increased -<br>Јас сум зг**о**лемил(а)<br>*Jas sum zg**o**lemil(a)* | We have increased -<br>Ние сме згол**е**миле<br>*Nie  sme zgol**e**mile* |

| | | |
|---|---|---|
| 2nd person | You have increased -<br>Ти си зг**о**лемил(а)<br>*Ti si zg**o**lemil(a)* | You have increased -<br>Вие сте згол**е**миле<br>*Vie ste zgol**e**mile* |
| 3rd person | He/She/It has increased -<br>Тој/Таа/Тоа зг**о**лемил(а)(о)<br>*Toj/Taa/Toa zg**o**lemil(a)(o)* | They have increased -<br>Тие згол**е**миле<br>*Tie zgol**e**mile* |

| Present Perfect Continuous Tense | | |
|---|---|---|
| *Person* | *Singular* | *Plural* |
| 1st person | I have been increasing -<br>Јас сум згол**е**мувал(а)<br>*Jas sum zgol**e**muval(a)* | We have been increasing -<br>Ние сме золем**у**вале<br>*Nie sme zgolem**u**vale* |
| 2nd person | You have been increasing -<br>Ти си згол**е**мувал(а)<br>*Ti si zgol**e**muval(a)* | You have been increasing -<br>Вие сте згол**е**м**у**вале<br>*Vie ste zgolem**u**vale* |
| 3rd person | He/She/It has been increasing<br>Тој/Таа/Тоа згол**е**мувал(а)(о)<br>*Toj/Taa/Toa zgol**e**muval(a)(o)* | They have been increasing -<br>Тие золем**у**вале<br>*Tie zgolem**u**vale* |

| Past Perfect Simple Tense | | |
|---|---|---|
| *Person* | *Singular* | *Plural* |
| 1st person | I had increased -<br>Јас бев зг**о**лемил(а)<br>*Jas bev zg**o**lemil(a)* | We had increased -<br>Ние бевме згол**е**миле<br>*Nie sme zgol**e**mile* |
| 2nd person | You had increased -<br>Ти беше зг**о**лемил(а)<br>*Ti beshe zg**o**lemil(a)* | You had increased -<br>Вие бевте згол**е**миле<br>*Vie bevte zgol**e**mile* |
| 3rd person | He/She/It had increased -<br>Тој/Таа/Тоа беше<br>зг**о**лемил(а)(о)<br>*Toj/Taa/Toa beshe zg**o**lemil(a)(o)* | They had increased -<br>Тие беа згол**е**миле<br>*Tie bea zgol**e**mile* |

| Future Simple Tense | | |
|---|---|---|
| *Person* | *Singular* | *Plural* |
| 1st person | I will increase -<br>Јас ќе згол**е**мувам/зг**о**лемам<br>*Jas kje zgol**e**muvam/zg**o**lemam* | We will increase -<br>Ние ќе золем**у**ваме/згол**е**миме<br>*Nie kje zgolem**u**vame/zgol**e**mime* |
| 2nd person | You will increase -<br>Ти ќе згол**е**муваш/зг**о**лемиш<br>*Ti kje zgol**e**muvash/zg**o**lemish* | You will increase -<br>Вие ќе золем**у**вате/згол**е**мите<br>*Vie kje zgolem**u**vate/zgol**e**mite* |
| 3rd person | He/She/It will increase -<br>Тој/Таа/Тоа ќе<br>згол**е**мува/зг**о**леми<br>*Toj/Taa/Toa kje*<br>*zgol**e**muva/zg**o**lemi* | They will increase -<br>Тие ќе золем**у**ваат/згол**е**мат<br>*Tie kje zgolem**u**vaat/zgol**e**mat* |

| **used to + infinitive or would + infinitive** | | |
|---|---|---|
| *Person* | *Singular* | *Plural* |
| 1st person | I would increase -<br>Јас ќе згол**е**мував/зг**о**лемев<br>*Jas kje zgol**e**muvav/zg**o**lemev* | We would increase -<br>Ние ќе<br>зголем**у**вавме/згол**е**мевме<br>*Nie kje*<br>*zgolem**u**vavme/zgolem**e**vme* |
| 2nd person | You would increase -<br>Ти ќе зголем**у**ваше/згол**е**меше<br>*Ti kje zgolem**u**vashe/zgol**e**meshe* | You would increase -<br>Вие ќе<br>зголем**у**вавте/згол**е**мевте<br>*Vie kje*<br>*zgolem**u**vavte/zgolem**e**vte* |
| 3rd person | He/She/It would increase -<br>Тој/Таа/Тоа ќе<br>зголем**у**ваше/згол**е**меше<br>*Toj/Taa/Toa kje*<br>*zgolem**u**vashe/zgol**e**meshe* | They would increase -<br>Тие ќе зголем**у**ваат/згол**е**меа<br>*Tie kje zgolem**u**vaat/zgol**e**mea* |

| **Personal endings for future perfect-in-the-past tense** | | |
|---|---|---|
| *Person* | *Singular* | *Plural* |
| 1st person | I would have increased -<br>Јас ќе сум<br>згол**е**мувал/зг**о**лемил(а)<br>*Jas kje sum*<br>*zgol**e**muval/zg**o**lemil(a)* | We would have increased -<br>Ние ќе сме<br>зголем**у**вале/згол**е**миле<br>*Nie kje sme*<br>*zgolem**u**vale/zgol**e**mile* |
| 2nd person | You would have increased -<br>Ти ќе си<br>зол**е**мувал/згол**е**мил(а)<br>*Ti kje si zgol**e**muval/zg**o**lemil(a)* | You would have increased -<br>Вие ќе сте<br>зголем**у**вале/згол**е**миле<br>*Vie kje ste*<br>*zgolem**u**vale/zgol**e**mile* |
| 3rd person | He/She/It would have increased -<br>Тој/Таа/Тоа ќе<br>згол**е**мувал/зг**о**лемил(а)(о)<br>*Toj/Taa/Toa kje*<br>*zgolemuval/zgolemil(a)(o)* | They would have increased -<br>Тие ќе зголем**у**вале/згол**е**миле<br>*Tie kje zgolem**u**vale/zgol**e**mile* |

***To introduce– Претставува/Претстави***

| | | |
|---|---|---|
| Infinitive | To introduce | Претст**а**вува<br>Pretst**a**vuva |

| Present Simple Tense | | |
|---|---|---|
| *Person* | *Singular* | *Plural* |
| 1st person | I introduce -<br>Јас претст**а**вувам<br>*Jas pretst**a**vuvam* | We introduce -<br>Ние претстав**у**ваме<br>*Nie pretstav**u**vame* |
| 2nd person | You introduce -<br>Ти претст**а**вуваш<br>*Ti pretst**a**vuvash* | You introduce -<br>Вие претстав**у**вате<br>*Vie pretstav**u**vate* |
| 3rd person | He/She/It introduces -<br>Тој/Таа/Тоа претст**а**вува<br>*Toj/Taa/Toa pretst**a**vuva* | They introduce -<br>Тие претстав**у**ваат<br>*Tie pretstav**u**vaat* |

| Past Simple Tense | | |
|---|---|---|
| *Person* | *Singular* | *Plural* |
| 1st person | I introduced -<br>Јас пр**е**тставив<br>*Jas pr**e**tstaviv* | We introduced -<br>Ние претст**а**вивме<br>*Nie pretst**a**vivme* |
| 2nd person | You introduced -<br>Ти пр**е**тстави<br>*Ti pr**e**tstavi* | You introduced -<br>Вие претст**а**вивте<br>*Vie pretst**a**vivte* |
| 3rd person | He/She/It introduced -<br>Тој/Таа/Тоа пр**е**тстави<br>*Toj/Taa/Toa pr**e**tstavi* | They introduced -<br>Тие претст**а**вија<br>*Tie pretst**a**vija* |

| Past Continuous Tense | | |
|---|---|---|
| *Person* | *Singular* | *Plural* |
| 1st person | I was introducing -<br>Јас претст**а**вував<br>*Jas pretst**a**vuvav* | We were introducing -<br>Ние претстав**у**вавме<br>*Nie pretstav**u**vame* |
| 2nd person | You were introducing -<br>Ти претстав**у**ваше<br>*Ti pretstav**u**vashe* | You were introducing -<br>Вие претстав**у**вавте<br>*Vi pretstav**u**vate* |
| 3rd person | He/She/It was introducing -<br>Тој/Таа/Тоа претстав**у**ваше<br>*Toj/Taa/Toa pretstav**u**vashe* | They were introducing -<br>Тие претстав**у**ваа<br>*Tie pretstav**u**vaa* |

| Present Perfect Simple Tense | | |
|---|---|---|
| *Person* | *Singular* | *Plural* |
| 1st person | I have introduced -<br>Јас сум претст**а**вувал(а)<br>*Jas sum pretst**a**vuval(a)* | We have introduced -<br>Ние сме претстав**у**вале<br>*Nie sme pretstav**u**vale* |

| | | |
|---|---|---|
| 2nd person | You have introduced - Ти си претст**а**вувал(а) *Ti si pretst**a**vuval(a)* | You have introduced - Вие сте претстав**у**вале *Vie ste pretstav**u**vale* |
| 3rd person | He/She/It has introduced - Тој/Таа/Тоа претст**а**вувал(а)(о) *Toj/Taa/Toa pretst**a**vuval(a)(o)* | They have introduced - Тие претстав**у**вале *Tie pretstav**u**vale* |

| Present Perfect Continuous Tense | | |
|---|---|---|
| *Person* | *Singular* | *Plural* |
| 1st person | I had introduced - Јас сум претст**а**вувал(а) *Jas sum pretst**a**vuval(a)* | We had introduced - Ние сме претстав**у**вале *Nie sme pretstav**u**vale* |
| 2nd person | You had introduced - Ти си претст**а**вувал(а) *Ti si pretst**a**vuval(a)* | You had introduced - Вие сте претстав**у**вале *Vie ste pretstav**u**vale* |
| 3rd person | He/She/It had introduced - Тој/Таа/Тоа претст**а**вувал(а)(о) *Toj/Taa/Toa pretst**a**vuval(a)(o)* | They had introduced - Тие претстав**у**вале *Tie pretstav**u**vale* |

| Past Perfect Simple Tense | | |
|---|---|---|
| *Person* | *Singular* | *Plural* |
| 1st person | I have been introducing - Јас бев пр**е**тставил(а) *Jas bev pr**e**tstavil(a)* | We have been introducing - Ние бевме претст**а**виле *Nie bevme pretst**a**vile* |
| 2nd person | You have been introducing - Ти бешепр**е**тставил(а) *Ti beshe pr**e**tstavil(a)* | You have been introducing - Вие бевте претст**а**виле *Vie bevte pretst**a**vile* |
| 3rd person | He/She/It has been introducing - Тој/Таа/Тоа бешепр**е**тставил(а),(о) *Toj/Taa/Toa beshe pr**e**tstavil(a),(o)* | They have been introducing - Тие беа претст**а**виле *Tie bea pretst**a**vile* |

| Future Simple Tense | | |
|---|---|---|
| *Person* | *Singular* | *Plural* |
| 1st person | I will introduce - Јас ќе претст**а**вувам/пр**е**тставам *Jas kje pretst**a**vuvam/pr**e**tstavam* | We will introduce - Ние ќе претстав**у**вавме/претст**а**виме *Nie kje pretstav**u**vame/pretst**a**vime* |
| 2nd person | You will introduce - Ти ќе претст**а**вуваш/пр**е**тставиш *Ti kje pretst**a**vuvash/pr**e**tstavish* | You will introduce - Вие ќе претстав**у**вавте/претст**а**вите *Vie kje pretstav**u**vate/pretst**a**vite* |
| 3rd person | He/She/It will introduce - Тој/Таа/Тоа претст**а**вува/пр**е**тстави *Toj/Taa/Toa kje pretst**a**vuva/pr**e**tstavi* | They will introduce - Тие ќе претстав**у**ваат/пр**е**тстават *Tie kje pretstav**u**vaat/pr**e**tstavat* |

| **used to + infinitive or would + infinitive** | | |
|---|---|---|
| *Person* | *Singular* | *Plural* |
| 1st person | I would introduce - Јас ќе претст**а**вував/пр**е**тставев *Jas kje pretst**a**vuvav/pr**e**tstavev* | We would introduce - Ние ќе претстав**у**вавме/претст**а**вевме *Nie kje pretstav**u**vavme/pretst**a**vivme* |
| 2nd person | You would introduce - Ти ќе претстав**у**ваше/претст**а**веше *Ti kje pretstav**u**vashe/pretst**a**veshe* | You would introduce - Вие ќе претстав**у**вавте/претст**а**вевте *Vie kje pretstavuvavte/pretst**a**vevte* |
| 3rd person | He/She/It would introduce - Тој/Таа/Тоа ќе претстав**у**ваше/претст**а**веше *Toj/Taa/Toa kje pretstav**u**vashe/pretst**a**veshe* | They would introduce - Тие ќе претстав**у**ваа/претст**а**веа *Tie kje pretstavuvavaa/pretst**a**vea* |

| **Personal endings for future perfect-in-the-past tense** | | |
|---|---|---|
| *Person* | *Singular* | *Plural* |
| 1st person | I would have introduced - Јас ќе сум претст**а**вувал/пр**е**тставил(а) *Jas kje sum pretst**a**vuval/pr**e**tstavil(a)* | We would have introduced - Ние ќе сме претстав**у**вале/претст**а**виле *Nie kje sme pretstav**u**vale/pretst**a**vile* |
| 2nd person | You would have introduced - Ти ќе си претст**а**вувал/пр**е**тставил(а) *Ti kje si pretst**a**vuval/pr**e**tstavil(a)* | You would have introduced - Вие ќе сте претстав**у**вале/претст**а**виле *Vie kje ste pretstav**u**vale/pretst**a**vile* |
| 3rd person | He/She/It would have introduced - Тој/Таа/Тоа претст**а**вувал/пр**е**тставил(а)(о) *Toj/Taa/Toa kje pretst**a**vuval/pr**e**tstavil(a)(o)* | They would have introduced - Тие ќе претстав**у**вале/претст**а**виле *Ti kje pretstav**u**vale/pretst**a**vile* |

***To invite - Поканува/Покани***

| | | |
|---|---|---|
| Infinitive | To invite | Пок**а**нува<br>Pok**a**nuva |

| Present Simple Tense | | |
|---|---|---|
| *Person* | *Singular* | *Plural* |
| 1st person | I invite -<br>Јас пок**а**нувам<br>*Jas pok**a**nuvam* | We invite -<br>Ние покан**у**ваме<br>*Nie pokan**u**vame* |
| 2nd person | You invite -<br>Ти пок**а**нуваш<br>*Ti pok**a**nuvash* | You invite -<br>Вие покан**у**вате<br>*Vie pokan**u**vate* |
| 3rd person | He/She/It invites -<br>Тој/Таа/Тоа пок**а**нува<br>*Toj/Taa/Toa pok**a**nuva* | They invite -<br>Тие покан**у**ваат<br>*Tie pokan**u**vaat* |

| Past Simple Tense | | |
|---|---|---|
| *Person* | *Singular* | *Plural* |
| 1st person | I invited -<br>Јас п**о**канив<br>*Jas p**o**kaniv* | We invited -<br>Ние пок**а**нивме<br>*Nie pok**a**nivme* |
| 2nd person | You invited -<br>Ти п**о**кани<br>*Ti p**o**kani* | You invited -<br>Вие пок**а**нивте<br>*Vie pok**a**nivte* |
| 3rd person | He/She/It invited -<br>Тој/Таа/Тоа п**о**кани<br>*Toj/Taa/Toa p**o**kani* | They invited -<br>Тие пок**а**нија<br>*Tie pok**a**nija* |

| Past Continuous Tense | | |
|---|---|---|
| *Person* | *Singular* | *Plural* |
| 1st person | I was inviting -<br>Јас пок**а**нував<br>*Jas pok**a**nuvav* | We were inviting -<br>Ние покан**у**вавме<br>*Nie pokan**u**vavme* |
| 2nd person | You were inviting -<br>Ти покан**у**ваше<br>*Ti pokan**u**vashe* | You were inviting -<br>Вие покан**у**вавте<br>*Vie pokan**u**vavte* |
| 3rd person | He/She/It was inviting -<br>Тој/Таа/Тоа покан**у**ваше<br>*Toj/Taa/Toa pokan**u**vashe* | They were inviting -<br>Тие покан**у**ваа<br>*Tie pokan**u**vaa* |

| Present Perfect Simple Tense | | |
|---|---|---|
| *Person* | *Singular* | *Plural* |
| 1st person | I have invited -<br>Јас сум п**о**канил(а)<br>*Jas sum p**o**kanil(a)* | We have invited -<br>Ние сме пок**а**ниле<br>*Nie sme pok**a**nile* |

| | | |
|---|---|---|
| 2nd person | You have invited - Ти си п**о**канил(а) *Ti si p**o**kanil(a)* | You have invited - Вие сте пок**а**ниле *Vie ste pok**a**nile* |
| 3rd person | He/She/It has invited - Тој/Таа/Тоа п**о**канил(а)(о) *Toj/Taa/Toa p**o**kanil(a)(o)* | They have invited - Тие пок**а**ниле *Tie pok**a**nile* |

| **Present Perfect Continuous Tense** | | |
|---|---|---|
| *Person* | *Singular* | *Plural* |
| 1st person | I have been inviting - Јас сум пок**а**нувал(а) *Jas sum pok**a**nuval(a)* | We have been inviting - Ние сме покан**у**вале *Nie sme pokan**u**vale* |
| 2nd person | You have been inviting - Ти си пок**а**нувал(а) *Ti si pok**a**nuval(a)* | You have been inviting - Вие сте покан**у**вале *Vie ste pokan**u**vale* |
| 3rd person | He/She/It has been inviting - Тој/Таа/Тоа пок**а**нувал(а)(о) *Toj/Taa/Toa pok**a**nuval(a)(o)* | They have been inviting - Тие покан**у**вале *Tie pokan**u**vale* |

| **Past Perfect Simple Tense** | | |
|---|---|---|
| *Person* | *Singular* | *Plural* |
| 1st person | I had invited - Јас бев п**о**канил(а) *Jas bev p**o**kanil(a)* | We had invited - Ние бевме пок**а**ниле *Nie bevme pok**a**nile* |
| 2nd person | You had invited - Ти беше п**о**канил(а) *Ti beshe p**o**kanil(a)* | You had invited - Вие бевте пок**а**ниле *Vie bevte pok**a**nile* |
| 3rd person | He/She/It had invited - Тој/Таа/Тоа беше п**о**канил(а)(о) *Toj/Taa/Toa beshe p**o**kanil(a)(o)* | They had invited - Тие беа пок**а**ниле *Tie bea pok**a**nile* |

| **Future Simple Tense** | | |
|---|---|---|
| *Person* | *Singular* | *Plural* |
| 1st person | I will invite - Јас ќе пок**а**нувам/п**о**канам *Jas kje pok**a**nuvam/p**o**kanam* | We will invite - Ние ќе покан**у**ваме/п**о**канеме *Nie kje pokan**u**vame/p**o**kaneme* |
| 2nd person | You will invite - Ти ќе пок**а**нуваш/п**о**канеш *Ti kje pok**a**nuvash/p**o**kanesh* | You will invite - Вие ќе покан**у**вате/п**о**канете *Vie kje pokan**u**vate/p**o**kanete* |
| 3rd person | He/She/It will invite - Тој/Таа/Тоа ќе пок**а**нува/п**о**кане *Toj/Taa/Toa pok**a**nuva/p**o**kane* | They will invite - Тие ќе покан**у**ваат/п**о**канат *Tie kje pokan**u**vaat/p**o**kanat* |

| **used to + infinitive or would + infinitive** | | |
|---|---|---|
| *Person* | *Singular* | *Plural* |
| 1st person | I would invite -<br>Јас ќе пок**а**нував/п**о**канев<br>*Jas kje pok**a**nuvav/p**o**kanev* | We would invite -<br>Ние ќе покан**у**вавме/пок**а**невме<br>*Nie kje pokan**u**vame/pok**a**nevme* |
| 2nd person | You would invite -<br>Ти ќе покан**у**ваше/пок**а**неше<br>*Ti kje pokan**u**vashe/pok**a**neshe* | You would invite -<br>Вие ќе покан**у**вавте/пок**а**невте<br>*Vie kje pokan**u**vavte/pok**a**nevte* |
| 3rd person | He/She/It would invite -<br>Тој/Таа/Тоа ќе<br>покан**у**ваше/пок**а**неше<br>*Toj/Taa/Toa*<br>*pokan**u**vashe/pok**a**neshe* | They would invite -<br>Тие ќе покан**у**ваа/пок**а**неа<br>*Tie kje pokan**u**vaa/pok**a**nea* |

| **Personal endings for future perfect-in-the-past tense** | | |
|---|---|---|
| *Person* | *Singular* | *Plural* |
| 1st person | I would have invited -<br>Јас ќе сум<br>пок**а**нувал/п**о**канил(а)<br>*Jas kje sum*<br>*pok**a**nuval/p**o**kanil(a)* | We would have invited -<br>Ние ќе сме<br>покан**у**вале/пок**а**ниле<br>*Nie kje sme pokan**u**vale/pok**a**nile* |
| 2nd person | You would have invited -<br>Ти ќе си пок**а**нувал/п**о**канил(а)<br>*Ti kje si pok**a**nuval/p**o**kanil(a)* | You would have invited -<br>Вие ќе сте<br>покан**у**вале/пок**а**ниле<br>*Vie kje ste pokan**u**vale/pok**a**nile* |
| 3rd person | He/She/It would have invited -<br>Тој/Таа/Тоа ќе<br>пок**а**нувал/п**о**канил(а)(о)<br>*Toj/Taa/Toa kje*<br>*pok**a**nuval/p**o**kanil(a)(o)* | They would have invited -<br>*Тие ќе* покан**у**вале/пок**а**ниле<br>*Tie kje pokan**u**vale/pok**a**nile* |

### *To kill - Убива/Убие*

| | | |
|---|---|---|
| Infinitive | Tokill | **У**бива<br>**U**biva |

| Present Simple Tense | | |
|---|---|---|
| *Person* | *Singular* | *Plural* |
| 1st person | I kill -<br>Јас **у**бивам<br>*Jas **u**bivam* | We kill -<br>Ние уб**и**ваме<br>*Nie ub**i**vame* |
| 2nd person | You kill -<br>Ти **у**биваш<br>*Ti **u**bivash* | You kill -<br>Вие уб**и**вате<br>*Vie ub**i**vate* |
| 3rd person | He/She/It kills -<br>Тој/Таа/Тоа **у**бива<br>Toj/Taa/Toa **u**biva | They kill -<br>Тие уб**и**ваат<br>*Tie ub**i**vaat* |

| Past Simple Tense | | |
|---|---|---|
| *Person* | *Singular* | *Plural* |
| 1st person | I killed -<br>Јас **у**бив<br>*Jas **u**biv* | We killed -<br>Ние **у**бивме<br>*Nie **u**bivme* |
| 2nd person | You killed -<br>Ти **у**би<br>*Ti **u**bi* | You killed -<br>Вие **у**бивте<br>*Vie **u**bivte* |
| 3rd person | He/She/It killed -<br>Тој/Таа/Тоа **у**би<br>*Toj/Taa/Toa **u**bi* | They killed -<br>Тие **у**бија<br>*Tie **u**bija* |

| Past Continuous Tense | | |
|---|---|---|
| *Person* | *Singular* | *Plural* |
| 1st person | I was killing -<br>Јас **у**бивав<br>*Jas **u**bivav* | We were killing -<br>Ние уб**и**вавме<br>*Nie ub**i**vavme* |
| 2nd person | You were killing -<br>Ти уб**и**ваше<br>*Ti ub**i**vashe* | You were killing -<br>Вие уб**и**вавте<br>*Vie ub**i**vavte* |
| 3rd person | He/She/It was killing -<br>Тој/Таа/Тоа уб**и**ваше<br>*Toj/Taa/Toa ub**i**vashe* | They were killing -<br>Тие уб**и**ваа<br>*Tie ub**i**vaa* |

| Present Perfect Simple Tense | | |
|---|---|---|
| *Person* | *Singular* | *Plural* |
| 1st person | I have been killing -<br>Јас сум **у**бил(а)<br>*Jas sum **u**bil(a)* | We have been killing -<br>Ние сме **у**биле<br>*Nie sme **u**bile* |

| | | |
|---|---|---|
| 2nd person | You have been killing -<br>Ти си **убил**(а)<br>*Ti si **ubil**(a)* | You have been killing -<br>Вие сте **убиле**<br>*Vie ste **ubile*** |
| 3rd person | He/She/It has been killing -<br>Тој/Таа/Тоа **убил**(а)(о)<br>*Toj/Taa/Toa **ubil**(a)(o)* | They have been killing -<br>Тие **убиле**<br>*Tie **ubile*** |

| **Present Perfect Continuous Tense** | | |
|---|---|---|
| *Person* | *Singular* | *Plural* |
| 1st person | I have killed -<br>Јас сум **убивал**(а)<br>*Jas sum **ubival**(a)* | We have killed -<br>Ние сме уб**и**вале<br>*Nie sme ub**i**vale* |
| 2nd person | You have killed -<br>Ти си **убивал**(а)<br>*Ti si **ubival**(a)* | You have killed -<br>Вие сте уб**и**вале<br>*Vie ste ub**i**vale* |
| 3rd person | He/She/It has killed -<br>Тој/Таа/Тоа **убивал**(а)(о)<br>*Toj/Taa/Toa **ubival**(a)(o)* | They have killed -<br>Тие уб**и**вале<br>*Tie ub**i**vale* |

| **Past Perfect Simple Tense** | | |
|---|---|---|
| *Person* | *Singular* | *Plural* |
| 1st person | I had killed -<br>Јас бев **убил**(а)<br>*Jas bev **ubil**(a)* | We had killed -<br>Ние бевме **убиле**<br>*Nie bevme **ubile*** |
| 2nd person | You had killed -<br>Ти беше **убил**(а)<br>*Ti beshe **ubill**(a)* | You had killed -<br>Вие бевте **убиле**<br>*Vie bevte **ubile*** |
| 3rd person | He/She/It had killed -<br>Тој/Таа/Тоа беше **убил**(а)(о)<br>*Toj/Taa/Toa beshe **ubil**(a)(o)* | They had killed -<br>Тие беа **убиле**<br>*Tie bea **ubile*** |

| **Future Simple Tense** | | |
|---|---|---|
| *Person* | *Singular* | *Plural* |
| 1st person | I will kill -<br>Јас ќе **убивам**/**убијам**<br>*Jas kje **ubivam**/**ubijam*** | We will kill -<br>Ние ќе уб**и**ваме/уб**и**еме<br>*Nie kje ub**i**vame/ub**i**eme* |
| 2nd person | You will kill -<br>Ти ќе **убиваш**/**убиеш**<br>*Ti kje **ubivash**/**ubiesh*** | You will kill -<br>Вие ќе уб**и**вате/уб**и**ете<br>*Vie kje ub**i**vate/ub**i**ete* |
| 3rd person | He/She/It will kill -<br>Тој/Таа/Тоа ќе **убива**/**убие**<br>*Toj/Taa/Toa kje **ubiva**/**ubie*** | They will kill -<br>Тие ќе уб**и**ваат/уб**и**јат<br>*Tie kje ub**i**vaat/ub**i**jat* |

| **used to + infinitive or would + infinitive** | | |
|---|---|---|
| *Person* | *Singular* | *Plural* |
| 1st person | I would kill -<br>Јас ќе **убивав**/**убиев**<br>*Jas kje **ubivav**/**ubiev*** | We would kill -<br>Ние ќе уб**и**вавме/уб**и**евме<br>*Nie kje ub**i**vavme/ub**i**evme* |

| | | |
|---|---|---|
| 2nd person | You would kill -<br>Ти ќе уб**и**ваше/уб**и**еше<br>*Ti kje ub**i**vashe/ub**i**eshe* | You would kill -<br>Вие ќе уб**и**вавте/уб**и**евте<br>*Vie kje ub**i**vavte/ub**i**evte* |
| 3rd person | He/She/It would kill -<br>Тој/Таа/Тоа ќе<br>уб**и**ваше/уб**и**еше<br>*Toj/Taa/Toa kje*<br>*ub**i**vashe/ub**i**eshe* | They would kill -<br>Тие ќе уб**и**ваа/уб**и**еја<br>*Tie kje ub**i**vaa/ub**i**eja* |

| **Personal endings for future perfect-in-the-past tense** | | |
|---|---|---|
| *Person* | *Singular* | *Plural* |
| 1st person | I would have killed -<br>Јас ќе сум **у**бивал/**у**биел(а)<br>*Jas kje sum **u**bival/**u**biel(a)* | We would have killed -<br>Ние ќе сме уб**и**вале/уб**и**еле<br>*Nie kje sme ub**i**vale/ub**i**ele* |
| 2nd person | You would have killed -<br>Ти ќе си **у**бивал/**у**биел(а)<br>*Ti kje si **u**bival/**u**biel(a)* | You would have killed -<br>Вие ќе сте уб**и**вале/уб**и**еле<br>*Vie kje ste ub**i**vale/ub**i**ele* |
| 3rd person | He/She/It would have killed -<br>Тој/Таа/Тоа ќе<br>**у**бивал/**у**биел(а)(о)<br>*Toj/Taa/Toa kje **u**bival/**u**biel(a)(o)* | They would have killed -<br>Тие ќе уб**и**вале/уб**и**еле<br>*Tie kje ub**i**vale/ub**i**ele* |

**To kiss - Бакнува/Бакне**

| | | |
|---|---|---|
| *Infinitive* | To kiss | Б**а**кнува<br>B**a**knuva |

| Present Simple Tense | | |
|---|---|---|
| *Person* | *Singular* | *Plural* |
| 1st person | I kiss -<br>Јас б**а**кнувам<br>*Jas b**a**knuvam* | We kiss -<br>Ние бакн**у**ваме<br>*Nie bakn**u**vame* |
| 2nd person | You kiss -<br>Ти б**а**кнуваш<br>*Ti b**a**knuvash* | You kiss -<br>Вие бакн**у**вате<br>*Vie bakn**u**vate* |
| 3rd person | He/She/It kisses -<br>Тој/Таа/Тоа б**а**кнува<br>*Toj/Taa/Toa b**a**knuva* | They kiss -<br>Тие бакн**у**ваат<br>*Tie bakn**u**vaat* |

| Past Simple Tense | | |
|---|---|---|
| *Person* | *Singular* | *Plural* |
| 1st person | I kissed -<br>Јас б**а**кнав<br>*Jas b**a**knav* | We kissed -<br>Ние б**а**кнавме<br>*Nie b**a**knavme* |
| 2nd person | You kissed -<br>Ти б**а**кна<br>*Ti b**a**kna* | You kissed -<br>Вие б**а**кнавте<br>*Vie b**a**knavte* |
| 3rd person | He/She/It kissed -<br>Тој/Таа/Тоа б**а**кна<br>*Toj/Taa/Toa b**a**kna* | They kissed -<br>Тие б**а**кнаа<br>*Tie b**a**knaa* |

| Past Continuous Tense | | |
|---|---|---|
| *Person* | *Singular* | *Plural* |
| 1st person | I was kissing -<br>Јас б**а**кнував<br>*Jas b**a**knuvav* | We were kissing -<br>Ние бакн**у**вавме<br>*Nie bakn**u**vavme* |
| 2nd person | You were kissing -<br>Ти бакн**у**ваше<br>*Ti bakn**u**vashe* | You were kissing -<br>Вие бакн**у**вавте<br>*Vie bakn**u**vavte* |
| 3rd person | He/She/It was kissing -<br>Тој/Таа/Тоа Тој бакн**у**ваше<br>*Toj/Taa/Toa bakn**u**vashe* | They were kissing -<br>Тие бакн**у**ваа<br>*Tie bak**u**vnaa* |

| Present Perfect Simple Tense | | |
|---|---|---|
| *Person* | *Singular* | *Plural* |
| 1st person | I have kissed -<br>Јас сум б**а**кнал(а)<br>*Jas sum b**a**knal(a)* | We have kissed -<br>Ние сме б**а**кнале<br>*Nie sme b**a**knale* |

| | | |
|---|---|---|
| 2nd person | You have kissed -<br>Ти си бакнал(а)<br>*Ti si baknal(a)* | You have kissed -<br>Вие сте бакнале<br>*Vie ste baknale* |
| 3rd person | He/She/It has kissed -<br>Тој/Таа/Тоа бакнал(а)(о)<br>*Toj/Taa/Toa baknal(a)(o)* | They have kissed -<br>Тие бакнале<br>*Tie baknale* |

| **Present Perfect Continuous Tense** | | |
|---|---|---|
| *Person* | *Singular* | *Plural* |
| 1st person | I have been kissing -<br>Јас сум бакнувал(а)<br>*Jas sum baknuval(a)* | We have been kissing -<br>Ние сме бакнувале<br>*Nie sme baknuvale* |
| 2nd person | You have been kissing -<br>Ти си бакнувал(а)<br>*Ti si baknuval(a)* | You have been kissing -<br>Вие сте бакнувале<br>*Vie ste baknuvale* |
| 3rd person | He/She/It has been kissing -<br>Тој/Таа/Тоа бакнувал(а)(о)<br>*Toj/Taa/Toa baknuval(a)(o)* | They have been kissing -<br>Тие бакнувале<br>*Tie baknuvale* |

| **Past Perfect Simple Tense** | | |
|---|---|---|
| *Person* | *Singular* | *Plural* |
| 1st person | I had kissed -<br>Јас бев бакнал(а)<br>*Jas bev baknal(a)* | We had kissed -<br>Ние бевме бакнале<br>*Nie bevme baknale* |
| 2nd person | You had kissed -<br>Ти беше бакнал(а)<br>*Ti beshe baknal(a)* | You had kissed -<br>Вие бевте бакнале<br>*Vie bevte baknale* |
| 3rd person | He/She/It had kissed -<br>Тој/Таа/Тоа беше бакнал(а)(о)<br>*Toj/Taa/Toa beshe baknal(a)(o)* | They had kissed -<br>Тие беа бакнале<br>*Tie bea baknale* |

| **Future Simple Tense** | | |
|---|---|---|
| *Person* | *Singular* | *Plural* |
| 1st person | I will kiss -<br>Јас ќе бакнувам/бакнам<br>*Jas kje baknuvam/baknam* | We will kiss -<br>Ние ќе бакнуваме/бакнеме<br>*Nie kje baknuvame/bakneme* |
| 2nd person | You will kiss -<br>Ти ќе бакнуваш/бакнеш<br>*Ti kje baknuvash/baknesh* | You will kiss -<br>Вие ќе бакнувате/бакнете<br>*Vie kje baknuvate/baknete* |
| 3rd person | He/She/It will kiss -<br>Тој/Таа/Тоа ќе банува/бакне<br>*Toj/Taa/Toa kje baknuva/bakne* | They will kiss -<br>Тие ќе бакнуваат/бакнат<br>*Tie kje baknuvaat/baknat* |

| **used to + infinitive or would + infinitive** | | |
|---|---|---|
| *Person* | *Singular* | *Plural* |
| 1st person | I would kiss -<br>Јас ќе бакнував/бакнав<br>*Jas kje baknuvav/baknav* | We would kiss -<br>Ние ќе бакнувавме/бакневме<br>*Nie kje baknuvavme/baknevme* |

| | | |
|---|---|---|
| 2nd person | You would kiss -<br>Ти ќе бакн**у**ваше/б**а**кнеше<br>*Ti kje bakn**u**vashe/b**a**kneshe* | You would kiss -<br>Вие ќе бакн**у**вавте/б**а**кневте<br>*Vie kje bakn**u**vavte/b**a**knevte* |
| 3rd person | He/She/It would kiss -<br>Тој/Таа/Тоа ќе<br>бакн**у**ваше/б**а**кнеше<br>*Toj/Taa/Toa kje*<br>*bakn**u**vashe/b**a**kneshe* | They would kiss -<br>Тие ќе бакн**у**ваа/б**а**кнеа<br>*Tie kje bakn**u**vaa/b**a**knea* |

| **Personal endings for future perfect-in-the-past tense** | | |
|---|---|---|
| *Person* | *Singular* | *Plural* |
| 1st person | I would have kissed -<br>Јас ќе сум б**а**кнувал/б**а**кнал(а)<br>*Jas kje sum b**a**knuval/b**a**knal(a)* | We would have kissed -<br>Ние ќе сме б**а**кнувале/б**а**кнале<br>*Nie kje sme b**a**knuvale/b**a**knele* |
| 2nd person | You would have kissed -<br>Ти ќе си б**а**кнувал/б**а**кнал(а)<br>*Ti kje si b**a**knuval/b**a**knal(a)* | You would have kissed -<br>Вие ќе сте б**а**кнувале/б**а**кнале<br>*Vie kje ste b**a**knuvale/b**a**knele* |
| 3rd person | He/She/It would have kissed -<br>Тој/Таа/Тоа ќе<br>б**а**кнувал/б**а**кнал(а)(о)<br>*Toj/Taa/Toa kje*<br>*b**a**knuval/b**a**knal(a)(o)* | They would have kissed -<br>Тие ќе б**а**кнувале/б**а**кнале<br>*Tie kje b**a**knuvale/b**a**knele* |

***To know - Знае/Дознае***

| | | |
|---|---|---|
| *Infinitive* | Toknow | Зн**а**е<br>Zn**a**e |

| Present Simple Tense | | |
|---|---|---|
| *Person* | *Singular* | *Plural* |
| 1st person | I know -<br>Јас зн**а**м<br>*Jas zn**a**m* | We know -<br>Ние зн**а**еме<br>*Nie zn**a**eme* |
| 2nd person | You know -<br>Ти зн**а**еш<br>*Ti zn**a**esh* | You know -<br>Вие зн**а**ете<br>*Vie zn**a**ete* |
| 3rd person | He/She/It knows -<br>Тој/Таа/Тоазн**а**е<br>*Toj/Taa/Toa zn**a**esh* | They know -<br>Тие зн**а**ат<br>*Tie zn**a**at* |

| Past Simple Tense | | |
|---|---|---|
| *Person* | *Singular* | *Plural* |
| 1st person | I knew -<br>Јас д**о**знав<br>*Jas d**o**znav* | We knew -<br>Ние д**о**знавме<br>*Nie d**o**znavme* |
| 2nd person | You knew -<br>Ти д**о**зна<br>*Ti d**o**zna* | You knew -<br>Вие д**о**знавте<br>*Vie d**o**znavte* |
| 3rd person | He/She/It knew -<br>Тој/Таа/Тоа д**о**зна<br>*Toj/Taa/Toa d**o**zna* | They knew -<br>Тие д**о**знаа<br>*Tie d**o**znaa* |

| Past Continuous Tense | | |
|---|---|---|
| *Person* | *Singular* | *Plural* |
| 1st person | I was knowing -<br>Јас зн**а**ев<br>*Jas zn**a**ev* | We were knowing -<br>Ние зн**а**евме<br>*Nie zn**a**evme* |
| 2nd person | You were knowing -<br>Ти зн**а**еше<br>*Ti zn**a**eshe* | You were knowing -<br>Вие зн**а**евте<br>*Vie zn**a**evte* |
| 3rd person | He/She/It was knowing -<br>Тој/Таа/Тоа зн**а**еше<br>*Toj/Taa/Toa zn**a**eshe* | They were knowing -<br>Тие зн**а**еја<br>*Tie zn**a**eja* |

| Present Perfect Simple Tense | | |
|---|---|---|
| *Person* | *Singular* | *Plural* |
| 1st person | I have known -<br>Јас сум д**о**знал(а)<br>*Jas sum d**o**znal(a)* | We have known -<br>Ние сме д**о**знале<br>*Nie sme d**o**znale* |

| | | |
|---|---|---|
| 2nd person | You have known - Ти си дознал(а) *Ti si doznal(a)* | You have known - Вие сте дознале *Vie ste doznale* |
| 3rd person | He/She/It has known - Тој/Таа/Тоа дознал(а)(о) *Toj/Taa/Toa doznal(a)(o)* | They have known - Тие дознале *Tie doznale* |

| Present Perfect Continuous Tense | | |
|---|---|---|
| *Person* | *Singular* | *Plural* |
| 1st person | I have been knowing - Јас сум знаел(а) *Jas sum znael(a)* | We have been kissing - Ние сме знаеле *Nie sme znaele* |
| 2nd person | You have been knowing - Ти си знаел(а) *Ti si znael(a)* | You have been knowing - Вие сте знаеле *Vie ste znaele* |
| 3rd person | He/She/It has been knowing - Тој/Таа/Тоа знаел(а)(о) *Toj/Taa/Toa znael(a)(o)* | They have been knowing - Тие знаеле *Tie znaele* |

| Past Perfect Simple Tense | | |
|---|---|---|
| *Person* | *Singular* | *Plural* |
| 1st person | I had known - Јас бев дознал(а) *Jas bev doznal(a)* | We had known - Ние бевме дознале *Nie bevme doznale* |
| 2nd person | You had known - Ти беше дознал(а) *Ti beshe doznal(a)* | You had known - Вие бевте дознале *Vie bevte doznale* |
| 3rd person | He/She/It had known - Тој/Таа/Тоа беше дознал(а)(о) *Toj/Taa/Toa beshe doznal(a)(o)* | They had known - Тие беа дознале *Tie bea doznale* |

| Future Simple Tense | | |
|---|---|---|
| *Person* | *Singular* | *Plural* |
| 1st person | I will know - Јас ќе знам/дознаам *Jas kje znam/doznaam* | We will know - Ние ќе знаеме/дознаеме *Nie kje znaeme/doznaeme* |
| 2nd person | You will know - Ти ќе знаеш/дознаеш *Ti kje znaesh/doznaesh* | You will know - Вие ќе знаете/дознаете *Vie kje znaete/doznaete* |
| 3rd person | He/She/It will know - Тој/Таа/Тоа ќе знае/дознае *Toj/Taa/Toa kje znae/doznae* | They will know - Тие ќе знаат/дознаат *Tiekje znaat/doznaat* |

| used to + infinitive or would + infinitive | | |
|---|---|---|
| *Person* | *Singular* | *Plural* |
| 1st person | I would know - Јас ќе знаев/дознаев *Jas kje znaev/doznaev* | We would know - Ние ќе знаевме/дознаевме *Nie kje znaevme/doznaevme* |

| | | |
|---|---|---|
| 2nd person | You would know -<br>Ти ќе зн**а**еше/дозн**а**еше<br>*Ti kje zn**a**eshe/dozn**a**eshe* | You would know -<br>Вие ќе зн**а**евте/дозн**а**евте<br>*Vie kje zn**a**evte/dozn**a**evte* |
| 3rd person | He/She/It would know -<br>Тој/Таа/Тоа ќе<br>зн**а**еше/дозн**а**еше<br>*Toj/Taa/Toa kje*<br>*zn**a**eshe/dozn**a**eshe* | They would know -<br>Тие ќе зн**а**еа/дозн**а**еа<br>*Tie kje zn**a**ea/dozn**a**ea* |

| **Personal endings for future perfect-in-the-past tense** | | |
|---|---|---|
| *Person* | *Singular* | *Plural* |
| 1st person | I would have known -<br>Јас ќе сум зн**а**ел/д**о**знаел(а)<br>*Jas kje sum zn**a**el/d**o**znael(a)* | We would have known -<br>Ние ќе сме зн**а**еле/дозн**а**еле<br>*Nie kje sme zn**a**ele/dozn**a**ele* |
| 2nd person | You would have known -<br>Ти ќе си зн**а**ел/д**о**знаел(а)<br>*Ti kje si zn**a**el/d**o**znael(a)* | You would have known -<br>Вие ќе сте зн**а**еле/дозн**а**еле<br>*Vie kje ste zn**a**ele/dozn**a**ele* |
| 3rd person | He/She/It would have known -<br>Тој/Таа/Тоа ќе<br>зн**а**ел/д**о**знаел(а)(о)<br>*Toj/Taa/Toa kje*<br>*zn**a**el/d**o**znael(a)(o)* | They would have known -<br>Тие ќе зн**а**еле/дозн**а**еле<br>*Tie kje zn**a**ele/dozn**a**ele* |

**To laugh – Се смее/Се изнасмее**

| | | |
|---|---|---|
| Infinitive | To laugh | Се смее<br>Se smee |

| Present Simple Tense | | |
|---|---|---|
| *Person* | *Singular* | *Plural* |
| 1st person | I laugh -<br>Јас се смеам<br>*Jas se smea* | We laugh -<br>Ние се смееме<br>*Nie se smeeme* |
| 2nd person | You laugh -<br>Ти се смееш<br>*Ti se smeesh* | You laugh -<br>Вие се смеете<br>*Vie se smeete* |
| 3rd person | He/She/It laughs -<br>Тој/Таа/Тоа се смее<br>Toj/Taa/Toa se smee | They laugh -<br>Тие се смеат<br>*Tie se smeat* |

| Past Simple Tense | | |
|---|---|---|
| *Person* | *Singular* | *Plural* |
| 1st person | I laughed -<br>Јас се изнасмеав<br>*Jas se iznasmeav* | We laughed -<br>Ние се изнасмеавме<br>*Nie se iznasmeavme* |
| 2nd person | You laughed -<br>Ти се изнасмеа<br>*Ti se iznasmea* | You laughed -<br>Вие се изнасмеавте<br>*Jas se iznasmeavte* |
| 3rd person | He/She/It laughed -<br>Тој/Таа/Тоа се изнасмеа<br>*Toj/Taa/Toa se iznasmea* | They laughed -<br>Тие се изнасмееа<br>*Tie se iznasmeea* |

| Past Continuous Tense | | |
|---|---|---|
| *Person* | *Singular* | *Plural* |
| 1st person | I was laughing -<br>Јас се смеев<br>*Jas se smeev* | We were laughing -<br>Ние се смеевме<br>*Nie se smeevme* |
| 2nd person | You were laughing -<br>Ти се смееше<br>*Ti se smeeshe* | You were laughing -<br>Вие се смеевте<br>*Vie se smeevte* |
| 3rd person | He/She/It was laughing -<br>Тој/Таа/Тоа се смееше<br>*Toj/Taa/Toa se smeeshe* | They were laughing -<br>Тие се смееа<br>*Tie se smeea* |

| Present Perfect Simple Tense | | |
|---|---|---|
| *Person* | *Singular* | *Plural* |
| 1st person | I have laughed -<br>Јас сум се изнасмеал(а)<br>*Jas sum se iznasmeal(a)* | We have laughed -<br>Ние сме се изнасмеале<br>*Nie sme se iznasmeale* |

| | | |
|---|---|---|
| 2nd person | You have laughed - Ти си се изнасмеал(а) *Ti si se iznasmeal(a)* | You have laughed - Вие сте се изнасмеале *Vie ste se iznasmeale* |
| 3rd person | He/She/It has laughed - Тој/Таа/Тоа се изнасмеал(а)(о) *Toj/Taa/Toa se iznasmeal(a)(o)* | They have laughed - Тие се изнасмеале *Tie se iznasmeale* |

| Present Perfect Continuous Tense | | |
|---|---|---|
| *Person* | *Singular* | *Plural* |
| 1st person | I have been laughing - Јас сум сесмеел(а) *Jas sum se smeel(a)* | We have been laughing - Ние сме се смееле *Nie sme se smeele* |
| 2nd person | You have been laughing - Ти си сесмеел(а) *Ti si se smeel(a)* | You have been laughing - Вие сте се смееле *Vie ste se smeele* |
| 3rd person | He/She/It has been laughing - Тој/Таа/Тоа се смеел(а)(о) *Toj/Taa/Toa se smeel(a)(o)* | They have been laughing - Тие се смееле *Tie se smeele* |

| Past Perfect Simple Tense | | |
|---|---|---|
| *Person* | *Singular* | *Plural* |
| 1st person | I had laughed - Јас бев се изнасмеал(а) *Jas bev se iznasmeal(a)* | We had laughed - Ние бевме се изнасмеале *Nie bevme se iznasmeale* |
| 2nd person | You had laughed - Ти беше се изнасмеал(а) *Ti beshe se iznasmeal(a)* | You had laughed - Вие бевте се изнасмеале *Vie bevte se iznasmeale* |
| 3rd person | He/She/It had laughed - Тој/Таа/Тоа се беше изнасмеал(а)(о) *Toj/Taa/Toa beshe se iznasmeal(a)(o)* | They had laughed - Тие беа се изнасмеале *Tie bea se iznasmeale* |

| Future Simple Tense | | |
|---|---|---|
| *Person* | *Singular* | *Plural* |
| 1st person | I will laugh - Јас ќе се смеам/се изнасмеам *Jas kje se smeam/se iznasmeam* | We will laugh - Ние ќе се смееме/се изнасмееме *Nie kje se smeeme/se iznasmeeme* |
| 2nd person | You will laugh - Ти ќе се смееш/се изнасмееш *Ti kje se smeesh/se iznasmeesh* | You will laugh Вие ќе се смеете/се изнасмеете *Vie kje se smeete/se iznasmeete* |

| | | |
|---|---|---|
| 3rd person | He/She/It will laugh -<br>Тој/Таа/Тоа ќе се смее/се изнасмее<br>*Toj/Taa/Toa kje se smee/se iznasmee* | They will laugh<br>Тие ќе се смеат/се изнасмеат<br>*Tie kje se smeat/se iznasmeat* |

| **used to + infinitive or would + infinitive** | | |
|---|---|---|
| *Person* | *Singular* | *Plural* |
| 1st person | I would laugh -<br>Јас ќе се смеев/се изнасмеев<br>Jas kje se smeev/se iznasmeev | We would laugh -<br>Ние ќе се смеевме/се изнасмеевме<br>Nie kje se smeevme/se iznasmeevme |
| 2nd person | You would laugh -<br>Ти ќе се смееше/се изнасмееше<br>Ti kje se smeeshe/se iznasmeeshe | You would laugh -<br>Вие ќе се смеевте/се изнасмеевте<br>Vie kje se smeevte/se iznasmeevte |
| 3rd person | He/She/It would laugh -<br>Тој/Таа/Тоа ќе се смееше/се изнасмееше<br>Toj/Taa/Toa kje se smeeshe/se iznasmeeshe | They would laugh -<br>Тие ќе се смееа/се изнасмееа<br>Tie kje se smeea/se iznasmeea |

| **Personal endings for future perfect-in-the-past tense** | | |
|---|---|---|
| *Person* | *Singular* | *Plural* |
| 1st person | I would have laughed -<br>Јас ќе сум се смеел/се изнасмеел(а)<br>*Jas kje sum se smeel/se iznasmeel(a)* | We would have laughed -<br>Ние ќе сме се смееле/се изнасмееле<br>*Nie kje sme se smeele/se iznasmeele* |
| 2nd person | You would have laughed -<br>Ти ќе си се смеел/се изнасмеел(а)<br>*Ti kje si se smeel/se iznasmeel(a)* | You would have laughed -<br>Вие ќе сте се смееле/се изнасмееле<br>*Vie kje ste se smeele/se iznasmeele* |
| 3rd person | He/She/It would have laughed<br>Тој/Таа/Тоа ќе се смеел/се изнасмеел(а)(о)<br>*Toj/Taa/Toa kje se smeel/se iznasmeel(a)(o)* | They would have laughed -<br>Тие ќе се смееле/се изнасмееле<br>*Tie kje se smeele/se iznasmeele* |

### *To learn - Учи/Научи*

| | | |
|---|---|---|
| Infinitive | To learn | **У**чи<br>**U**chi |

| Present Simple Tense | | |
|---|---|---|
| *Person* | *Singular* | *Plural* |
| 1st person | I learn -<br>Јас уч**ам**<br>*Jas uch**am*** | We learn -<br>Ние уч**и**ме<br>*Nie uch**i**me* |
| 2nd person | You learn -<br>Ти уч**и**ш<br>*Ti uch**i**sh* | You learn -<br>Вие уч**и**те<br>*Vie uch**i**te* |
| 3rd person | He/She/It learns -<br>Тој/Таа/Тоа уч**и**<br>*Toj/Taa/Toa uchi* | They learn -<br>Тие уч**а**т<br>*Tie uch**a**t* |

| Past Simple Tense | | |
|---|---|---|
| *Person* | *Singular* | *Plural* |
| 1st person | I learnt -<br>Јас н**а**учив<br>*Jas n**a**uchiv* | We learnt -<br>Ние на**у**чивме<br>*Nie na**u**chivme* |
| 2nd person | You learnt -<br>Ти н**а**учи<br>*Ti n**a**uchi* | You learnt -<br>Вие на**у**чивте<br>*Vie na**u**chivte* |
| 3rd person | He/She/It learnt -<br>Тој/Таа/Тоа н**а**учи<br>*Toj/Taa/Toa n**a**uchi* | They learnt -<br>Тие на**у**чија<br>*ie na**u**chija* |

| Past Continuous Tense | | |
|---|---|---|
| *Person* | *Singular* | *Plural* |
| 1st person | I was learning -<br>Јас уч**е**в<br>*Jas uch**e**v* | We were learning -<br>Ние уч**е**вме<br>*Nie uch**e**vme* |
| 2nd person | You were learning -<br>Ти уч**е**ше<br>*Ti uch**e**she* | You were learning -<br>Вие уч**е**вте<br>*Vie uch**e**vte* |
| 3rd person | He/She/It was learning -<br>Тој/Таа/ТоаТој уч**е**ше<br>*Toj/Taa/Toa uch**e**she* | They were learning -<br>Тие уч**е**а<br>*Tie uch**e**a* |

| Present Perfect Simple Tense | | |
|---|---|---|
| *Person* | *Singular* | *Plural* |
| 1st person | I have learnt -<br>Јас сум на**у**чил(а)<br>*Jas sum na**u**chil(a)* | We have learnt -<br>Ние сме на**у**чиле<br>*Nie sme na**u**chile* |

| | | |
|---|---|---|
| 2nd person | You have learnt -<br>Ти си н**а**учил(а)<br>*Ti si n**a**uchil(a)* | You have learnt -<br>Вие сте на**у**чиле<br>*Vie ste na**u**chile* |
| 3rd person | He/She/It has learnt -<br>Тој/Таа/Тоа н**а**учил(а)(о)<br>*Toj/Taa/Toa n**a**uchil(a)(o)* | They have learnt -<br>Тие на**у**чиле<br>*Tie na**u**chile* |

| Present Perfect Continuous Tense | | |
|---|---|---|
| *Person* | *Singular* | *Plural* |
| 1st person | I have been learning -<br>Јас сум **у**чел(а)<br>*Jas sum **u**chel(a)* | We have been learning -<br>Ние сме **у**челе<br>*Nie sme **u**chele* |
| 2nd person | You have been learning -<br>Ти си **у**чел(а)<br>*Ti si **u**chel(a)* | You have been learning -<br>Вие сте **у**челе<br>*Vie ste **u**chele* |
| 3rd person | He/She/It has been learning -<br>Тој/Таа/Тоа **у**чел(а)(о)<br>*Toj/Taa/Toa **u**chel(a)(o)* | They have been learning -<br>Тие **у**челе<br>*Tie **u**chele* |

| Past Perfect Simple Tense | | |
|---|---|---|
| *Person* | *Singular* | *Plural* |
| 1st person | I had learnt -<br>Јас бев н**а**учил(а)<br>*Jas bev n**a**uchil(a)* | We had learnt -<br>Ние бевме на**у**чиле<br>*Nie bevme na**u**chile* |
| 2nd person | You had learnt -<br>Ти беше н**а**учил(а)<br>*Ti beshe n**a**uchil(a)* | You had learnt -<br>Вие бевте на**у**чиле<br>*Vie bevte na**u**chile* |
| 3rd person | He/She/It had learnt -<br>Тој/Таа/Тоа беше н**а**учил(а)(о)<br>*Toj/Taa/Toa beshe n**a**uchil(a)(o)* | They had learnt -<br>Тие беа на**у**чиле<br>*Tie bea na**u**chile* |

| Future Simple Tense | | |
|---|---|---|
| *Person* | *Singular* | *Plural* |
| 1st person | I will learn -<br>Јас ќе **у**чам/н**а**учам<br>*Jas kje **u**cham/n**a**ucham* | We will learn -<br>Ние ќе **у**чиме/на**у**чиме<br>*Nie kje **u**chime/na**u**chime* |
| 2nd person | You will learn -<br>Ти ќе **у**чиш/н**а**учиш<br>*Ti kje **u**chish/n**a**uchish* | You will learn -<br>Вие ќе **у**чите/на**у**чите<br>*Vie kje **u**chite/na**u**chite* |
| 3rd person | He/She/It will learn -<br>Тој/Таа/Тоа ќе **у**чи н**а**учи<br>*Toj/Taa/Toa kje **u**chi/n**a**uchi* | They will learn -<br>Тие ќе **у**чат/н**а**учат<br>*Tie kje **u**chat/n**a**uchat* |

| used to + infinitive or would + infinitive | | |
|---|---|---|
| *Person* | *Singular* | *Plural* |
| 1st person | I would learn -<br>Јас ќе **у**чев/н**а**учев<br>*Jas kje **u**chev/n**a**uchev* | We would learn -<br>Ние ќе **у**чевме/на**у**чевме<br>*Nie kje **u**chevme/na**u**chevme* |

| | | |
|---|---|---|
| 2nd person | You would learn - Ти ќе **у**чеше/ на**у**чеше *Ti kje **u**cheshe/na**u**cheshe* | You would learn - Вие ќе **у**чевте /на**у**чевте *Vie kje **u**chevte/na**u**chevte* |
| 3rd person | He/She/It would learn - Тој/Таа/Тоа ќе **у**чеше/ на**у**чеше *Toj/Taa/Toa kje **u**cheshe/na**u**cheshe* | They would learn - Тие ќе **у**чеа/на**у**чеа *Tie kje **u**chea/na**u**chea* |

| **Personal endings for future perfect-in-the-past tense** | | |
|---|---|---|
| *Person* | *Singular* | *Plural* |
| 1st person | I would have learnt - Јас ќе сум **у**чел/н**а**учил(а) *Jas kje sum **u**chel/n**a**uchil(a)* | We would have learnt - ние ќе сме **у**челе/на**у**чиле *Nie kje sme **u**chele/na**u**chile* |
| 2nd person | You would have learnt - Ти ќе си **у**чел/н**а**учил(а) *Ti kje si **u**chel/n**a**uchil(a)* | You would have learnt - Вие ќе сте **у**челе/на**у**чиле *Vie kje ste **u**chele/na**u**chile* |
| 3rd person | He/She/It would have learnt - Тој/Таа/Тоа ќе **у**чел/н**а**учил(а)(о) *Toj/Taa/Toa kje **u**chel/n**a**uchil(a)(o)* | They would have learnt - Тие ќе **у**челе/на**у**чиле *Tie kje **u**chele/na**u**chile* |

**To lie down – Лежи/Легне**

| | | |
|---|---|---|
| Infinitive | To lie | Лежи<br>Lezi |

| Present Simple Tense | | |
|---|---|---|
| *Person* | *Singular* | *Plural* |
| 1st person | I lie down -<br>Јас лежам<br>*Jas lezham* | We lie down -<br>Ние лежиме<br>*Nie lezhime* |
| 2nd person | You lie down -<br>Ти лежиш<br>*Ti lezhish* | You lie down -<br>Вие лежите<br>*Vie lezhite* |
| 3rd person | He/She/It lies down -<br>Тој/Таа/Тоа лежи<br>*Toj/Taa/Toa lezhi* | They lie down -<br>Тие лежат<br>*Tie lezhat* |

| Past Simple Tense | | |
|---|---|---|
| *Person* | *Singular* | *Plural* |
| 1st person | I lied down -<br>Јас легнав<br>*Jas legnav* | We lied down -<br>Ние легнавме<br>*Nie legnavme* |
| 2nd person | You lied down -<br>Ти легна<br>*Ti legna* | You lied down -<br>Вие легнавте<br>*Vie legnavte* |
| 3rd person | He/She/It lied down -<br>Тој/Таа/Тоа легна<br>*Toj/Taa/Toa legna* | They lied down -<br>Тие легнаа<br>*Tie legnaa* |

| Past Continuous Tense | | |
|---|---|---|
| *Person* | *Singular* | *Plural* |
| 1st person | I was laying down -<br>Јас лежев<br>*Jas lezhev* | We were laying down -<br>Ние лежевме<br>*Nie lezhevme* |
| 2nd person | You were laying down -<br>Ти лежеше<br>*Ti lezheshe* | You were laying down -<br>Вие лежевте<br>*Vie lezhvte* |
| 3rd person | He/She/It was laying down -<br>Тој/Таа/Тоа лежеше<br>*Toj/Taa/Toa lezheshe* | They were laying down -<br>Тие лежеа<br>*Tie lezhea* |

| Present Perfect Simple Tense | | |
|---|---|---|
| *Person* | *Singular* | *Plural* |
| 1st person | I have lied down -<br>Јас сум легнал(а)<br>*Jas sum legnal(a)* | We have lied down -<br>Ние сме легнале<br>*Nie sme legnale* |

| | | |
|---|---|---|
| 2nd person | You have lied down -<br>Ти си легнал(а)<br>*Ti si legnal(a)* | You have lied down -<br>Вие сте легнале<br>*Vie ste legnale* |
| 3rd person | He/She/It has lied down -<br>Тој/Таа/Тоа легнал(а)(о)<br>*Toj/Taa/Toa legnal(a)(o)* | They have lied down -<br>Тие легнале<br>*Tie legnale* |

| **Present Perfect Continuous Tense** | | |
|---|---|---|
| *Person* | *Singular* | *Plural* |
| 1st person | I have been laying down -<br>Јас сум лежел(а)<br>*Jas sum lezhel(a)* | We have been laying down -<br>Ние сме лежеле<br>*Nie sme lezhele* |
| 2nd person | You have been laying down -<br>Ти си лежел(а)<br>*Ti si lezhel(a)* | You have been laying down -<br>Вие сте лежеле<br>*Vie ste lezhele* |
| 3rd person | He/She/It has been laying down -<br>Тој/Таа/Тоа лежел(а)(о)<br>*Toj/Taa/Toa lezhel(a)(o)* | They have been laying down -<br>Тие лежеле<br>*Tie lezhele* |

| **Past Perfect Simple Tense** | | |
|---|---|---|
| *Person* | *Singular* | *Plural* |
| 1st person | I had lied down -<br>Јас бев легнал(а)<br>*Jas bev legnal(a)* | We had lied down -<br>Ние бевме легнале<br>*Nie bevme legnale* |
| 2nd person | You had lied down -<br>Ти беше легнал(а)<br>*Ti beshe legnal(a)* | You had lied down -<br>Вие бевте легнале<br>*Vie bevte legnale* |
| 3rd person | He/She/It had lied down -<br>Тој/Таа/Тоа беше легнале(а)(о)<br>*Toj/Taa/Toa beshe legnal(a)(o)* | They had lied down -<br>Тие беа легнале<br>*Tie bea legnale* |

| **Future Simple Tense** | | |
|---|---|---|
| *Person* | *Singular* | *Plural* |
| 1st person | I will lie down -<br>Јас ќе лежам/легнам<br>*Jas kje lezham/legnam* | We will lie down -<br>Ние ќе лежиме/легнеме<br>*Nie kje lezhime/legneme* |
| 2nd person | You will lie down -<br>Ти ќе лежиш/легнеш<br>*Ti kje lezhish/lezhnesh* | You will lie down -<br>Вие ќе лежите/легнете<br>*Vie kje lezhite/legnete* |
| 3rd person | He/She/It will lie down -<br>Тој/Таа/Тоа ќе лежи/легне<br>*Toj/Taa/Toa kje lezhi/legne* | They will lie down -<br>Тие ќе лежат/легнат<br>*Tie kje lezhat/legnat* |

| **used to + infinitive or would + infinitive** | | |
|---|---|---|
| *Person* | *Singular* | *Plural* |
| 1st person | I would lie down -<br>Јас ќе лежев/легнев<br>*Jas kje lezhev/legnev* | We would lie down -<br>Ние ќе лежевме/легневме<br>*Nie kje lezhevme/legnevme* |

| | | |
|---|---|---|
| 2nd person | You would lie down - Ти ќе лежеше/легнеше *Ti kje lezheshe/legneshe* | You would lie down - Вие ќе лежевте/легневте *Vie kje lezhevte/legnevte* |
| 3rd person | He/She/It would lie down - Тој/Таа/Тоа ќе лежеше/легнеше *Toj/Taa/Toa kje lezheshe/legneshe* | They would lie down - Тие ќе лежеат/легнаа *Tie kje lezheat/legnaa* |

| **Personal endings for future perfect- in - the - past tense** | | |
|---|---|---|
| *Person* | *Singular* | *Plural* |
| 1st person | I would have lied down - Јас ќе сум лежел/легнал(а) *Jas kje sum lezhel/ legnal(a)* | We would have lied down - Ние ќе сме лежеле/легнале *Nie kje sme lezhele/ legnale* |
| 2nd person | You would have lied down - Ти ќе силежел/легнал(а) *Ti kje si lezhel/ legnal(a)* | You would have lied down - Вие ќе сте лежеле/легнале *Vie kje ste lezhele/ legnale* |
| 3rd person | He/She/It would have lied down - Тој/Таа/Тоа ќе лежел/легнал(а)(о) *Toj/Taa/Toa kje lezhel/legnal(a)(o)* | They would have lied down - ие ќележеле/легнале *Tie kje lezhele/legnale* |

### *To like– Сака/Засака*

| | | |
|---|---|---|
| *Infinitive* | To like | Сака<br>Saka |

| Present Simple Tense | | |
|---|---|---|
| *Person* | *Singular* | *Plural* |
| 1st person | I like -<br>Јас сакам<br>*Jas sakam* | We like -<br>Ние сакаме<br>*Nie sakame* |
| 2nd person | You like -<br>Ти сакаш<br>*Ti sakash* | You like -<br>Вие сакате<br>*Vie sakate* |
| 3rd person | He/She/It likes -<br>Тој/Таа/Тоа сака<br>*Toj/Taa/Toa saka* | They like -<br>Тие сакаат<br>*Tie sakaat* |

| Past Simple Tense | | |
|---|---|---|
| *Person* | *Singular* | *Plural* |
| 1st person | I liked -<br>Јас засакав<br>*Jas zasakav* | We liked -<br>Ние засакавме<br>*Nie zasakavme* |
| 2nd person | You liked -<br>Ти засака<br>*Ti zasaka* | You liked -<br>Вие засакавте<br>*Vie zasakavte* |
| 3rd person | He/She/It liked -<br>Тој/Таа/Тоа засака<br>*Toj/Taa/Toa zasaka* | They liked -<br>Тие засакаа<br>*Tie zasakaa* |

| Past Continuous Tense | | |
|---|---|---|
| *Person* | *Singular* | *Plural* |
| 1st person | I was liking -<br>Јас сакав<br>*Jas sakav* | We were liking -<br>Ние сакавме<br>*Nie sakavme* |
| 2nd person | You were liking -<br>Ти сакаше<br>*Ti sakashe* | You were liking -<br>Вие сакавме<br>*Vie sakavte* |
| 3rd person | He/She/It was liking -<br>Тој/Таа/Тоа сакаше<br>*Toj/Taa/Toa sakashe* | They were liking -<br>Тие сакаа<br>*Tie sakaa* |

| Present Perfect Simple Tense | | |
|---|---|---|
| *Person* | *Singular* | *Plural* |
| 1st person | I have liked -<br>Јас сум засакал(а)<br>*Jas sum zasakal(a)* | We have liked -<br>Ние сме засакале<br>*Nie sme zasakale* |

| | | |
|---|---|---|
| 2nd person | You have liked - <br> Ти си засакал(а) <br> *Ti si zasakal(a)* | You have liked - <br> Вие сте засакале <br> *Vie ste zasakale* |
| 3rd person | He/She/It has liked - <br> Тој/Таа/Тоа засакал(а)(о) <br> *Toj/Taa/Toa zasakal(a)(o)* | They have liked - <br> Тие засакале <br> *Tie zasakale* |

| **Present Perfect Continuous Tense** | | |
|---|---|---|
| *Person* | *Singular* | *Plural* |
| 1st person | I have been liking - <br> Јас сум сакал(а) <br> *Jas sum sakal(a)* | We have been liking - <br> Ние сме сакале <br> *Nie sme sakale* |
| 2nd person | You have been liking - <br> Ти си сакал(а) <br> *Ti si sakal(a)* | You have been liking - <br> Вие сте сакале <br> *Vie ste sakale* |
| 3rd person | He/She/It has been liking - <br> Тој/Таа/Тоа сакал(а)(о) <br> *Toj/Taa/Toa sakal(a)(o)* | They have been liking - <br> Тие сакале <br> *Tie sakale* |

| **Past Perfect Simple Tense** | | |
|---|---|---|
| *Person* | *Singular* | *Plural* |
| 1st person | I had liked - <br> Јас бев засакал(а) <br> *Jas bev zasakal(a)* | We had liked - <br> Ние сме засакале <br> *Nie bevme zasakale* |
| 2nd person | You had liked - <br> Ти беше засакал(а) <br> *Ti beshe zasakal(a)* | You had liked - <br> Вие сте засакале <br> *Vie bevte zasakale* |
| 3rd person | He/She/It had liked - <br> Тој/Таа/Тоа засакал(а)(о) <br> *Toj/Taa/Toa zasakal(a)(o)* | They had liked - <br> Тие засакале <br> *Tie zasakale* |

| **Future Simple Tense** | | |
|---|---|---|
| *Person* | *Singular* | *Plural* |
| 1st person | I will like - <br> Јас ќе сакам/засакам <br> *Jas kje sakam/zasakam* | We will like - <br> Ние ќе сакаме/засакаме <br> *Nie kje sakame/zasakame* |
| 2nd person | You will like - <br> Ти ќе сакаш/засакаш <br> *Ti kje sakash/zasakash* | You will like - <br> Вие ќе сакате/засакате <br> *Vie kje sakate/zasakate* |
| 3rd person | He/She/It will like - <br> Тој/Таа/Тоа ќе сака/засака <br> *Toj/Taa/Toa kje saka/zasaka* | They will like - <br> Тие ќе сакаат/засакаат <br> *Tie kje sakaat/zasakaat* |

| **used to + infinitive or would + infinitive** | | |
|---|---|---|
| *Person* | *Singular* | *Plural* |
| 1st person | I would like - <br> Јас ќе сакав/засакав <br> *Jas kje sakav/zasakav* | We would like - <br> Ние ќе сакавме/засакавме <br> *Nie kje sakavme/zasakavme* |

| | | |
|---|---|---|
| 2nd person | You would like - Ти ќе с**а**каше/зас**а**каше *Ti kje s**a**kashe/zas**a**kashe* | You would like - Вие ќе с**а**кавте/зас**а**кавте *Vie kje s**a**kavte/zas**a**kavte* |
| 3rd person | He/She/It would like - Тој/Таа/Тоа ќе с**а**каше/зас**а**каше *Toj/Taa/Toa kje s**a**kashe/zas**a**kashe* | They would like - Тие ќе с**а**каа/зас**а**каа *Tie kje s**a**kaa/zas**a**kaa* |

| Personal endings for future perfect-in-the-past tense | | |
|---|---|---|
| *Person* | *Singular* | *Plural* |
| 1st person | I would have liked - Јас ќе сум с**а**кал/з**а**сакал(а) *Jas kje sum s**a**kal/z**a**sakal(a)* | We would have liked - Ние ќе сме с**а**кале/зас**а**кале *Nie kje sme s**a**kale/z**a**sakale* |
| 2nd person | You would have liked - Ти ќе си с**а**кал/з**а**сакал(а) *Ti kje si s**a**kal/z**a**sakal(a)* | You would have liked - Ви ќе сте с**а**кале/зас**а**кале *Vie kje ste s**a**kale/z**a**sakale* |
| 3rd person | He/She/It would have liked - Тој/Таа/Тоа ќе с**а**кал/з**а**сакал(а)(о) *Toj/Taa/Toa kje s**a**kal/z**a**sakal(a)(a)* | They would have liked - Тие ќе с**а**кале/з**а**сакале *Tie kje s**a**kale/z**a**sakale* |

***To listen – Слуша/Послуша***

| | | |
|---|---|---|
| *Infinitive* | To listen | Сл**у**ша<br>Sl**u**sha |

| Present Simple Tense | | |
|---|---|---|
| *Person* | *Singular* | *Plural* |
| 1st person | I listen -<br>Јас сл**у**шам<br>*Jas sl**u**sham* | We listen -<br>Ние сл**у**шаме<br>*Nie sl**u**shame* |
| 2nd person | You listen -<br>Ти сл**у**шаш<br>*Ti sl**u**shash* | You listen -<br>Вие сл**у**шате<br>*Vie sl**u**shate* |
| 3rd person | He/She/It listens -<br>Тој/Таа/Тоа сл**у**ша<br>*Toj/Taa/Toa sl**u**sha* | They listen -<br>Тие сл**у**шаат<br>*Tie sl**u**shaat* |

| Past Simple Tense | | |
|---|---|---|
| *Person* | *Singular* | *Plural* |
| 1st person | I listened -<br>Јас п**о**слушав<br>*Jas p**o**slushav* | We listened -<br>Ние посл**у**шавме<br>*Nie posl**u**shavme* |
| 2nd person | You listened -<br>Ти п**о**слуша<br>*Ti p**o**slusha* | You listened -<br>Вие посл**у**шавте<br>*Vie posl**u**shavte* |
| 3rd person | He/She/It listened -<br>Тој/Таа/Тоа п**о**слуша<br>*Toj/Taa/Toa p**o**slusha* | They listened -<br>Тие посл**у**шаа<br>*Tie posl**u**shaa* |

| Past Continuous Tense | | |
|---|---|---|
| *Person* | *Singular* | *Plural* |
| 1st person | I was listening -<br>Јас сл**у**шав<br>*Jas sl**u**shav* | We were listening -<br>Ние сл**у**шавме<br>*Nie sl**u**shavme* |
| 2nd person | You were listening -<br>Ти сл**у**шаше<br>*Ti sl**u**shashe* | You were listening -<br>Вие сл**у**шавте<br>*Vie sl**u**shavte* |
| 3rd person | He/She/It was listening-<br>Тој/Таа/Тоа сл**у**шаше<br>*Toj/Taa/Toa sl**u**shashe* | They were listening -<br>Тие сл**у**шаа<br>*Tie sl**u**shaa* |

| Present Perfect Simple Tense | | |
|---|---|---|
| *Person* | *Singular* | *Plural* |
| 1st person | I have listened -<br>Јас сум п**о**слушал(а)<br>*Jas sum p**o**slushal(a)* | We have listened -<br>Ние сме посл**у**шале<br>*Nie sme posl**u**shale* |

| | | |
|---|---|---|
| 2nd person | You have listed -<br>Ти си п**о**слушал(а)<br>*Ti si p**o**slushal(a)* | You have listened -<br>Вие сте посл**у**шале<br>*Vie ste posl**u**shale* |
| 3rd person | He/She/It has listened<br>Тој/Таа/Тоа п**о**слушал(а)(о)<br>*Toj/Taa/Toa p**o**slushal(a)(o)* | They have listened -<br>Тие посл**у**шале<br>*Tie posl**u**shale* |

| **Present Perfect Continuous Tense** | | |
|---|---|---|
| *Person* | *Singular* | *Plural* |
| 1st person | I have been listening -<br>Јас сум сл**у**шал(а)<br>*Jas sum sl**u**shal(a)* | We have been listening -<br>Ние сме сл**у**шале<br>*Nie sme sl**u**shale* |
| 2nd person | You have been listening -<br>Ти си сл**у**шал(а)<br>*Ti si sl**u**shal(a)* | You have been listening -<br>Вие сте сл**у**шале<br>*Vie ste sl**u**shale* |
| 3rd person | He/She/It has been listening -<br>Тој/Таа/Тоа сл**у**шал(а)(о)<br>*Toj/Taa/Toa sl**u**shal(a)(o)* | They have been listening -<br>Тие сл**у**шале<br>*Tie sl**u**shale* |

| **Past Perfect Simple Tense** | | |
|---|---|---|
| *Person* | *Singular* | *Plural* |
| 1st person | I had listened -<br>Јас бев п**о**слушал(а)<br>*Jas bev p**o**slushal(a)* | We had listened -<br>Ние бевме посл**у**шале<br>*Nie bevme posl**u**shale* |
| 2nd person | You had listened -<br>Ти беше п**о**слушал(а)<br>*Ti beshe p**o**slushal(a)* | You had listened -<br>Вие бевте посл**у**шале<br>*Vie bevte posl**u**shale* |
| 3rd person | He/She/It had listened -<br>Тој/Таа/Тоа беше п**о**слушал(а)(о)<br>*Toj/Taa/Toa beshe p**o**slushal(a)(o)* | They had listened -<br>Тие беа посл**у**шале<br>*Tie bea posl**u**shale* |

| **Future Simple Tense** | | |
|---|---|---|
| *Person* | *Singular* | *Plural* |
| 1st person | I will listen<br>Јас ќе сл**у**шам/п**о**слушам<br>*Jas kje sl**u**sham/p**o**slusham* | We will listen<br>Ние ќе сл**у**шаме/посл**у**шаме<br>*Nie kje sl**u**shame/posl**u**shame* |
| 2nd person | You will listen<br>Ти ќе сл**у**шаш/п**о**слушаш<br>*Ti kje sl**u**shash/p**o**slushash* | You will listen<br>Вие ќе сл**у**шате/посл**у**шате<br>*Vie kje sl**u**shate/posl**u**shate* |
| 3rd person | He/She/It will listen<br>Тој/Таа/Тоа ќе сл**у**ша/п**о**слуша<br>*Toj/Taa/Toa kje sl**u**sha/p**o**slusha* | They will listen<br>Тие ќе сл**у**шаат/посл**у**шаат<br>*Tie kje sl**u**shaat/posl**u**shaat* |

| **used to + infinitive or would + infinitive** | | |
|---|---|---|
| *Person* | *Singular* | *Plural* |
| 1st person | I would listen -<br>Јас ќе сл**у**шав/посл**у**шав<br>*Jas kje sl**u**shav/posl**u**shav* | We would listen -<br>Ние ќе сл**у**шавме/посл**у**шавме<br>*Nie kje sl**u**shavme/posl**u**shavme* |
| 2nd person | You would listen -<br>Ти ќе сл**у**шаше/посл**у**шаше<br>*Ti kje sl**u**shashe/posl**u**shashe* | You would listen -<br>Вие ќе сл**у**шавте/посл**у**шавте<br>*Vie kje sl**u**shavte/posl**u**shavte* |
| 3rd person | He/She/It would listen -<br>Тој/Таа/Тоа ќе<br>сл**у**шаше/посл**у**шаше<br>*Toj/Taa/Toa kje*<br>*sl**u**shashe/posl**u**shashe* | They would listen -<br>Тие ќе сл**у**шаа/посл**у**шаа<br>*Tie kje sl**u**shaa/posl**u**shaa* |

| **Personal endings for future perfect-in-the-past tense** | | |
|---|---|---|
| *Person* | *Singular* | *Plural* |
| 1st person | I would have listened -<br>Јас ќе сум сл**у**шал/п**о**слушал(а)<br>*Jas kje sum sl**u**shal/p**o**slushal(a)* | We would have listened -<br>Ние ќе сме<br>сл**у**шале/посл**у**шале<br>*Nie kje sme sl**u**shale/posl**u**shale* |
| 2nd person | You would have listened -<br>Ти ќе си сл**у**шал/п**о**слушал(а)<br>*Ti kje si sl**u**shal/p**o**slushal(a)* | You would have listened -<br>Вие ќе сте сл**у**шале/посл**у**шале<br>*Vie kje ste sl**u**shale/posl**u**shale* |
| 3rd person | He/She/It would have listened<br>Тој/Таа/Тоа ќе<br>сл**у**шал/п**о**слушал(а)(о)<br>*Toj/Taa/Toa kje*<br>*sl**u**shal/p**o**slushal(a)(o)* | They would have listened -<br>Тие ќе сл**у**шале/посл**у**шале<br>*Tie kje sl**u**shale/posl**u**shale* |

***To live – Живее/Изживеа***

| | | |
|---|---|---|
| *Infinitive* | To live | Ж**и**вее<br>Zh**i**vee |

| Present Simple Tense | | |
|---|---|---|
| *Person* | *Singular* | *Plural* |
| 1st person | I live -<br>Јас ж**и**веам<br>*Jas zh**i**veam* | We live -<br>Ние ж**и**вееме<br>*Nie zh**i**veeme* |
| 2nd person | You live -<br>Ти ж**и**вееш<br>*Ti zh**i**veesh* | You live -<br>Вие ж**и**веете<br>*Vie zh**i**veete* |
| 3rd person | He/She/It lives -<br>Тој/Таа/Тоа ж**и**вее<br>*Toj/Taa/Toa zh**i**vee* | They live -<br>Тие ж**и**веат<br>*Tie zh**i**veat* |

| Past Simple Tense | | |
|---|---|---|
| *Person* | *Singular* | *Plural* |
| 1st person | I lived -<br>Јас изж**и**веав<br>*Jas izzh**i**veav* | We lived -<br>Ние изживе**а**вме<br>*Nie izzhive**a**me* |
| 2nd person | You lived -<br>Ти изж**и**веа<br>*Ti izzh**i**vea* | You lived -<br>Вие изживе**а**вте<br>*Vie izzhive**a**vte* |
| 3rd person | He/She/It lived -<br>Тој/Таа/Тоа изж**и**веа<br>*Toj/Taa/Toa izzh**i**vea* | They lived -<br>Тие изживе**е**ја<br>*Tie izzhive**e**ja* |

| Past Continuous Tense | | |
|---|---|---|
| *Person* | *Singular* | *Plural* |
| 1st person | I was living -<br>Јас ж**и**веев<br>*Jas zh**i**veev* | We were living -<br>Ние живе**е**вме<br>Nie zhive**e**vme |
| 2nd person | You were living -<br>Ти живе**е**ше<br>*Ti zhive**e**she* | You were living -<br>Вие живе**е**вте<br>Vie zhive**e**vte |
| 3rd person | He/She/It was living -<br>Тој/Таа/Тоа живе**е**ше<br>*Toj/Taa/Toa zhive**e**she* | They were living -<br>Тие живе**е**ја<br>Tie zhive**e**ja |

| Present Perfect Simple Tense | | |
|---|---|---|
| *Person* | *Singular* | *Plural* |
| 1st person | I have lived -<br>Јас сум изж**и**веal(a)<br>*Jas sum izzh**i**veal(a)* | We have lived -<br>Ние сме изживе**а**ле<br>*Nie sme izzhive**a**le* |

| | | |
|---|---|---|
| 2nd person | You have lived -<br>Ти си изж**и**веal(a)<br>*Ti si izzh**i**veal(a)* | You have lived -<br>Вие сте изжив**е**але<br>*Vie ste izzhiv**e**ale* |
| 3rd person | He/She/It has lived -<br>Toj/Taa/Toa изж**и**веal(a)(o)<br>*Toj/Taa/Toa izzh**i**veal(a)(o)* | They have lived -<br>Тие изжив**е**але<br>*Tie izzhiv**e**ale* |

| Present Perfect Continuous Tense | | |
|---|---|---|
| *Person* | *Singular* | *Plural* |
| 1st person | I have been living -<br>Јас сум ж**и**веел(a)<br>*Jas sum zh**i**veel(a)* | We have been living -<br>Ние сме жив**е**еле<br>*Nie sme zhiv**e**ele* |
| 2nd person | You have been living -<br>Ти си ж**и**веел(a)<br>*Ti si zh**i**veel(a)* | You have been living -<br>Вие сте жив**е**еле<br>*Vie ste zhiv**e**ele* |
| 3rd person | He/She/It has been living -<br>Toj/Taa/Toa си ж**и**веел(a)(o)<br>*Toj/Taa/Toa zh**i**veel(a)(o)* | They have been living -<br>Тие жив**е**еле<br>*Tie zhiv**e**ele* |

| Past Perfect Simple Tense | | |
|---|---|---|
| *Person* | *Singular* | *Plural* |
| 1st person | I had lived -<br>Јас бев изж**и**веал(a)<br>*Jas bev izzh**i**veal(a)* | We had lived -<br>Ние бевме изжив**е**але<br>*Nie bevme izzhiv**e**ale* |
| 2nd person | You had lived -<br>Ти беше изж**и**веal(a)<br>*Ti beshe izzh**i**veal(a)* | You had lived -<br>Вие сте изжив**е**але<br>*Vie bevte izzhiv**e**ale* |
| 3rd person | He/She/It had lived -<br>Toj/Taa/Toa беше<br>изж**и**веal(a)(o)<br>*Toj/Taa/Toa beshe*<br>*izzh**i**veal(a)(o)* | They had lived -<br>Тие изжив**е**але<br>*Tie bea izzhiv**e**ale* |

| Future Simple Tense | | |
|---|---|---|
| *Person* | *Singular* | *Plural* |
| 1st person | I will live -<br>Јас ќе ж**и**веам/изж**и**веам<br>*Jas kje zh**i**veam/ si zh**i**veam* | We will live -<br>Ние ќе жив**е**еме/изжив**е**еме<br>*Nie kje zhiv**e**eme/si zhiv**e**eme* |
| 2nd person | You will live -<br>Ти ќе ж**и**вееш/изж**и**вееш<br>*Ti kje zh**i**veesh/ si zh**i**veeshe* | You will live -<br>Вие ќе жив**е**ете/изжив**е**ете<br>*Vie kje zhiv**e**ete/izhiv**e**ete* |
| 3rd person | He/She/It will live -<br>Toj/Taa/Toa ќе ж**и**вее/изж**и**веа<br>*Toj/Taa/Toa kje zh**i**vee/si zh**i**vee* | They will live -<br>Тие ќе ж**и**веат/изж**и**веat<br>*Tie kje zh**i**veat/izh**i**veat* |

| used to + infinitive or would + infinitive | | |
|---|---|---|
| *Person* | *Singular* | *Plural* |
| 1st person | I would live -<br>Јас ќе ж**и**веев/ изж**и**веев<br>*Jas kje zh**i**veev/izzh**i**veev* | We would live -<br>Ние ќе жив**е**евме/изжив**е**евме<br>*Nie kje zhiv**e**eme/izzhiv**e**evme* |
| 2nd person | You would live -<br>Ти ќе ж**и**вееше/изжив**е**еше<br>*Ti kje zh**i**veeshe/izzhiv**e**eshe* | You would live -<br>Вие ќе жив**е**евте/изжив**е**евте<br>*Vie kje zhiv**e**ete/izzhiv**e**evte* |
| 3rd person | He/She/It would live -<br>Тој/Таа/Тоа ќе<br>жив**е**еше/изжив**е**еше<br>*Toj/Taa/Toa kje*<br>*zhiv**e**eshe/izzhiv**e**eshe* | They would live -<br>Тие ќе жив**е**еја/изжив**е**еја<br>*Tie kje zhiv**e**eja/izzhiv**e**eja* |

| Personal endings for future perfect-in-the-past tense | | |
|---|---|---|
| *Person* | *Singular* | *Plural* |
| 1st person | I would have lived -<br>Јас ќе сум ж**и**веел/изж**и**веел(а)<br>*Jas kje sum zh**i**veel/izzh**i**veel(a)* | We would have lived -<br>Ние ќе сме жив**е**еле/изжив**е**еле<br>*Nie kje sme zhiv**e**ele/izzhiv**e**ele* |
| 2nd person | You would have lived -<br>Ти ќе си ж**и**веел/изж**и**веел(а)<br>*Ti kje si zh**i**veel/izzh**i**veel(a)* | You would have lived -<br>Вие ќе сте жив**е**еле/изжив**е**еле<br>*Vie kje ste zhiv**e**ele/izzhiv**e**ele* |
| 3rd person | He/She/It would have lived -<br>Тој/Таа/Тоа ќе<br>ж**и**веел/изж**и**веел(а)(о)<br>*Toj/Taa/Toa kje*<br>*zh**i**veel/izzh**i**veel(a)(o)* | They would have lived -<br>Тие ќе жив**е**еле/изжив**е**еле<br>*Tie kje zhiv**e**ele/izzhiv**e**ele* |

### *To lose – Губи/Изгуби*

| | | |
|---|---|---|
| *Infinitive* | To lose | Губи<br>G**u**bi |

| Present Simple Tense | | |
|---|---|---|
| *Person* | *Singular* | *Plural* |
| 1st person | I lose -<br>Јас г**у**бам<br>*Jas g**u**bam* | We lose -<br>Ние г**у**биме<br>*Nie g**u**bime* |
| 2nd person | You lose -<br>Ти г**у**биш<br>*Ti g**u**bish* | You lose -<br>Вие г**у**бите<br>*Vie g**u**bite* |
| 3rd person | He/She/It loses -<br>Тој/Таа/Тоа г**у**би<br>*Toj/Taa/Toa g**u**bi* | They lose -<br>Тие г**у**бат<br>*Tie g**u**bat* |

| Past Simple Tense | | |
|---|---|---|
| *Person* | *Singular* | *Plural* |
| 1st person | I lost -<br>Јас **и**згубив<br>*Jas **i**zgubiv* | We lost -<br>Ние изг**у**бивме<br>*Nie izg**u**bivme* |
| 2nd person | You lost -<br>Ти **и**згуби<br>*Ti **i**zgubi* | You lost -<br>Вие изг**у**бивте<br>*Vie izg**u**bivte* |
| 3rd person | He/She/It lost -<br>Тој/Таа/Тоа**и**згуби<br>*Toj/Taa/Toa **i**zgubi* | They lost -<br>Тие изг**у**бија<br>*Tie izg**u**bija* |

| Past Continuous Tense | | |
|---|---|---|
| *Person* | *Singular* | *Plural* |
| 1st person | I was losing -<br>Јас г**у**бев<br>*Jas g**u**bev* | We were losing -<br>Ние г**у**бевме<br>*Nie g**u**bevme* |
| 2nd person | You were losing -<br>Ти г**у**беше<br>*Ti g**u**beshe* | You were losing -<br>Вие г**у**бевте<br>*Vie g**u**bevte* |
| 3rd person | He/She/It was losing -<br>Тој/Таа/Тоа г**у**беше<br>*Toj/Taa/Toa g**u**beshe* | They were losing -<br>Тие г**у**беа<br>*Tie g**u**bat* |

| Present Perfect Simple Tense | | |
|---|---|---|
| *Person* | *Singular* | *Plural* |
| 1st person | I have lost -<br>Јас сум **и**згубил(а)<br>*Jas sum **i**zgubil(a)* | We have lost -<br>Ние сме изг**у**биле<br>*Nie sme izg**u**bile* |

| | | |
|---|---|---|
| 2nd person | You have lost -<br>Ти си **из**губил(а)<br>*Ti si **iz**gubil(a)* | You have lost -<br>Вие сте изг**у**биле<br>*Vie ste izg**u**bile* |
| 3rd person | He/She/It has lost -<br>Тој/Таа/Тоа**из**губил(а)(о)<br>*Toj/Taa/Toa **iz**gubil(a)(o)* | They have lost -<br>Тие изг**у**биле<br>*Tie izg**u**bile* |

| **Present Perfect Continuous Tense** | | |
|---|---|---|
| *Person* | *Singular* | *Plural* |
| 1st person | I have been losing -<br>Јас сум **гу**бел(а)<br>*Jas sum **gu**be(a)* | We have been losing -<br>Ние сме **гу**беле<br>*Nie sme **gu**bele* |
| 2nd person | You have been losing -<br>Ти си **гу**бел(а)<br>*Ti si **gu**bel(a)* | You have been losing -<br>Вие сте **гу**беле<br>*Vie ste **gu**bele* |
| 3rd person | He/She/It has been losing -<br>Тој/Таа/Тоа **гу**бел(а)(о)<br>*Toj/Taa/Toa **gu**bel(a)(o)* | They have been losing -<br>Тие **гу**беле<br>*Tie **gu**bele* |

| **Past Perfect Simple Tense** | | |
|---|---|---|
| *Person* | *Singular* | *Plural* |
| 1st person | I had lost -<br>Јас бев **из**губил(а)<br>*Jas bev **iz**gubil(a)* | We had lost -<br>Ние бевме изг**у**биле<br>*Nie bevme izg**u**bile* |
| 2nd person | You had lost -<br>Ти беше **из**губил(а)<br>*Ti beshe **iz**gubil(a)* | You had lost -<br>Вие бевте изг**у**биле<br>*Vie bevte izg**u**bile* |
| 3rd person | He/She/It had lost -<br>Тој/Таа/Тоа беше **из**губил(а)(о)<br>*Toj/Taa/Toa beshe **iz**gubil(a)(o)* | They had lost -<br>Тие беа изг**у**биле<br>*Tie bea izg**u**bile* |

| **Future Simple Tense** | | |
|---|---|---|
| *Person* | *Singular* | *Plural* |
| 1st person | I will lose -<br>Јас ќе **гу**бам/**из**губам<br>*Jas kje **gu**bam/**iz**gubam* | We will lose -<br>Ние ќе **гу**биме/изг**у**биме<br>*Nie kje **gu**bime/izg**u**bime* |
| 2nd person | You will lose -<br>Ти ќе **гу**биш/**из**губиш<br>*Ti kje **gu**bish/**iz**gubish* | You will lose -<br>Вие ќе **гу**бите/изг**у**бите<br>*Vie kje **gu**bite/izg**u**bite* |
| 3rd person | He/She/It will lose -<br>Тој/Таа/Тоа ќе **гу**би/**из**губи<br>Toj/Taa/Toa kje **gu**bi/**iz**gubi | They will lose -<br>Тие ќе **гу**бат/**из**губат<br>Tie kje **gu**bat/**iz**gubat |

| **used to + infinitive or would + infinitive** | | |
|---|---|---|
| *Person* | *Singular* | *Plural* |
| 1st person | I would lose -<br>Јас ќе **гу**бев/**из**губев<br>*Jas kje **gu**bev/**iz**gubev* | We would lose -<br>Ние ќе **гу**бевме/изг**у**бевме<br>*Nie kje **gu**bevme/izg**u**bevme* |

| | | |
|---|---|---|
| 2nd person | You would lose -<br>Ти ќе г**у**беше/изг**у**беше<br>*Ti kje g**u**beshe/izg**u**beshe* | You would lose -<br>Вие ќе г**у**бевте/изг**у**бевте<br>*Vie kje g**u**bevte/izg**u**bevte* |
| 3rd person | He/She/It would lose -<br>Тој/Таа/Тоа ќе<br>г**у**беше/изг**у**беше<br>*Toj/Taa/Toa kje*<br>*g**u**beshe/izg**u**beshe* | They would lose -<br>Тие ќе г**у**бат/**и**згубат<br>*Tie kje g**u**bat/**i**zgubat* |

| **Personal endings for future perfect-in-the-past tense** | | |
|---|---|---|
| *Person* | *Singular* | *Plural* |
| 1st person | I would have lost -<br>Јас ќе сум г**у**бел/**и**згубел(а)<br>*Jas kje sum g**u**bel/**i**zgubel(a)* | We would have lost -<br>Ние ќе сме г**у**беле/изг**у**беле<br>*Nie kje sme g**u**bele/iz**g**ubele* |
| 2nd person | You would have lost -<br>Ти ќе си г**у**бел/**и**згубел(а)<br>*Ti kje si g**u**bel/**i**zgubel(a)* | You would have lost -<br>Вие ќе сте г**у**беле/изг**у**беле<br>*Vie kje ste g**u**bele/iz**g**ubele* |
| 3rd person | He/She/It would have lost -<br>Тој/Таа/Тоа ќе<br>г**у**бел/**и**згубел(а)(о)<br>*Toj/Taa/Toa kje*<br>*g**u**bel/**i**zgubel(a)(o)* | They would have lost -<br>Тие ќе г**у**беле/изг**у**беле<br>*Tie kje g**u**bele/iz**g**ubele* |

## *To love – Љуби/Заљуби*

| | | |
|---|---|---|
| *Infinitive* | To love | Љ**у**би<br>Lj**u**bi |

| Present Simple Tense | | |
|---|---|---|
| *Person* | *Singular* | *Plural* |
| 1st person | I love -<br>Јас љ**у**бам<br>*Jas lj**u**bam* | We love -<br>Ние љ**у**биме<br>*Nie lj**u**bime* |
| 2nd person | You love -<br>Ти љ**у**биш<br>*Ti lj**u**bish* | You love -<br>Вие љ**у**бите<br>*Vie lj**u**bite* |
| 3rd person | He/She/It loves -<br>Тој/Таа/Тоа љ**у**би<br>*Toj/Taa/Toa lj**u**bi* | They love -<br>Тие љ**у**бат<br>*Tie lj**u**bat* |

| Past Simple Tense | | |
|---|---|---|
| *Person* | *Singular* | *Plural* |
| 1st person | I loved -<br>Јас з**а**љубив<br>*Jas z**a**ljubiv* | We loved -<br>Ние зали**у**бивме<br>*Nie zalj**u**bivme* |
| 2nd person | You loved -<br>Ти з**а**љуби<br>*Ti z**a**ljubi* | You loved -<br>Вие заљ**у**бивте<br>*Vie zalj**u**bivte* |
| 3rd person | He/She/It loved –<br>Тој/Таа/Тоа з**а**љуби<br>*Toj/Taa/Toa z**a**ljubi* | They loved -<br>Тие заљ**у**бија<br>*Tie zalj**u**bija* |

| Past Continuous Tense | | |
|---|---|---|
| *Person* | *Singular* | *Plural* |
| 1st person | I was loving -<br>Јас љ**у**бев<br>*Jas lj**u**bev* | We were loving -<br>Ние љ**у**бевме<br>*Nie lj**u**bevme* |
| 2nd person | You were loving -<br>Ти љ**у**беше<br>*Ti lj**u**beshe* | You were loving -<br>Вие љ**у**бевте<br>*Vie lj**u**bevte* |
| 3rd person | He/She/It was loving -<br>Тој/Таа/Тоа љ**у**беше<br>Toj/Taa/Toa lj**u**beshe | They were loving -<br>Тие љ**у**беа<br>*Tie lj**u**bea* |

| Present Perfect Simple Tense | | |
|---|---|---|
| *Person* | *Singular* | *Plural* |
| 1st person | I have been loving -<br>Јас сум з**а**љубил(а)<br>Jas sum z**a**ljubil(a) | We have been loving -<br>Ние сме заљ**у**биле<br>Nie sme zalj**u**bile |

| | | |
|---|---|---|
| 2nd person | You have been loving -<br>Ти си **за**љубил(а)<br>Ti si **za**ljubil(a) | You have been loving -<br>Вие сте заљ**у**биле<br>Vie ste zalj**u**bile |
| 3rd person | He/She/It has been loving -<br>Тој/Таа/Тоа **за**љубил(а)(о)<br>Тој/Таа/Тоа **za**ljubil(a)(o) | They have been loving -<br>Тие заљ**у**биле<br>Tie zalj**u**bile |

| Present Perfect Continuous Tense | | |
|---|---|---|
| *Person* | *Singular* | *Plural* |
| 1st person | I have loved -<br>Јас сум љ**у**бел(а)<br>*Jas sum lj**u**bel(a)* | We have loved -<br>Ние сме љ**у**беле<br>*Nie sme lj**u**bele* |
| 2nd person | You have loved -<br>Ти си љ**у**бел(а)<br>*Ti si lj**u**bel(a)* | You have loved -<br>Вие сте љ**у**беле<br>*Vie ste lj**u**bele* |
| 3rd person | He/She/It has loved -<br>Тој/Таа/Тоа љ**у**бел(а)(о)<br>*Toj/Taa/Toa lj**u**bel(a)(o)* | They have loved -<br>Тие љ**у**беле<br>*Tie lj**u**bele* |

| Past Perfect Simple Tense | | |
|---|---|---|
| *Person* | *Singular* | *Plural* |
| 1st person | I had loved -<br>Јас бев **за**љубил(а)<br>*Jas bev **za**ljubil(a)* | We had loved -<br>Ние бевме заљ**у**биле<br>*Nie bevme zalj**u**bile* |
| 2nd person | You had loved -<br>Ти беше **за**љубил(а)<br>*Ti beshe **za**ljubil(a)* | You had loved -<br>Вие бевте заљ**у**биле<br>*Vie bevte zalj**u**bile* |
| 3rd person | He/She/It had loved -<br>Тој/Таа/Тоа беше<br>**за**љубил(а)(о)<br>*Toj/Taa/Toa beshe **za**ljubil(a)(o)* | They had loved -<br>Тие беа заљ**у**биле<br>*Tie bea zalj**u**bile* |

| Future Simple Tense | | |
|---|---|---|
| *Person* | *Singular* | *Plural* |
| 1st person | I will love -<br>Јас ќе љ**у**бам/**за**љубам<br>*Jas kje lj**u**bam/**za**ljubam* | We will love -<br>Ние ќе љ**у**биме/заљ**у**биме<br>*Nie kje lj**u**bime/zalj**u**bime* |
| 2nd person | You will love -<br>Ти ќе љ**у**биш/**за**љубиш<br>*Ti kje lj**u**bish/**za**ljubish* | You will love -<br>Вие ќе љ**у**бите/заљ**у**бите<br>*Vie kje lj**u**bite/zalj**u**bite* |
| 3rd person | He/She/It will love -<br>Тој/Таа/Тоа ќе љ**у**би/**за**љуби<br>*Toj/Taa/Toa kje lj**u**bi/**za**ljubi* | They will love -<br>Тие ќе љ**у**бат/заљ**у**бат<br>*Tie kje lj**u**bat/zalj**u**bat* |

| **used to + infinitive or would + infinitive** | | |
|---|---|---|
| *Person* | *Singular* | *Plural* |
| 1st person | I would love -<br>Јас ќе љ**у**бев/з**а**љубев<br>*Jas kje lj**u**bev/z**a**ljubev* | We would love -<br>Ние ќе љ**у**бевме/залј**у**бевме<br>*Nie kje lj**u**bevme/zalj**u**bevme* |
| 2nd person | You would love -<br>Ти ќе љ**у**беше/залј**у**беше<br>*Ti kje lj**u**beshe/zalj**u**beshe* | You would love -<br>Вие ќе љ**у**бевте/залј**у**бевте<br>*Vie kje lj**u**bevte/zalj**u**bevte* |
| 3rd person | He/She/It would love -<br>Тој/Таа/Тоа ќе<br>љ**у**беше/залј**у**беше<br>*Toj/Taa/Toa kje*<br>*lj**u**beshe/zalj**u**beshe* | They would love -<br>Тие ќе љ**у**беа/залј**у**беа<br>*Tie kje lj**u**bea/zalj**u**bea* |

| **Personal endings for future perfect-in-the-past tense** | | |
|---|---|---|
| *Person* | *Singular* | *Plural* |
| 1st person | I would have loved -<br>Јас ќе сум љ**у**бел/з**а**љубел(а)<br>*Jas kje sum lj**u**bel/z**a**ljubel(a)* | We would have loved -<br>Ние ќе сме љ**у**беле/залј**у**беле<br>*Nie kje sme lj**u**bele/zalj**u**bele* |
| 2nd person | You would have loved -<br>Ти ќе си љ**у**бел/з**а**љубел(а)<br>*Ti kje si lj**u**bel/z**a**ljubel(a)* | You would have loved –<br>Вие ќе сте љ**у**беле/залј**у**беле<br>*Vie kje ste lj**u**bele/zalj**u**bele* |
| 3rd person | He/She/It would have loved -<br>Тој/Таа/Тоа ќе<br>љ**у**бел/з**а**љубел(а)(о)<br>*Toj/Taa/Toa kje*<br>*lj**u**bel/z**a**ljubel(a)(o)* | They would have loved -<br>Тие ќе љ**у**беле/залј**у**беле<br>Tie kje *lj**u**bele/zalj**u**bele* |

***To meet– Се сретнува/Се сретне***

| *Infinitive* | To meet | Се сретнува<br>Se sretnuva |
|---|---|---|

| **Present Simple Tense** | | |
|---|---|---|
| *Person* | *Singular* | *Plural* |
| 1st person | I meet -<br>Јас се сретнувам<br>Jas se sretnuvam | We meet -<br>Ние се сретнуваме<br>Nie se sretnuvame |
| 2nd person | You meet -<br>Ти се сретнуваш<br>Ti se sretnuvash | You meet -<br>Вие се сретнувате<br>Vie se sretnuvate |
| 3rd person | He/She/It meets -<br>Тој/Таа/Тоа се сретнува<br>Toj/Taa/Toa se sretnuva | They meet -<br>Тие се сретнуваат<br>Tie se sretnuvaat |

| **Past Simple Tense** | | |
|---|---|---|
| *Person* | *Singular* | *Plural* |
| 1st person | I met -<br>Јас се сретнав<br>*Jas se sretnav* | We met -<br>Ние се сретнавме<br>*Nie se sretnavme* |
| 2nd person | You met -<br>Ти се сретна<br>*Ti se sretna* | You met -<br>Вие се сретнавте<br>*Vie se sretnavte* |
| 3rd person | He/She/It met -<br>Тој/Таа/Тоа се сретна<br>*Toj/Taa/Toa se sretna* | They met -<br>Тие се сретнаа<br>*Tie se sretnaa* |

| **Past Continuous Tense** | | |
|---|---|---|
| *Person* | *Singular* | *Plural* |
| 1st person | I was meeting -<br>Јас се сретнував<br>*Jas se sretnuvav* | We were meeting -<br>Ние се сретнувавме<br>*Nie se sretnuvavme* |
| 2nd person | You were meeting -<br>Ти се сретнуваше<br>*Ti se sretnuvashe* | You were meeting -<br>Вие се сретнувате<br>*Vie se sretnuvavte* |
| 3rd person | He/She/It was meeting -<br>Тој/Таа/Тоа сретнуваше<br>*Toj/Taa/Toa se sretnuvashe* | They were meeting -<br>Тие се сретнуваа<br>*Tie se sretnuvaa* |

| **Present Perfect Simple Tense** | | |
|---|---|---|
| *Person* | *Singular* | *Plural* |
| 1st person | I have met -<br>Јас сум се сретнал(а)<br>*Jas sum sretnal(a)* | We have met -<br>Ние сме се сретнале<br>*Nie sme sretnale* |

| | | |
|---|---|---|
| 2nd person | You have met -<br>Ти си се ср**е**тнал(а)<br>*Ti si sr**e**tnal(a)* | You have met -<br>Вие сте се ср**е**тнале<br>*Vie ste sr**e**tnale* |
| 3rd person | He/She/It has met -<br>Тој/Таа/Тоа се ср**е**тнал(а)(о)<br>*Toj/Taa/Toa sr**e**tnal(a)(o)* | They have met -<br>Тие се ср**е**тнале<br>*Tie se sr**e**tnale* |

| **Present Perfect Continuous Tense** | | |
|---|---|---|
| *Person* | *Singular* | *Plural* |
| 1st person | I have been meeting -<br>Јас сум се ср**е**тнувал(а)<br>*Jas sum se sr**e**tnuval(a)* | We have been meeting -<br>Ние сме се сретн**у**вале<br>*Nie sme se sretn**u**vale* |
| 2nd person | You have been meeting -<br>Ти си се ср**е**тнувал(а)<br>*Ti si se sr**e**tnuval(a)* | You have been meeting -<br>Вие сте се сретн**у**вале<br>*Vie ste se sretn**u**vale* |
| 3rd person | He/She/It has been meeting -<br>Тој/Таа/Тоа се ср**е**тнувал(а)(о)<br>*Toj/Taa/Toa se sr**e**tnuval(a)(o)* | They have been meeting -<br>Тие се сретн**у**вале<br>*Tie se sretn**u**vale* |

| **Past Perfect Simple Tense** | | |
|---|---|---|
| *Person* | *Singular* | *Plural* |
| 1st person | I had met -<br>Јас сум се ср**е**тнал(а)<br>*Jas bev se sr**e**tnal(a)* | We had met -<br>Ние сме се ср**е**тнале<br>*Nie bevme se sr**e**tnale* |
| 2nd person | You had met -<br>Ти си се ср**е**тнал(а)<br>*Ti beshe se sr**e**tnal(a)* | You had met -<br>Вие сте се ср**е**тнале<br>*Vie ste se sr**e**tnale* |
| 3rd person | He/She/It had met -<br>Тој/Таа/Тоа се ср**е**тнал(а)(о)<br>*Toj/Taa/Toa se sr**e**tnal(a)(o)* | They had met -<br>Тие се ср**е**тнале<br>*Tie se sr**e**tnale* |

| **Future Simple Tense** | | |
|---|---|---|
| *Person* | *Singular* | *Plural* |
| 1st person | I will meet -<br>Јас ќе се ср**е**тнувам/се сретнам<br>*Jas kje se sr**e**tnuvam/ se sretnam* | We will meet -<br>Ние ќе се сретн**у**ваме/се ср**е**тнеме<br>*Nie kje se sretn**u**vame/ se sr**e**tname* |
| 2nd person | You will meet -<br>Ти ќе се ср**е**тнуваш/се ср**е**тнеш<br>*Ti kje se sr**e**tnuvash/se sr**e**tnesh* | You will meet -<br>Вие ќе се сретн**у**вате/ср**е**тнете<br>*Vie kje se sretn**u**vate/ se sr**e**tnate* |
| 3rd person | He/She/It will meet -<br>Тој/Таа/Тоа ќе се ср**е**тнува/се ср**е**тне<br>*Toj/Taa/Toa kje se sr**e**tnuva/se sr**e**tne* | They will meet -<br>Тие ќе се сретн**у**ваат/се ср**е**тнат<br>*Tie kje se sretn**u**vaat/ se sr**e**tnat* |

| used to + infinitive or would + infinitive | | |
|---|---|---|
| *Person* | *Singular* | *Plural* |
| 1st person | I would meet -<br>Јас ќе се сретнував/ се сретнев<br>*Jas kje se sretnuvav/se sretnev* | We would meet -<br>Ние ќе се сретнувавме/се сретневме<br>*Nie kje se sretnuvavme/se sretnevme* |
| 2nd person | You would meet -<br>Ти ќе се сретнуваше/ се сретнеше<br>*Ti kje se sretnuvashe/se sretneshe* | You would meet -<br>Вие ќе се сретнувавте/се сретневте<br>*Vie kje se sretnuvavte/se sretnevte* |
| 3rd person | He/She/It would meet -<br>Тој/Таа/Тоа ќе се сретнуваше/ се сретнеше<br>Toj/Taa/Toa kje se *sretnuvashe/se sretneshe* | They would meet -<br>Тие ќе се сретнуваа/сретнеа<br>*Tie kje se sretnuvaa/se sretnea* |

| Personal endings for future perfect-in-the-past tense | | |
|---|---|---|
| *Person* | *Singular* | *Plural* |
| 1st person | I would have met -<br>Јас ќе сум се сретнувал/се сретнал(а)<br>*Jas kje sum se sretnuval/sretnal(a)* | We would have met -<br>Ние ќе сме сретнувале/се сретнале<br>*Nie kje sme se sretnuvale/sretnale* |
| 2nd person | You would have met -<br>Ти ќе си сретнувал/се сретнал(а)<br>*Ti kje si se sretnuval/sretnal(a)* | You would have met -<br>Вие ќе сте сретнувале/се сретнале<br>*Vie kje ste se sretnuvale/sretnale* |
| 3rd person | He/She/It would have met -<br>Тој/Таа/Тоа ќе сретнувал/се сретнал(а)(о)<br>*Toj/Taa/Toa kje se sretnuval/sretnal(a)(o)* | They would have met -<br>Тие ќе се сретнувале/се сретнале<br>*Tie kje se sretnuvale/sretnale* |

***To need – Треба/Притреба***

| | | |
|---|---|---|
| *Infinitive* | To need | Тр**е**ба<br>Tr**e**ba |

| Present Simple Tense | | |
|---|---|---|
| *Person* | *Singular* | *Plural* |
| 1st person | I need -<br>Јас тр**е**бам<br>*Jas tr**e**bam* | We need -<br>Ние тр**е**баме<br>*Nie tr**e**bame* |
| 2nd person | You need -<br>Ти тр**е**баш<br>*Ti tr**e**bash* | You need -<br>Вие тр**е**бате<br>*Vie tr**e**bate* |
| 3rd person | He/She/It needs -<br>Тој/Таа/Тоа тр**е**ба<br>*Toj/Taa/Toa tr**e**ba* | They need -<br>Тие тр**е**баат<br>*Tie tr**e**baat* |

| Past Simple Tense | | |
|---|---|---|
| *Person* | *Singular* | *Plural* |
| 1st person | I needed -<br>Јас пр**и**требав<br>*Jas pr**i**trebav* | We needed -<br>Ние притр**е**бавме<br>*Nie pritr**e**bavme* |
| 2nd person | You needed -<br>Ти пр**и**треба<br>*Ti pr**i**treba* | You needed -<br>Вие притр**е**бавате<br>*Vie pritr**e**bavte* |
| 3rd person | He/She/It needed -<br>Тој/Таа/Тоа пр**и**треба<br>*Toj/Taa/Toa pr**i**treba* | They needed -<br>Тие притр**е**баа<br>*Tie pritr**e**baa* |

| Past Continuous Tense | | |
|---|---|---|
| *Person* | *Singular* | *Plural* |
| 1st person | I was needing-<br>Јас тр**е**бав<br>*Jas tr**e**bav* | We were needing -<br>Ние тр**е**бавме<br>*Nie tr**e**bavme* |
| 2nd person | You were needing -<br>Ти тр**е**баше<br>*Ti tr**e**bashe* | You were needing -<br>Вие тр**е**бавте<br>*Vie tr**e**bavte* |
| 3rd person | He/She/It was needing -<br>Тој/Таа/Тоа тр**е**баше<br>*Toj/Taa/Toa tr**e**bashe* | They were needing -<br>Тие тр**е**баа<br>*Tie tr**e**baa* |

| Present Perfect Simple Tense | | |
|---|---|---|
| *Person* | *Singular* | *Plural* |
| 1st person | I have needed -<br>Јас сум пр**и**требал(а)<br>*Jas sum pr**i**trebal(a)* | We have needed -<br>Ние сме притр**е**бале<br>*Nie sme prit**e**rbale* |

| | | |
|---|---|---|
| 2nd person | You have needed - Ти си притребал(а) *Ti si pritrebal(a)* | You have needed - Вие сте притребале *Vie ste pritrebale* |
| 3rd person | He/She/It has needed - Тој/Таа/Тоа притребал(а)(о) *Toj/Taa/Toa pritrebal(a)(o)* | They have needed - Тие притребале *Tie pritrebale* |

| Present Perfect Continuous Tense | | |
|---|---|---|
| *Person* | *Singular* | *Plural* |
| 1st person | I have been needing - Јас сум требал(а) *Jas sum trebal(a)* | We have been needing - Ние сме требале *Nie sme trebale* |
| 2nd person | You have been needing - Ти си требал(а) *Ti si trebal(a)* | You have been needing - -Вие сте требале *Vie ste trebale* |
| 3rd person | He/She/It has been needing - Тој/Таа/Тоа требал(а)(о) *Toj/Taa/Toa trebal(a)(o)* | They have been needing - Тие требале *Tie trebale* |

| Past Perfect Simple Tense | | |
|---|---|---|
| *Person* | *Singular* | *Plural* |
| 1st person | I had needed - Јас бев притребал(а) *Jas bev pritrebal(a)* | We had needed - Ние бевме притребале *Nie bevme pritrebale* |
| 2nd person | You had needed - Ти беше притребал(а) *Ti beshe pritrebal(a)* | You had needed - Вие бевте притребале *Vie bevte pritrebale* |
| 3rd person | He/She/It had needed - Тој/Таа/Тоа беше притребал(а)(о) *Toj/Taa/Toa beshe pritrebal(a)(o)* | They had needed - Тие беа притребале *Tie bea pritrebale* |

| Future Simple Tense | | |
|---|---|---|
| *Person* | *Singular* | *Plural* |
| 1st person | I will need - Јас ќе требам/притребам *Jas kje terbam/pritrebam* | We will need - Ние ќе требаме/притребаме *Nie kje trebame/pritrebame* |
| 2nd person | You will need - Ти ќе требаш/притребаш *Ti kje trebash/pritrebash* | You will need - Вие ќе требате/притребате *Vie kje trebate/pritrebate* |
| 3rd person | He/She/It will need - Тој/Таа/Тоа Тој ќе треба/притреба *Toj/Taa/Toa kje treba/pritreba* | They will need - Тие ќе требат/притребат *Tie kje trebat/pritrebat* |

| used to + infinitive or would + infinitive | | |
|---|---|---|
| *Person* | *Singular* | *Plural* |
| 1st person | I would need -<br>Јас ќе тр**е**бав/пр**и**требав<br>*Jas kje tr**e**bav/pr**i**trebav* | We would need -<br>Ние ќе тр**е**бавме/притр**е**бавте<br>*Nie kje tr**e**bavme/pritr**e**bavme* |
| 2nd person | You would need -<br>Ти ќе тр**е**баше/притр**е**баше<br>*Ti kje tr**e**bashe/pritr**e**bashe* | You would need -<br>Вие ќе тр**е**бавте/притр**е**бавте<br>*Vie kje tr**e**bavte/pritr**e**bavte* |
| 3rd person | He/She/It would need -<br>Тој/Таа/Тоа ќе<br>тр**е**баше/притр**е**баше<br>*Toj/Taa/Toa kje*<br>*tr**e**bashe/pritr**e**bashe* | They would need -<br>Тие ќе тр**е**баа/притр**е**баа<br>*Tie kje tr**e**baa/pritr**e**baa* |

| Personal endings for future perfect-in-the-past tense | | |
|---|---|---|
| *Person* | *Singular* | *Plural* |
| 1st person | I would have needed -<br>Јас ќе сум тр**е**бал/пр**и**требал(а)<br>*Jas kje sum tr**e**bal/pr**i**trebal(a)* | We would have needed -<br>Ние ќе сме<br>тр**е**бале/притр**е**бале<br>*Nie kje sme tr**e**bale/pritr**e**bale* |
| 2nd person | You would have needed -<br>Ти ќе си тр**е**бал/пр**и**требал(а)<br>*Ti kje si tr**e**bal/pr**i**trebal(a)* | You would have needed -<br>Вие ќе сте тр**е**бале/притр**е**бале<br>*Vie kje ste tr**e**bale/pritr**e**bale* |
| 3rd person | He/She/It would have needed<br>Тој/Таа/Тоа ќе<br>тр**е**бал/пр**и**требал(а)(о)<br>*Toj/Taa/Toa kje*<br>*tr**e**bal/pr**i**trebal(a)(o)* | They would have needed -<br>Тие ќе тр**е**бале/притр**е**бале<br>*Tie kje tr**e**bale/pritr**e**bale* |

***To notice– Забележува/Забележи***

| | | |
|---|---|---|
| *Infinitive* | To notice | Забел**е**жува<br>Zabel**e**zuva |

| Present Simple Tense | | |
|---|---|---|
| *Person* | *Singular* | *Plural* |
| 1st person | I notice -<br>Јас забел**е**жувам<br>*Jas zabel**e**zhuvam* | We notice -<br>Ние забележ**у**ваме<br>*Nie zabelezh**u**vame* |
| 2nd person | You notice -<br>Ти забел**е**жуваш<br>*Ti zabel**e**zhuvash* | You notice -<br>Вие забележ**у**вате<br>*Vie zabelezh**u**vate* |
| 3rd person | He/She/It notices -<br>Тој/Таа/Тоа забел**е**жува<br>*Toj/Taa/Toa zab**e**lezhuva* | They notice -<br>Тие забележ**у**ваат<br>*Tie zabelezh**u**vaat* |

| Past Simple Tense | | |
|---|---|---|
| *Person* | *Singular* | *Plural* |
| 1st person | I noticed -<br>Јас заб**е**лежав<br>*Jas zab**e**lezhav* | We noticed -<br>Ние забел**е**жавме<br>*Nie zabel**e**zhavme* |
| 2nd person | You noticed -<br>Ти заб**е**лежа<br>*Ti zab**e**lezha* | You noticed -<br>Вие забел**е**жавте<br>*Vie zabel**e**zhavte* |
| 3rd person | He/She/It noticed -<br>Тој/Таа/Тоа заб**е**лежа<br>*Toj/Taa/Toa zab**e**lezha* | They noticed -<br>Тие заб**е**лежаа<br>*Tie zabel**e**zhaa* |

| Past Continuous Tense | | |
|---|---|---|
| *Person* | *Singular* | *Plural* |
| 1st person | I was noticing -<br>Јас забел**е**жував<br>Jas zabel**e**zhuvav | We were noticing -<br>Ние забележ**у**вавме<br>*Nie zabelezh**u**vavme* |
| 2nd person | You were noticing -<br>Ти забележ**у**ваше<br>Ti zabelezh**u**vashe | You were noticing -<br>Вие забележ**у**вавте<br>*Vie zabelezh**u**vavte* |
| 3rd person | He/She/It was noticing -<br>Тој/Таа/Тоа забележ**у**ваше<br>Toj/Taa/Toa zabelezh**u**vashe | They were noticing -<br>Тие забележ**у**ваа<br>*Tie zabelezh**u**vaa* |

| Present Perfect Simple Tense | | |
|---|---|---|
| *Person* | *Singular* | *Plural* |
| 1st person | I have noticed-<br>Јас сум заб**е**лежал(а)<br>*Jas sumzab**e**lezhal(a)* | We have noticed -<br>Ние сме забел**е**жале<br>*Nie sme zabel**e**zhale* |

| | | |
|---|---|---|
| 2nd person | You have noticed - Ти си заб**е**лежал(а) *Ti si zab**e**lezhal(a)* | You have noticed - Вие сте забел**е**жале *Vie ste zabel**e**zhale* |
| 3rd person | He/She/It has noticed - Тој/Таа/Тоа заб**е**лежал(а)(о) *Тој/Таа/Тоа zab**e**lezhal(a)(o)* | They have noticed - Тие забел**е**жале *Tie zabel**e**zhale* |

| Present Perfect Continuous Tense | | |
|---|---|---|
| *Person* | *Singular* | *Plural* |
| 1st person | I have been noticing - Јас сум забел**е**жувал(а) *Jas sum zabe**le**zhuval(a)* | We have been noticing - Ние сме забележ**у**вале *Nie sme zabelezh**u**vale* |
| 2nd person | You have been noticing - Ти си забел**е**жувал(а) *Ti si zabel**e**zhuval(a)* | You have been noticing - Вие сте забележ**у**вале *Vie ste zabelezh**u**vale* |
| 3rd person | He/She/It has been noticing - Тој/Таа/Тоа забел**е**жувал(а)(о) *Тој/Таа/Тоа zabel**e**zhuval(a)(o)* | They have been noticing - Тие забележ**у**вале *Tie zabelezh**u**vale* |

| Past Perfect Simple Tense | | |
|---|---|---|
| *Person* | *Singular* | *Plural* |
| 1st person | I had noticed- Јас сум заб**е**лежал(а) *Jas sum zab**e**lezhal(a)* | We had noticed - Ние сме забел**е**жале *Nie sme zabel**e**zhale* |
| 2nd person | You had noticed - Ти си заб**е**лежал(а) *Ti si zab**e**lezhal(a)* | You had noticed - Вие сте забел**е**жале *Vie ste zabel**e**zhale* |
| 3rd person | He/She/It had noticed - Тој/Таа/Тоа заб**е**лежал(а)(о) *Тој/Таа/Тоа zab**e**lezhal(a)(o)* | They had noticed - Тие забел**е**жале *Tie zabel**e**zhale* |

| Future Simple Tense | | |
|---|---|---|
| *Person* | *Singular* | *Plural* |
| 1st person | I will notice - Јас ќе забел**е**жувам/заб**е**лежам *Jas kje zabel**e**zhuvam/zab**e**lezham* | We will notice - Ние ќе забележ**у**ваме/забел**е**жиме *Nie kje zabelezh**u**vame/zabel**e**zhime* |
| 2nd person | You will notice - Ти ќе забел**е**жуваш/заб**е**лежиш *Ti kje zabel**e**zhuvash/zab**e**lezhish* | You will notice - Вие ќе забележ**у**вате/забел**е**жите *Vie kje zabelezh**u**vate/zabel**e**zhite* |

| | | |
|---|---|---|
| 3rd person | He/She/It will notice - Тој/Таа/Тоа ќе забел**е**жува/заб**е**лежи *Toj/Taa/Toa kje zabel**e**zhuva/zab**e**lezhi* | They will notice - Тие ќе забележ**у**ваат/заб**е**лежат *Tie kje zabelezh**u**vaat/zab**e**lezhat* |

| used to + infinitive or would + infinitive | | |
|---|---|---|
| *Person* | *Singular* | *Plural* |
| 1st person | I would notice- Јас ќе забел**е**жував/заб**е**лежав *Jas kje zabel**e**zhuvav/zab**e**lezhav* | We would notice - Ние ќе забележ**у**вавме/забел**е**жавме *Nie kje zabelezh**u**vavme/zabel**e**zhavme* |
| 2nd person | You would notice - Ти ќе забел**е**жуваше/забел**е**жаше *Ti kje zabel**e**zhuvash/zabel**e**zhashe* | You would notice - Вие ќе забележ**у**вавте/забел**е**жавте *Vie kje zabelezh**u**vavte/zabel**e**zhavte* |
| 3rd person | He/She/It would notice - Тој/Таа/Тоа ќе забел**е**жуваше/забел**е**жаше *Toj/Taa/Toa kje zabel**e**zhuvash/zabel**e**zhashe* | They would notice - Тие ќе забележ**у**ваа/забел**е**жаа *Tie kje zabelezh**u**vaa/zabel**e**zhaa* |

| Personal endings for future perfect-in-the-past tense | | |
|---|---|---|
| *Person* | *Singular* | *Plural* |
| 1st person | I would have noticed - Јас ќе сумзабел**е**жувал/заб**е**лежил(а) *Jas kje sumzabel**e**zhuval/zab**e**lezhil(a)* | We would have noticed - Ние ќе сме забележ**у**вале/забел**е**жиле *Nie kje sme zabelezh**u**vale/zabel**e**zhile* |
| 2nd person | You would have noticed - Ти ќе си забел**е**жувал/заб**е**лежил(а) *Ti kje si zabel**e**zhuval/zab**e**lezhil(a)* | You would have noticed - Вие ќе сте забележ**у**вале/забел**е**жиле *Vie kje ste zabelezh**u**vale/zabel**e**zhile* |
| 3rd person | He/She/It would have noticed - Тој/Таа/Тоа ќе забел**е**жувал/заб**е**лежил(а)(о) *Toj/Taa/Toa kje zabel**e**zhuval/zab**e**lezhil(a)(o)* | They would have noticed - Тие ќе забележ**у**вале/забел**е**жиле *Tie kje zabelezh**u**vale/zabel**e**zhile* |

***To open – Отвара/Отвори***

| | | |
|---|---|---|
| *Infinitive* | To open | **О**твара<br>**O**tvara |

| Present Simple Tense | | |
|---|---|---|
| *Person* | *Singular* | *Plural* |
| 1st person | I open -<br>Јас **о**тварам<br>*Jas **o**tvaram* | We open -<br>Ние отв**а**раме<br>*Nie otv**a**rame* |
| 2nd person | You open -<br>Ти **о**твараш<br>*Ti **o**tvarash* | You open -<br>Вие отв**а**рате<br>*Vie otv**a**rate* |
| 3rd person | He/She/It opens -<br>Тој/Таа/Тоа **о**твара<br>*Toj/Taa/Toa**o**tvara* | They open -<br>Тие отв**а**раат<br>*Tie otv**a**raat* |

| Past Simple Tense | | |
|---|---|---|
| *Person* | *Singular* | *Plural* |
| 1st person | I opened -<br>Јас **о**творив<br>*Jas **o**tvoriv* | We opened -<br>Ние отв**о**ривме<br>*Nie otv**o**rivme* |
| 2nd person | You opened -<br>Ти **о**твори<br>*Ti **o**tvori* | You opened -<br>Вие отв**о**ривте<br>*Vie otv**o**rivte* |
| 3rd person | He/She/It opened -<br>Тој/Таа/Тоа **о**твори<br>*Toj/Taa/Toa**o**tvori* | They opened -<br>Тие отв**о**рија<br>*Tie otv**o**rija* |

| Past Continuous Tense | | |
|---|---|---|
| *Person* | *Singular* | *Plural* |
| 1st person | I was opening -<br>Јас **о**тварав<br>*Jas **o**tvarav* | We were opening -<br>Ние отв**а**равме<br>*Nie otv**a**ravme* |
| 2nd person | You were opening -<br>Ти отв**а**раше<br>*Ti otv**a**rashe* | You were opening -<br>Вие отв**а**равте<br>*Vie otv**a**ravte* |
| 3rd person | He/She/It was opening -<br>Тој/Таа/Тоа отв**а**раше<br>*Toj/Taa/Toa otv**a**rashe* | They were opening -<br>Тие отв**а**раа<br>*Tie otv**a**raa* |

| Present Perfect Simple Tense | | |
|---|---|---|
| *Person* | *Singular* | *Plural* |
| 1st person | I have opened -<br>Јас сум **о**творил(а)<br>*Jas sum **o**tvoril(a)* | We have opened -<br>Ние сме отв**о**риле<br>*Nie sme otv**o**rile* |

| | | |
|---|---|---|
| 2nd person | You have opened -<br>Ти си **о**творил(а)<br>*Ti si **o**tvoril(a)* | You have opened -<br>Вие сте отв**о**риле<br>*Vie ste otv**o**rile* |
| 3rd person | He/She/It has opened -<br>Тој/Таа/Тоа **о**творил(а)(о)<br>*Toj/Taa/Toa**o**tvoril(a)(o)* | They have opened -<br>Тие отв**о**риле<br>*Tie otv**o**rile* |

| **Present Perfect Continuous Tense** | | |
|---|---|---|
| *Person* | *Singular* | *Plural* |
| 1st person | I have been opening -<br>Јас сум **о**тварал(а)<br>*Jas sum **o**tvaral(a)* | We have been opening -<br>Ние сме отв**а**рале<br>*Nie sme otv**a**rale* |
| 2nd person | You have been opening -<br>Ти си **о**тварал(а)<br>*Ti si **o**tvaral(a)* | You have been opening -<br>Вие сте отв**а**рале<br>*Vie ste otv**a**rale* |
| 3rd person | He/She/It has been opening -<br>Тој/Таа/Тоа **о**тварал(а)(о)<br>*Toj/Taa/Toa**o**tvaral(a)(o)* | They have been opening -<br>Тие отв**а**рале<br>*Tie otv**a**rale* |

| **Past Perfect Simple Tense** | | |
|---|---|---|
| *Person* | *Singular* | *Plural* |
| 1st person | I had opened -<br>Јас бев **о**творил(а)<br>*Jas bev **o**tvoril(a)* | We had opened -<br>Ние бвме отв**о**риле<br>*Nie bevme otv**o**rile* |
| 2nd person | You had opened -<br>Ти беше **о**творил(а)<br>*Ti beshe **o**tvoril(a)* | You had opened -<br>Вие бевте отв**о**риле<br>*Vie bevte otv**o**rile* |
| 3rd person | He/She/It had opened -<br>Тој/Таа/Тоа беше **о**творил(а)(о)<br>*Toj/Taa/Toa beshe **o**tvoril(a)(o)* | They had opened -<br>Тие беа отв**о**риле<br>*Tie bea otv**o**rile* |

| **Future Simple Tense** | | |
|---|---|---|
| *Person* | *Singular* | *Plural* |
| 1st person | I will open -<br>Јас ќе **о**тварам/**о**творам<br>*Jas kje **o**tvaram/**o**tvoram* | We will open -<br>Ние ќе отв**а**раме/отв**о**риме<br>*Nie kje otv**a**rame/otv**o**rime* |
| 2nd person | You will open -<br>Ти ќе **о**твараш/**о**твориш<br>*Ti kje **o**tvarish/**o**tvorash* | You will open -<br>Вие ќе отв**а**рате/отв**о**рите<br>*Vie kje otv**a**rate/otv**o**rite* |
| 3rd person | He/She/It will open -<br>Тој/Таа/Тоа ќе **о**твара/**о**твори<br>*Toj/Taa/Toa kje **o**tvara/**o**tvori* | They will open -<br>Тие ќе **о**твараат/**о**творат<br>*Tie kje **o**tvaraat/**o**tvorat* |

| **used to + infinitive or would + infinitive** | | |
|---|---|---|
| *Person* | *Singular* | *Plural* |
| 1st person | I would open -<br>Јас ќе **о**тварав/**о**творев<br>*Jas kje **o**tvarav/**o**tvoriv* | We would open -<br>Ние ќе отв**а**равме/отв**о**ревме<br>*Nie kje otv**a**ravme/otv**o**rivme* |

| | | |
|---|---|---|
| 2nd person | You would open -<br>Ти ќе отв**а**раше/отв**о**реше<br>*Ti kje otv**a**rashe/otv**o**reshe* | You would open -<br>Вие ќе отв**а**равте/отв**о**ревте<br>*Vie kje otv**a**ravte/otv**o**rivte* |
| 3rd person | He/She/It would open -<br>Тој/Таа/Тоа ќе<br>отв**а**раше/отв**о**реше<br>*Toj/Taa/Toa kje*<br>*otv**a**rashe/otv**o**reshe* | They would open -<br>Тие ќе отв**а**раа/отв**о**реа<br>*Tie kje otv**a**raa/otv**o**rea* |

| **Personal endings for future perfect-in-the-past tense** | | |
|---|---|---|
| *Person* | *Singular* | *Plural* |
| 1st person | I would have opened -<br>Јас ќе сум **о**тварал/**о**творил(а)<br>*Jas kje sum **o**tvaral/**o**tvoril(a)* | We would have opened -<br>Ние ќе сме отв**а**рале/отв**о**риле<br>*Nie kje sme otv**a**rale/otv**o**rile* |
| 2nd person | You would have opened -<br>Ти ќе си **о**тварал/**о**творил(а)<br>*Ti kje si **o**tvaral/**o**tvoril(a)* | You would have opened -<br>Вие ќе сте отв**а**рале/отв**о**риле<br>*Vie kje ste otv**a**rale/otv**o**rile* |
| 3rd person | He/She/It would have opened-<br>Тој/Таа/Тоа ќе<br>**о**тварал/**о**творил(а)(о)<br>*Toj/Taa/Toa kje*<br>*__o__tvaral/__o__tvoril(a)(o)* | They would have opened -<br>Тие ќе отв**а**рале/отв**о**риле<br>*Tie kje otv**a**rale/otv**o**rile* |

***To play – Игра/Изигра***

| | | |
|---|---|---|
| *Infinitive* | Toplay | **Игра**<br>**I**gra |

| Present Simple Tense | | |
|---|---|---|
| *Person* | *Singular* | *Plural* |
| 1st person | I play -<br>Јас **играм**<br>*Jas **igram*** | We play -<br>Ние **играме**<br>*Nie **igrame*** |
| 2nd person | You play -<br>Ти **играш**<br>*Ti **igrash*** | You play -<br>Вие **играте**<br>*Vie **igrate*** |
| 3rd person | He/She/It plays -<br>Тој/Таа/Тоа**игра**<br>*Toj/Taa/Toa **igra*** | They play -<br>Тие **играат**<br>*Tie **igraat*** |

| Past Simple Tense | | |
|---|---|---|
| *Person* | *Singular* | *Plural* |
| 1st person | I played -<br>Јас **изиграв**<br>*Jas **izigrav*** | We played -<br>Ние изи**гра**вме<br>*Nie izi**gra**vme* |
| 2nd person | You played -<br>Ти **изигра**<br>*Ti **izigra*** | You played -<br>Вие изи**гра**вте<br>*Vie izi**gra**vte* |
| 3rd person | He/She/It played -<br>Тој/Таа/Тоа**изигра**<br>*Toj/Taa/Toa **izigra*** | They played -<br>Тие изи**гра**а<br>*Tie izi**gra**a* |

| Past Continuous Tense | | |
|---|---|---|
| *Person* | *Singular* | *Plural* |
| 1st person | I was playing -<br>Јас **играв**<br>*Jas **igrav*** | We were playing -<br>Ние **играв**ме<br>*Nie **igrav**me* |
| 2nd person | You were playing -<br>Ти **играше**<br>*Ti **igrashe*** | You were playing -<br>Вие **игра**вте<br>*Vie **igra**vte* |
| 3rd person | He/She/It was playing -<br>Тој/Таа/Тоа **играше**<br>*Toj/Taa/Toa **igrashe*** | They were playing -<br>Тие **игра**а<br>*Tie **igra**a* |

| Present Perfect Simple Tense | | |
|---|---|---|
| *Person* | *Singular* | *Plural* |
| 1st person | I have played -<br>Јас сум **изиграл**(а)<br>*Jas sum **izigral**(a)* | We have played -<br>Ние сме изи**гра**ле<br>*Nie sme izi**gra**le* |

| | | |
|---|---|---|
| 2nd person | You have played -<br>Ти си **изиграл**(а)<br>*Ti si **izigral**(a)* | You have played -<br>Вие сте изиграле<br>*Vie ste izigrale* |
| 3rd person | He/She/It has played -<br>Тоj/Таа/Тоа **изиграл**(а)(о)<br>*Toj/Taa/Toa **izigral**(a)(o)* | They have played -<br>Тие изиграле<br>*Tie izigrale* |

| Present Perfect Continuous Tense | | |
|---|---|---|
| *Person* | *Singular* | *Plural* |
| 1st person | I have been playing -<br>Јас сум **играл**(а)<br>*Jas sum **igral**(a)* | We have been playing -<br>Ние сме **играле**<br>*Nie sme **igrale*** |
| 2nd person | You have been playing -<br>Ти си **играл**(а)<br>*Ti si **igral**(a)* | You have been playing -<br>Вие сте **играле**<br>*Vie ste **igrale*** |
| 3rd person | He/She/It has been playing<br>Тоj/Таа/Тоа**играл**(а)(о)<br>*Toj/Taa/Toa **igral**(a)(o)* | They have been playing -<br>Тие **играле**<br>*Tie **igrale*** |

| Past Perfect Simple Tense | | |
|---|---|---|
| *Person* | *Singular* | *Plural* |
| 1st person | I had played -<br>Јас бев **изиграл**(а)<br>*Jas bev **izigral**(a)* | We had played -<br>Ние бевме изиграле<br>*Nie bevme izigrale* |
| 2nd person | You had played -<br>Ти беше **изиграл**(а)<br>*Ti beshe **izigral**(a)* | You had played -<br>Вие бевте изиграле<br>*Vie bevte izigrale* |
| 3rd person | He/She/It had played -<br>Тоj/Таа/Тоа беше **изиграл**(а)(о)<br>*Toj/Taa/Toa beshe **izigral**(a)(o)* | They had played -<br>Тие беа изиграле<br>*Tie bea izigrale* |

| Future Simple Tense | | |
|---|---|---|
| *Person* | *Singular* | *Plural* |
| 1st person | I will play -<br>Јас ќе **играм**/**изиграм**<br>*Jas kje **igram**/**izigram*** | We will play -<br>Ние ќе **играме**/**изиграме**<br>*Nie kje **igrame**/**izigrame*** |
| 2nd person | You will play -<br>Ти ќе **играш**/**изиграш**<br>*Ti kje **igrash**/**izigrash*** | You will play -<br>Вие ќе **играте**/**изиграте**<br>*Vie kje **igrate**/**izigrate*** |
| 3rd person | He/She/It will play -<br>Тоj/Таа/Тоа ќе **игра**/**изигра**<br>*Toj/Taa/Toa kje **igra**/**izigra*** | They will play -<br>Тие ќе **играат**/**изиграат**<br>*Tie kje **igraat**/**izigraat*** |

| used to + infinitive or would + infinitive | | |
|---|---|---|
| *Person* | *Singular* | *Plural* |
| 1st person | I would play -<br>Јас ќе **игра**в/**изигра**в<br>*Jas kje **igra**v/**izigra**v* | We would play -<br>Ние **игра**вме/из**и**гравме<br>*Nie kje **igra**vme/**izigra**vme* |
| 2nd person | You would play -<br>Ти ќе **игра**ше/из**и**граше<br>*Ti kje **igra**she/iz**i**grashe* | You would play -<br>Вие **игра**вте/из**и**гравте<br>*Vie kje **igra**vte/iz**i**gravte* |
| 3rd person | He/She/It would play -<br>Тој/Таа/Тоа **игра**ше/из**и**граше<br>*Тој/Таа/Тоа kje*<br>***igra**she/iz**i**grashe* | They would play -<br>Тие ќе **игра**а/из**и**граа<br>*Tie kje **igra**a/iz**i**graa* |

| Personal endings for future perfect-in-the-past tense | | |
|---|---|---|
| *Person* | *Singular* | *Plural* |
| 1st person | I would have played<br>Јас ќе сум **игра**л/**и**зигрaл(а)<br>*Jas kje sum **igra**l/**i**zigral(a)* | We would have played<br>Ние ќе сме **игра**ле/из**и**грале<br>*Nie kje sme **igra**le/iz**i**grale* |
| 2nd person | You would have played<br>Ти ќе си **игра**л/**и**зигрaл(а)<br>*Ti kje si **igra**l/**i**zigral(a)* | You would have played<br>Вие ќе сте **игра**ле/из**и**грале<br>*Vie kje ste **igra**le/iz**i**grale* |
| 3rd person | He/She/It would have played<br>Тој/Таа/Тоа ќе<br>**игра**л/**и**зигрaл(а)(о)<br>*Тој/Таа/Тоа kje **igra**l/**i**zigral(a)(o)* | They would have played<br>Тие ќе **игра**ле/из**и**грале<br>*Tie kje **igra**le/iz**i**grale* |

***To put – Става/Остави***

| | | |
|---|---|---|
| *Infinitive* | To put | Ст**а**ва<br>St**a**va |

| **Present Simple Tense** | | |
|---|---|---|
| *Person* | *Singular* | *Plural* |
| 1st person | I put -<br>Јасст**а**вам<br>*Jas st**a**vam* | We put -<br>Ние ст**а**ваме<br>*Nie st**a**vame* |
| 2nd person | You put -<br>Ти ст**а**ваш<br>*Ti st**a**vash* | You put -<br>Вие ст**а**вате<br>*Vie st**a**vate* |
| 3rd person | He/She/It puts -<br>Тој/Таа/Тоа ст**а**ва<br>*Toj/Taa/Toa st**a**va* | They put -<br>Тие ст**а**ваат<br>*Tie st**a**vaat* |

| **Past Simple Tense** | | |
|---|---|---|
| *Person* | *Singular* | *Plural* |
| 1st person | I put -<br>Јас **о**ставив<br>*Jas **o**staviv* | We put -<br>Ние ост**а**вивме<br>*Nie ost**a**vivme* |
| 2nd person | You put -<br>Ти **о**стави<br>*Ti **o**stavi* | You put -<br>Вие ост**а**вивте<br>*Vie ost**a**vivte* |
| 3rd person | He/She/It put -<br>Тој/Таа/Тоа**о**стави<br>*Toj/Taa/Toa **o**stavi* | They put -<br>Тие ост**а**вија<br>*Tie ost**a**vija* |

| **Past Continuous Tense** | | |
|---|---|---|
| *Person* | *Singular* | *Plural* |
| 1st person | I was putting -<br>Јас ст**а**вив<br>*Jas st**a**vav* | We were putting -<br>-Ние ст**а**вивме<br>*Nie st**a**vivme* |
| 2nd person | You were putting -<br>Ти ст**а**ви<br>*Tu st**a**vi* | You were putting -<br>-Вие ст**а**вивте<br>*Vie st**a**vivte* |
| 3rd person | He/She/It was putting -<br>Тој/Таа/Тоа ст**а**ви<br>*Toj/Taa/Toa st**a**vi* | They were putting -<br>Тие ст**а**вија<br>*Tie st**a**vija* |

| **Present Perfect Simple Tense** | | |
|---|---|---|
| *Person* | *Singular* | *Plural* |
| 1st person | I have put -<br>Јас сум **о**ставил(а)<br>*Jas sum **o**stavil(a)* | We have put -<br>Ние сме ост**а**виле<br>*Nie sme ost**a**vile* |

| | | |
|---|---|---|
| 2nd person | You have put -<br>Ти си **о**ставил(а)<br>*Ti si **o**stavil(a)* | You have put -<br>Вие сте ост**а**виле<br>*Vie ste ost**a**vile* |
| 3rd person | He/She/It has put -<br>Тој/Таа/Тоа**о**ставил(а)(о)<br>*Toj/Taa/Toa**o**stavil(a)(o)* | They have put -<br>Тие ост**а**виле<br>*Tie ost**a**vile* |

| **Present Perfect Continuous Tense** | | |
|---|---|---|
| *Person* | *Singular* | *Plural* |
| 1st person | I have been putting -<br>Јас сум ст**а**вал(а)<br>*Jas sum st**a**val(a)* | We have been putting -<br>Ние сме ст**а**вале<br>*Nie sme st**a**vale* |
| 2nd person | You have been putting -<br>Ти си ст**а**вал(а)<br>*Ti si st**a**val(a)* | You have been putting -<br>Вие сте ст**а**вале<br>*Vie ste st**a**vale* |
| 3rd person | He/She/It has been putting -<br>Тој/Таа/Тоа ст**а**вал(а)(о)<br>*Toj/Taa/Toa st**a**val(a)(o)* | They have been putting -<br>Тие ст**а**вале<br>*Tie st**a**vale* |

| **Past Perfect Simple Tense** | | |
|---|---|---|
| *Person* | *Singular* | *Plural* |
| 1st person | I had put -<br>Јас бев **о**ставил(а)<br>*Jas bev **o**stavil(a)* | We had put -<br>Ние бевме ост**а**виле<br>*Nie bevme ost**a**vile* |
| 2nd person | You had put -<br>Ти беше **о**ставил(а)<br>*Ti beshe **o**stavil(a)* | You had put -<br>Вие бевте ост**а**виле<br>*Vie bevte ost**a**vile* |
| 3rd person | He/She/It had put -<br>Тој/Таа/Тоа беше **о**ставил(а)(о)<br>*Toj/Taa/Toa beshe **o**stavil(a)(o)* | They had put -<br>Тие беа ост**а**виле<br>*Tie bea ost**a**vile* |

| **Future Simple Tense** | | |
|---|---|---|
| *Person* | *Singular* | *Plural* |
| 1st person | I will put -<br>Јас ќе ст**а**вам/**о**ставам<br>*Jas kje st**a**vam/**o**stavam* | We will put -<br>Ние ќе ст**а**ваме/ост**а**виме<br>*Nie kje st**a**vame/ost**a**vime* |
| 2nd person | You will put -<br>Ти ќе ст**а**ваш/**о**ставиш<br>*Ti kje st**a**vash/**o**stavish* | You will put -<br>Вие ќе ст**а**вате/ост**а**вите<br>*Vie kje st**a**vate/ost**a**vite* |
| 3rd person | He/She/It will put -<br>Тој/Таа/Тоа ќе ст**а**ва/**о**стави<br>*Toj/Taa/Toa kje st**a**ve/**o**stavi* | They will put -<br>Тие ќе ст**а**ваат/**о**стават<br>*Tie kje st**a**vaat/**o**stavat* |

| **used to + infinitive or would + infinitive** | | |
|---|---|---|
| *Person* | *Singular* | *Plural* |
| 1st person | I would put -<br>Јас ќе ст**а**вав/**о**ставев<br>*Jas kje st**a**vav/**o**stavev* | We would put -<br>Ние ќе ст**а**вавме/ост**а**вевме<br>*Nie kje st**a**vavme/ost**a**vevme* |

| | | |
|---|---|---|
| 2nd person | You would put -<br>Ти ќе ст**а**ваше/ост**а**веше<br>*Ti kje st**a**veshe/ost**a**veshe* | You would put -<br>Вие ќе ст**а**вавте/ост**а**вевте<br>*Vie kje st**a**vavte/ost**a**vevte* |
| 3rd person | He/She/It would put -<br>Тој/Таа/Тоа ќе<br>ст**а**ваше/ост**а**веше<br>*Toj/Taa/Toa kje*<br>*st**a**vashe/ost**a**veshe* | They would put -<br>Тие ќе ст**а**ваа/ост**а**веа<br>*Tie kje st**a**vaa/ost**a**vea* |

| **Personal endings for future perfect-in-the-past tense** | | |
|---|---|---|
| *Person* | *Singular* | *Plural* |
| 1st person | I would have put -<br>Јас ќе сум ст**а**вал/**о**ставил(а)<br>*Jas kje sum st**a**val/**o**stavil(a)* | We would have put -<br>Ние ќе сме ќе<br>ст**а**вале/**о**ставиле<br>*Nie kje sme st**a**vale/**o**stavile* |
| 2nd person | You would have put -<br>Ти ќе си ст**а**вал/**о**ставил(а)<br>Ti kje si *st**a**val/**o**stavil(a)* | You would have put -<br>Вие ќе сте ќе ст**а**вале/**о**ставиле<br>*Vie kje ste st**a**vale/ost**a**vile* |
| 3rd person | He/She/It would have put -<br>Тој/Таа/Тоа ќе<br>ст**а**вал/**о**ставил(а)(о)<br>*Toj/Taa/Toa kje*<br>*st**a**val/**o**stavil(a)(o)* | They would have put -<br>Тие ќе ст**а**вале/**о**ставиле<br>*Tie kje st**a**vale/**o**stavile* |

***To read – Чита/Прочита***

| *Infinitive* | Toread | Ч**и**та<br>Ch**i**ta |
|---|---|---|

| **Present Simple Tense** | | |
|---|---|---|
| *Person* | *Singular* | *Plural* |
| 1st person | I read -<br>Јас ч**и**там<br>*Jas ch**i**tam* | We read -<br>Ние ч**и**таме<br>*Nie ch**i**tame* |
| 2nd person | You read -<br>Ти ч**и**таш<br>*Ti ch**i**tash* | You read -<br>Вие ч**и**тате<br>*Vie ch**i**tate* |
| 3rd person | He/She/It reads -<br>Тој/Таа/Тоа ч**и**та<br>*Toj/Taa/Toa ch**i**ta* | They read -<br>Тие ч**и**таат<br>*Tie ch**i**taat* |

| **Past Simple Tense** | | |
|---|---|---|
| *Person* | *Singular* | *Plural* |
| 1st person | I read -<br>Јас пр**о**читав<br>*Jas pr**o**chitav* | We read -<br>Ние проч**и**тавме<br>*Nie proch**i**tavme* |
| 2nd person | You read -<br>Ти пр**о**чита<br>*Ti pr**o**chita* | You read -<br>Вие проч**и**тавте<br>*Vie proch**i**tavte* |
| 3rd person | He/She/It read -<br>Тој/Таа/Тоа пр**о**чита<br>*Toj/Taa/Toa pr**o**chita* | They read -<br>Тие проч**и**таа<br>*Tie proch**i**taa* |

| **Past Continuous Tense** | | |
|---|---|---|
| *Person* | *Singular* | *Plural* |
| 1st person | I was reading -<br>Јас ч**и**тав<br>*Jas ch**i**tav* | We were reading -<br>Ние ч**и**тавме<br>*Nie ch**i**tavme* |
| 2nd person | You were reading -<br>Ти ч**и**таше<br>*Ti ch**i**tashe* | You were reading -<br>Вие ч**и**тавте<br>*Vie ch**i**tavte* |
| 3rd person | He/She/It was reading -<br>Тој/Таа/Тоа ч**и**таше<br>*Toj/Taa/Toa ch**i**tashe* | They were reading -<br>Тие ч**и**таа<br>*Tie ch**i**taa* |

| **Present Perfect Simple Tense** | | |
|---|---|---|
| *Person* | *Singular* | *Plural* |
| 1st person | I have read -<br>Јас сум пр**о**читал(а)<br>*Jas sum pr**o**chital(a)* | We have read -<br>Ние сме проч**и**тале<br>*Nie sme proch**i**tale* |

| | | |
|---|---|---|
| 2nd person | You have read -<br>Ти си прочитал(а)<br>*Ti si prochital(a)* | You have read -<br>Вие сте прочитале<br>*Vie ste prochitale* |
| 3rd person | He/She/It has read -<br>Тој/Таа/Тоа прочитал(а)(о)<br>*Toj/Taa/Toa prochital(a)(o)* | They have read -<br>Тие прочитале<br>*Tie prochitale* |

| **Present Perfect Continuous Tense** | | |
|---|---|---|
| *Person* | *Singular* | *Plural* |
| 1st person | I have been reading -<br>Јас сум читал(а)<br>*Jas sum chital(a)* | We have been reading -<br>Ние сме читале<br>*Nie sme chitale* |
| 2nd person | You have been reading -<br>Ти си читал(а)<br>*Ti si chital(a)* | You have been reading -<br>Вие сте читале<br>*Vie ste chitale* |
| 3rd person | He/She/It has been reading -<br>Тој/Таа/Тоа читал(а)(о)<br>*Toj/Taa/Toa chital(a)(o)* | They have been reading -<br>Тие читале<br>*Tie chitale* |

| **Past Perfect Simple Tense** | | |
|---|---|---|
| *Person* | *Singular* | *Plural* |
| 1st person | I had read -<br>Јас бев прочитал(а)<br>*Jas bev prochital(a)* | We had read -<br>Ние бевме прочитале<br>*Nie bevme prochitale* |
| 2nd person | You had read -<br>Ти беше прочитал(а)<br>*Ti beshe prochital(a)* | You had read -<br>Вие бевте прочитале<br>*Vie bevte prochitale* |
| 3rd person | He/She/It had read -<br>Тој/Таа/Тоа беше<br>прочитал(а)(о)<br>*Toj/Taa/Toa beshe*<br>*prochital(a)(o)* | They had read -<br>Тие беа прочитале<br>*Tie bea prochitale* |

| **Future Simple Tense** | | |
|---|---|---|
| *Person* | *Singular* | *Plural* |
| 1st person | I will read -<br>Јас ќе читам/прочитам<br>*Jas kje chitam/prochitam* | We will read -<br>Ние ќе читаме/прочитаме<br>*Nie kje chitame/prochitame* |
| 2nd person | You will read -<br>Ти ќе читаш/прочиташ<br>*Ti kje chitash/prochitash* | You will read -<br>Вие ќе читате/прочитате<br>*Vie kje chitate/prochitate* |
| 3rd person | He/She/It will read -<br>Тој/Таа/Тоа ќе чита/прочита<br>*Toj/Taa/Toa kje chita/prochita* | They will read -<br>Тие ќе читаат/прочитаат<br>*Tie kje chitaat/prochitaat* |

| used to + infinitive or would + infinitive | | |
|---|---|---|
| *Person* | *Singular* | *Plural* |
| 1st person | I would read - Јас ќе ч**и**тав/пр**о**читав *Jas kje ch**i**tav/pr**o**chitav* | We would read - Ние ќе ч**и**тавме/проч**и**тавме *Nie kje ch**i**tavme/proch**i**tavme* |
| 2nd person | You would read - Ти ќе ч**и**таше/проч**и**таше *Ti kje ch**i**tashe/proch**i**tashe* | You would read - Вие ќе ч**и**тавте/проч**и**тавте *Vie kje ch**i**tavte/proch**i**tavte* |
| 3rd person | He/She/It would read - Тој/Таа/Тоа ќе ч**и**таше/проч**и**таше *Toj/Taa/Toa kje ch**i**tashe/proch**i**tashe* | They would read - Тие ќе ч**и**таа/пр**о**читаа *Tie kje ch**i**taa/pr**o**chitaa* |

| Personal endings for future perfect-in-the-past tense | | |
|---|---|---|
| *Person* | *Singular* | *Plural* |
| 1st person | I would have read - Јас ќе сум ч**и**тал/пр**о**читал(а) *Jas kje sum ch**i**tal/pr**o**chital(a)* | We would have read - Ние ќе сме ч**и**тале/проч**и**тале *Nie kje sme ch**i**tale/proch**i**tale* |
| 2nd person | You would have read - Ти ќе си ч**и**тал/пр**о**читал(а) *Ti kje si ch**i**tal/pr**o**chital(a)* | You would have read - Вие ќе сте ч**и**тале/проч**и**тале *Vie kje ste ch**i**tale/proch**i**tale* |
| 3rd person | He/She/It would have read - Тој/Таа/Тоа ќе ч**и**тал/пр**о**читал(а)(о) *Toj/Taa/Toa kje ch**i**tal/pr**o**chital(a)(o)* | They would have read - Тие ќе ч**и**тале/проч**и**тале *Tie kje ch**i**tale/proch**i**tale* |

## *To receive– Прима/Прими*

| | | |
|---|---|---|
| *Infinitive* | To receive | Прима<br>Prima |

| Present Simple Tense | | |
|---|---|---|
| *Person* | *Singular* | *Plural* |
| 1st person | I receive -<br>Јас примам<br>*Jas primam* | We receive -<br>Ние примаме<br>*Nie primame* |
| 2nd person | You receive -<br>Ти примаш<br>*Ti primash* | You receive -<br>Вие примате<br>*Vie primate* |
| 3rd person | He/She/It receives -<br>Тој/Таа/Тоа прима<br>*Toj/Taa/Toa prima* | They receive -<br>Тие примаат<br>*Tie primaat* |

| Past Simple Tense | | |
|---|---|---|
| *Person* | *Singular* | *Plural* |
| 1st person | I received -<br>Јас примив<br>*Jas primiv* | We received -<br>Ние примивме<br>*Nie primivme* |
| 2nd person | You received -<br>Ти прими<br>*Ti primi* | You received -<br>Вие примивте<br>*Vie primivte* |
| 3rd person | He/She/It received -<br>Тој/Таа/Тоа прими<br>*Toj/Taa/Toa primi* | They received -<br>Тие примија<br>*Ti primija* |

| Past Continuous Tense | | |
|---|---|---|
| *Person* | *Singular* | *Plural* |
| 1st person | I was receiving -<br>Јас примав<br>*Jas primav* | We were receiving -<br>Ние примавме<br>*Nie primavme* |
| 2nd person | You were receiving -<br>Ти примаше<br>*Ti primashe* | You were receiving -<br>Вие примавте<br>*Vie primavte* |
| 3rd person | He/She/It was receiving -<br>Тој/Таа/Тоа примаше<br>*Toj/Taa/Toa primashe* | They were receiving -<br>Тие примаа<br>*Tie primaa* |

| Present Perfect Simple Tense | | |
|---|---|---|
| *Person* | *Singular* | *Plural* |
| 1st person | I have received -<br>Јас сум примил(а)<br>*Jas sum primil(a)* | We have received -<br>Ние сме примиле<br>*Nie sme primile* |

| | | |
|---|---|---|
| 2nd person | You have received -<br>Ти си пр**и**мил(а)<br>*Ti si primil(a)* | You have received -<br>Вие сте пр**и**миле<br>*Vie ste primile* |
| 3rd person | He/She/It has received -<br>Тој/Таа/Тоа пр**и**мил(а)(о)<br>*Toj/Taa/Toa primil(a)(o)* | They have received -<br>Тие пр**и**миле<br>*Tie primile* |

| **Present Perfect Continuous Tense** | | |
|---|---|---|
| *Person* | *Singular* | *Plural* |
| 1st person | I have been receiving -<br>Јас сум пр**и**мал(а)<br>*Jas sum primal(a)* | We have been receiving -<br>Ние сме пр**и**мале<br>*Nie sme primale* |
| 2nd person | You have been receiving -<br>Ти си пр**и**мал(а)<br>*Ti si primal(a)* | You have been receiving -<br>Вие сте пр**и**мале<br>*Vie ste primale* |
| 3rd person | He/She/It has been receiving -<br>Тој/Таа/Тоа пр**и**мал(а)(о)<br>*Toj/Taa/Toa primal(a)(o)* | They have been receiving -<br>Тие пр**и**мале<br>*Tie primale* |

| **Past Perfect Simple Tense** | | |
|---|---|---|
| *Person* | *Singular* | *Plural* |
| 1st person | I had received -<br>Јас бев пр**и**мила(а)<br>*Jas bev primil(a)* | We had received -<br>Ние бевме пр**и**миле<br>*Nie bevme primile* |
| 2nd person | You had received -<br>Ти беше пр**и**мила(а)<br>*Ti beshe primil(a)* | You had received -<br>Вие бевте пр**и**миле<br>*Vie bevte primile* |
| 3rd person | He/She/It had received -<br>Тој/Таа/Тоа беше пр**и**мила(а)(о)<br>*Toj/Taa/Toa beshe primil(a)(o)* | They had received -<br>Тие беа пр**и**миле<br>*Tie bea primile* |

| **Future Simple Tense** | | |
|---|---|---|
| *Person* | *Singular* | *Plural* |
| 1st person | I will receive -<br>Јас ќе пр**и**мам/пр**и**мам<br>*Jas kje primam/primam* | We will receive -<br>Ние ќе пр**и**маме/пр**и**миме<br>*Nie kje primame/primime* |
| 2nd person | You will receive -<br>Ти ќе пр**и**маш/пр**и**миш<br>*Ti kje primash/primish* | You will receive -<br>Вие ќе пр**и**мате/пр**и**мите<br>*Vie kje primate/primite* |
| 3rd person | He/She/It will receive -<br>Тој/Таа/Тоа ќе пр**и**ма/пр**и**ми<br>*Toj/Taa/Toa kje prima/primi* | They will receive -<br>Тие ќе пр**и**маат/пр**и**мат<br>*Tie kje primaat/primat* |

| used to + infinitive or would + infinitive | | |
|---|---|---|
| *Person* | *Singular* | *Plural* |
| 1st person | I would receive -<br>Јас ќе пр**и**мав/пр**и**мив<br>*Jas kje primav/primiv* | We would receive -<br>Ние ќе пр**и**мавме/пр**и**мивме<br>*Nie kje primavme/primivme* |
| 2nd person | You would receive -<br>Ти ќе пр**и**маше/пр**и**мише<br>*Ti kje primashe/primishe* | You would receive -<br>Вие ќе пр**и**мавте/пр**и**мивте<br>*Vie kje primavte/primivte* |
| 3rd person | He/She/It would receive -<br>Тој/Таа/Тоа пр**и**маше/пр**и**мише<br>*Toj/Taa/Toa primashe/primishe* | They would receive -<br>Тие ќе пр**и**маа/пр**и**мија<br>*Tie kje primaa/primija* |

| Personal endings for future perfect-in-the-past tense | | |
|---|---|---|
| *Person* | *Singular* | *Plural* |
| 1st person | I would have received<br>Јас ќе сум пр**и**мал/пр**и**мил(а)<br>*Jas kje sum primal/primil(a)* | We would have received<br>Ние ќе сме пр**и**мале/пр**и**миле<br>*Nie kje sme primale/primile* |
| 2nd person | You would have received<br>Ти ќе си пр**и**мал/пр**и**мил(а)<br>*Ti kje si primal/primil(a)* | You would have received<br>Вие ќе сте пр**и**мале/пр**и**миле<br>*Vie kje ste primale/primile* |
| 3rd person | He/She/It would have received<br>Тој/Таа/Тоа ќе<br>пр**и**мал/пр**и**мил(а)(о)<br>*Toj/Taa/Toa kje*<br>*primal/primil(a)(o)* | They would have received<br>Тие ќе пр**и**мале/пр**и**миле<br>*Tie kje primale/primile* |

***To remember – Помни/Запомни***

| | | |
|---|---|---|
| *Infinitive* | To remember | П**о**мни<br>P**o**mni |

| **Present Simple Tense** | | |
|---|---|---|
| *Person* | *Singular* | *Plural* |
| 1st person | I remember -<br>Јас п**о**мнам<br>*Jas p**o**mnam* | We remember -<br>Ние п**о**мниме<br>*Nie p**o**mnime* |
| 2nd person | You remember -<br>Ти п**о**мниш<br>*Ti p**o**nish* | You remember -<br>Вие п**о**мните<br>*Vie p**o**mnite* |
| 3rd person | He/She/It remembers -<br>Тој/Таа/Тоа п**о**мни<br>*Toj/Taa/Toa p**o**mni* | They remember -<br>Тие п**о**мнат<br>*Tie p**o**mnat* |

| **Past Simple Tense** | | |
|---|---|---|
| *Person* | *Singular* | *Plural* |
| 1st person | I remembered -<br>Јас з**а**помнив<br>*Jas z**a**pomniv* | We remembered -<br>Ние зап**о**мнивме<br>*Nie zap**o**mnivme* |
| 2nd person | You remembered -<br>Ти з**а**помни<br>*Ti z**a**pomni* | You remembered -<br>Вие зап**о**мнивте<br>*Vie zap**o**mnivte* |
| 3rd person | He/She/It remembered -<br>Тој/Таа/Тоа з**а**помни<br>*Toj/Taa/Toa z**a**pomni* | They remembered -<br>Тие зап**о**мнија<br>*Tie zap**o**mnija* |

| **Past Continuous Tense** | | |
|---|---|---|
| *Person* | *Singular* | *Plural* |
| 1st person | I was remembering -<br>Јас п**о**мнев<br>*Jas p**o**mnev* | We were remembering -<br>Ние п**о**мневме<br>*Nie p**o**mnevme* |
| 2nd person | You were remembering -<br>Ти п**о**мнеше<br>*Ti p**o**mneshe* | You were remembering -<br>Вие п**о**мневте<br>*Vie p**o**mnevte* |
| 3rd person | He/She/It was remembering -<br>Тој/Таа/Тоа п**о**мнеше<br>*Toj/Taa/Toa p**o**mneshe* | They were remembering -<br>Тие п**о**мнеа<br>*Tie p**o**mnea* |

| **Present Perfect Simple Tense** | | |
|---|---|---|
| *Person* | *Singular* | *Plural* |
| 1st person | I have remembered -<br>Јас сум з**а**помнил(а)<br>*Jas sum z**a**pomnil(a)* | We have remembered -<br>Ние сме зап**о**мниле<br>*Nie sm zap**o**mnile* |
| 2nd person | You have remembered -<br>Ти си з**а**помнил(а)<br>*Ti si z**a**pomnil(a)* | You have remembered -<br>Вие сте зап**о**мниле<br>*Vie ste zap**o**mnile* |

| | | |
|---|---|---|
| 3rd person | He/She/It has remembered -<br>Тој/Таа/Тоа запомнил(а)(о)<br>*Toj/Taa/Toa zapomnil(a)(o)* | They have remembered -<br>Тие запомниле<br>*Tie zapomnile* |

| **Present Perfect Continuous Tense** | | |
|---|---|---|
| *Person* | *Singular* | *Plural* |
| 1st person | I have been remembering -<br>Јас сум помнел(а)<br>*Jas sum pomnel(a)* | We have been remembering -<br>Ние сме помнеле<br>*Nie sme pomnele* |
| 2nd person | You have been remembering -<br>Ти си помнел(а)<br>*Ti si pomnel(a)* | You have been remembering -<br>Вие сте помнеле<br>*Vie ste pomnele* |
| 3rd person | He/She/It has been remembering<br>-<br>Тој/Таа/Тоа помнел(а)(о)<br>*Toj/Taa/Toa pomnelo(a)(o)* | They have been remembering<br>Тие помнеле<br>*Tie pomnele* |

| **Past Perfect Simple Tense** | | |
|---|---|---|
| *Person* | *Singular* | *Plural* |
| 1st person | I had remembered -<br>Јас бев запомнил(а)<br>*Jas bev zapomnil(a)* | We had remembered -<br>Ние бевме запомниле<br>*Nie bevme zapomnile* |
| 2nd person | You had remembered -<br>Ти беше запомнил(а)<br>*Ti beshe zapomnil(a)* | You had remembered -<br>Вие бевте запомниле<br>*Vie bevte zapomnile* |
| 3rd person | He/She/It had remembered -<br>Тој/Таа/Тоа беше запомнил(а)<br>*Toj/Taa/Toa beshe zapomnil(a)* | They had remembered -<br>Тие беа запомниле<br>*Tie bea zapomnile* |

| **Future Simple Tense** | | |
|---|---|---|
| *Person* | *Singular* | *Plural* |
| 1st person | I will remember -<br>Јас ќе помнам/запомнам<br>*Jas kje pomnam/zapomnam* | We will remember -<br>Ние ќе помниме/запомниме<br>*Nie kje pomnime/zapomnime* |
| 2nd person | You will remember -<br>Ти ќе помнеш/запомниш<br>*Ti kje pomesh/zapomnish* | You will remember -<br>Вие ќе помните/запомните<br>*Vie kje pomnite zapomnite* |
| 3rd person | He/She/It will remember -<br>Тој/Таа/Тоа ќе помне/запомни<br>*Toj/Taa/Toa kje pomne/zapomni* | They will remember -<br>Тие ќе помнат/запомнат<br>*Tie kje pomnat/zapomnat* |

| **used to + infinitive or would + infinitive** | | |
|---|---|---|
| *Person* | *Singular* | *Plural* |
| 1st person | I would remember -<br>Јас ќе помнев/запомнев<br>*Jas kje pomnev/zapomnev* | We would remember -<br>Ние ќе помневме/запомнивме<br>Nie kje *ponevme/zapomnivme* |

| | | |
|---|---|---|
| 2nd person | You would remember - Ти ќе п**о**мнеше/зап**о**мнише *Ti kje p**o**mneshe/zap**o**mnishe* | You would remember - Вие ќе п**о**мневте/зап**о**мнивте *Vie kjep**o**mnevte/zap**o**mnivte* |
| 3rd person | He/She/It would remember - Тој/Таа/Тоаќе п**о**мнеше/зап**о**мнише *Toj/Taa/Toakje p**o**mneshe/zap**o**mnishe* | They would remember - Тие ќе п**о**мнеа/зап**о**мнија *Tie kje p**o**mnat/zap**o**mnija* |

| Personal endings for future perfect-in-the-past tense | | |
|---|---|---|
| *Person* | *Singular* | *Plural* |
| 1st person | I would have remembered - Јас ќе сум п**о**мнел/з**а**помнил(а) *Jas kj sum p**o**mnel/z**a**pomnil(a)* | We would have remembered - Ние ќе сме п**о**мнеле/зап**о**мниле *Nie kje sme p**o**mnele/zap**o**mnile* |
| 2nd person | You would have remembered-Ти ќе си п**о**мнел/з**а**помнил(а) *Ti kje si p**o**mnel/z**a**pomnil(a)* | You would have remembered- Вие ќе сте п**о**мнеле/зап**о**мниле *Vie kje ste p**o**mnele/zap**o**mnile* |
| 3rd person | He/She/It would have remembered - Тој/Таа/Тоа ќе п**о**мнел/з**а**помнил(а)(о) *Toj/Taa/Toa kje p**o**mnel/z**a**pomnil(a)(o)* | They would have remembered Тие ќе п**о**мнеле/зап**о**мниле *Tie kje p**o**mnele/zap**o**mnile* |

***To repeat– Повторува/Повтори***

| | | |
|---|---|---|
| Infinitive | To repeat | Повт**о**рува<br>Povt**o**ruva |

| Present Simple Tense | | |
|---|---|---|
| *Person* | *Singular* | *Plural* |
| 1st person | I repeat -<br>Јас повт**о**рувам<br>*Jas povt**o**ruvam* | We repeat -<br>Ние повтор**у**ваме<br>*Nie povtor**u**vame* |
| 2nd person | You repeat -<br>Ти повт**о**руваш<br>*Ti povt**o**ruvash* | You repeat -<br>Вие повтор**у**вате<br>*Vie povtor**u**vate* |
| 3rd person | He/She/It repeats -<br>Тој/Таа/Тоа повт**о**рува<br>*Toj/Taa/Toa povt**o**ruva* | They repeat -<br>Тие повтор**у**ваат<br>*Tie povtor**u**vaat* |

| Past Simple Tense | | |
|---|---|---|
| *Person* | *Singular* | *Plural* |
| 1st person | I repeated -<br>Јас п**о**вторив<br>*Jas p**o**vtoriv* | We repeated -<br>Ние повт**о**ривме<br>*Nie povt**o**rivme* |
| 2nd person | You repeated -<br>Ти п**о**втори<br>*Ti p**o**vtori* | You repeated -<br>Вие повт**о**рувавте<br>*Vie povt**o**rivte* |
| 3rd person | He/She/It repeated -<br>Тој/Таа/Тоа п**о**втори<br>*Toj/Taa/Toa p**o**vtori* | They repeated -<br>Тие повт**о**рија<br>*Tie povt**o**rija* |

| Past Continuous Tense | | |
|---|---|---|
| *Person* | *Singular* | *Plural* |
| 1st person | I was repeating -<br>Јас повт**о**рував<br>*Jas povt**o**ruvav* | We were repeating -<br>Ние повтор**у**вавме<br>*Nie povtor**u**vavme* |
| 2nd person | You were repeating -<br>Ти повтор**у**ваше<br>*Ti povtor**u**vashe* | You were repeating -<br>Вие повтор**у**вавте<br>*Vie povtor**u**vavte* |
| 3rd person | He/She/It was repeating -<br>Тој/Таа/Тоа повтор**у**ваше<br>*Toj/Taa/Toapovtor**u**vashe* | They were repeating -<br>Тие повтор**у**ваа<br>*Tie povtor**u**vaa* |

| Present Perfect Simple Tense | | |
|---|---|---|
| *Person* | *Singular* | *Plural* |
| 1st person | I have repeated -<br>Јас сум п**о**вторил(а)<br>*Jas sum p**o**vtoril(a)* | We have repeated -<br>Ние сме повт**о**риле<br>*Nie sme povt**o**rile* |

| | | |
|---|---|---|
| 2nd person | You have repeated -<br>Ти си повторил(а)<br>*Ti si povtoril(a)* | You have repeated -<br>Вие сте повториле<br>*Vie ste povtorile* |
| 3rd person | He/She/It has repeated -<br>Тој/Таа/Тоа повторил(а)(о)<br>*Toj/Taa/Toa povtoril(a)(o)* | They have repeated -<br>Тие повториле<br>*Tie povtorile* |

| **Present Perfect Continuous Tense** | | |
|---|---|---|
| *Person* | *Singular* | *Plural* |
| 1st person | I have been repeating -<br>Јас сум повторувал(а)<br>*Jas sum povtoruval(a)* | We have been repeating -<br>Ние сме повторувале<br>*Nie sme povtoruvale* |
| 2nd person | You have been repeating -<br>Ти сиповторувал(а)<br>*Ti si povtoruval(a)* | You have been repeating -<br>Вие сте повторувале<br>*Vie ste povtoruvale* |
| 3rd person | He/She/It has been repeating-<br>Тој/Таа/Тоа повторувал(а)(о)<br>*Toj/Taa/Toa povtoruval(a)(o)* | They have been repeating -<br>Тие повторувале<br>*Tie povtoruvale* |

| **Past Perfect Simple Tense** | | |
|---|---|---|
| *Person* | *Singular* | *Plural* |
| 1st person | I had repeated -<br>Јас бев повторил(а)<br>*Jas bev povtoril(a)* | We had repeated -<br>Ние бевме повториле<br>*Nie bevme povtorile* |
| 2nd person | You had repeated -<br>Ти беше повторил(а)<br>*Ti beshe povtoril(a)* | You had repeated -<br>Вие бевте повториле<br>*Vie bevte povtorile* |
| 3rd person | He/She/It had repeated -<br>Тој/Таа/Тоа беше<br>повторил(а)(о)<br>*Toj/Taa/Toa beshe povtoril(a)(o)* | They had repeated -<br>Тиебеа повториле<br>*Tie bea povtorile* |

| **Future Simple Tense** | | |
|---|---|---|
| *Person* | *Singular* | *Plural* |
| 1st person | I will repeat -<br>Јас ќе повторувам/повторам<br>*Jas kje povtoruvam/povtoram* | We will repeat -<br>Ние ќе повторуваме/повториме<br>*Nie kje povtoruvame/povtorime* |
| 2nd person | You will repeat -<br>Ти ќе повторуваш/повториш<br>*Ti kje povtoruvash/povtorish* | You will repeat -<br>Вие ќе повторувате/повторите<br>*Vie kje povtoruvate/povtorite* |
| 3rd person | He/She/It will repeat -<br>Тој/Таа/Тоа ќе<br>повторува/повтори<br>*Toj/Taa/Toa kje*<br>*povtoruva/povtori* | They will repeat -<br>Тие ќе повторуваат/повторија<br>*Tie kje povtoruvaat/povtorat* |

| **used to + infinitive or would + infinitive** | | |
|---|---|---|
| *Person* | *Singular* | *Plural* |
| 1st person | I would repeat - Јас ќе повт**о**рував/п**о**вторив *Jas kje povt**o**ruvav/p**o**vtoriv* | We would repeat - Ние ќе повтор**у**вавме/повт**о**ривме *Nie kje povtor**u**vavme/povt**o**rivme* |
| 2nd person | You would repeat - Ти ќе повтор**у**ваше/повт**о**реше *Ti kje povtor**u**vashe/povt**o**reshe* | You would repeat - Вие ќе повтор**у**вавте/повт**о**ривте *Vie kje povtor**u**vavte/povt**o**rivte* |
| 3rd person | He/She/It would repeat - Тој/Таа/Тоа ќе повтор**у**ваше/повт**о**реше *Тој/Таа/Тоа kje povtor**u**vashe/povt**o**reshe* | They would repeat - Тие ќе повтор**у**ваа/повт**о**реа -*Tie kje povtor**u**vaa/povt**o**rea* |

| **Personal endings for future perfect-in-the-past tense** | | |
|---|---|---|
| *Person* | *Singular* | *Plural* |
| 1st person | I would have repeated - Јас ќе сум повт**о**рувал/п**о**вторил(а) *Jas kje sum povt**o**ruval/p**o**vtoril(a)* | We would have repeated - Ние ќе сме повтор**у**вале/повт**о**риле *Nie kje sme povtor**u**vale/povt**o**rile* |
| 2nd person | You would have repeated - Ти ќе си повт**о**рувал/п**о**вторил(а) *Tie kje si povt**o**ruval/p**o**vtoril(a)* | You would have repeated - Вие ќе сте повтор**у**вале/повт**о**риле *Vie kje ste povtor**u**vale/povt**o**rile* |
| 3rd person | He/She/It would have repeated - Тој/Таа/Тоа ќе повт**о**рувал/п**о**вторил(а)(о) *Тој/Таа/Тоа kje povt**o**ruval/p**o**vtoril(a)(o)* | They would have repeated - Тие ќе повтор**у**вале/повт**о**риле *Tie kje povtor**u**vale/povt**o**rile* |

***To return –Враќа/Врати***

| | | |
|---|---|---|
| *Infinitive* | To return | Вр**а**ќа<br>Vr**a**kja |

| Present Simple Tense | | |
|---|---|---|
| *Person* | *Singular* | *Plural* |
| 1st person | I return -<br>Јас вр**а**ќам<br>*Jas vr**a**kjam* | We return -<br>Ние вр**а**ќаме<br>*Nie vr**a**kjame* |
| 2nd person | You return -<br>Ти вр**а**ќаш<br>*Ti vr**a**kjash* | You return -<br>Вие вр**а**ќате<br>*Vie vr**a**kjate* |
| 3rd person | He/She/It returns -<br>Тој/Таа/Тоа вр**а**ќа<br>*Toj/Taa/Toa vr**a**kja* | They return -<br>Тие вр**а**ќаат<br>*Tie vr**a**kjaat* |

| Past Simple Tense | | |
|---|---|---|
| *Person* | *Singular* | *Plural* |
| 1st person | I returned -<br>Јас вр**а**тив<br>*Jas vr**a**tiv* | We returned -<br>Ние вр**а**тивме<br>*Nie vr**a**tivme* |
| 2nd person | You returned -<br>Ти вр**а**ти<br>*Ti vr**a**ti* | You returned -<br>Вие вр**а**тивте<br>*Vie vr**a**tivte* |
| 3rd person | He/She/It returned -<br>Тој/Таа/Тоа вр**а**ти<br>*Toj/Taa/Toa vr**a**ti* | They returned -<br>Тие вр**а**тија<br>*Tie vr**a**tija* |

| Past Continuous Tense | | |
|---|---|---|
| *Person* | *Singular* | *Plural* |
| 1st person | I was returning -<br>Јас вр**а**ќав<br>*Jas vr**a**kjav* | We were returning -<br>Ние вр**а**ќавме<br>*Nie vr**a**kjavme* |
| 2nd person | You were returning -<br>Ти вр**а**ќаше<br>*Ti vr**a**kjashe* | You were returning -<br>Вие вр**а**ќавте<br>*Vie vr**a**kjavte* |
| 3rd person | He/She/It was returning -<br>Тој/Таа/Тоа вр**а**ќаше<br>*Toj/Taa/Toa vr**a**kjashe* | They were returning -<br>Тие вр**а**ќаа<br>*Tie vr**a**kjat* |

| Present Perfect Simple Tense | | |
|---|---|---|
| *Person* | *Singular* | *Plural* |
| 1st person | I have returned -<br>Јас сум вр**а**тил(а)<br>*Jas sum vr**a**til(a)* | We have returned -<br>Ние сме вр**а**тиле<br>*Nie sme vr**a**tile* |

| | | |
|---|---|---|
| 2nd person | You have returned - Ти си вратил(а) *Ti si vratil(a)* | You have returned - Вие сте вратиле *Vie ste vratile* |
| 3rd person | He/She/It has returned - Тој/Таа/Тоа вратил(а)(о) *Toj/Taa/Toa vratil(a)(o)* | They have returned - Тие вратиле *Tie vratile* |

| **Present Perfect Continuous Tense** | | |
|---|---|---|
| *Person* | *Singular* | *Plural* |
| 1st person | I have been returning - Јас сум враќал(а) *Jas sum vrakjal(a)* | We have been returning - Ние сме враќале *Nie sme vrakjale* |
| 2nd person | You have been returning - Ти си враќал(а) *Ti si vrakjal(a)* | You have been returning - Вие сте враќале *Vie ste vrakjale* |
| 3rd person | He/She/It has been returning - Тој/Таа/Тоа враќал(а)(о) *Toj/Taa/Toa vrakjal(a)(o)* | They have been returning - Тие враќале *Tie vrakjale* |

| **Past Perfect Simple Tense** | | |
|---|---|---|
| *Person* | *Singular* | *Plural* |
| 1st person | I had returned - Јас бев вратил(а) *Jas bev vratil(a)* | We had returned - Ние бевме вратиле *Nie bevme vratile* |
| 2nd person | You had returned - Ти беше вратил(а) *Ti beshe vratil(a)* | You had returned - Вие бевте вратиле *Vie bevte vratile* |
| 3rd person | He/She/It had returned - Тој/Таа/Тоа беше вратил(а)(о) *Toj/Taa/Toa beshe vratil(a)(o)* | They had returned - Тие беа вратиле *Tie bea vratile* |

| **Future Simple Tense** | | |
|---|---|---|
| *Person* | *Singular* | *Plural* |
| 1st person | I will return - Јас ќе враќам/вратам *Jas kje vrakjam/vratam* | We will return - Ние ќе враќаме/вратиме *Nie kje vrakjame/vratime* |
| 2nd person | You will return - Ти ќе враќаш/вратиш *Ti kje vrakjash/vratish* | You will return - Вие ќе враќате/вратите *Vie kje vrakjate/vratite* |
| 3rd person | He/She/It will return - Тој/Таа/Тоа ќе враќа/врати *Toj/Taa/Toa kje vrakja/vrati* | They will return - Тие ќе враќаат/вратат *Tie kje vrakjaat/vratat* |

| **used to + infinitive or would + infinitive** | | |
|---|---|---|
| *Person* | *Singular* | *Plural* |
| 1st person | I would return - Јас ќе враќав/вратев *Jas kje vrakjav/vratev* | We would return - Ние ќе враќавме/вратевме *Nie kje vrakjavme/vratevme* |

| | | |
|---|---|---|
| 2nd person | You would return -<br>Ти ќе враќаше/вратеше<br>*Ti kje vrakjashe/vrateshe* | You would return -<br>Вие ќе враќавте/вратевте<br>*Vie kje vrakjavte/vratevme* |
| 3rd person | He/She/It would return -<br>Тој/Таа/Тоа ќе враќаше/вратеше<br>*Toj/Taa/Toa vrakjashe/vrateshe* | They would return -<br>Тие ќе враќаа/вратеа<br>*Tie kje vrakjaa/vratea* |

| Personal endings for future perfect-in-the-past tense | | |
|---|---|---|
| *Person* | *Singular* | *Plural* |
| 1st person | I would have returned -<br>Јас ќе сум враќал/врател(а)<br>*Jas kje sum vrakjal/vratel(a)* | We would have returned -<br>Ние ќе сме враќале/врателе<br>*Nie kje sme vrakjale/vratele* |
| 2nd person | You would have returned -<br>Ти ќе си враќал/врател(а)<br>*Ti kje si vrakjal/vratel(a)* | You would have returned -<br>Вие ќе сте враќале/врателе<br>*Vie kje ste vrakjale/vratele* |
| 3rd person | He/She/It would have returned<br>Тој/Таа/Тоа ќе враќал/врател(а)(о)<br>*Toj/Taa/Toa kje vrakjal/vratel(a)(o)* | They would have returned -<br>Тие ќе враќале/врателе<br>*Tie kjevrakjale/vratele* |

**To run – Трча/Истрча**

| | | |
|---|---|---|
| Infinitive | To run | Т**р**ча<br>T**r**cha |

| Present Simple Tense | | |
|---|---|---|
| *Person* | *Singular* | *Plural* |
| 1st person | I run -<br>Јас т**р**чам<br>*Jas trcham* | *We run -*<br>Ние т**р**чаме<br>*Nie trchame* |
| 2nd person | You run -<br>Ти т**р**чаш<br>*Ti trchash* | You run -<br>Вие т**р**чате<br>*Vie trchate* |
| 3rd person | He/She/It runs -<br>Тој/Таа/Тоа т**р**ча<br>*Toj/Taa/Toa trcha* | They run -<br>Тие т**р**чат<br>*Tie trchaat* |

| Past Simple Tense | | |
|---|---|---|
| *Person* | *Singular* | *Plural* |
| 1st person | I ran -<br>Јас **и**стрчав<br>*Jas istrchav* | We ran -<br>Ние ист**р**чавме<br>*Nie istrchavme* |
| 2nd person | You ran -<br>Ти **и**стрча<br>*Ti istrcha* | You ran -<br>Вие ист**р**чавте<br>*Vie istrchavte* |
| 3rd person | He/She/It ran -<br>Тој/Таа/Тоа **и**стрча<br>*Toj/Taa/Toa istrcha* | They ran -<br>Тие ист**р**чаа<br>*Tie istrchaa* |

| Past Continuous Tense | | |
|---|---|---|
| *Person* | *Singular* | *Plural* |
| 1st person | I was running -<br>Јас т**р**чав<br>*Jas trchav* | We were running -<br>Ние т**р**чавме<br>*Nie trchavme* |
| 2nd person | You were running -<br>Ти т**р**чаше<br>*Ti trchashe* | You were running -<br>Вие т**р**чавте<br>*Vie trchavte* |
| 3rd person | He/She/It was running -<br>Тој/Таа/Тоа т**р**чаше<br>*Toj/Taa/Toa trchashe* | They were running -<br>Тие т**р**чаа<br>*Tie trcaa* |

| Present Perfect Simple Tense | | |
|---|---|---|
| *Person* | *Singular* | *Plural* |
| 1st person | I have run -<br>Јас сум **и**стрчал(а)<br>*Jas sum istrchal(a)* | We have run -<br>Ние сме ист**р**чале<br>*Nie sme istrchale* |

| | | |
|---|---|---|
| 2nd person | You have run -<br>Ти си **и**стрчал(а)<br>*Ti si **i**strchal(a)* | You have run -<br>Вие сте ист**р**чале<br>*Vie ste ist**r**chale* |
| 3rd person | He/She/It has run -<br>Тој/Таа/Тоа **и**стрчал(а)(о)<br>*Toj/Taa/Toa **i**strchal(a)(o)* | They have run -<br>Тие ист**р**чале<br>*Tie ist**r**chale* |

| Present Perfect Continuous Tense | | |
|---|---|---|
| *Person* | *Singular* | *Plural* |
| 1st person | I have been running -<br>Јас сум т**р**чал(а)<br>*Jas sum t**r**chal(a)* | We have been running -<br>Ние сме т**р**чале<br>*Nie sme t**r**chale* |
| 2nd person | You have been running -<br>Ти си т**р**чал(а)<br>*Ti si t**r**chal(a)* | You have been running -<br>Вие сте т**р**чале<br>*Vie ste t**r**chale* |
| 3rd person | He/She/It has been running -<br>Тој/Таа/Тоа т**р**чал(а)(о)<br>*Toj/Taa/Toa t**r**chal(a)(o)* | They have been running -<br>Тие т**р**чале<br>*Tie t**r**chale* |

| Past Perfect Simple Tense | | |
|---|---|---|
| *Person* | *Singular* | *Plural* |
| 1st person | I had run -<br>Јас бев **и**стрчал(а)<br>*Jas bev **i**strchal(a)* | We had run -<br>Ние бевме ист**р**чале<br>*Nie bevme ist**r**chale* |
| 2nd person | You had run -<br>Ти беше **и**стрчал(а)<br>*Ti beshe **i**strchal(a)* | You had run -<br>Вие бевте ист**р**чале<br>*Vie bevte ist**r**chale* |
| 3rd person | He/She/It had run -<br>Тој/Таа/Тоа беше **и**стрчал(а)(о)<br>*Toj/Taa/Toa beshe **i**strchal(a)(o)* | They had run -<br>Тие беа ист**р**чале<br>*Tie bea ist**r**chale* |

| Future Simple Tense | | |
|---|---|---|
| *Person* | *Singular* | *Plural* |
| 1st person | I will run -<br>Јас ќе т**р**чам/**и**стрчам<br>*Jas kje t**r**cham/**i**strcham* | We will run -<br>Ние ќе т**р**чаме/ист**р**чаме<br>*Nie kje t**r**chame/ist**r**chame* |
| 2nd person | You will run -<br>Ти ќе т**р**чаш/**и**стрчаш<br>*Ti kje t**r**chash/**i**strchash* | You will run -<br>Вие ќе т**р**чате/ист**р**чате<br>*Vie kje t**r**chate/ist**r**chate* |
| 3rd person | He/She/It will run -<br>Тој/Таа/Тоа ќе т**р**ча/**и**стрча<br>*Toj/Taa/Toa kje t**r**cha/**i**strcha* | They will run -<br>Тие ќе т**р**чаат/ист**р**чаат<br>*Tie kje t**r**chaat/ist**r**chaat* |

| used to + infinitive or would + infinitive | | |
|---|---|---|
| *Person* | *Singular* | *Plural* |
| 1st person | I would run -<br>Јас ќе т**р**чав/**и**стрчав<br>*Jas kje t**r**chav/**i**strchav* | We would run -<br>Ние ќе т**р**чавме/ист**р**чавме<br>*Nie kje t**r**chavme/ist**r**chavme* |

| | | |
|---|---|---|
| 2nd person | You would run -<br>Ти ќе т**р**чаше/ист**р**чаше<br>*Ti kje t**r**chashe/ist**r**chashe* | You would run -<br>Вие ќе т**р**чавте/ист**р**чавте<br>*Vie kje t**r**chavte/ist**r**chavte* |
| 3rd person | He/She/It would run -<br>Тој/Таа/Тоа ќе<br>тр**ч**аше/ист**р**чаше<br>*Toj/Taa/Toa kje*<br>*t**r**chashe/ist**r**chashe* | They would run -<br>Тие ќе т**р**чаа/ист**р**чаа<br>*Tie kje t**r**chaa/ist**r**chaa* |

| **Personal endings for future perfect-in-the-past tense** | | |
|---|---|---|
| *Person* | *Singular* | *Plural* |
| 1st person | I would have run -<br>Јас ќе сум т**р**чал/**и**стрчал(а)<br>*Jas kje sum t**r**chal/**i**strchal(a)* | We would have run -<br>Ние ќе сме т**р**чале/ист**р**чале<br>*Nie kje sme t**r**chale/ist**r**chale* |
| 2nd person | You would have run -<br>Ти ќе си т**р**чал/**и**стрчал(а)<br>*Ti kje si t**r**chal/**i**strchal(a)* | You would have run -<br>Вие ќе сте т**р**чале/ист**р**чале<br>*Vie kje ste t**r**chale/ist**r**chale* |
| 3rd person | He/She/It would have run -<br>Тој/Таа/Тоа ќе<br>т**р**чал/**и**стрчал(а)(о)<br>*Toj/Taa/Toa kje*<br>*t**r**chal/**i**strchal(a)(o)* | They would have run -<br>Тие ќе т**р**чале/ист**р**чале<br>*Tie kje t**r**chale/ist**r**chale* |

***To say – Кажува/Кажа***

| | | |
|---|---|---|
| *Infinitive* | To say | Ка**ж**ува<br>Ka**z**huva |

| Present Simple Tense | | |
|---|---|---|
| *Person* | *Singular* | *Plural* |
| 1st person | I say -<br>Јас к**а**жувам<br>*Jas k**a**zhuvam* | We say<br>Ние кажу**в**аме<br>*Nie kazh**u**vame* |
| 2nd person | You say -<br>Ти к**а**жуваш<br>*Ti k**a**zhuvash* | You say<br>Вие кажу**в**ате<br>*Vie kazh**u**vate* |
| 3rd person | He/She/It says -<br>Тој/Таа/Тоа к**а**жува<br>*Toj/Taa/Toa k**a**zhuva* | They say<br>Тие кажу**в**аат<br>*Tie kazh**u**vaat* |

| Past Simple Tense | | |
|---|---|---|
| *Person* | *Singular* | *Plural* |
| 1st person | I said -<br>Јас к**а**жав<br>*Jas k**a**zhav* | We said -<br>Ние к**а**жавме<br>*Nie k**a**zhavme* |
| 2nd person | You said -<br>Ти к**а**жа<br>*Ti k**a**sha* | You said -<br>Вие к**а**жавте<br>*Vie k**a**zhavte* |
| 3rd person | He/She/It said -<br>Тој/Таа/Тоа к**а**жа<br>*Toj/Taa/Toa k**a**zha* | They said -<br>Тие к**а**жаа<br>*Tie k**a**zhaa* |

| Past Continuous Tense | | |
|---|---|---|
| *Person* | *Singular* | *Plural* |
| 1st person | I was saying -<br>Јас к**а**жував<br>*Jas k**a**zhuvav* | We were saying -<br>Ние кажу**в**авме<br>Nie kazh**u**vavme |
| 2nd person | You were saying -<br>Ти кажу**в**аше<br>*Ti kazh**u**vashe* | You were saying -<br>Вие кажу**в**авте<br>Vie kazh**u**vavte |
| 3rd person | He/She/It was saying -<br>Тој/Таа/Тоа кажу**в**аше<br>*Toj/Taa/Toa kazh**u**vashe* | They were saying -<br>Тие кажу**в**аа<br>Tie kazh**u**vaa |

| Present Perfect Simple Tense | | |
|---|---|---|
| *Person* | *Singular* | *Plural* |
| 1st person | I have said -<br>Јас сум к**а**жал(а)<br>*Jas sum k**a**zhal(a)* | We have said -<br>Ние сме к**а**жале<br>*Nie sme k**a**zhale* |

| | | |
|---|---|---|
| 2nd person | You have said -<br>Ти си к**а**жал(а)<br>*Ti si k**a**zhal(a)* | You have said -<br>Вие сте к**а**жале<br>*Vie ste k**a**zhale* |
| 3rd person | He/She/It has said -<br>Тој/Таа/Тоа к**а**жал(а)(о)<br>*Toj/Taa/Toa k**a**zhal(a)(o)* | They have said -<br>Тие к**а**жале<br>*Tie k**a**zhale* |

| **Present Perfect Continuous Tense** | | |
|---|---|---|
| *Person* | *Singular* | *Plural* |
| 1st person | I have been saying -<br>Јас сум к**а**жувал(а)<br>*Jas sum k**a**zhuval(a)* | We have been saying -<br>Ние сме каж**у**вале<br>Nie sme kazh**u**vale |
| 2nd person | You have been saying -<br>Ти си к**а**жувал(а)<br>*Ti si k**a**zhuval(a)* | You have been saying -<br>Вие сте каж**у**вале<br>*Vie ste kazh**u**vale* |
| 3rd person | He/She/It has been saying -<br>Тој/Таа/Тоа к**а**жувал(а)(о)<br>*Toj/Taa/Toa k**a**zhuval(a)(o)* | They have been saying -<br>Тие каж**у**вале<br>*Tie kazh**u**vale* |

| **Past Perfect Simple Tense** | | |
|---|---|---|
| *Person* | *Singular* | *Plural* |
| 1st person | I had said -<br>Јас бев к**а**жал(а)<br>*Jas bev k**a**zhal(a)* | We had said -<br>Ние бевме к**а**жале<br>*Nie bevme k**a**zhale* |
| 2nd person | You had said -<br>Ти беше к**а**жал(а)<br>*Ti beshe k**a**zhal(a)* | You had said -<br>Вие бевте к**а**жале<br>*Vie bevte k**a**zhale* |
| 3rd person | He/She/It had said -<br>Тој/Таа/Тоа беше к**а**жал(а)(о)<br>*Toj/Taa/Toa beshe k**a**zhal(a)(o)* | They had said -<br>Тие беа к**а**жале<br>*Tie bea k**a**zhale* |

| **Future Simple Tense** | | |
|---|---|---|
| *Person* | *Singular* | *Plural* |
| 1st person | I will say -<br>Јас ќе к**а**жувам/к**а**жам<br>Јас кје k**a**zhuvam/k**a**zhaм | We will say -<br>Ние ќе каж**у**ваме/к**а**жаме<br>Nie kje kazh**u**vame/k**a**zhame |
| 2nd person | You will say<br>Ти ќе к**а**жуваш/к**а**жеш<br>*Ti kjek**a**zhuvash/k**a**zhesh* | You will say<br>Вие ќе каж**у**вате/к**а**жате<br>*Vie kje kazh**u**vate/k**a**zhate* |
| 3rd person | He/She/It will say -<br>Тој/Таа/Тоа ќе к**а**жува/к**а**жа<br>*Toj/Taa/Toa kje k**a**zhuva/k**a**zha* | They will say -<br>Тие ќе каж**у**ваат/к**а**жат<br>*Tie kje kazh**u**vaat/k**a**zhat* |

| **used to + infinitive or would + infinitive** | | |
|---|---|---|
| *Person* | *Singular* | *Plural* |
| 1st person | I would say -<br>Јас ќе к**а**жував/к**а**жав<br>*Jas kje k**a**zhuvav/k**a**zhav* | We would say -<br>Ние ќе каж**у**вавме/к**а**жавме<br>*Nie kje kazh**u**vavme/k**a**zhavme* |

| | | |
|---|---|---|
| 2[nd] person | You would say -<br>Ти ќе каж**у**ваше/к**а**жеше<br>*Ti kje kazh**u**vashe/k**a**zheshe* | You would say -<br>Вие ќе каж**у**вавте/к**а**жавте<br>*Vie kje kazh**u**vavte/k**a**zhavte* |
| 3[rd] person | He/She/It would say -<br>Тој/Таа/Тоа ќе<br>каж**у**ваше/к**а**жеше<br>*Toj/Taa/Toa kje*<br>*kazh**u**vashe/k**a**zheshe* | They would say -<br>Тие ќе к**а**жуваа/к**а**жаа<br>*Tie kje k**a**zhuvaa/k**a**zhaa* |

| **Personal endings for future perfect-in-the-past tense** | | |
|---|---|---|
| *Person* | *Singular* | *Plural* |
| 1[st] person | I would have said -<br>Јас ќе сум к**а**жувал/к**а**жал(а)<br>*Jas kje sum k**a**zhuval/k**a**zhal(a)* | We would have said -<br>Ние ќе сме каж**у**вале/к**а**жале<br>*Nie kje sme kazh**u**vale/k**a**zhale* |
| 2[nd] person | You would have said -<br>Ти ќе си к**а**жувал/к**а**жал(а)<br>*Ti kje si k**a**zhuval/k**a**zhal(a)* | You would have said -<br>Вие ќе сте каж**у**вале/к**а**жале<br>*Vie kje ste kazh**u**vale/k**a**zhale* |
| 3[rd] person | He/She/It would have said -<br>Тој/Таа/Тоа ќе<br>к**а**жувал/к**а**жал(а)(о)<br>*Toj/Taa/Toa kje*<br>*k**a**zhuval/k**a**zhal(a)(o)* | They would have said -<br>Тие ќе каж**у**вале/к**а**жале<br>*Tie kje kazh**u**vale/k**a**zhale* |

### *To scream – Вика/Извика*

| | | |
|---|---|---|
| *Infinitive* | To scream | В**и**ка<br>V**i**ka |

| Present Simple Tense | | |
|---|---|---|
| *Person* | *Singular* | *Plural* |
| 1st person | I scream -<br>Јас **ви**кам<br>*Jas **vi**kam* | We scream -<br>Ние **ви**каме<br>*Nie **vi**kame* |
| 2nd person | You scream -<br>Ти **ви**каш<br>*Ti **vi**kash* | You scream -<br>Вие **ви**кате<br>*Vie **vi**kate* |
| 3rd person | He/She/It screams -<br>Тој/Таа/Тоа **ви**ка<br>*Toj/Taa/Toa **vi**ka* | They scream -<br>Тие **ви**каат<br>*Tie **vi**kaat* |

| Past Simple Tense | | |
|---|---|---|
| *Person* | *Singular* | *Plural* |
| 1st person | I screamed -<br>Јас **из**викав<br>*Jas **iz**vikav* | We screamed -<br>Ние изв**и**кавме<br>*Nie izv**i**kavme* |
| 2nd person | You screamed -<br>Ти **из**вика<br>*Ti **iz**vika* | You screamed -<br>Вие изв**и**кавте<br>*Vie izv**i**kavte* |
| 3rd person | He/She/It screamed -<br>Тој/Таа/Тоа **из**вика<br>*Toj/Taa/Toa **iz**vika* | They screamed -<br>Тие изв**и**каа<br>*Tie izv**i**kaa* |

| Past Continuous Tense | | |
|---|---|---|
| *Person* | *Singular* | *Plural* |
| 1st person | I was screaming -<br>Јас **ви**кав<br>*Jas **vi**kav* | We were screaming -<br>Ние в**и**кавме<br>*Nie v**i**kavme* |
| 2nd person | You were screaming -<br>Ти **ви**каше<br>*Ti **vi**kashe* | You were screaming -<br>Вие в**и**кавте<br>*Vie v**i**kavte* |
| 3rd person | He/She/It was screaming -<br>Тој/Таа/Тоа **ви**каше<br>*Toj/Taa/Toa **vi**kashe* | They were screaming -<br>Тие **ви**каа<br>*Tie **vi**kaa* |

| Present Perfect Simple Tense | | |
|---|---|---|
| *Person* | *Singular* | *Plural* |
| 1st person | I have screamed<br>Јас сум **из**викал(а)<br>*Jas sum **iz**vikal(a)* | We have screamed<br>Ние сме изв**и**кале<br>*Nie sme izv**i**kale* |

| | | |
|---|---|---|
| 2nd person | You have screamed<br>Ти си **извикал(а)**<br>*Ti si **izvikal(a)*** | You have screamed<br>Вие сте изв**и**кале<br>*Vie ste izv**i**kale* |
| 3rd person | He/She/It has screamed<br>Тој/Таа/Тоа **извикал(а)(о)**<br>*Toj/Toa/Taa/Toa **izvikal(a))o)*** | They have screamed<br>Тие изв**и**кале<br>*Tie izv**i**kale* |

| Present Perfect Continuous Tense | | |
|---|---|---|
| *Person* | *Singular* | *Plural* |
| 1st person | I have been screaming -<br>Јас сум **в**икал(а)<br>*Jas sum **v**ikal(a)* | We have been screaming -<br>Ние сме **в**икале<br>*Nie sme **v**ikale* |
| 2nd person | You have been screaming -<br>Ти си **в**икал(а)<br>*Ti si **v**ikal(a)* | You have been screaming -<br>Вие сте **в**икале<br>*Vie ste **v**ikale* |
| 3rd person | He/She/It has been screaming<br>Тој/Таа/Тоа **в**икал(а)(о)<br>*Toj/Taa/Toa **v**ikal(a)(o)* | They have been screaming -<br>Тие **в**икале<br>*Tie **v**ikale* |

| Past Perfect Simple Tense | | |
|---|---|---|
| *Person* | *Singular* | *Plural* |
| 1st person | I had screamed -<br>Јас бев **извикал(а)**<br>Jas bev **izvikal(a)** | We had screamed -<br>Ние бевмеизв**и**кале<br>Nie bevme izv**i**kale |
| 2nd person | You had screamed -<br>Ти беше **извикал(а)**<br>Ti beshe **izvikal(a)** | You had screamed -<br>Вие бевте изв**и**кале<br>Vie bevte izv**i**kale |
| 3rd person | He/She/It had screamed -<br>Тој/Таа/Тоа беше **извикал(а)(о)**<br>Toj/Taa/Toa beshe **i**zvikal(a)(o) | They had screamed -<br>Тие беа изв**и**кале<br>Tie bea izv**i**kale |

| Future Simple Tense | | |
|---|---|---|
| *Person* | *Singular* | *Plural* |
| 1st person | I will scream -<br>Јас ќе **в**икам/**и**звикам<br>Jas kje v**i**kam/**i**zvikam | We will scream -<br>Ние ќе **в**икаме/изв**и**каме<br>Nie kje v**i**kame/izv**i**kame |
| 2nd person | You will scream -<br>Ти ќе **в**икаш/**и**звикаш<br>Ti kje v**i**kash/**i**zvikash | You will scream -<br>-Вие ќе в**и**кате/изв**и**кате<br>Vie kje v**i**kate/izv**i**kate |
| 3rd person | He/She/It will scream -<br>Тој/Таа/Тоа ќе **в**ика/**и**звика<br>Toa/Taa/Toa kje v**i**ka/**i**zvika | They will scream -<br>Тие ќе **в**икаат/изв**и**каат<br>Tie kje v**i**kaat/izv**i**kaat |

| used to + infinitive or would + infinitive | | |
|---|---|---|
| *Person* | *Singular* | *Plural* |
| 1st person | I would scream -<br>Јас ќе **в**икав/изв**и**кав<br>Jas kje v**i**kav/izv**i**kav | We would scream -<br>Ние ќе **в**икавме/изв**и**кавме<br>Nie kje v**i**kavme/izv**i**kavme |

| | | |
|---|---|---|
| 2nd person | You would scream -<br>Ти ќе **ви**каше/изв**и**каше<br>Ti kje v**i**kashe/izvik**a**she | You would scream -<br>Вие ќе **ви**кавте/изв**и**кавте<br>Vie kje v**i**kavte/izv**i**kavte |
| 3rd person | He/She/It would scream -<br>Тој/Таа/Тоа ќе<br>**ви**каше/изв**и**каше<br>Toj/Taa/Toa kje<br>vikashe/izv**i**kuvashe | They would scream -<br>Тие ќе **ви**каа/изв**и**каа<br>ie kje v**i**kaa/izv**i**kaa |

| Personal endings for future perfect-in-the-past tense | | |
|---|---|---|
| *Person* | *Singular* | *Plural* |
| 1st person | I would have screamed -<br>Јас ќе сум **ви**кал/изв**и**кал(а)<br>Jas kje sum v**i**kal/izv**i**kal(a) | We would have screamed -<br>Ние ќе сме **ви**кале/изв**и**кале<br>Nie kje sme v**i**kale/izv**i**kale |
| 2nd person | You would have screamed -<br>Ти ќе си **ви**кал/изв**и**кал(а)<br>Ti kje si v**i**kal/izv**i**kal(a) | You would have screamed -<br>Вие ќе сте **ви**кале/изв**и**кале<br>Vie kje ste v**i**kale/izv**i**kale |
| 3rd person | He/She/It would have screamed -<br>Тој/Таа/Тоа ќе<br>**ви**кал/изв**и**кал(а)(о)<br>Toj/Taa/Toa/Toa kje<br>v**i**kal/izv**i**kal(a)(o) | They would have screamed -<br>Тие ќе **ви**кале/изв**и**кале<br>Tie kje v**i**kale/izv**i**kale |

## *To see – Гледа/Здогледа*

| *Infinitive* | To see | Гл**е**да<br>Gl**e**da |
|---|---|---|

| **Present Simple Tense** | | |
|---|---|---|
| *Person* | *Singular* | *Plural* |
| 1st person | I see -<br>Јас гл**е**дам<br>*Jas gl**e**dam* | We see -<br>Ние гл**е**даме<br>*Nie gl**e**dame* |
| 2nd person | You see -<br>Ти гл**е**даш<br>*Ti gl**e**dash* | You see -<br>Вие гл**е**дате<br>*Vie gl**e**date* |
| 3rd person | He/She/It sees -<br>Тој/Таа/Тоа гл**е**да<br>*Toj/Taa/Toa gl**e**da* | They see -<br>Тие гл**е**даат<br>*Tie gl**e**dat* |

| **Past Simple Tense** | | |
|---|---|---|
| *Person* | *Singular* | *Plural* |
| 1st person | I saw -<br>Јас зд**о**гледав<br>*Jas zd**o**gledav* | We saw -<br>Ние здогл**е**давме<br>*Nie zdogl**e**davme* |
| 2nd person | You saw -<br>Ти зд**о**гледа<br>*Ti zd**o**gleda* | You saw -<br>Вие здогл**е**давте<br>*Vie zdogl**e**davte* |
| 3rd person | He/She/It saw -<br>Тој/Таа/Тоа зд**о**гледа<br>*Toj/Taa/Toa zd**o**gleda* | They saw -<br>Тие здогл**е**даа<br>*Tie zdogl**e**daa* |

| **Past Continuous Tense** | | |
|---|---|---|
| *Person* | *Singular* | *Plural* |
| 1st person | I was seeing -<br>Јас гл**е**дав<br>*Jas gl**e**dav* | We were seeing -<br>Ние гл**е**давме<br>Nie gl**e**davme |
| 2nd person | You were seeing -<br>Ти гл**е**даше<br>*Ti gl**e**dashe* | You were seeing -<br>Вие гл**е**давте<br>*Vie gl**e**davte* |
| 3rd person | He/She/It was seeing -<br>Тој/Таа/Тоа гл**е**даше<br>*Toj/Taa/Toa gl**e**dashe* | They were seeing -<br>Тие гл**е**даа<br>*Tie gl**e**daa* |

| **Present Perfect Simple Tense** | | |
|---|---|---|
| *Person* | *Singular* | *Plural* |
| 1st person | I have seen -<br>Јас сум зд**о**гледал(а)<br>*Jas sum zd**o**gledal(a)* | We have seen -<br>Ние сме здогл**е**дале<br>*Nie sme zdogl**e**dale* |

| | | |
|---|---|---|
| 2nd person | You have seen -<br>Ти си зд**о**гледал(а)<br>*Ti si zd**o**gledal(a)* | You have seen -<br>Вие сте здогл**е**дале<br>*Vie ste zdogl**e**dale* |
| 3rd person | He/She/It has seen -<br>Тој/Таа/Тоа зд**о**гледал(а)(о)<br>*Toj/Taa/Toa zd**o**gledal(a)(o)* | They have seen -<br>Тие здогл**е**дале<br>*Tie zdogl**e**dale* |

| **Present Perfect Continuous Tense** | | |
|---|---|---|
| *Person* | *Singular* | *Plural* |
| 1st person | I have been seeing -<br>Јас сум гл**е**дал(а)<br>*Jas sum gl**e**dal(a)* | We have been seeing -<br>Ние сме гл**е**дале<br>*Nie sme gl**e**dale* |
| 2nd person | You have been seeing -<br>Ти си гл**е**дал(а)<br>*Ti si gl**e**dal(a)* | You have been seeing -<br>Вие сте гл**е**дале<br>*Vie ste gl**e**dale* |
| 3rd person | He/She/It has been seeing -<br>Тој/Таа/Тоа гл**е**дал(а)(о)<br>*Toj/Taa/Toa gl**e**dal(a)(o)* | They have been seeing -<br>Тие гл**е**дале<br>*Tie gl**e**dale* |

| **Past Perfect Simple Tense** | | |
|---|---|---|
| *Person* | *Singular* | *Plural* |
| 1st person | I had seen -<br>Јас бев зд**о**гледал(а)<br>*Jas bev zd**o**gledal(a)* | We had seen -<br>Ние бевме здогл**е**дале<br>*Nie bevme zdogl**e**dale* |
| 2nd person | You had seen -<br>Ти беше зд**о**гледал(а)<br>*Ti beshe zd**o**gledal(a)* | You had seen -<br>Вие бевте здогл**е**дале<br>*Vie bevte zdogl**e**dale* |
| 3rd person | He/She/It had seen - Тој/Таа/Тоа<br>зд**о**гледал(а)(о)<br>*Toj/Taa/Toa beshe*<br>*zd**o**gledal(a)(o)* | They had seen -<br>Тие беа здогл**е**дале<br>*Tie bea zdogl**e**dale* |

| **Future Simple Tense** | | |
|---|---|---|
| *Person* | *Singular* | *Plural* |
| 1st person | I will see-<br>Јас ќе гл**е**дам/зд**о**гледам<br>*Jas kje gl**e**dam/zd**o**gledam* | We will see -<br>Ние ќе гл**е**даме/здогл**е**даме<br>*Nie kje gl**e**dame/zdogl**e**dame* |
| 2nd person | You will see-<br>Ти ќе гл**е**даш/зд**о**гледаш<br>*Ti kje gl**e**dash/zd**o**gledash* | You will see -<br>Вие ќе гл**е**дате/здогл**е**дате<br>*Vie kje gl**e**date/zd**o**gledate* |
| 3rd person | He/She/It will see -<br>Тој/Таа/Тоа ќе гл**е**да/зд**о**гледа<br>*Toj/Taa/Toa kje gl**e**da/zd**o**gleda* | They will see -<br>Тие ќе гл**е**даат/здогл**е**даат<br>*Tie kje gl**e**daat/zdogl**e**daat* |

| **used to + infinitive or would + infinitive** | | |
|---|---|---|
| *Person* | *Singular* | *Plural* |
| 1st person | I would see-<br>Јас ќе гл**е**дав/зд**о**гледав<br>*Jas kje gl**e**dav/zd**o**gledav* | We would see -<br>Ние ќе гл**е**давме/здогл**е**давме<br>*Nie kje gl**e**davme/zdogl**e**davme* |
| 2nd person | You would see -<br>Ти ќе гл**е**даше/здогл**е**даше<br>*Ti kje gl**e**dashe/zdogl**e**dashe* | You would see -<br>Вие ќе гл**е**давте/здогл**е**давте<br>*Vie kje gl**e**davte/zdogl**e**davte* |
| 3rd person | He/She/It would see -<br>Тој/Таа/Тоа<br>глед**а**ше/здогл**е**даше<br>*Toj/Taa/Toa kje*<br>*gl**e**dashe/zdogl**e**dashe* | They would see -<br>Тие ќе гл**е**даа/здогл**е**даа<br>*Tie kje gl**e**daa/zdogl**e**daa* |

| **Personal endings for future perfect-in-the-past tense** | | |
|---|---|---|
| *Person* | *Singular* | *Plural* |
| 1st person | I would have seen -<br>Јас ќе сум гл**е**дал/зд**о**гледал(а)<br>*Jas kje sum gl**e**dal/zd**o**gledal(a)* | We would have seen -<br>Ние ќе сме гл**е**дале/здогл**е**дале<br>*Nie kje sme gl**e**dale/zdogl**e**dale* |
| 2nd person | You would have seen -<br>Ти ќе си гл**е**дал/зд**о**гледал(а)<br>*Ti kje si gl**e**dal/zd**o**gledal(a)* | You would have seen -<br>Вие ќе сте гл**е**дале/здогл**е**дале<br>*Vie kje ste gl**e**dale/zdogl**e**dale* |
| 3rd person | He/She/It would have seen -<br>Тој/Таа/Тоа ќе<br>гл**е**дал/зд**о**гледал(а)(о)<br>*Toj/Taa/Toa kje*<br>*gl**e**dal/zdogl**e**dal(a)(o)* | They would have seen -<br>Тие ќе гл**е**дале/здогл**е**дале<br>*Tie kje gl**e**dale/zdogl**e**dale* |

***To seem – Изгледа***

| | | |
|---|---|---|
| *Infinitive* | To seem | **И**зледа<br>**I**zgleda |

| Present Simple Tense | | |
|---|---|---|
| *Person* | *Singular* | *Plural* |
| 1st person | I seem -<br>Јас **и**згледам<br>*Jas **i**zgledam* | We seem<br>Ние изгл**е**даме<br>*Nie izgl**e**dame* |
| 2nd person | You seem -<br>Ти **и**згледаш<br>*Ti **i**zgledash* | You seem<br>Вие изгл**е**дате<br>*Vie izgl**e**date* |
| 3rd person | He/She/It seems -<br>Тој/Таа/Тоа **и**згледа<br>*Toj/Taa/Toa **i**zgleda* | They seem<br>Тие изгл**е**даат<br>*Tie izgl**e**dat* |

| Past Simple Tense | | |
|---|---|---|
| *Person* | *Singular* | *Plural* |
| 1st person | / | / |
| 2nd person | / | / |
| 3rd person | / | / |

**this verb does not have a perfective form*

| Past Continuous Tense | | |
|---|---|---|
| *Person* | *Singular* | *Plural* |
| 1st person | I was seeming -<br>Јас **и**згледав<br>*Jas **i**zgledav* | We were seeming -<br>Ние изгл**е**давме<br>Nie izgl**e**davme |
| 2nd person | You were seeming -<br>Ти изгл**е**даше<br>*Ti izgl**e**dashe* | You were seeming -<br>Вие изгл**е**давте<br>*Vie izgl**e**davte* |
| 3rd person | He/She/It was seeming -<br>Тој/Таа/Тоа изгл**е**даше<br>*Toj/Taa/Toa izgl**e**dashe* | They were seeming -<br>Тие изгл**е**даа<br>*Tie izgl**e**daa* |

| Present Perfect Simple Tense | | |
|---|---|---|
| *Person* | *Singular* | *Plural* |
| 1st person | / | / |
| 2nd person | / | / |
| 3rd person | / | / |

| Present Perfect Continuous Tense | | |
|---|---|---|
| *Person* | *Singular* | *Plural* |
| 1st person | I have been seeming -<br>Јас сум **и**згледал(а)<br>*Jas sum **i**zgledal(a)* | We have been seeming -<br>Ние сме изгл**е**дале<br>*Nie sme izgl**e**dale* |

| | | |
|---|---|---|
| 2nd person | You have been seeming -<br>Ти си **и**згледал(а)<br>*Ti si **i**zgledal(a)* | You have been seeming -<br>Вие сте изгл**е**дале<br>*Vie ste izgl**e**dale* |
| 3rd person | He/She/It has been seeming -<br>Тој/Таа/Тоа **и**згледал(а)(о)<br>*Toj/Taa/Toa **i**zgledal(a)(o)* | They have been seeming -<br>Тие изгл**е**дале<br>*Tie izgl**e**dale* |

| Past Perfect Simple Tense | | |
|---|---|---|
| *Person* | *Singular* | *Plural* |
| 1st person | I had seemed -<br>Јас бев **и**згледал(а)<br>*Jas bev **i**zgledal(a)* | We had seemed -<br>Ние бевме изгл**е**дале<br>*Nie bevme izgl**e**dale* |
| 2nd person | You had seemed -<br>Јас бев **и**згледал(а)<br>*Ti beshe **i**zgledal(a)* | You had seemed -<br>Вие бевте изгл**е**дале<br>*Vie bevte izgl**e**dale* |
| 3rd person | He/She/It had seemed -<br>Тој/Таа/Тоа беше<br>**и**згледал(а)(о)<br>*Toj/Taa/Toa beshe **i**zgledal(a)(o)* | They had seemed -<br>Тие беа изгл**е**дале<br>*Tie bea izgl**e**dale* |

| Future Simple Tense | | |
|---|---|---|
| *Person* | *Singular* | *Plural* |
| 1st person | I will seem -<br>Јас ќе **и**згледам<br>*Jas kje **i**zgledam* | We will seem -<br>Ние ќе изгл**е**даме<br>*Nie kje izgl**e**dame* |
| 2nd person | You will seem -<br>Ти ќе **и**згледаш<br>*Ti kje **i**zgledash* | You will seem -<br>Вие ќе изгл**е**дате<br>*Vie kje izgl**e**date* |
| 3rd person | He/She/It will seem -<br>Тој/Таа/Тоа ќе **и**згледа<br>*Toj/Taa/Toa kje **i**zgleda* | They will seem -<br>Тие ќе изгл**е**даат<br>*Tie kje izgl**e**daat* |

| used to + infinitive or would + infinitive | | |
|---|---|---|
| *Person* | *Singular* | *Plural* |
| 1st person | I would seem -<br>Јас ќе **и**згледав<br>*Jas kje **i**zgledav* | We would seem -<br>Ние ќе изгл**е**давме<br>*Nie kje izgl**e**davme* |
| 2nd person | You would seem -<br>Ти ќе изгл**е**даше<br>*Ti kje izgl**e**dashe* | You would seem -<br>Вие ќе изгл**е**давте<br>*Vie kje izgl**e**davte* |
| 3rd person | He/She/It would seem -<br>Тој/Таа/Тоа ќе изгл**е**даше<br>*Toj/Taa/Toa kje izgl**e**dashe* | They would seem -<br>Тие ќе изгл**е**даа<br>*Tie kje izgl**e**daa* |

| **Personal endings for future perfect-in-the-past tense** | | |
|---|---|---|
| *Person* | *Singular* | *Plural* |
| 1st person | I would have seemed -<br>Јас ќе сум **и**зглeдал(а)<br>*Jas kje sum izgl**e**dal(a)* | We would have seemed -<br>Ние ќе сме изгл**е**дале<br>*Nie kje sme izgl**e**dale* |
| 2nd person | You would have seemed -<br>Ти ќе си изгл**е**дал(а)<br>*Ti kje si izgl**e**dal(a)* | You would have seemed -<br>Вие ќе сте изгл**е**дале<br>*Vie kje ste izgl**e**dale* |
| 3rd person | He/She/It would have seemed<br>Тој/Таа/Тоа ќе изгл**е**дал(а)(о)<br>*Toj/Taa/Toa kje izgl**e**dal(a)(o)* | They would have seemed -<br>Тие ќе изгл**е**дале<br>*Tie kje izgl**e**dale* |

***To sell – Продава/Продаде***

| | | |
|---|---|---|
| *Infinitive* | Tosell | Пр**о**дава<br>Pr**o**dava |

| Present Simple Tense | | |
|---|---|---|
| *Person* | *Singular* | *Plural* |
| 1st person | I sell-<br>Јас пр**о**давам<br>*Jas pr**o**davam* | We sell-<br>Ние прод**а**ваме<br>*Nie prod**a**vame* |
| 2nd person | You sell-<br>Ти пр**о**даваш<br>*Ti pr**o**davash* | You sell -<br>Вие прод**а**вате<br>*Vie prod**a**vate* |
| 3rd person | He/She/It sells-<br>Тој/Таа/Тоа пр**о**дава<br>*Toj/Taa/Toa pr**o**dava* | They sell -<br>Тие прод**а**ваат<br>*Tie prod**a**vaat* |

| Past Simple Tense | | |
|---|---|---|
| *Person* | *Singular* | *Plural* |
| 1st person | I sold -<br>Јас пр**о**дадов<br>*Jas pr**o**dadov* | We sold -<br>Ние прод**а**довме<br>*Nie prod**a**dovme* |
| 2nd person | You sold -<br>Ти пр**о**даде<br>*Ti pr**o**dade* | You sold -<br>Вие прод**а**довте<br>*Vie prod**a**dovte* |
| 3rd person | He/She/It sold -<br>Тој/Таа/Тоа пр**о**даде<br>*Toj/Taa/Toa pr**o**dade* | They sold -<br>Тие прод**а**доа<br>*Tie prod**a**doa* |

| Past Continuous Tense | | |
|---|---|---|
| Person | Singular | Plural |
| 1st person | I was selling -<br>Јас пр**о**давав<br>*Jas pr**o**davav* | We were selling -<br>Ние прод**а**вавме<br>*Nie prod**a**vavme* |
| 2nd person | You were selling -<br>Ти прод**а**ваше<br>*Ti prod**a**vashe* | You were selling -<br>Вие прод**а**вавте<br>*Vie prod**a**vavte* |
| 3rd person | He/She/It was selling -<br>Тој/Таа/Тоа прод**а**ваше<br>*Toj/Taa/Toa prod**a**vashe* | They were selling -<br>Тие прод**а**ваа<br>*Tie prod**a**vaa* |

| Present Perfect Simple Tense | | |
|---|---|---|
| *Person* | *Singular* | *Plural* |
| 1st person | I have sold -<br>Јас сум пр**о**дал(а)<br>*Jas sum pr**o**dal(a)* | We have sold -<br>Ние сме пр**о**дале<br>*Nie sme pr**o**dale* |

| | | |
|---|---|---|
| 2nd person | You have sold -<br>Ти си пр**о**дал(а)<br>*Ti si pr**o**dal(a)* | You have sold -<br>Вие сте пр**о**дале<br>*Nie sme pr**o**dale* |
| 3rd person | He/She/It has sold - Тој/Таа/Тоа<br>пр**о**дал(а)(о)<br>*Toj/Taa/Toa pr**o**dal(a)(o)* | They have sold -<br>Тие пр**о**дале<br>*Tie pr**o**dale* |

| **Present Perfect Continuous Tense** | | |
|---|---|---|
| *Person* | *Singular* | *Plural* |
| 1st person | I have been selling-<br>Јас сум пр**о**давал(а)<br>*Jas sum pr**o**daval(a)* | We have been selling -<br>Ние сме прод**а**вале<br>*Nie sme prod**a**vale* |
| 2nd person | You have been selling-<br>Ти си пр**о**давал(а)<br>*Ti si pr**o**daval(a)* | You have been selling -<br>Вие сте прод**а**вале<br>*Vie ste prod**a**vale* |
| 3rd person | He/She/It has been selling -<br>Тој/Таа/Тоа<br>пр**о**давал(а)(о)*Toj/Taa/Toa*<br>*pr**o**daval(a)(o)* | They have been selling -<br>Тие прод**а**вале<br>*Tie prod**a**vale* |

| **Past Perfect Simple Tense** | | |
|---|---|---|
| *Person* | *Singular* | *Plural* |
| 1st person | I had sold -<br>Јас бев пр**о**дал(а)<br>*Jas bev pr**o**dal(a)* | We had sold -<br>Ние бевме пр**о**дале<br>*Nie bevme pr**o**dale* |
| 2nd person | You had sold -<br>Ти беше пр**о**дал(а)<br>*Ti beshe pr**o**dal(a)* | You had sold -<br>Вие бевте пр**о**дале<br>*Vie bevte pr**o**dale* |
| 3rd person | He/She/It had sold - Тој/Таа/Тоа<br>беше пр**о**дал(а)(о)<br>*Toj/Taa/Toa beshe pr**o**dal(a)(o)* | They had sold -<br>Тие беа пр**о**дале<br>*Tie bea pr**o**dale* |

| **Future Simple Tense** | | |
|---|---|---|
| *Person* | *Singular* | *Plural* |
| 1st person | I will sell-<br>Јас ќе пр**о**давам/пр**о**дадам<br>*Jas kje pr**o**davam/pr**o**dadam* | We will sell -<br>Ние ќе прод**а**ваме/прод**а**деме<br>*Nie kje prod**a**vame/prod**a**deme* |
| 2nd person | You will sell -<br>Ти ќе пр**о**даваш/пр**о**дадеш<br>Ti kje pr**o**davash/pr**o**dadesh | You will sell -<br>Вие ќе прод**а**вате/прод**а**дете<br>Vie kje prod**a**vate/prod**a**dete |
| 3rd person | He/She/It will sell - Тој/Таа/Тоа<br>ќе пр**о**дава/пр**о**даде<br>Toj/Taa/Toa kje<br>pr**o**dava/pr**o**dade | They will sell-<br>Тие ќе прод**а**ваат/пр**о**дадат<br>Tie kje prod**a**vaat/pr**o**dadat |

| **used to + infinitive or would + infinitive** | | |
|---|---|---|
| *Person* | *Singular* | *Plural* |
| 1st person | I would sell -<br>Јас ќе пр**о**давав/пр**о**дадов<br>Jas kje pr**o**davav/pr**o**dadov | We would sell -<br>Ние ќе<br>прод**а**вавме/прод**а**довме<br>Nie kje prod**a**vavme/prod**a**dovme |
| 2nd person | You would sell -<br>Ти ќе прод**а**ваше/прод**а**деше<br>Ti kje prod**a**vashe/prod**a**deshe | You would sell -<br>Вие ќе прод**а**вавте/прод**а**довте<br>Vie kje prod**a**vavte/prod**a**dovte |
| 3rd person | He/She/It would sell -<br>Тој/Таа/Тоа ќе<br>прод**а**ваше/прод**а**деше<br>Toj/Taa/Toa kje<br>prod**a**vashe/prod**a**deshe | They would sell -<br>Тие ќе прод**а**ваа/прод**а**доа<br>Tie kje prod**a**vaa/prod**a**doa |

| **Personal endings for future perfect-in-the-past tense** | | |
|---|---|---|
| *Person* | *Singular* | *Plural* |
| 1st person | I would have sold -<br>Јас ќе сум<br>пр**о**давал/пр**о**дадел(а)<br>Jas kje sum<br>pr**o**daval/pr**o**dadel(a) | We would have sold -<br>Ние ќе сме<br>прод**а**вале/прод**а**деле<br>Nie kje sme prod**a**vale/prod**a**dele |
| 2nd person | You would have sold -<br>Ти ќе си пр**о**давал/пр**о**дадел(а)<br>Ti kje si pr**o**daval/pr**o**dadel(a) | You would have sold -<br>Вие ќе сте<br>прод**а**вале/прод**а**деле<br>Vie kje ste prod**a**vale/prod**a**dele |
| 3rd person | He/She/It would have sold -<br>Тој/Таа/Тоа ќе<br>пр**о**давал/пр**о**дадел(а)(о)<br>Toj/Taa/Toa kje<br>pr**o**daval/pr**o**dadel(a)(o) | They would have sold -<br>Тие ќе прод**а**вале/прод**а**деле<br>Tie kje prod**a**vale/prod**a**dele |

***To send – Праќа/Прати***

| | | |
|---|---|---|
| *Infinitive* | To send | Праќа<br>Prakja |

| Present Simple Tense | | |
|---|---|---|
| *Person* | *Singular* | *Plural* |
| 1st person | I send -<br>Јас праќам<br>*Jas prakjam* | We send -<br>Ние праќаме<br>*Nie prakjame* |
| 2nd person | You send -<br>Ти праќаш<br>*Ti prakjash* | You send -<br>Вие праќате<br>*Vie prakjate* |
| 3rd person | He/She/It sends -<br>Тој/Таа/Тоа праќа<br>*Toj/Taa/Toa prakja* | They send -<br>Тие праќаат<br>*Tie prakjaat* |

| Past Simple Tense | | |
|---|---|---|
| *Person* | *Singular* | *Plural* |
| 1st person | I sent -<br>Јас пратив<br>*Jas prativ* | We sent -<br>Ние пративме<br>*Nie prativme* |
| 2nd person | You sent -<br>Ти прати<br>*Ti prati* | You sent -<br>Вие пративте<br>*Vie prativte* |
| 3rd person | He/She/It sent -<br>Тој/Таа/Тоа прати<br>*Toj/Taa/Toa prati* | They sent -<br>Тие пратија<br>*Tie pratija* |

| Past Continuous Tense | | |
|---|---|---|
| *Person* | *Singular* | *Plural* |
| 1st person | I was sending -<br>Јас праќав<br>*Jas prakjav* | We were sending -<br>Ние праќавме<br>*Nie prakjavme* |
| 2nd person | You were sending -<br>Ти праќаше<br>*Ti prakjashe* | You were sending -<br>Вие праќавте<br>*Vie prakjavte* |
| 3rd person | He/She/It was sending -<br>Тој/Таа/Тоа праќаше<br>*Toj/Taa/Toa prakjashe* | They were sending -<br>Тие праќаа<br>*Tie prakjaa* |

| Present Perfect Simple Tense | | |
|---|---|---|
| *Person* | *Singular* | *Plural* |
| 1st person | I have sent -<br>Јас сум пратил(а)<br>*Jas sum pratil(a)* | We have sent -<br>Ние сме пратиле<br>*Nie sme pratile* |

| | | |
|---|---|---|
| 2nd person | You have sent -<br>Ти си пр**а**тил(а)<br>*Ti si pr**a**til(a)* | You have sent-<br>Вие сте пр**а**тиле<br>*Vie ste pr**a**tile* |
| 3rd person | He/She/It has sent –<br>Тој/Таа/Тоа пр**а**тил(а)(о)<br>*Toj/Taa/Toa pr**a**til(a)(o)* | They have sent -<br>Тие пр**а**тиле<br>*Tie pr**a**tile* |

| **Present Perfect Continuous Tense** | | |
|---|---|---|
| *Person* | *Singular* | *Plural* |
| 1st person | I have been sending-<br>Јас сум пр**а**ќал(а)<br>*Jas sum pr**a**kjal(a* | We have been sending-<br>Ние сме пр**а**ќале<br>*Nie sme pr**a**kjale* |
| 2nd person | You have been sending-<br>Ти си пр**а**ќал(а)<br>*Ti si pr**a**kjal(a)* | You have been sending-<br>Вие сте пр**а**ќале<br>*Vie ste pr**a**kjale* |
| 3rd person | He/She/It has been sending-<br>Тој/Таа/Тоа пр**а**ќал(а)(о)<br>*Toj/Taa/Toa pr**a**kjal(a)(o)* | They have been sending-<br>Тие пр**а**ќале<br>*Tie pr**a**kjale* |

| **Past Perfect Simple Tense** | | |
|---|---|---|
| *Person* | *Singular* | *Plural* |
| 1st person | I had sent-<br>Јас бев пр**а**тил(а)<br>*Jas bev pr**a**til(a)* | We had sent-<br>Ние бевме пр**а**тиле<br>*Nie bevme pr**a**tile* |
| 2nd person | You had sent -<br>Ти беше пр**а**тил(а)<br>*Ti beshe pr**a**til(a)* | You had sent-<br>Вие бевте пр**а**тиле<br>*Vie bevte pr**a**tile* |
| 3rd person | He/She/It had sent -<br>Тој/Таа/Тоа беше пр**а**тил(а)(о)<br>*Toj/Taa/Toa beshe pr**a**til(a)(o)* | They had sent-<br>Тие беа пр**а**тиле<br>*Tie bea pr**a**tile* |

| **Future Simple Tense** | | |
|---|---|---|
| *Person* | *Singular* | *Plural* |
| 1st person | I will send-<br>Јас ќе пр**а**ќам/пр**а**там<br>Jas kje pr**a**kjam/pr**a**tam | We will send -<br>Ние ќе пр**а**ќаме/пр**а**тиме<br>Nie kje pr**a**kjame/pr**a**time |
| 2nd person | You will send -<br>Ти ќе пр**а**ќаш/пр**а**тиш<br>*Ti kje pr**a**kjash/pr**a**tish* | You will send-<br>Вие ќе пр**а**ќате/пр**а**тите<br>*Vie kje pr**a**kjate/pr**a**tite* |
| 3rd person | He/She/It will send -<br>Тој/Таа/Тоа ќе пр**а**ќа/пр**а**ти<br>*Toj/Taa/Toa kje pr**a**kja/pr**a**ti* | They will send -<br>Тие ќе пр**а**ќаат/пр**а**тат<br>*Tie kje pr**a**kjaat/pr**a**tat* |

| **used to + infinitive or would + infinitive** | | |
|---|---|---|
| *Person* | *Singular* | *Plural* |
| 1st person | I would send-<br>Јас ќе пр**а**ќав/пр**а**тив<br>*Jas kje pr**a**kjav/pr**a**tiv* | We would send -<br>Ние ќе пр**а**ќавме/пр**а**тивме<br>*Nie kje pr**a**kjavme/pr**a**tivme* |
| 2nd person | You would send -<br>Ти ќе пр**а**ќаше/пр**а**тише<br>*Ti kje pr**a**kjashe/pr**a**tishe* | You would send -<br>Вие ќе пр**а**ќавте/пр**а**тивте<br>*Vie kje pr**a**kjavte/pr**a**tivte* |
| 3rd person | He/She/It would send -<br>Тој/Таа/Тоа ќе<br>пр**а**ќаше/пр**а**тише<br>*Toj/Taa/Toa kje<br>pr**a**kjashe/pr**a**tishe* | They would send -<br>Тие ќе пр**а**ќаа/пр**а**тија<br>*Tie kje pr**a**kjaa/pr**a**tija* |

| **Personal endings for future perfect-in-the-past tense** | | |
|---|---|---|
| *Person* | *Singular* | *Plural* |
| 1st person | I would have sent -<br>Јас ќе сум пр**а**ќал/пр**а**тил(а)<br>*Jas kje sum pr**a**kjal/pr**a**til(a)* | We would have sent -<br>Ние ќе сме пр**а**ќале/пр**а**тиле<br>*Nie kje sme pr**a**kjale/pr**a**tile* |
| 2nd person | You would have sent -<br>Тие ќе си пр**а**ќал/пр**а**тил(а)<br>*Ti kje si pr**a**kjal/pr**a**til(a)* | You would have sent -<br>Вие ќе сте пр**а**ќале/пр**а**тиле<br>*Vie kje ste pr**a**kjale/pr**a**tile* |
| 3rd person | He/She/It would have sent -<br>Тој/Таа/Тоа ќе<br>пр**а**ќал/пр**а**тил(а)(о)<br>*Toj/Taa/Toa kje<br>pr**a**kjal/pr**a**til(a)(o)* | They would have sent -<br>Тие ќе пр**а**ќале/пр**а**тиле<br>*Tie kje pr**a**kjale/pr**a**tile* |

***To show – Покажува/Покажа***

| | | |
|---|---|---|
| *Infinitive* | To show | Пок**а**жува<br>Pok**a**zhuva |

| Present Simple Tense | | |
|---|---|---|
| *Person* | *Singular* | *Plural* |
| 1st person | I show -<br>Јас пок**а**жувам<br>*Jas pok**a**zhuvam* | We show -<br>Ние покаж**у**ваме<br>*Nie pokazh**u**vame* |
| 2nd person | You show -<br>Ти пок**а**жуваш<br>*Ti pok**a**zhuvash* | You show -<br>Вие покаж**у**вате<br>*Vie pokazh**u**vate* |
| 3rd person | He/She/It shows -<br>Тој/Таа/Тоа пок**а**жува<br>Toj/Taa/Toa pok**a**zhuva | They show -<br>Тие покаж**у**ваат<br>*Tie pokazh**u**vaat* |

| Past Simple Tense | | |
|---|---|---|
| *Person* | *Singular* | *Plural* |
| 1st person | I showed -<br>Јас п**о**кажав<br>*Jas p**o**kazhav* | We showed -<br>Ние пок**а**жавме<br>*Nie pok**a**zhavme* |
| 2nd person | You showed -<br>Ти пок**а**жа<br>*Ti pok**a**zha* | You showed -<br>Вие пок**а**жавте<br>*Vie pok**a**zhavte* |
| 3rd person | He/She/It showed -<br>Тој/Таа/Тоа п**о**кажа<br>*Toj/Taa/Toa p**o**kazha* | They showed -<br>Тие пок**а**жаа<br>*Tie pok**a**zhaa* |

| Past Continuous Tense | | |
|---|---|---|
| *Person* | *Singular* | *Plural* |
| 1st person | I was showing -<br>Јас пок**а**жував<br>*Jas pok**a**zhuvav* | We were showing -<br>Ние покаж**у**вавме<br>*Nie pokazh**u**vavme* |
| 2nd person | You were showing -<br>Ти пок**а**жуваше<br>*Ti pok**a**zhuvashe* | You were showing -<br>Вие покаж**у**вавте<br>*Vie pokazh**u**vate* |
| 3rd person | He/She/It was showing -<br>Тој/Таа/Тоа покаж**у**ваше<br>*Toj/Taa/Toa pokazh**u**vashe* | They were showing -<br>Тие покаж**у**ваа<br>*Tie pokazh**u**vaa* |

| Present Perfect Simple Tense | | |
|---|---|---|
| *Person* | *Singular* | *Plural* |
| 1st person | I have showed -<br>Јас сум п**о**кажал(а)<br>*Jas sum p**o**kazhal(a)* | We have showed -<br>Ние сме пок**а**жале<br>*Nie sme pok**a**zhale* |

| | | |
|---|---|---|
| 2nd person | You have showed -<br>Ти си п**о**кажал(а)<br>*Ti si p**o**kazhal(a)* | You have showed -<br>Вие сте пок**а**жале<br>*Vie ste pok**a**zhale* |
| 3rd person | He/She/It has showed -<br>Тој/Таа/Тоа п**о**кажал(а)(о)<br>*Toj/Taa/Toa p**o**kazhal(a)(o)* | They have showed -<br>Тие пок**а**жале<br>*Tie pok**a**zhale* |

| Present Perfect Continuous Tense | | |
|---|---|---|
| *Person* | *Singular* | *Plural* |
| 1st person | I have been showing -<br>Јас сум пок**а**жувал(а)<br>*Jas sum pok**a**zhuval(a)* | We have been showing -<br>Ние сме покаж**у**вале<br>*Nie sme pokazh**u**vale* |
| 2nd person | You have been showing -<br>Ти си пок**а**жувал(а)<br>*Ti si pok**a**zhuval(a)* | You have been showing -<br>Вие сте покаж**у**вале<br>*Vie ste pokazh**u**vale* |
| 3rd person | He/She/It has been showing -<br>Тој/Таа/Тоа пок**а**жувал(а)(о)<br>*Toj/Taa/Toa pok**a**zhuva(a)(o)* | They have been showing -<br>Тие покаж**у**вале<br>*Tie pokazh**u**vale* |

| Past Perfect Simple Tense | | |
|---|---|---|
| *Person* | *Singular* | *Plural* |
| 1st person | I had showed -<br>Јас бев п**о**кажал(а)<br>*Jas bev p**o**kazhal(a)* | We had showed -<br>Ние бевме пок**а**жале<br>*Nie bevme pok**a**zhale* |
| 2nd person | You had showed -<br>Ти беше п**о**кажал(а)<br>*Ti beshe p**o**kazhal(a)* | You had showed -<br>Вие бевте пок**а**жале<br>*Vie bevte pok**a**zhale* |
| 3rd person | He/She/It had showed -<br>Тој/Таа/Тоа беше п**о**кажал(а)(о)<br>*Toj/Taa/Toa beshe p**o**kazhal(a)(o)* | They had showed -<br>Тие беа пок**а**жале<br>*Tie bea pok**a**zhale* |

| Future Simple Tense | | |
|---|---|---|
| *Person* | *Singular* | *Plural* |
| 1st person | I will show-<br>Јас ќе пок**а**жувам/п**о**кажам<br>*Jas kje pok**a**zhuvam/p**o**kazham* | We will show -<br>Ние ќе покаж**у**ваме/пок**а**жеме<br>*Nie kje pokazh**u**vame/pok**a**zheme* |
| 2nd person | You will show -<br>Ти ќе пок**а**жуваш/п**о**кажеш<br>*Ti kje pok**a**zhuvash/p**o**kazhesh* | You will show -<br>Вие ќе покажувате/покажете<br>*Vie kje pokazh**u**vate/pok**a**zhete* |
| 3rd person | He/She/It will show -<br>Тој/Таа/Тоа пок**а**жува/п**о**каже<br>*Toj/Taa/Toa kje pok**a**zhuva/p**o**kazhe* | They will show -<br>Тие ќе покаж**у**ваат/п**о**кажат<br>*Tie kje pokazh**u**vaat/p**o**kazhat* |

| **used to + infinitive or would + infinitive** | | |
|---|---|---|
| *Person* | *Singular* | *Plural* |
| 1st person | I would show - Јасќе пок**а**жував/п**о**кажев *Jas kje pok**a**zhuvav/p**o**kazhav* | We would show - Ние ќе покаж**у**вавме/пок**а**жевме *Nie kje pokazh**u**vavme/pok**a**zhevme* |
| 2nd person | You would show - Ти ќе покаж**у**ваше/пок**а**жеше *Ti kje pokazh**u**vashe/pok**a**zheshe* | You would show - Вие ќе покаж**у**вавте/пок**а**жевте *Vie kje pokazh**u**vavte/pok**a**zhevte* |
| 3rd person | He/She/It would show - Тој/Таа/Тоа ќе покаж**у**ваше/пок**а**жеше *Toj/Taa/Toa kje pokazh**u**vashe/pok**a**zheshe* | They would show - Тие кје покаж**у**ваа/пок**а**жеа *Tie kje pokazh**u**vaa/pok**a**zhea* |

| **Personal endings for future perfect-in-the-past tense** | | |
|---|---|---|
| *Person* | *Singular* | *Plural* |
| 1st person | I would have showed - Јас ќе сум пок**а**жувал/п**о**кажал(а) Jas kje sum pok**a**zhuval/p**o**kazhal(a) | We would have showed - Ние ќе сме покаж**у**вале/пок**а**жале Nie kje sme pokazh**u**vale/pok**a**zhale |
| 2nd person | You would have showed - Ти ќе си пок**а**жувал/п**о**кажал(а) Ti kje si pok**a**zhuval/p**o**kazhal(a) | You would have showed - Вие ќе сте покаж**у**вале/пок**а**жале Vie ste kje pokazh**u**vale/pok**a**zhale |
| 3rd person | He/She/It would have showed Тој/Таа/Тоа ќе пок**а**жувал/п**о**кажал(а)(о) Тој/Таа/Тоа kje pok**a**zhuval/p**o**kazhal(a)(o) | They would have showed - Тие ќе покаж**у**вале/пок**а**жале Tie kje pokazh**u**vale/pok**a**zhale |

***To sing – Пее/Испеа***

| | | |
|---|---|---|
| *Infinitive* | To sing | Пее<br>Pee |

| Present Simple Tense | | |
|---|---|---|
| *Person* | *Singular* | *Plural* |
| 1st person | I sing -<br>Јас **пеам**<br>*Jas **peam*** | We sing -<br>Ние **пееме**<br>*Nie **peeme*** |
| 2nd person | You sing -<br>Ти **пееш**<br>*Ti **peesh*** | You sing -<br>Вие пеете<br>*Vie peete* |
| 3rd person | He/She/It sings -<br>Тој/Таа/Тоа **пее**<br>*Toj/Taa/Toa **pee*** | They sing -<br>Тие п**е**јат<br>*Tie p**e**jat* |

| Past Simple Tense | | |
|---|---|---|
| *Person* | *Singular* | *Plural* |
| 1st person | I sang -<br>Јас **и**спеав<br>*Jas **i**speav* | We sang -<br>Ние испеавме<br>*Nie ispeavme* |
| 2nd person | You sang -<br>Ти **и**спеа<br>*Ti **i**spea* | You sang -<br>Вие испеавте<br>*Vie ispeavte* |
| 3rd person | He/She/It sang -<br>Тој/Таа/Тоа **и**спеа<br>*Toj/Taa/Toa **i**spea* | They sang -<br>Тие исп**е**аја<br>*Tie isp**e**aja* |

| Past Continuous Tense | | |
|---|---|---|
| *Person* | *Singular* | *Plural* |
| 1st person | I was singing -<br>Јас пеев<br>*Jas peev* | We were singing -<br>Ние пеевме<br>*Nie peevme* |
| 2nd person | You were singing -<br>Ти пееше<br>*Ti peeshe* | You were singing -<br>Вие пеевте<br>*Vie peevte* |
| 3rd person | He/She/It was singing -<br>Тој/Таа/Тоа пееше<br>*Toj/Taa/Toa peeshe* | They were singing -<br>Тие пеea<br>*Tie peea* |

| Present Perfect Simple Tense | | |
|---|---|---|
| *Person* | *Singular* | *Plural* |
| 1st person | I have sung -<br>Јас сум **и**спеал(а)<br>*Jas sum **i**speal(a)* | We have sung -<br>Ние сме исп**е**але<br>*Nie sme isp**e**ale* |

| | | |
|---|---|---|
| 2nd person | You have sung -<br>Ти си испеал(а)<br>*Ti si ispeal(a)* | You have sung -<br>Вие сте испеале<br>*Vie ste ispeale* |
| 3rd person | He/She/It has sung -<br>Тој/Таа/Тоа испеал(а)(о)<br>*Toj/Taa/Toa ispeal(a)(o)* | They have sung -<br>Тие испеале<br>*Tie ispeale* |

| Present Perfect Continuous Tense | | |
|---|---|---|
| *Person* | *Singular* | *Plural* |
| 1st person | I have been singing -<br>Јас сум пеел(а)<br>*Jas sum peel(a)* | We have been singing -<br>Ние сме пееле<br>*Nie sme peele* |
| 2nd person | You have been singing -<br>Ти си пеел(а)<br>*Ti si peel(a)* | You have been singing -<br>Вие сте пееле<br>*Vie ste peele* |
| 3rd person | He/She/It has been singing -<br>Тој/Таа/Тоа пеел(а)(о)<br>*Toj/Taa/Toa peel(a)(o)* | They have been singing -<br>Тие пееле<br>*Tie peele* |

| Past Perfect Simple Tense | | |
|---|---|---|
| *Person* | *Singular* | *Plural* |
| 1st person | I had sung -<br>Јас бев испеал(а)<br>*Jas bev ispeal(a)* | We had sung -<br>Ние бевме испеале<br>*Nie bevme ispeale* |
| 2nd person | You had sung -<br>Ти беше испеал(а)<br>*Ti beshe ispeal(a)* | You had sung -<br>Вие бевте испеале<br>*Vie bevte ispeale* |
| 3rd person | He/She/It had sung -<br>Тој/Таа/Тоа испеал(а)(о)<br>*Toj/Taa/Toa beshe ispeal(a)(o)* | They had sung -<br>Тие беа испеале<br>*Tie bea ispeale* |

| Future Simple Tense | | |
|---|---|---|
| *Person* | *Singular* | *Plural* |
| 1st person | I will sing -<br>Јас ќе пеам/испеам<br>*Jas kje peam/ispeam* | We will sing -<br>Ние ќе пееме/испееме<br>*Nie kje peeme/ispeeme* |
| 2nd person | You will sing -<br>Ти ќе пееш/испееш<br>*Ti kje peesh/ispeesh* | You will sing -<br>Вие ќе пеете/испеете<br>*Vie kje peete/ispeete* |
| 3rd person | He/She/It will sing -<br>Тој/Таа/Тоа ќе пее/испее<br>*Toj/Taa/Toa kje pee/ispee* | They will sing -<br>Тие ќе пеат/испеат<br>*Tie kje peat/ispeat* |

| used to + infinitive or would + infinitive | | |
|---|---|---|
| *Person* | *Singular* | *Plural* |
| 1st person | I would sing -<br>Јас ќе пеев/испеев<br>*Jas kje peev/ispeev* | We would sing -<br>Ние ќе пеевме/испеевме<br>*Nie kje peevme/ispeevme* |

| | | |
|---|---|---|
| 2nd person | You would sing -<br>Ти ќе пееше/испееше<br>*Ti kje peeshe/ispeeshe* | You would sing -<br>Вие ќе пеевте/испеевте<br>*Vie kje peevte/ispeevte* |
| 3rd person | He/She/It would sing -<br>Тој/Таа/Тоа ќе пееше/испееше<br>*Toj/Taa/Toa kje peeshe/ispeeshe* | They would sing -<br>Тие ќе пееја/испееја<br>*Tie kje peeja/ispeeja* |

| **Personal endings for future perfect-in-the-past tense** | | |
|---|---|---|
| *Person* | *Singular* | *Plural* |
| 1st person | I would have sung -<br>Јас ќе сум пеел/**и**спеал(а)<br>Jas kje sum peel/**i**speal(a) | We would have sung -<br>Ние ќе сме пееле/испеале<br>*Nie kje sme peele/ispeale* |
| 2nd person | You would have sung -<br>Ти ќе си пеел/**и**спеал(а)<br>*Ti kje si* peel/**i**speal(a) | You would have sung -<br>Вие ќе сте пееле/испеале<br>*Vie kje ste peele/ispeale* |
| 3rd person | He/She/It would have sung -<br>Тој/Таа/Тоа ќе<br>пеел/**и**спеал(а)(о)<br>*Toj/Taa/Toa kje* peel/**i**speal(a)(o) | They would have sung -<br>Тие ќе пееле/испеале<br>*Tie kje peele/ispeale* |

### *To sit down – Седи/Седна*

| | | |
|---|---|---|
| *Infinitive* | To sit down | Седи<br>Sedi |

| Present Simple Tense | | |
|---|---|---|
| *Person* | *Singular* | *Plural* |
| 1st person | I sit down -<br>Јас седам<br>*Jas sedam* | We sit down -<br>Ние седиме<br>*Nie sedime* |
| 2nd person | You sit down -<br>Ти седиш<br>*Ti sedish* | You sit down -<br>Вие седите<br>*Vie sedite* |
| 3rd person | He/She/It sits down -<br>Тој/Таа/Тоа седи<br>*Toj/Taa/Toa sedi* | They sit down -<br>Тие седат<br>*Tie sedat* |

| Past Simple Tense | | |
|---|---|---|
| *Person* | *Singular* | *Plural* |
| 1st person | I sat down -<br>Јас седнав<br>*Jas sednav* | We sat down -<br>Ние седнавме<br>*Nie sednavme* |
| 2nd person | You sat down -<br>Ти седна<br>*Ti sedna* | You sat down -<br>Вие седнавте<br>*Vie sednavte* |
| 3rd person | He/She/It sat down -<br>Тој/Таа/Тоа седна<br>*Toj/Taa/Toa sedna* | They sat down -<br>Тие седнаа<br>*Tie sednaa* |

| Past Continuous Tense | | |
|---|---|---|
| *Person* | *Singular* | *Plural* |
| 1st person | I was sitting down -<br>Јас седев<br>*Jas sedev* | We were sitting down -<br>Ние седевме<br>*Nie sedevme* |
| 2nd person | You were sitting down -<br>Ти седеше<br>*Ti sedeshe* | You were sitting down -<br>Вие седевте<br>*Vie sedevte* |
| 3rd person | He/She/It was sitting down -<br>Тој/Таа/Тоа седеше<br>*Toj/Taa/Toa sedeshe* | They were sitting down -<br>Тие седеа<br>*Tie sedea* |

| Present Perfect Simple Tense | | |
|---|---|---|
| *Person* | *Singular* | *Plural* |
| 1st person | I have sat down -<br>Јас сум седнал(а)<br>*Jas sum sednal(a)* | We have sat down -<br>Ние сме седнале<br>*Nie sme sednale* |

| | | |
|---|---|---|
| 2nd person | You have sat down -<br>Ти си седнал(а)<br>*Ti si sednal(a)* | You have sat down -<br>Вие сте седнале<br>*Vie ste sednale* |
| 3rd person | He/She/It has sat down -<br>Тој/Таа/Тоа седнал(а)(о)<br>*Toj/Taa/Toa sednal(a)(o)* | They have sat down -<br>Тие седнале<br>*Tie sednale* |

| **Present Perfect Continuous Tense** | | |
|---|---|---|
| *Person* | *Singular* | *Plural* |
| 1st person | I have been sitting down -<br>Јас сум седел(а)<br>*Jas sum sedel(a)* | We have been sitting down -<br>Ние сме седеле<br>*Nie sme sedele* |
| 2nd person | You have been sitting down -<br>Ти си седел(а)<br>*Ti si sedel(a)* | You have been sitting down -<br>Вие сте седеле<br>*Vie ste sedele* |
| 3rd person | He/She/It has been sitting down -<br>Тој/Таа/Тоа седел(а)(о)<br>*Toj/Taa/Toa sedel(a)(o)* | They have been sitting down -<br>Тие седеле<br>*Tie sedele* |

| **Past Perfect Simple Tense** | | |
|---|---|---|
| *Person* | *Singular* | *Plural* |
| 1st person | I had sat down -<br>Јас бев седнал(а)<br>*Jas bev sednal(a)* | We had sat down -<br>Ние бевме седнале<br>*Nie bevme sednale* |
| 2nd person | You had sat down -<br>Ти беше седнал(а)<br>*Ti beshe sednal(a)* | You had sat down -<br>Вие бевте седнале<br>*Vie bevte sednale* |
| 3rd person | He/She/It had sat down -<br>Тој/Таа/Тоа беше седнал(а)(о)<br>*Toj/Taa/Toa beshe sednal(a)(o)* | They had sat down -<br>Тие беа седнале<br>*Tie bea sednale* |

| **Future Simple Tense** | | |
|---|---|---|
| *Person* | *Singular* | *Plural* |
| 1st person | I will sit down -<br>Јас ќе седам/седнам<br>*Jas kje sedam/sednam* | We will sit down -<br>Ние ќе седиме/седнеме<br>*Nie kje sedime/sedneme* |
| 2nd person | You will sit down -<br>Ти ќе седиш/седнеш<br>*Ti kje sedish/sednesh* | You will sit down -<br>Вие ќе седите/седнете<br>*Vie kje sedite/sednete* |
| 3rd person | He/She/It will sit down -<br>Тој/Таа/Тоа ќе седи/седне<br>*Toj/Taa/Toa kje sedi/sedne* | They will sit down -<br>Тие ќе седат/седнат<br>*Tie kje sedat/sednat* |

| **used to + infinitive or would + infinitive** | | |
|---|---|---|
| *Person* | *Singular* | *Plural* |
| 1st person | I would sit down -<br>Јас ќе седев/седнев<br>*Jas kje sedev/sednev* | We would sit down -<br>Ние ќе седевме/седневме<br>*Nie kje sedevme/sednevme* |

| | | |
|---|---|---|
| 2nd person | You would sit down -<br>Ти ќе седеше/седнеше<br>*Ti kje sedeshe/sedneshe* | You would sit down -<br>Вие ќе седевте/седневте<br>*Vie kje sedevte/sednevte* |
| 3rd person | He/She/It would sit down -<br>Тој/Таа/Тоа ќе седеше/седнеше<br>*Toj/Taa/Toa kje sedeshe/sedneshe* | They would sit down -<br>Тие ќе седеа/седнеа<br>*Tie kje sedea/sednea* |

| **Personal endings for future perfect-in-the-past tense** | | |
|---|---|---|
| *Person* | *Singular* | *Plural* |
| 1st person | I would have sat down -<br>Јас ќе сум седел/седнал(а)<br>*Jas kje sum sedel/sednal(a)* | We would have sat down -<br>Ние ќе сме седеле/седнале<br>*Nie kje sme sedele/sednale* |
| 2nd person | You would have sat down -<br>Ти ќе си седел/седнал(а)<br>*Ti kje si sedel/sednal(a)* | You would have sat down -<br>Вие ќе сте седеле/седнале<br>*Vie kje ste sedele/sednale* |
| 3rd person | He/She/It would have sat down -<br>Тој/Таа/Тоа ќе седел/седнал(а)(о)<br>*Toj/Taa/Toa kje sedel/sednal(a)(o)* | They would have sat down -<br>Тие ќе седеле/седнале<br>*Tie kje sedele/sednale* |

### *To sleep – Спие/Заспа*

| | | |
|---|---|---|
| *Infinitive* | To sleep | Спие<br>Spie |

| **Present Simple Tense** | | |
|---|---|---|
| *Person* | *Singular* | *Plural* |
| 1st person | I sleep -<br>Јас спијам<br>*Jas spijam* | We sleep -<br>Ние спиеме<br>*Nie spieme* |
| 2nd person | You sleep -<br>Ти спиеш<br>*Ti spiesh* | You sleep -<br>Вие спиете<br>*Vie spiete* |
| 3rd person | He/She/It sleeps -<br>Тој/Таа/Тоа спие<br>*Toj/Taa/Toa spie* | They sleep -<br>Тие спијат<br>*Tie spijat* |

| **Past Simple Tense** | | |
|---|---|---|
| *Person* | *Singular* | *Plural* |
| 1st person | I slept -<br>Јас заспав<br>*Jas zaspav* | We slept -<br>Ние заспавме<br>*Ni zaspavme* |
| 2nd person | You slept -<br>Ти заспа<br>*Ti zaspa* | You slept -<br>Вие заспавте<br>*Vie zaspavte* |
| 3rd person | He/She/It slept -<br>Тој/Таа/Тоа заспа<br>*Toj/Taa/Toa zaspa* | They slept -<br>Тие заспаа<br>*Tie zaspaa* |

| **Past Continuous Tense** | | |
|---|---|---|
| *Person* | *Singular* | *Plural* |
| 1st person | I was sleeping -<br>Јас спиев<br>*Jas spiev* | We were sleeping -<br>Ние спиевме<br>*Nie spievme* |
| 2nd person | You were sleeping -<br>Ти спиеше<br>*Ti spieshe* | You were sleeping -<br>Вие спиевте<br>*Vie spievte* |
| 3rd person | He/She/It was sleeping -<br>Тој/Таа/Тоа спиеше<br>*Toj/Taa/Toa spishe* | They were sleeping -<br>Тие спиеја<br>*Tie spieja* |

| **Present Perfect Simple Tense** | | |
|---|---|---|
| *Person* | *Singular* | *Plural* |
| 1st person | I have slept -<br>Јас сум заспал(а)<br>*Jas sum zaspal(a)* | We have slept -<br>Ние сме заспале<br>*Nie sme zaspale* |

| | | |
|---|---|---|
| 2nd person | You have slept -<br>Ти си **за**спал(а)<br>*Ti si **za**spala(a)* | You have slept -<br>Вие сте **за**спале<br>*Vie ste **za**spale* |
| 3rd person | He/She/It has slept -<br>Тој/Таа/Тоа **за**спал(а)(о)<br>*Toj/Taa/Toa **za**spal(a)(o)* | They have slept -<br>Тие **за**спале<br>*Tie **za**spale* |

| **Present Perfect Continuous Tense** | | |
|---|---|---|
| *Person* | *Singular* | *Plural* |
| 1st person | I have been sleeping -<br>Јас сум сп**и**ел(а)<br>*Jas sum sp**i**el(a)* | We have been sleeping -<br>Ние сме сп**и**еле<br>*Nie sme sp**i**ele* |
| 2nd person | You have been sleeping -<br>Ти си сп**и**ел(а)<br>*Ti si sp**i**el(a)* | You have been sleeping -<br>Вие сте сп**и**еле<br>*Vie ste sp**i**ele* |
| 3rd person | He/She/It has been sleeping -<br>Тој/Таа/Тоа сп**и**ел(а)(о)<br>*Toj/Taa/Toa sp**i**el(a)(o)* | They have been sleeping -<br>Тие сп**и**еле<br>*Tie sp**i**ele* |

| **Past Perfect Simple Tense** | | |
|---|---|---|
| *Person* | *Singular* | *Plural* |
| 1st person | I had slept -<br>Јас бев **за**спал(а)<br>*Jas bev **za**spal(a)* | We had slept -<br>Ние бевме **за**спале<br>*Nie bevme **za**spale* |
| 2nd person | You had slept -<br>Ти беше **за**спал(а)<br>*Ti beshe **za**spal(a)* | You had slept -<br>Вие бевте **за**спале<br>*Vie bevte **za**spale* |
| 3rd person | He/She/It had slept -<br>Тој/Таа/Тоа беше **за**спал(а)(о)<br>*Toj/Taa/Toa beshe **za**spal(a)(o)* | They had slept -<br>Тие беа **за**спале<br>*Tie bea **za**spale* |

| **Future Simple Tense** | | |
|---|---|---|
| *Person* | *Singular* | *Plural* |
| 1st person | I will sleep -<br>Јас ќе сп**и**јам/**за**спиам<br>*Jas kje sp**i**jam/**za**spiam* | We will sleep -<br>Ние ќе сп**и**еме/засп**и**еме<br>*Nie kje sp**i**eme/zasp**i**eme* |
| 2nd person | You will sleep -<br>Ти ќе сп**и**еш/**за**спиеш<br>*Ti kje sp**i**esh/**za**spiesh* | You will sleep -<br>Вие ќе сп**и**ете/засп**и**ете<br>*Vie kje sp**i**ete/zasp**i**ete* |
| 3rd person | He/She/It will sleep -<br>Тој/Таа/Тоа ќе сп**и**е/**за**спие<br>*Toj/Taa/Toa kje sp**i**e/**za**spie* | They will sleep -<br>Тие ќе сп**иј**ат/засп**иј**ат<br>*Tie kje sp**ij**at/zasp**ij**at* |

| **used to + infinitive or would + infinitive** | | |
|---|---|---|
| *Person* | *Singular* | *Plural* |
| 1st person | I would sleep -<br>Јас ќе сп**и**ев/**за**спиев<br>*Jas kje sp**i**ev/**za**spiev* | We would sleep -<br>Ние ќе сп**и**евме/засп**и**евме<br>*Nie kje sp**i**evme/zasp**i**evme* |

| | | |
|---|---|---|
| 2nd person | You would sleep - Ти ќе сп**и**еше/засп**и**еше *Ti kje sp**i**eshe/zasp**i**eshe* | You would sleep - Вие ќе сп**и**евте/засп**и**евте *Vie kje sp**i**evte/zasp**i**evte* |
| 3rd person | He/She/It would sleep - Тој/Таа/Тоа ќе сп**и**еше/засп**и**еше *Toj/Taa/Toa kje sp**i**eshe/zasp**i**eshe* | They would sleep - Тие ќе сп**и**јеа/засп**и**јеа *Tie kje sp**i**jea/zasp**i**jea* |

| Personal endings for future perfect-in-the-past tense | | |
|---|---|---|
| *Person* | *Singular* | *Plural* |
| 1st person | I would have slept - Јас ќе сум сп**и**ел/з**а**спиел(а) *Jas kje sum sp**i**el/z**a**spiel(a)* | We would have slept - Ние ќе сме сп**и**еле/засп**и**еле *Nie kje sme sp**i**ele/zasp**i**ele* |
| 2nd person | You would have slept - Ти ќе си сп**и**ел/з**а**спиел(а) *Ti kje si sp**i**el/z**a**spiel(a)* | You would have slept - Вие ќе сте сп**и**еле/засп**и**еле *Vie kje ste sp**i**ele/zasp**i**ele* |
| 3rd person | He/She/It would have slept - Тој/Таа/Тоа ќе сп**и**ел/з**а**спиел(а)(о) *Toj/Taa/Toa kje si sp**i**el/z**a**spiel(a)(o)* | They would have slept - Тие ќе сп**и**еле/засп**и**еле *Tie kje sp**i**ele/zasp**i**ele* |

***To smile – Се насмевнува/Се насмевна***

| | | |
|---|---|---|
| Infinitive | Tosmile | Се насмевнува<br>Se nasmevnuva |

| **Present Simple Tense** | | |
|---|---|---|
| *Person* | *Singular* | *Plural* |
| 1st person | I smile-<br>Јас се насмевнувам<br>*Jas se nasmevnuvam* | We smile-<br>Ние се насмевнуваме<br>*Nie se nasmevnuvame* |
| 2nd person | You smile-<br>Ти се насмевнуваш<br>*Ti se nasmevnuvash* | You smile-<br>Вие се насмевнувате<br>*Vie se nasmevnuvate* |
| 3rd person | He/She/It smiles -<br>Тој/Таа/Тоа се насмевнува<br>*Toj/Taa/Toa se nasmevmuva* | They smile-<br>Тие се насмевнуваат<br>*Tie se nasmevnuvaat* |

| **Past Simple Tense** | | |
|---|---|---|
| *Person* | *Singular* | *Plural* |
| 1st person | I smiled-<br>Јас се насмевнав<br>*Jas se nasmevnav* | We smiled -<br>Ние се насмевнавме<br>*Nie se nasmevnavme* |
| 2nd person | You smiled -<br>Ти се насмевна<br>*Ti se nasmevna* | You smiled -<br>Вие се насмевнавте<br>*Vie se nasmevnavte* |
| 3rd person | He/She/It smiled -<br>Тој/Таа/Тоа се насмевна<br>*Toj/Taa/Toa se nasmevna* | They smiled -<br>Тие се насмевнаа<br>*Tie se nasmevnaa* |

| **Past Continuous Tense** | | |
|---|---|---|
| *Person* | *Singular* | *Plural* |
| 1st person | I was smiling-<br>Јас се насмевнував<br>*Jas se nasmevnuvav* | We were smiling-<br>Ние се насмевнуваме<br>*Nie se nasmevnuvavme* |
| 2nd person | You were smiling-<br>Ти се насмевнуваш<br>*Ti se nasmevnuvashe* | You were smiling-<br>Вие се насмевнувате<br>*Vie se nasmevnuvavte* |
| 3rd person | He/She/It was smiling -<br>Тој/Таа/Тоа се насмевнуваш<br>*Toj/Taa/Toa se nasmevnuvashe* | They were smiling-<br>Тие се насмевнуваа<br>*Tie se nasmevnuvaa* |

| **Present Perfect Simple Tense** | | |
|---|---|---|
| *Person* | *Singular* | *Plural* |
| 1st person | I have smiled-<br>Јас сум се насмевнал(а)<br>*Ja sum se nasmevnal(a)* | We have smiled -<br>Ние сме се насмевнале<br>*Nie sme se nasmevnale* |

| | | |
|---|---|---|
| 2nd person | You have smiled -<br>Ти си се н**а**смевнал(а)<br>*Ti si se n**a**smevnal(a)* | You have smiled -<br>Вие сте се насм**е**внале<br>*Vie ste se nasm**e**vnale* |
| 3rd person | He/She/It has smiled -<br>Тој/Таа/Тоа се н**а**смевнал(а)(о)<br>*Toj/Taa/Toa se n**a**smevnal(a)(o)* | They have smiled -<br>Тие се насм**е**внале<br>*Tie se nasm**e**vnale* |

| **Present Perfect Continuous Tense** | | |
|---|---|---|
| *Person* | *Singular* | *Plural* |
| 1st person | I have been smiling-<br>Јас сум се насм**е**внувал(а)<br>*Jas sum se nasm**e**vnuval(a)* | We have been smiling -<br>Ние сме се насмевн**у**вале<br>*Nie sme se nasmevn**u**vale* |
| 2nd person | You have been smiling-<br>Ти си се насм**е**внувал(а)<br>*Ti si se nasm**e**vnuval(a)* | You have been smiling-<br>Вие сте се насмевн**у**вале<br>*Vie ste se nasmevn**u**vale* |
| 3rd person | He/She/It has been smiling -<br>Тој/Таа/Тоа се<br>насм**е**внувал(а)(о)<br>*Toj/Taa/Toa se*<br>*nasm**e**vnuval(a)(o)* | They have been smiling -<br>Тие се насмевн**у**вале<br>*Tie se nasmevn**u**vale* |

| **Past Perfect Simple Tense** | | |
|---|---|---|
| *Person* | *Singular* | *Plural* |
| 1st person | I had smiled -<br>Јас бев се н**а**смевнал(а)<br>*Jas bev se n**a**smevnal(a)* | We had smiled -<br>Ние бевме се насм**е**внале<br>*Nie bevme se nasm**e**vnale* |
| 2nd person | You had smiled -<br>Ти беше се н**а**смевнал(а)<br>*Ti beshe se n**a**smevnal(a)* | You had smiled -<br>Вие бевте се насм**е**внале<br>*Vie bevte se nasm**e**vnale* |
| 3rd person | He/She/It had smiled -<br>Тој/Таа/Тоа беше се<br>н**а**смевнал(а)(о)<br>*Toj/Taa/Toa beshe se*<br>*n**a**smevnal(a)(o)* | They had smiled -<br>Тие беа се насм**е**внале<br>*Tie bea se nasm**e**vnale* |

| **Future Simple Tense** | | |
|---|---|---|
| *Person* | *Singular* | *Plural* |
| 1st person | I will smile -<br>Јас ќе се насм**е**внувам/<br>се н**а**смевнам<br>*Jas kje se nasm**e**vnuvam/*<br>*se n**a**smevnam* | We will smile -<br>Ние ќе се насмевн**у**ваме/<br>се насм**е**вneme<br>*Nie kje se nasmevn**u**vame/*<br>*se nasm**e**vneme* |
| 2nd person | You will smile -<br>Ти ќе се насм**е**внуваш/<br>се н**а**смевнеш<br>*Ti kje se nasm**e**vnuvash/*<br>*se n**a**smevnesh* | You will smile -<br>Вие ќе се се насмевн**у**вате/<br>се насм**е**внете<br>*Vie kje se nasmevn**u**vate/*<br>*se nasm**e**vnete* |

| | | |
|---|---|---|
| 3rd person | He/She/It will smile -<br>Тој/Таа/Тоа ќе се<br>насм**е**внува/се н**а**смевне<br>*Toj/Taa/Toa kje se*<br>*nasm**e**vnuva/se n**a**smevne* | They will smile -<br>Тие ќе се насмевн**у**вааате/<br>се н**а**смевнат<br>*Tie kje se nasmevn**u**vaat/*<br>*se n**a**smevnat* |

| **used to + infinitive or would + infinitive** | | |
|---|---|---|
| *Person* | *Singular* | *Plural* |
| 1st person | I would smile -<br>Јас ќе се насм**е**внував/<br>се н**а**смевнев<br>*Jas kje se nasmevnuvav/*<br>*se n**a**smevnev* | We would smile -<br>Ние ќе се насмевн**у**вавме/<br>се насм**е**вневме<br>*Nie kje se nasmevn**u**vavme/*<br>*se nasm**e**vnevme* |
| 2nd person | You would smile -<br>Ти ќе се насмевн**у**ваше/<br>се насм**е**внеше<br>*Ti kje se nasmevn**u**vashe/*<br>*se nasm**e**vneshe* | You would smile -<br>Вие ќе се насмевн**у**вавте/<br>се насм**е**вневте<br>*Vie kje se nasmevn**u**vavte/*<br>*se nasm**e**vnevte* |
| 3rd person | He/She/It would smile -<br>Тој/Таа/Тоа ќе<br>се насмевн**у**ваше/<br>се насм**е**внеше<br>*Toj/Taa/Toa kje se*<br>*nasmevn**u**vashe/*<br>*senasm**e**vneshe* | They would smile-<br>Тие ќе се насмевн**у**ваа/<br>се насм**е**внаа<br>*Tie kje se nasmevn**u**vaa/se*<br>*nasm**e**vnaa* |

| **Personal endings for future perfect-in-the-past tense** | | |
|---|---|---|
| *Person* | *Singular* | *Plural* |
| 1st person | I would have smiled -<br>Јас ќе сум се насм**е**внувал/<br>се н**а**смевнал(а)<br>*Jas kje sum se nasm**e**vnuval/*<br>*se n**a**smevnal(a)* | We would have smiled -<br>Ние ќе сме се насмевн**у**вале/<br>се насм**е**внале<br>*Nie kje sme*<br>*se nasmevn**u**vale/*<br>*se nasm**e**vnale* |
| 2nd person | You would have smiled-<br>Ти ќе си се насм**е**внувал/<br>се н**а**смевнал(а)<br>*Ti kje si nasm**e**vnuval/*<br>*se n**a**smevnal(a)* | *You would have smiled -*<br>*Вие ќе сте се насмевн**у**вале/*<br>*се насм**е**внале*<br>Vie kje ste<br>se nasmevn**u**vale/<br>se nasm**e**vnale |
| 3rd person | He/She/It would have smiled -<br>Тој/Таа/Тоа ќе<br>се насм**е**внувал<br>/се н**а**смевнал(а)(о)<br>*Toj/Taa/Toa kje*<br>*se nasm**e**vnuval/*<br>*se n**a**smevnal(a)(o)* | They would have smiled -<br>Тие ќе се насмевн**у**вале/<br>се насм**е**внале<br>*Tie kje se nasmevn**u**vale/*<br>*se nasm**e**vnale* |

***To speak – Зборува/Позборува***

| | | |
|---|---|---|
| *Infinitive* | To speak | Зб**о**рува<br>Zb**o**ruva |

| **Present Simple Tense** | | |
|---|---|---|
| *Person* | *Singular* | *Plural* |
| 1st person | I speak -<br>Јас зб**о**рувам<br>*Jas zb**o**ruvam* | We speak -<br>Ние збор**у**ваме<br>*Nie zbor**u**vame* |
| 2nd person | You speak -<br>Ти зб**о**руваш<br>*Ti zb**o**ruvash* | You speak -<br>Вие збор**у**вате<br>*Vie zbor**u**vate* |
| 3rd person | He/She/It speaks -<br>Тој/Таа/Тоа зб**о**рува<br>*Toj/Taa/Toa zb**o**ruva* | They speak -<br>Тие збор**у**ваат<br>*Tie zbor**u**vaat* |

| **Past Simple Tense** | | |
|---|---|---|
| *Person* | *Singular* | *Plural* |
| 1st person | I spoke -<br>Јас позб**о**рував<br>*Jas pozb**o**ruvav* | We spoke -<br>Ние позбор**у**вавме<br>*Nie pozbor**u**vavme* |
| 2nd person | You spoke -<br>Ти позб**о**рува<br>*Ti pozb**o**ruva* | You spoke -<br>Вие позбор**у**вавте<br>*Vie pozbor**u**vavte* |
| 3rd person | He/She/It spoke -<br>Тој/Таа/Тоа позб**о**рува<br>*Toj/Taa/Toa pozb**o**ruva* | They spoke -<br>Тие позбор**у**ваа<br>*Tie pozbor**u**vaa* |

| **Past Continuous Tense** | | |
|---|---|---|
| *Person* | *Singular* | *Plural* |
| 1st person | I was speaking -<br>Јас зб**о**рував<br>*Jas zb**o**ruvav* | We were speaking -<br>Ние збор**у**вавме<br>*Nie zbor**u**vavme* |
| 2nd person | You were speaking -<br>Ти збор**у**ваше<br>*Ti zbor**u**vashe* | You were speaking -<br>Вие збор**у**вавте<br>*Vie zbor**u**vavte* |
| 3rd person | He/She/It was speaking -<br>Тој/Таа/Тоа збор**у**ваше<br>*Toj/Taa/Toa zbor**u**vashe* | They were speaking -<br>Тие збор**у**ваа<br>*Tie zbor**u**vaa* |

| **Present Perfect Simple Tense** | | |
|---|---|---|
| *Person* | *Singular* | *Plural* |
| 1st person | I have spoken -<br>*Јас сум позб**о**рувал(а)*<br>*Jas sum pozb**o**ruval(a)* | We have spoken -<br>Ние сме позбор**у**вале<br>*Nie sme pozbor**u**vale* |

| | | |
|---|---|---|
| 2nd person | You have spoken -<br>Ти си позб**о**рувал(а)<br>*Ti si pozb**o**ruval(a)* | You have spoken -<br>Вие сте позбор**у**вале<br>*Vie ste pozbor**u**vale* |
| 3rd person | He/She/It has spoken -<br>Тој/Таа/Тоа позб**о**рувал(а)(о)<br>*Toj/Taa/Toa pozb**o**ruval(a)(o)* | They have spoken -<br>Тие позбор**у**вале<br>*Tie pozbor**u**vale* |

| **Present Perfect Continuous Tense** | | |
|---|---|---|
| *Person* | *Singular* | *Plural* |
| 1st person | *I have been speaking -*<br>*Јас сум зб**о**рувал(а)*<br>*Jas sum zb**o**ruval(a)* | We have been speaking -<br>Ние сме збор**у**вале<br>*Nie sme zbor**u**vale* |
| 2nd person | You have been speaking -<br>Ти си зб**о**рувал(а)<br>*Ti si zb**o**ruval(a)* | You have been speaking -<br>Вие сте збор**у**вале<br>*Vie ste zbor**u**vale* |
| 3rd person | He/She/It has been speaking -<br>Тој/Таа/Тоа зб**о**рувал(а)(о)<br>*Toj/Taa/Toa zb**o**ruval(a)(o)* | They have been speaking -<br>Тие збор**у**вале<br>*Tie zbor**u**vale* |

| **Past Perfect Simple Tense** | | |
|---|---|---|
| *Person* | *Singular* | *Plural* |
| 1st person | I had spoken -<br>Јас бев позб**о**рувал(а)<br>*Jas bev pozb**o**ruval(a)* | We had spoken -<br>Ние бевме позбор**у**вале<br>*Nie bevme pozbor**u**vale* |
| 2nd person | You had spoken -<br>Ти беше позб**о**рувал(а)<br>*Ti beshe pozb**o**ruval(a)* | You had spoken -<br>Вие бевте позбор**у**вале<br>*Vie bevte pozbor**u**vale* |
| 3rd person | He/She/It had spoken -<br>Тој/Таа/Тоа беше позб**о**рувал(а)(о)<br>*Toj/Taa/Toa beshe pozb**o**ruval(a)(o)* | They had spoken -<br>Тие беа позбор**у**вале<br>*Tie bea pozbor**u**vale* |

| **Future Simple Tense** | | |
|---|---|---|
| *Person* | *Singular* | *Plural* |
| 1st person | I will speak -<br>Јас ќе зб**о**рувам/позб**о**рувам<br>*Jas kje zb**o**ruvam/pozb**o**ruvam* | We will speak -<br>Ние ќе збор**у**ваме/позбор**у**ваме<br>Nie kje *zbor**u**vame/pozbor**u**vavme* |
| 2nd person | You will speak -<br>Ти ќе зб**о**руваше/позб**о**руваше<br>*Ti kje zb**o**ruvashe/pozb**o**ruvashe* | You will speak -<br>Вие ќе збор**у**вате/позбор**у**вате<br>*Vie zbor**u**vate/pozbor**u**vavte* |
| 3rd person | He/She/It will speak –<br>Тој/Таа/Тоа ќе зб**о**руваше/позб**о**руваше<br>*Toj/Taa/Toa kje zb**o**ruvashe/pozb**o**ruvashe* | They will speak -<br>Тие ќе збор**у**ваат/ позбор**у**ваат<br>*Tie kje zbor**u**vaat/ pozbor**u**vaat* |

| **used to + infinitive or would + infinitive** | | |
|---|---|---|
| *Person* | *Singular* | *Plural* |
| 1st person | I would speak -<br>Јас ќе зб**о**рував/позб**о**рував<br>*Jas kje zb**o**ruvav/pozb**o**ruvav* | We would speak -<br>Ние ќе<br>збор**у**вавме/позбор**у**вавме<br>*Nie kje*<br>*zbor**u**vavme/pozbo**ru**vavme* |
| 2nd person | You would speak -<br>Ти ќе збор**у**ваше/позбор**у**ваше<br>*Ti kje zbor**u**vashe/pozbor**u**vashe* | You would speak -<br>Вие ќе<br>збор**у**вавте/позбор**у**вавте<br>*Vie kje zbor**u**vavte/pozbor**u**vavte* |
| 3rd person | He/She/It would speak -<br>Тој/Таа/Тоа<br>збор**у**ваше/позбор**у**ваше<br>*Toj/Taa/Toa*<br>*zbor**u**vashe/pozbor**u**vashe* | They would speak -<br>Тие ќе збор**у**ваа/позбор**у**ваа<br>*Tie kje zbor**u**vaa/pozbor**u**vaa* |

| **Personal endings for future perfect-in-the-past tense** | | |
|---|---|---|
| *Person* | *Singular* | *Plural* |
| 1st person | I would have spoken -<br>Јас ќе сум<br>зб**о**рувал/позб**о**рувал(а)<br>*Jas kje sum*<br>*zb**o**ruval/pozb**o**ruval(a)* | We would have spoken -<br>Ние ќе сме<br>збор**у**вале/позбор**у**вале<br>*Nie kje sme*<br>*zbor**u**vale/pozbor**u**vale* |
| 2nd person | You would have spoken -<br>Ти ќе си<br>зб**о**рувал/позб**о**рувал(а)<br>*Ti kje si zb**o**ruval/pozb**o**ruval(a)* | You would have spoken -<br>Вие ќе сте<br>збор**у**вале/позбор**у**вале<br>*Vie kje ste*<br>*zbor**u**vale/pozbor**u**vale* |
| 3rd person | He/She/It would have spoken<br>Тој/Таа/Тоа ќе<br>зб**о**рувал/позб**о**рувал(а)(о)<br>*Toj/Taa/Toa kje*<br>*zb**o**ruval/p**o**zboruval(a)(o)* | They would have spoken -<br>Тие ќе збор**у**вале/позбор**у**вале<br>*Tie kje zbor**u**vale/pozbor**u**vale* |

***To stand – Стои/Постоја***

| | | |
|---|---|---|
| *Infinitive* | To stand | Стои<br>Stoi |

| Present Simple Tense | | |
|---|---|---|
| *Person* | *Singular* | *Plural* |
| 1st person | I stand-<br>Јас стојам<br>*Jas stojam* | We stand-<br>Ние стоиме<br>*Nie stoime* |
| 2nd person | You stand-<br>Ти стоиш<br>*Ti stoish* | You stand -<br>Ве стоите<br>*Vie stoite* |
| 3rd person | He/She/It stands -<br>Тој/Таа/Тоастои<br>*Toj/Taa/Toa stoi* | They stand-<br>Тие стојат<br>*Tie stojat* |

| Past Simple Tense | | |
|---|---|---|
| *Person* | *Singular* | *Plural* |
| 1st person | I stood-<br>Јас постојав<br>*Jas postojav* | We stood -<br>Ние постојавме<br>*Nie postojavme* |
| 2nd person | You stood-<br>Ти постоја<br>*Ti postoja* | You stood -<br>Вие постојавте<br>*Vie postojavte* |
| 3rd person | He/She/It stood -<br>Тој/Таа/Тоа постоја<br>*Toj/Taa/Toa postoja* | They stood -<br>Тие постојаа<br>*Tie postojaa* |

| Past Continuous Tense | | |
|---|---|---|
| Person | Singular | Plural |
| 1st person | I was standing-<br>Јас стоев<br>*Jas stov* | We were standing -<br>Ние стоевме<br>*Nie stoevme* |
| 2nd person | You were standing-<br>Ти стоеше<br>*Ti stoeshe* | You were standing -<br>Вие стоевте<br>*Vie stoevte* |
| 3rd person | He/She/It was standing-<br>Тој/Таа/Тоа стоеше<br>*Toj/Taa/Toa stoeshe* | They were standing -<br>Тие стоеја<br>*Tie stoeja* |

| Present Perfect Simple Tense | | |
|---|---|---|
| *Person* | *Singular* | *Plural* |
| 1st person | I have stood -<br>Јас сум постојал(а)<br>*Jas sum postojal(a)* | We have stood -<br>Ние сме постојале<br>*Nie sme postojale* |

| | | |
|---|---|---|
| 2nd person | You have stood -<br>Ти си п**о**стојал(а)<br>*Ti si p**o**stojal(a)* | You have stood -<br>Вие сте п**о**стојале<br>*Vie ste p**o**stojale* |
| 3rd person | He/She/It has stood -<br>Тој/Таа/Тоа п**о**стојал(а)(о)<br>*Toj/Taa/Toa p**o**stojal(a)(o)* | They have stood -<br>Тие п**о**стојале<br>*Tie p**o**stojale* |

| Present Perfect Continuous Tense | | |
|---|---|---|
| *Person* | *Singular* | *Plural* |
| 1st person | I have been standing -<br>Јас сум ст**о**ел(а)<br>*Jas sum st**o**el(a)* | We have been standing -<br>Ние сме ст**о**еле<br>*Nie sme st**o**ele* |
| 2nd person | You have been standing -<br>Ти си ст**о**ел(а)<br>*Ti si st**o**el(a)* | You have been standing -<br>Вие сте ст**о**еле<br>*Vie ste st**o**ele* |
| 3rd person | He/She/It has been standing -<br>Тој/Таа/Тоа ст**о**ел(а)(о)<br>*Toj/Taa/Toa st**o**el(a)(o)* | They have been standing -<br>Тие ст**о**еле<br>*Tie st**o**ele* |

| Past Perfect Simple Tense | | |
|---|---|---|
| *Person* | *Singular* | *Plural* |
| 1st person | I had stood -<br>Јас бев п**о**стојал(а)<br>*Jas bev p**o**stojal(a)* | We had stood -<br>Ние бевме пост**о**јале<br>*Nie bevme post**o**jale* |
| 2nd person | You had stood -<br>Ти беше п**о**стојал(а)<br>*Ti beshe p**o**stojal(a)* | You had stood -<br>Вие бевте пост**о**јале<br>*Vie bevte post**o**jale* |
| 3rd person | He/She/It had stood -<br>Тој/Таа/Тоа беше<br>п**о**стојал(а)(о)<br>*Toj/Taa/Toa beshe*<br>*p**o**stojal(a)(o)* | They had stood -<br>Тие беа пост**о**јале<br>*Tie bea post**o**jale* |

| Future Simple Tense | | |
|---|---|---|
| *Person* | *Singular* | *Plural* |
| 1st person | I will stand -<br>Јас ќе ст**о**јам/п**о**стојам<br>*Jas kje st**o**jam/p**o**stojam* | We will stand -<br>Ние ќе ст**о**име/пост**о**име<br>*Nie kje st**o**ime/post**o**ime* |
| 2nd person | You will stand -<br>Ти ќе ст**о**иш/пост**о**иш<br>*Ti kje st**o**ish/post**o**ish* | You will stand -<br>Вие ќе ст**о**ите/пост**о**ите<br>*Vie kje st**o**ite/post**o**ite* |
| 3rd person | He/She/It will stand -<br>Тој/Таа/Тоа ќе ст**о**и/п**о**стои<br>*Toj/Taa/Toa kje st**o**i/p**o**stoi* | They will stand -<br>Тие ќе ст**о**јат/пост**о**јат<br>*Tie kje st**o**eja/post**o**eja* |

| **used to + infinitive or would + infinitive** | | |
|---|---|---|
| *Person* | *Singular* | *Plural* |
| 1st person | I would stand -<br>Јас ќе стоев/постоев<br>*Jas kje stovev/postoev* | We would stand -<br>Ние ќе стоевме/постоевме<br>*Nie kje stoevme/postoivme* |
| 2nd person | You would stand -<br>Ти ќе стоеше/постоеше<br>*Ti kje stoeshe/postoeshe* | You would stand -<br>Вие ќе стоевте/постоевте<br>*Vie kje stoevte/postoivte* |
| 3rd person | He/She/It would stand -<br>Тој/Таа/Тоа ќе стоеше/постоеше<br>*Toj/Taa/Toa stoeshe/postoeshe* | They would stand -<br>Тие ќе стоеја/постоеа<br>*Tie stoeja/postoea* |

| **Personal endings for future perfect-in-the-past tense** | | |
|---|---|---|
| *Person* | *Singular* | *Plural* |
| 1st person | I would have stood -<br>Јас ќе сум стоел/постоел(а)<br>*Jas kje sum stoel/postoel(a)* | We would have stood -<br>Ние ќе сме стоеле/постоеле<br>*Nie kje sme stoele/postoele* |
| 2nd person | You would have stood -<br>Ти ќе си стоел/постоел(а)<br>*Ti kje si stoel/postoel(a)* | You would have stood -<br>Вие ќе сте стоеле/постоеле<br>*Vie kje ste stoele/postoele* |
| 3rd person | He/She/It would have stood-<br>Тој/Таа/Тоа ќе стоел/постоел(а)(о)<br>*Toj/Taa/Toa kje stoel/postoel(a)(o)* | They would have stood -<br>Тие ќе стоеле/постоеле<br>*Tie kje stoele/postoele* |

***To start – Почнува/Почна***

| | | |
|---|---|---|
| *Infinitive* | To start | П**о**чнува<br>P**o**cnhuva |

| **Present Simple Tense** | | |
|---|---|---|
| *Person* | *Singular* | *Plural* |
| $1^{st}$ person | I start -<br>Јас п**о**чнувам<br>*Jas p**o**chnuvam* | We start -<br>Ние п**о**чнуваме<br>*Nie p**o**chnuvame* |
| $2^{nd}$ person | You start -<br>Ти п**о**чнуваш<br>*Ti p**o**chnuvash* | You start -<br>Вие п**о**чнувате<br>*Vie p**o**chnuvate* |
| $3^{rd}$ person | He/She/It starts -<br>Тој/Таа/Тоа п**о**чнува<br>*Toj/Taa/Toa p**o**chnuva* | They start -<br>Тие п**о**чнуваат<br>*Tie p**o**chnuvaat* |

| **Past Simple Tense** | | |
|---|---|---|
| *Person* | *Singular* | *Plural* |
| $1^{st}$ person | I started -<br>Јас п**о**чнав<br>*Jas p**o**chnav* | We started -<br>Ние п**о**чнавме<br>*Nie p**o**chnavme* |
| $2^{nd}$ person | You started -<br>Ти п**о**чна<br>*Tie p**o**chna* | You started -<br>Вие п**о**чнавте<br>*Vie p**o**chnavte* |
| $3^{rd}$ person | He/She/It started -<br>Тој/Таа/Тоа п**о**чна<br>*Toj/Taa/Toa p**o**chna* | They started -<br>Тие п**о**чнаа<br>*Tie p**o**chnaa* |

| **Past Continuous Tense** | | |
|---|---|---|
| *Person* | *Singular* | *Plural* |
| $1^{st}$ person | I was starting -<br>Јас п**о**чнував<br>*Jas p**o**chnuvav* | We were starting -<br>Ние почн**у**вавме<br>*Nie pochn**u**vavme* |
| $2^{nd}$ person | You were starting -<br>Ти почн**у**ваше<br>*Ti pochn**u**vashe* | You were starting -<br>Вие почн**у**вавте<br>*Vie pochn**u**vavte* |
| $3^{rd}$ person | He/She/It was starting -<br>Тој/Таа/Тоа почн**у**ваше<br>*Toj/Taa/Toa pochn**u**vashe* | They were starting -<br>Тие почн**у**ваа<br>*Tie pochn**u**vaa* |

| **Present Perfect Simple Tense** | | |
|---|---|---|
| *Person* | *Singular* | *Plural* |
| $1^{st}$ person | I have started -<br>Јас сум п**о**чнал(а)<br>*Jas sum p**o**chnal(a)* | We have started -<br>Ние сме п**о**чнале<br>*Nie sme p**o**chnale* |
| $2^{nd}$ person | You have started -<br>Ти си п**о**чнал(а)<br>*Ti si p**o**chnal(a)* | You have started -<br>Вие сте п**о**чнале<br>*Vie ste p**o**chnale* |

| | | |
|---|---|---|
| 3rd person | He/She/It has started -<br>Тој/Таа/Тоа почнал(а)(о)<br>*Toj/Taa/Toa pochnal(a)(o)* | They have started -<br>Тие почнале<br>*Ti pochnale* |

| **Present Perfect Continuous Tense** | | |
|---|---|---|
| *Person* | *Singular* | *Plural* |
| 1st person | I have been starting -<br>Јас сум почнувал(а)<br>*Jas sum pochnuval(a)* | We have been starting -<br>Ние сме почнувале<br>*Nie sme pochnuvale* |
| 2nd person | You have been starting -<br>Ти си почнувал(а)<br>*Ti si pochnuval(a)* | You have been starting -<br>Вие сте почнувале<br>*Vie ste pochnuvale* |
| 3rd person | He/She/It has been starting -<br>Тој/Таа/Тоа почнувал(а)(о)<br>*Toj/Taa/Toa pochnuval(a)(o)* | They have been starting -<br>Тие почнувале<br>*Tie pochnuvale* |

| **Past Perfect Simple Tense** | | |
|---|---|---|
| *Person* | *Singular* | *Plural* |
| 1st person | I had started -<br>Јас бев почнал(а)<br>*Jas bev pochnal(a)* | We had started -<br>Ние бевме почнале<br>*Nie bevme pochnale* |
| 2nd person | You had started -<br>Ти беше почнал(а)<br>*Ti beshe pochnal(a)* | You had started -<br>Вие бевте почнале<br>*Vie bevte pochnale* |
| 3rd person | He/She/It had started -<br>Тој/Таа/Тоа беше почнал(а)(о)<br>*Toj/Taa/Toa beshe pochnal(a)(o)* | They had started -<br>Тие беа почнале<br>*Tie bea pochnale* |

| **Future Simple Tense** | | |
|---|---|---|
| *Person* | *Singular* | *Plural* |
| 1st person | I will start -<br>Јас ќе почнувам/почнам<br>*Jas kje pochnuvam/pochnam* | We will start -<br>Ние ќе почнуваме/почнаме<br>*Nie kje pochnuvame/pochname* |
| 2nd person | You will start -<br>Ти ќе почнуваш/почнеш<br>*Ti kje pochnuvash/pochnash* | You will start -<br>Вие ќе почнувате/почнете<br>*Vie kje pochnuvate/pochnate* |
| 3rd person | He/She/It will start -<br>Тој/Таа/Тоа ќе почнува/почне<br>*Toj/Taa/Toa kje pochnuva/pochna* | They will start -<br>Тие ќе почнуваат/почнат<br>*Tie kje pochnuvaat/pochnat* |

| **used to + infinitive or would + infinitive** | | |
|---|---|---|
| *Person* | *Singular* | *Plural* |
| 1st person | I would start -<br>Јас ќе почнував/почнев<br>*Jas kje pochnuvav/pochnev* | We would start -<br>Ние ќе почнувавме/почневме<br>*Nie kje pochnuvavme/pochnevme* |

| | | |
|---|---|---|
| 2nd person | You would start -<br>Ти ќе почн**у**ваше/п**о**чнеше<br>*Ti kje pochn**u**vashe/p**o**chneshe* | You would start -<br>Вие ќе почн**у**вавте/п**о**чневте<br>*Vie kje pochn**u**vavte/p**o**chnevete* |
| 3rd person | He/She/It would start -<br>Тој/Таа/Тоа ќе<br>почн**у**ваше/п**о**чнеше<br>*Toj/Taa/Toa kje*<br>*pochn**u**vashe/p**o**chneshe* | They would start -<br>Тие ќе почн**у**ваа/п**о**чнеа<br>*Tie kje pochn**u**vaa/p**o**chnea* |

| **Personal endings for future perfect-in-the-past tense** | | |
|---|---|---|
| *Person* | *Singular* | *Plural* |
| 1st person | I would have started -<br>Јас ќе сум п**о**чнувал/п**о**чнал(а)<br>Jas kje sum<br>p**o**chnuval/p**o**chnal(a) | We would have started -<br>Ние ќе сме почн**у**вале/п**о**чнале<br>*Nie kje sme*<br>*pochn**u**vale/p**o**chnale* |
| 2nd person | You would have started -<br>Ти ќе си п**о**чнувал/п**о**чнал(а)<br>*Ti kje si p**o**chnuval/p**o**chnal(a)* | You would have started -<br>Вие ќе сте почн**у**вале/п**о**чнале<br>*Vie kje ste pochn**u**vale/p**o**chnale* |
| 3rd person | He/She/It would have started -<br>Тој/Таа/Тоа ќе<br>п**о**чнувал/п**о**чнал(а)(о)<br>*Toj/Taa/Toa kje*<br>*p**o**chnuval/p**o**chnal(a)(o)* | They would have started -<br>Тие ќе почн**у**вале/п**о**чнале<br>*Tie kje pochn**u**vale/ p**o**chnale* |

### *To stay – Останува/Остана*

| Infinitive | To stay | Останува<br>Ostanuva |
|---|---|---|

| Present Simple Tense | | |
|---|---|---|
| *Person* | *Singular* | *Plural* |
| 1st person | I stay -<br>Јас останувам<br>*Jas ostanuvam* | We stay -<br>Ние останувамe<br>*Nie ostanuvame* |
| 2nd person | You stay -<br>Ти останувaш<br>*Ti ostanuvash* | You stay -<br>Вие останувате<br>*Vie ostanuvate* |
| 3rd person | He/She/It stays -<br>Тој/Таа/Тоаостанува<br>*Toj/Taa/Toa ostanuva* | They stay -<br>Тие останувaат<br>*Tie ostanuvaat* |

| Past Simple Tense | | |
|---|---|---|
| *Person* | *Singular* | *Plural* |
| 1st person | I stayed -<br>Јас останав<br>*Jas ostanav* | We stayed -<br>Ние останавме<br>*Nie ostanavme* |
| 2nd person | You stayed -<br>Ти остана<br>*Ti ostana* | You stayed -<br>Вие останавте<br>*Vie ostanavte* |
| 3rd person | He/She/It stayed -<br>Тој/Таа/Тоа остана<br>*Toj/Taa/Toa ostana* | They stayed -<br>Тие останаа<br>*Tie ostanaa* |

| Past Continuous Tense | | |
|---|---|---|
| *Person* | *Singular* | *Plural* |
| 1st person | I was staying -<br>Јас останував<br>*Jas ostanuvav* | We were staying -<br>Ние останувавме<br>*Nie ostanuvavme* |
| 2nd person | You were staying -<br>Ти останувaше<br>*Ti ostanuvashe* | You were staying -<br>Вие останувавте<br>*Vie ostanuvavte* |
| 3rd person | He/She/It was staying -<br>Тој/Таа/Тоа останувaше<br>*Toj/Taa/Toa ostanuvashe* | They were staying -<br>Тие останувaа<br>*Tie ostanuvaa* |

| Present Perfect Simple Tense | | |
|---|---|---|
| *Person* | *Singular* | *Plural* |
| 1st person | I have stayed -<br>Јас сум останал(а)<br>*Jas sum ostanal(a)* | We have stayed -<br>Ние сме останале<br>*Nie sme ostanale* |

| | | |
|---|---|---|
| 2nd person | You have stayed -<br>Ти си ост**а**нал(а)<br>*Ti si ost**a**nal(a)* | You have stayed -<br>Вие сте ост**а**нале<br>*Vie ste ost**a**nale* |
| 3rd person | He/She/It has stayed -<br>Тој/Таа/Тоа ост**а**нал(а)(о)<br>*Toj/Taa/Toa ost**a**nal(a)(o)* | They have stayed -<br>Тие ост**а**нале<br>*Tie ost**a**nale* |

| **Present Perfect Continuous Tense** | | |
|---|---|---|
| *Person* | *Singular* | *Plural* |
| 1st person | I have been staying -<br>Јас сум ост**а**нувал(а)<br>*Jas sum ost**a**nuval(a)* | We have been staying -<br>Ние сме остан**у**вале<br>*Nie sme ostan**u**vale* |
| 2nd person | You have been staying -<br>Ти си ост**а**нувал(а)<br>*Ti si ost**a**nuval(a)* | You have been staying -<br>Вие сте остан**у**вале<br>*Vie ste ostan**u**vale* |
| 3rd person | He/She/It has been staying -<br>Тој/Таа/Тоа ост**а**нувал(а)(о)<br>*Toj/Taa/Toa ost**a**nuval(a)(o)* | They have been staying -<br>Тие остан**у**вале<br>*Tie ostan**u**vale* |

| **Past Perfect Simple Tense** | | |
|---|---|---|
| *Person* | *Singular* | *Plural* |
| 1st person | I had stayed -<br>Јас бев **о**станал(а)<br>*Jas bev **o**stanal(a)* | We had stayed -<br>Ние бевме ост**а**нале<br>*Nie bevme ost**a**nale* |
| 2nd person | You had stayed -<br>Ти беше **о**станал(а)<br>*Ti beshe **o**stanal(a)* | You had stayed -<br>Вие бевте ост**а**нале<br>*Vie bevte ost**a**nale* |
| 3rd person | He/She/It had stayed -<br>Тој/Таа/Тоа беше **о**станал(а)(о)<br>*Toj/Taa/Toa beshe **o**stanal(a)(o)* | They had stayed -<br>Тие беа ост**а**нале<br>*Tie bea oat**a**nale* |

| **Future Simple Tense** | | |
|---|---|---|
| *Person* | *Singular* | *Plural* |
| 1st person | I will stay -<br>Јас ќе ост**а**нувам/**о**станам<br>*Jas kje ost**a**nuvam/**o**stanam* | We will stay -<br>Ние ќе остан**у**ваме/ост**а**неме<br>*Nie kje ostan**u**vame/ost**a**neme* |
| 2nd person | You will stay -<br>Ти ќе ост**а**нуваш/**о**станеш<br>*Ti kje ost**a**nuvash/**o**stanesh* | You will stay -<br>Вие ќе остан**у**вате/ост**а**нете<br>*Vie ostan**u**vate/ost**a**nete* |
| 3rd person | He/She/It will stay -<br>Тој/Таа/Тоа ќе ост**а**нува/**о**стане<br>*Toj/Taa/Toa kje ost**a**nuva/**o**stane* | They will stay -<br>Тие ќе остан**у**ваат/ост**а**нат<br>*Tie kje ostan**u**vaat/ost**a**nat* |

| **used to + infinitive or would + infinitive** | | |
|---|---|---|
| *Person* | *Singular* | *Plural* |
| 1st person | I would stay -<br>Јас ќе ост**а**нував/**о**станев<br>*Jas kje ost**a**nuvav/**o**stanev* | We would stay -<br>Ние ќе остан**у**вавме/ост**а**невме<br>*Nie kje ostan**u**vavme/ost**a**nevme* |

| | | |
|---|---|---|
| 2nd person | You would stay -<br>Ти ќе остан**у**ваше/ост**а**неше<br>*Ti kje ostan**u**vashe/ost**a**neshe* | You would stay -<br>Вие ќе остан**у**вавте/ост**а**невте<br>*Vie kje ostan**u**vavte/ost**a**nevte* |
| 3rd person | He/She/It would stay -<br>Тој/Таа/Тоа ќе<br>остан**у**ваше/ост**а**неше<br>*Toj/Taa/Toa kje*<br>*ostan**u**vashe/ost**a**neshe* | They would stay -<br>Тие ќе ост**а**нуваа/ост**а**неа<br>*Tie kje ostan**u**vaa/ost**a**nea* |

| **Personal endings for future perfect-in-the-past tense** | | |
|---|---|---|
| *Person* | *Singular* | *Plural* |
| 1st person | I would have stayed -<br>Јас ќе сум<br>ост**а**нувал/**о**станал(а)<br>*Jas kje sum ost**a**nuval/**o**stanal(a)* | We would have stayed -<br>Ние ќе сме<br>ост**а**нувале/ост**а**нале<br>Nie kje sme *ost**a**nuvale/ost**a**nale* |
| 2nd person | You would have stayed -<br>Ти ќе си ост**а**нувал/**о**станал(а)<br>*Ti kje si ost**a**nuval/**o**stanal(a)* | You would have stayed -<br>Вие ќе сте<br>остан**у**вале/ост**а**нале<br>*Vie kje ste ostan**u**vale/ost**a**nale* |
| 3rd person | He/She/It would have stayed -<br>Тој/Таа/Тоа ќе<br>ост**а**нувал/**о**станал(а)(о)<br>*Toj/Taa/Toa kje*<br>*ost**a**nuval/**o**stanal(a)(a)* | They would have stayed -<br>Тие ќе остан**у**вале/ост**а**нале<br>*Tie kje ostan**u**vale/ost**a**nale* |

***To take – Зема/Зеде***

| | | |
|---|---|---|
| *Infinitive* | To take | Зема<br>Zema |

| Present Simple Tense | | |
|---|---|---|
| *Person* | *Singular* | *Plural* |
| 1st person | I take -<br>Јас земам<br>Jas zemam | We take -<br>Ние земаме<br>*Nie zemame* |
| 2nd person | You take-<br>Ти земаш<br>*Ti zemash* | You take -<br>Вие земате<br>*Vie zemate* |
| 3rd person | He/She/It takes -<br>Тој/Таа/Тоа зема<br>*Toj/Taa/Toa zema* | They take-<br>Тие земаат<br>*Tie zemaat* |

| Past Simple Tense | | |
|---|---|---|
| *Person* | *Singular* | *Plural* |
| 1st person | I took-<br>Јас зедов<br>*Jas zedov* | We took -<br>Ние зедовме<br>*Nie zedovme* |
| 2nd person | You took-<br>Ти зеде<br>*Ti zede* | You took -<br>Вие зедовте<br>*Vie zedovte* |
| 3rd person | He/She/It took-<br>Тој/Таа/Тоа зеде<br>*Toj/Taa/Toa zede* | They took -<br>Тие зедоа<br>*Tie zedoa* |

| Past Continuous Tense | | |
|---|---|---|
| *Person* | *Singular* | *Plural* |
| 1st person | I was taking-<br>Јас земав<br>*Jas zemav* | We were taking-<br>Ние земавме<br>*Nie zemavme* |
| 2nd person | You were taking-<br>Ти земаше<br>*Ti zemashe* | You were taking-<br>Вие земавте<br>*Vie zemavte* |
| 3rd person | He/She/It was taking-<br>Тој/Таа/Тоа земаше<br>*Toj/Taa/Toa zemashe* | They were taking-<br>Тие земаа<br>*Tie zemaa* |

| Present Perfect Simple Tense | | |
|---|---|---|
| *Person* | *Singular* | *Plural* |
| 1st person | I have took -<br>Јас сум земал(а)<br>*Jas sum zemal(a)* | We have took -<br>Ние сме земале<br>*Nie sme zemale* |

| | | |
|---|---|---|
| 2nd person | You have took -<br>Ти си **зем**ал(а)<br>*Ti si **zem**al(a)* | You have took -<br>Вие сте **зем**але<br>*Vie ste **zem**ale* |
| 3rd person | He/She/It has took -<br>Тој/Таа/Тоа **зем**ал(а)(о)<br>*Toj/Taa/Toa **zem**al(a)(o)* | They have took -<br>Тие **зем**але<br>*Tie **zem**ale* |

| **Present Perfect Continuous Tense** | | |
|---|---|---|
| *Person* | *Singular* | *Plural* |
| 1st person | I have been taking-<br>Јас сум **зе**л(а)<br>*Jas sum **ze**l(a)* | We have been taking-<br>Ние сме **зе**ле<br>*Nie sme **ze**le* |
| 2nd person | You have been taking-<br>Ти си **зе**л(а)<br>*Ti si **ze**l(a)* | You have been taking-<br>Вие сте **зе**ле<br>*Vie ste **ze**le* |
| 3rd person | He/She/It has been taking-<br>Тој/Таа/Тоа **зе**л(а)(о)<br>*Toj/Taa/Toa **ze**l(a)(o)* | They have been taking-<br>Тие **зе**ле<br>*Tie **ze**le* |

| **Past Perfect Simple Tense** | | |
|---|---|---|
| *Person* | *Singular* | *Plural* |
| 1st person | I had took -<br>Јас бев **зем**ал(а)<br>*Jas bev **zem**al(a)* | We had took -<br>Ние бевме **зем**але<br>*Nie sme **zem**ale* |
| 2nd person | You had took-<br>Ти беше **зем**ал(а)<br>*Ti beshe **zem**al(a)* | You had took -<br>Вие бевте **зем**але<br>*Vie ste **zem**ale* |
| 3rd person | He/She/It had took -<br>Тој/Таа/Тоа беше **зем**ал(а),(о)<br>*Toj/Taa/Toa **zem**al(a)(o)* | They had took -<br>Тие беа **зем**але<br>*Tie **zem**ale* |

| **Future Simple Tense** | | |
|---|---|---|
| *Person* | *Singular* | *Plural* |
| 1st person | I will took-<br>Јас ќе **зем**ам/**зед**ам<br>*Jas kje **zem**am/**zed**am* | We will took-<br>Ние ќе **зем**еме/**зед**еме<br>*Nie kje **zem**eme/**zed**eme* |
| 2nd person | You will took -<br>*Ти ќе **зем**еш/**зед**еш*<br>*Ti kje **zem**esh/**zed**esh* | You will took -<br>*Вие ќе **зем**ете/**зед**ете*<br>Vie kje **zem**ete/**zed**ete |
| 3rd person | He/She/It will took-<br>Тој/Таа/Тоа ќе **зем**е/**зед**е<br>*Toj/Taa/Toa kje **zem**e/**zed**e* | They will took-<br>Тие ќе **зем**аат/**зед**ат<br>*Tie kje **zem**at/**zed**at* |

| **used to + infinitive or would + infinitive** | | |
|---|---|---|
| *Person* | *Singular* | *Plural* |
| 1st person | I would take-<br>Јас ќе **зем**ев/**зед**ов<br>*Jas kje **zem**ev/**zed**ov* | We would take -<br>Ние ќе **зем**евме/**зед**овме<br>*Nie kje **zem**evme/**zed**ovme* |

| | | |
|---|---|---|
| 2nd person | You would take -<br>Ти ќе **зе**меше/**зе**деше<br>*Ti kje **ze**meshe/**ze**deshe* | You would take -<br>Вие ќе **зе**мевте/**зе**довте<br>*Vie kje **ze**mevte/**ze**dovte* |
| 3rd person | He/She/It would take -<br>Тој/Таа/Тоа ќе **зе**меше/**зе**деше<br>Toj/Taa/Toa kje<br>**ze**meshe/**ze**deshe | They would take -<br>Тие ќе **зе**маа/**зе**доа<br>*Tie kje **ze**maa/**ze**doa* |

| **Personal endings for future perfect-in-the-past tense** | | |
|---|---|---|
| *Person* | *Singular* | *Plural* |
| 1st person | I would have took -<br>Јас ќе сум **зе**мал/**зе**л(а)<br>*Jas kje sum **ze**mal/**ze**l(a)* | We would have took -<br>Ние ќе смезе**ма**ле/**зе**ле<br>*Nie kje sme **ze**male/**ze**le* |
| 2nd person | You would have took -<br>Ти ќе си **зе**мал/**зе**л(а)<br>*Ti kje si **ze**mal/**ze**l(a)* | You would have took -<br>Вие ќе сте **зе**мале/**зе**ле<br>*Vie kje ste **ze**male/**ze**le* |
| 3rd person | He/She/It would have took-<br>Тој/Таа/Тоа ќе **зе**мал/**зе**л(а)(о)<br>*Toj/Taa/Toa kje **ze**mal/**ze**l(a)(o)* | They would have took-<br>Тие ќе **зе**мале/**зе**ле<br>*Tie kje **ze**male/**ze**le* |

***To talk – Разговара/Поазговора***

| | | |
|---|---|---|
| Infinitive | To talk | Разг**о**вара<br>Razg**o**vara |

| Present Simple Tense | | |
|---|---|---|
| *Person* | *Singular* | *Plural* |
| 1st person | I talk-<br>Јас разг**о**варам<br>*Jas razg**o**varam* | We talk-<br>Ние разгов**а**раме<br>*Nie razgov**a**rame* |
| 2nd person | You talk-<br>Ти разг**о**вараш<br>*Ti razg**o**varash* | You talk-<br>Вие разгов**а**рате<br>*Vie razgov**a**rate* |
| 3rd person | He/She/It talks-<br>Тој/Таа/Тоа разг**о**вара<br>*Toj/Taa/Toa razg**o**vara* | They talk-<br>Тие разгов**а**раат<br>*Tie razgov**a**raat* |

| Past Simple Tense | | |
|---|---|---|
| *Person* | *Singular* | *Plural* |
| 1st person | I talked-<br>Јас поразг**о**варав<br>*Jas porazg**o**varav* | We talked -<br>Ние поразгов**а**равме<br>*Nie porazgov**a**ravme* |
| 2nd person | You talked-<br>Ти поразг**о**вара<br>*Ti poazg**o**vara* | You talked -<br>Вие поразгов**а**равте<br>*Vie porazgov**a**ravte* |
| 3rd person | He/She/It talked -<br>Тој/Таа/Тоа поразг**о**вара<br>*Toj/Taa/Toa poazg**o**vara* | They talked -<br>Тие поразгов**а**раа<br>*Tie porazgov**a**raa* |

| Past Continuous Tense | | |
|---|---|---|
| *Person* | *Singular* | *Plural* |
| 1st person | I was talking -<br>Јас разг**о**варав<br>*Jas razg**o**varav* | We were talking -<br>Ние разгов**а**равме<br>*Nie razgov**a**ravme* |
| 2nd person | You were talking -<br>Ти разгов**а**раше<br>*Ti razgov**a**rashe* | You were talking -<br>Вие разгов**а**равте<br>*Vie razgov**a**ravte* |
| 3rd person | He/She/It was talking -<br>Тој/Таа/Тоа разгов**а**раше<br>*Toj/Taa/Toa razgov**ar**ashe* | They were talking -<br>Тие разгов**а**раа<br>*Tie razgov**a**raa* |

| Present Perfect Simple Tense | | |
|---|---|---|
| *Person* | *Singular* | *Plural* |
| 1st person | I have talked-<br>Јас сум поразг**о**ворил(а)<br>*Jas sum porazg**o**voril(a)* | We have talked-<br>Ние сме поразгов**о**риле<br>*Ni sme porazg**o**vorile* |

| | | |
|---|---|---|
| 2nd person | You have talked-<br>Ти си поразг**о**ворил(а)<br>*Ti si porazg**o**voril(a)* | You have talked-<br>Вие сте поразгов**о**риле<br>*Vie ste porazg**o**vorile* |
| 3rd person | He/She/It has talked-<br>Тој/Таа/Тоа поразг**о**ворил(а)(о)<br>*Toj/Taa/Toa porazg**o**voril(a)(o)* | They have talked-<br>Тие поразгов**о**риле<br>*Tie porazg**o**vorile* |

| **Present Perfect Continuous Tense** | | |
|---|---|---|
| *Person* | *Singular* | *Plural* |
| 1st person | I have been talking -<br>Јас сумразг**о**варал(а)<br>Jas sum razg**o**varal(a) | We have been talking -<br>Ние сме разгов**а**рале<br>*Nie sme razgov**a**rale* |
| 2nd person | You have been talking -<br>Ти си разг**о**варал(а)<br>Ti si razg**o**varal(a) | You have been talking -<br>Вие сте разгов**а**рале<br>*Vie ste razgov**a**rale* |
| 3rd person | He/She/It has been talking -<br>Тој/Таа/Тоа разг**о**варал(а)(о)<br>Toj/Taa/Toa razg**o**varal(a)(o) | They have been talking -<br>Тие разгов**а**рале<br>*Tie razgov**a**rale* |

| **Past Perfect Simple Tense** | | |
|---|---|---|
| *Person* | *Singular* | *Plural* |
| 1st person | I had talked -<br>Јас бев поразг**о**ворил(а)<br>*Jas bev porazg**o**voril(a)* | We had talked-<br>Ние бевме поразгов**о**риле<br>*Nie bevme porazgov**o**rile* |
| 2nd person | You had talked-<br>Ти беше поразг**о**ворил(а)<br>*Ti beshe porazg**o**voril(a)* | You had talked-<br>Вие бевте поразгов**о**риле<br>*Vie bevte porazgov**o**rile* |
| 3rd person | He/She/It had talked-<br>Тој/Таа/Тоа беше<br>поразг**о**ворил(а)(о)<br>*Toj/Taa/Toa beshe*<br>*porazg**o**voril(a)(o)* | They had talked-<br>Тие беа поразгов**о**риле<br>*Tie bea porazgov**o**rile* |

| **Future Simple Tense** | | |
|---|---|---|
| *Person* | *Singular* | *Plural* |
| 1st person | I will talk -<br>Јас ќе<br>разг**о**варам/поразг**о**ворам<br>*Jas kje*<br>*razg**o**varam/porazg**o**voram* | We will talk -<br>Ние ќе<br>разгов**а**раме/поразгов**о**риме<br>*Nie kje*<br>*razgov**a**rame/porazgov**o**rime* |
| 2nd person | You will talk -<br>Ти ќе<br>разг**о**вараш/поразг**о**вориш<br>*Ti kje razg**o**varash/porazg**o**vorish* | You will talk -<br>Вие ќе<br>разгов**а**рате/поразгов**о**рите<br>*Vie kje*<br>*razgov**a**rate/porazgov**o**rite* |

| | | |
|---|---|---|
| 3rd person | He/She/It will talk - Тој/Таа/Тоа разг**о**вара/поразг**о**вори *Toj/Taa/Toa kje razg**o**vara/porazg**o**vori* | They will talk - Тие ќе разгов**а**раат/поразг**о**ворат *Tie kje razgov**a**raat/porazg**o**vorat* |

| **used to + infinitive or would + infinitive** | | |
|---|---|---|
| *Person* | *Singular* | *Plural* |
| 1st person | I would talk - Јас ќе разг**о**варав/поразг**о**ворив *Jas kje razg**o**varav/ porazg**o**voriv* | We would talk - Ние ќе разгов**а**равме/поразгов**о**ривме *Nie kje razgov**a**ravme/ porazgov**o**rivme* |
| 2nd person | You would talk - Ти ќе разгов**а**раше/поразгов**о**рише *Ti kje razgov**a**rashe/ porazgov**o**rilshe* | You would talk - Вие ќе разгов**а**равте/поразгов**о**ривте *Vie kje razgov**a**ravte/ porazgov**o**rivte* |
| 3rd person | He/She/It would talk - Тој/Таа/Тоа разгов**а**раше/поразгов**о**рише *Toj/Taa/Toa kje razgov**a**rashe/porazgov**o**rishe* | They would talk - Тие ќе разгов**а**раа/разгов**о**рија *Tie kje razgov**a**raa/porazgov**o**rija* |

| **Personal endings for future perfect-in-the-past tense** | | |
|---|---|---|
| *Person* | *Singular* | *Plural* |
| 1st person | I would have talked - Јас ќе сум разг**о**варал/поразг**о**ворил *Jas kje sum razg**o**varal/ porazg**o**voril(a)* | We would have talked- Ние ќе сме разгов**а**рале/поразгов**о**риле *Nie kje sme razgov**a**rale/ porazgov**o**rile* |
| 2nd person | You would have talked- Ти ќе си разг**о**варал/ поразг**о**ворил *Ti kje si razg**o**varal/ porazg**o**voril(a)* | You would have talked- Вие ќе сте разгов**а**рале/ поразгов**о**риле *Vie kje ste razgov**a**rale/ porazgov**o**rile* |
| 3rd person | He/She/It would have talked- Тој/Таа/Тоа ќе разг**о**варал/ поразг**о**ворил(а)(о) *Toj/Taa/Toa kje razg**o**varal/ porazg**o**voril(a)(o)* | They would have talked- Тие ќе разгов**а**рале/ поразгов**о**риле *Tie kje razgov**a**rale/ porazgov**o**rile* |

***To teach – Предава/Предаде***

| | | |
|---|---|---|
| *Infinitive* | To teach | Пред**а**ва<br>Pr**e**dava |

| Present Simple Tense | | |
|---|---|---|
| *Person* | *Singular* | *Plural* |
| 1st person | I teach -<br>Јас пр**е**давам<br>*Jas pr**e**davam* | We teach -<br>Ние пред**а**ваме<br>*Nie pred**a**vame* |
| 2nd person | You teach -<br>Ти пр**е**даваш<br>*Ti pr**e**davash* | You teach -<br>Вие пред**а**вате<br>*Vie pred**a**vate* |
| 3rd person | He/She/It teaches -<br>Тој/Таа/Тоа пр**е**дава<br>*Toj/Taa/Toa pr**e**dava* | They teach -<br>Тие пред**а**ваат<br>*Tie pred**a**vaat* |

| Past Simple Tense | | |
|---|---|---|
| *Person* | *Singular* | *Plural* |
| 1st person | I taught -<br>Јас пр**е**дадов<br>*Jas pr**e**dadov* | We taught -<br>Ние пред**а**довме<br>*Nie pred**a**dovme* |
| 2nd person | You taught -<br>Ти пр**е**даде<br>*Ti pr**e**dade* | You taught -<br>Вие пред**а**довте<br>*Vie pred**a**dovte* |
| 3rd person | He/She/It taught -<br>Тој/Таа/Тоа пр**е**даде<br>*Toj/Taa/Toa pr**e**dade* | They taught -<br>Тие пред**а**доа<br>*Tie pred**a**doa* |

| Past Continuous Tense | | |
|---|---|---|
| *Person* | *Singular* | *Plural* |
| 1st person | I was teaching -<br>Јас пр**е**давав<br>*Jas pr**e**dava* | We were teaching -<br>Ние пред**а**вавме<br>*Nie pred**a**vavme* |
| 2nd person | You were teaching -<br>Ти пред**а**ваше<br>*Ti pred**a**vashe* | You were teaching -<br>Вие пред**а**вавте<br>*Vie pred**a**vavte* |
| 3rd person | He/She/It was teaching -<br>Тој/Таа/Тоа пред**а**ваше<br>*Toj/Taa/Toa pred**a**vashe* | They were teaching -<br>Те пред**а**ваа<br>*Tie pred**a**vaa* |

| Present Perfect Simple Tense | | |
|---|---|---|
| *Person* | *Singular* | *Plural* |
| 1st person | I have taught -<br>Јас сум пр**е**дал(а)<br>*Jas sum pr**e**dal(a)* | We have taught-<br>Ние сме пред**а**ле<br>*Nie sme pred**a**le* |

| | | |
|---|---|---|
| 2nd person | You have taught -<br>Ти си пр**е**дал(а)<br>*Ti si pr**e**dal(a)* | You have taught-<br>Вие сте пред**а**ле<br>*Vie sye pred**a**le* |
| 3rd person | He/She/It has taught-<br>Тој/Таа/Тоа пр**е**дал(а)(о)<br>*Toj/Taa/Toa pr**e**dal(a)(o)* | They have taught-<br>Тие пред**а**ле<br>*Tie pred**a**le* |

| **Present Perfect Continuous Tense** | | |
|---|---|---|
| *Person* | *Singular* | *Plural* |
| 1st person | I have been teaching-<br>Јас сум пр**е**давал(а)<br>*Jas sum pr**e**daval(a)* | We have been teaching-<br>Ние сме пр**е**давале<br>*Nie sme pr**e**davale* |
| 2nd person | You have been teaching-<br>Ти си пр**е**давал(а)<br>*Ti si pr**e**daval(a)* | You have been teaching-<br>Вие сте пр**е**давале<br>*Vie ste pr**e**davale* |
| 3rd person | He/She/It has been teaching-<br>Тој/Таа/Тоа пр**е**давал(а)(о)<br>*Toj/Taa/Toa pr**e**daval(a)(o)* | They have been teaching-<br>Тие пр**е**давале<br>*Tie pr**e**davale* |

| **Past Perfect Simple Tense** | | |
|---|---|---|
| *Person* | *Singular* | *Plural* |
| 1st person | I had taught-<br>Јас бев пр**е**дал(а)<br>*Jas bev pr**e**dal(a)* | We had taught-<br>Ние бевме пред**а**ле<br>*Nie bevme pred**a**le* |
| 2nd person | You had taught-<br>Ти беше пр**е**дал(а)<br>*Ti beshe pr**e**dal(a)* | You had taught-<br>Вие бевте пред**а**ле<br>*Vie bevte pred**a**le* |
| 3rd person | He/She/It had taught-<br>Тој/Таа/Тоа беше пр**е**дал(а)(о)<br>*Toj/Taa/Toa beshe pr**e**dal(a)(o)* | They had taught-<br>Тие беа пред**а**ле<br>*Tie bea pred**a**le* |

| **Future Simple Tense** | | |
|---|---|---|
| *Person* | *Singular* | *Plural* |
| 1st person | I will teach-<br>Јас ќе пр**е**давам/пр**е**дадам<br>*Jas kje pr**e**davam/pr**e**dadam* | We will teach-<br>Ние ќе пред**а**ваме/пред**а**деме<br>*Nie kje pred**a**vame/pred**a**deme* |
| 2nd person | You will teach-<br>Ти ќе пр**е**даваш/пр**е**дадеш<br>*Ti kje pr**e**davash/pr**e**dadesh* | You will teach-<br>Вие ќе пред**а**вате/пред**а**дете<br>*Vie kje pred**a**vate/pred**a**dete* |
| 3rd person | He/She/It will teach-<br>Тој/Таа/Тоа<br>пр**е**даваш/пр**е**дадеш<br>*Toj/Taa/Toa kje*<br>*pr**e**dava/pr**e**dade* | They will teach-<br>Тие ќе пред**а**ваат/пр**е**дадат<br>*Tie kje pred**a**vaat/pr**e**dadat* |

| used to + infinitive or would + infinitive | | |
|---|---|---|
| *Person* | *Singular* | *Plural* |
| 1st person | I would teach-<br>Јас ќе пр**е**давав/пр**е**дадев<br>*Jas kje pr**e**davav/pr**e**dadev* | We would teach-<br>Ние ќе<br>пред**а**вавме/пред**а**девме<br>*Nie kje pred**a**vavme/pred**a**devme* |
| 2nd person | You would teach-<br>Ти ќе пред**а**ваше/пред**а**деше<br>*Ti kje pred**a**vashe/pred**a**deshe* | You would teach-<br>Вие ќе пред**а**вавте/пред**а**девте<br>*Vie kje pred**a**vavte/pred**a**devte* |
| 3rd person | He/She/It would teach-<br>Тој/Таа/Тоа<br>пред**а**ваше/пред**а**деше<br>*Toj/Taa/Toa kje*<br>*pred**a**vashe/pred**a**deshe* | They would teach-<br>Тие ќе пред**а**ваа/пред**а**деа<br>*Tie kje pred**a**vaa/pred**a**dea* |

| Personal endings for future perfect-in-the-past tense | | |
|---|---|---|
| *Person* | *Singular* | *Plural* |
| 1st person | I would have taught-<br>Јас ќе сум пр**е**давал/пр**е**дал(а)<br>*Jas kje su pr**e**daval/pr**e**dal(a)* | We would have taught-<br>Ние ќе сме пред**а**вал/пред**а**ле<br>*Nie kje sme pred**a**vale/ pred**a**le* |
| 2nd person | You would have taught-<br>Ти ќе си пр**е**давал/ пр**е**дал(а)<br>*Ti kje si pr**e**daval/pr**e**dal(a)* | You would have taught-<br>Вие ќе сте пред**а**вал/пред**а**ле<br>*Vie kje ste pred**a**vale/ pred**a**le* |
| 3rd person | He/She/It would have taught-<br>Тој/Таа/Тоа ќе пр**е**давал/<br>пр**е**дал(а)(о)<br>*Toj/Taa/Toa kje pr**e**daval/*<br>*pr**e**dal(a)(o)* | They would have taught-<br>Тие ќе пред**а**вал/пред**а**ле<br>*Tie kje se pred**a**vale/pred**a**le* |

***To think – Мисли/Измисли***

| | | |
|---|---|---|
| *Infinitive* | To think | Мисли<br>Misli |

| Present Simple Tense | | |
|---|---|---|
| *Person* | *Singular* | *Plural* |
| 1st person | I think -<br>Јас **ми**слам<br>*Jas **mi**slam* | We think -<br>Ние **ми**слиме<br>*Nie **mi**slime* |
| 2nd person | You think -<br>Ти **ми**слиш<br>*Ti **mi**slish* | You think -<br>Вие **ми**слите<br>*Vie **mi**slite* |
| 3rd person | He/She/It thinks -<br>Тој/Таа/Тоа **ми**сли<br>*Toj/Taa/Toa **mi**sli* | They think -<br>Тие **ми**слат<br>*Tie **mi**slat* |

| Past Simple Tense | | |
|---|---|---|
| *Person* | *Singular* | *Plural* |
| 1st person | I thought -<br>Јас **изми**слив<br>*Jas **izmi**sliv* | We thought -<br>Ние изм**и**сливме<br>*Nie izm**i**slivme* |
| 2nd person | You thought -<br>Ти **изми**сли<br>*Ti **izmi**sli* | You thought -<br>Вие изм**и**сливте<br>*Ve izm**i**slivte* |
| 3rd person | He/She/It thought -<br>Тој/Таа/Тоа **изми**сли<br>*Toj/Taa/Toa **izmi**sli* | They thought -<br>Тие изм**и**слија<br>*Tie izm**i**slija* |

| Past Continuous Tense | | |
|---|---|---|
| *Person* | *Singular* | *Plural* |
| 1st person | I was thinking -<br>Јас **ми**слев<br>*Jas **mi**slev* | We were thinking -<br>Ние **ми**слевме<br>*Nie **mi**slevme* |
| 2nd person | You were thinking -<br>Ти **ми**слеше<br>*Ti **mi**sleshe* | You were thinking -<br>Вие **ми**слевте<br>*Vie **mi**slevte* |
| 3rd person | He/She/It was thinking -<br>Тој/Таа/Тоа **ми**слеше<br>*Toj/Taa/Toa **mi**sleshe* | They were thinking -<br>Тие **ми**слеа<br>*Tie **mi**slea* |

| Present Perfect Simple Tense | | |
|---|---|---|
| *Person* | *Singular* | *Plural* |
| 1st person | I have thought -<br>Јас сум **изми**слил(а)<br>*Jas sum **izmi**slil(a)* | We have thought -<br>Ние сме **изми**слиле<br>*Nie sme **izmi**slile* |
| 2nd person | You have thought -<br>Ти сум **изми**слил(а)<br>*Ti si **izmi**slil(a* | You have thought -<br>Вие сте **изми**слиле<br>*Vie ste **izmi**slile* |

| | | |
|---|---|---|
| 3rd person | He/She/It has thought -<br>Тој/Таа/Тоа измислил(а)(о)<br>*Toj/Taa/Toa izmislil(a)(o)* | They have thought -<br>Тие измислиле<br>*Tie izmislile* |

| **Present Perfect Continuous Tense** | | |
|---|---|---|
| *Person* | *Singular* | *Plural* |
| 1st person | I have been thinking -<br>Јас сум мислел(а)<br>*Jas sum mislel(a)* | We have been thinking -<br>Ние сме мислеле<br>*Nie sme mislele* |
| 2nd person | You have been thinking -<br>Ти си мислел(а)<br>*Ti si mislel(a)* | You have been thinking -<br>Вие сте мислеле<br>*Vie ste mislele* |
| 3rd person | He/She/It has been thinking -<br>Тој/Таа/Тоа мислел(а)(о)<br>*Toj/Taa/Toa mislel(a)(o)* | They have been thinking -<br>Тие мислеле<br>*Tie mislele* |

| **Past Perfect Simple Tense** | | |
|---|---|---|
| *Person* | *Singular* | *Plural* |
| 1st person | I had thought -<br>Јас бев измислил(а)<br>*Jas bev izmislil(a)* | We had thought -<br>Ние бевме измислиле<br>*Nie bevme izmislile* |
| 2nd person | You had thought -<br>Ти беше измислил(а)<br>*Ti beshe izmislil(a)* | You had thought -<br>Вие бевте измислиле<br>*Vie bevte izmislile* |
| 3rd person | He/She/It had thought -<br>Тој/Таа/Тоа беше измислил(а)(о)<br>*Toj/Taa/Toa beshe izmislil(a)(o)* | They had thought -<br>Тие беа измислиле<br>*Tie bea izmislile* |

| **Future Simple Tense** | | |
|---|---|---|
| *Person* | *Singular* | *Plural* |
| 1st person | I will think -<br>Јас ќе мислам/измислам<br>*Jas kje mislam/izmislam* | We will think -<br>Ние ќе мислиме/измислиме<br>*Nie kje mislime/izmislime* |
| 2nd person | You will think -<br>Ти ќе мислиш/измислиш<br>*Ti kje mislish/izmislish* | You will think -<br>Вие ќе мислите/измислите<br>*Vie kje mislite/izmislime* |
| 3rd person | He/She/It will think -<br>Тој/Таа/Тоа ќе мисли/измисли<br>*Toj/Taa/Toa misli/izmisli* | They will think -<br>Тие ќе мислат/измислат<br>*Tie kje mislat/izmislat* |

| **used to + infinitive or would + infinitive** | | |
|---|---|---|
| *Person* | *Singular* | *Plural* |
| 1st person | I would think -<br>Јас ќе мислев/измислев<br>*Jas kje mislev/izmislev* | We would think -<br>Ние ќе мислевме/измислевме<br>*Nie kje mislevme/izmislevme* |

| | | |
|---|---|---|
| 2nd person | You would think - Ти ќе мислеше/измислеше *Ti kje misleshe/izmisleshe* | You would think - Вие ќе мислевте/измислевте *Vie kje mislevte/izmislevte* |
| 3rd person | He/She/It would think - Тој/Таа/Тоа ќе мислеше/измислеше *Toj/Taa/Toa kje misleshe/izmisleshe* | They would think - Тие ќе мислеа/измислеа *Tie kje mislea/izmislea* |

| **Personal endings for future perfect-in-the-past tense** | | |
|---|---|---|
| *Person* | *Singular* | *Plural* |
| 1st person | I would have thought - Јас ќе сум мислел/измислел(а) *Jas kje sum mislel/izmislel*(a) | We would have thought - Ние ќе сме мислеле/измислеле *Nie kje sme mislele/izmislele* |
| 2nd person | You would have thought - Ти ќе си мислел/измислел(а) *Ti kje si mislel/izmislel (a)* | You would have thought - Вие ќе сте мислеле/измислеле *Vie kje ste mislele/izmislele* |
| 3rd person | He/She/It would have thought Тој/Таа/Тоа ќе мислел/измислел(а)(о) *Toj/Taa/Toa kje mislel/izmislel (a)(o)* | They would have thought - Тие ќе мислеле/измислеле *Tie kje mislele/izmislele* |

***To touch – Допира/Допре***

| | | |
|---|---|---|
| *Infinitive* | To touch | Допира<br>Dopira |

| Present Simple Tense | | |
|---|---|---|
| *Person* | *Singular* | *Plural* |
| 1st person | I touch -<br>Јас допирам<br>*Jas dopiram* | We touch-<br>Ние допираме<br>*Nie dopirame* |
| 2nd person | You touch-<br>Ти допираш<br>*Ti dopirash* | You touch -<br>Вие допирате<br>*Vie dopirate* |
| 3rd person | He/She/It touches -<br>Тој/Таа/Тоа допира<br>*Toj/Taa/Toa dopira* | They touch-<br>Тие допираат<br>*Tie dopiraat* |

| Past Simple Tense | | |
|---|---|---|
| *Person* | *Singular* | *Plural* |
| 1st person | I touched -<br>Јас допрев<br>*Jas doprev* | We touched -<br>Ние допревме<br>*Nie doprevme* |
| 2nd person | You touched -<br>Ти допре<br>*Ti dopre* | You touched -<br>Вие допревте<br>*Vie doprevte* |
| 3rd person | He/She/It touched -<br>Тој/Таа/Тоа допре<br>*Toj/Taa/Toa dopre* | They touched -<br>Тие допреа<br>*Tie doprea* |

| Past Continuous Tense | | |
|---|---|---|
| *Person* | *Singular* | *Plural* |
| 1st person | I was touching -<br>Јас допирав<br>*Jas dopirav* | We were touching -<br>Ние допиравме<br>*Nie dopiravme* |
| 2nd person | You were touching -<br>Ти допираше<br>*Ti dopirashe* | You were touching -<br>Вие допиравте<br>*Vie dopiravte* |
| 3rd person | He/She/It was touching -<br>Тој/Таа/Тоа допираше<br>*Toj/Taa/Toa dopirashe* | They were touching -<br>Тие допираа<br>*Tie dopiraa* |

| Present Perfect Simple Tense | | |
|---|---|---|
| *Person* | *Singular* | *Plural* |
| 1st person | I have touched -<br>Јас сум допрел(а)<br>*Jas sum doprel(a)* | We have touched -<br>Ние сме допреле<br>*Nie sme doprele* |

| | | |
|---|---|---|
| 2nd person | You have touched- Ти си до**п**рел(а) *Ti si doprel(a)* | You have touched - Вие сте **допреле** *Vie ste doprele* |
| 3rd person | He/She/It has touched - Тој/Таа/Тоа допрел(а)(о) *Toj/Taa/Toa doprel(a)(o)* | They have touched - Тие **допреле** *Tie doprele* |

| **Present Perfect Continuous Tense** | | |
|---|---|---|
| *Person* | *Singular* | *Plural* |
| 1st person | I have been touching - Јас сум допирал(а) *Jas sum dopiral(a)* | We have been touching - Ние сме допирале *Nie sme dopirale* |
| 2nd person | You have been touching - Ти сидопирал(а) *Ti si dopiral(a)* | You have been touching - Вие сте допирале *Vie ste dopirale* |
| 3rd person | He/She/It has been touching - Тој/Таа/Тоа допирал(а) *Toj/Taa/Toa dopiral(a)* | They have been touching - Тие допирале *Tie dopirale* |

| **Past Perfect Simple Tense** | | |
|---|---|---|
| *Person* | *Singular* | *Plural* |
| 1st person | I had touched - Јас бев допирал(а) *Jas bev dopiral(a)* | We had touched - Ние бевме допирале *Nie bevme dopirale* |
| 2nd person | You had touched - Ти беше допирал(а) *Ti beshe dopiral(a)* | You had touched - Вие бевте допирале *Vie bevte dopirale* |
| 3rd person | He/She/It had touched- Тој/Таа/Тоа беше допирал(а)(о) *Toj/Taa/Toa beshe dopiral(a)(o)* | They had touched - Тие беа допирале *Tie bea dopirale* |

| **Future Simple Tense** | | |
|---|---|---|
| *Person* | *Singular* | *Plural* |
| 1st person | I will touch - Јас ќе допирам/допрам *Jas kje dopiram/dopram* | We will touch - Ние ќе допираме/допреме *Nie kje dopirame/dopreme* |
| 2nd person | You will touch - Ти ќе допираш/допреш *Ti kje dopirash/dopresh* | You will touch - Вие ќе допирате/допрете *Vie kje dopirate/doprete* |
| 3rd person | He/She/It will touch- Тој/Таа/Тоа ќе допира/допре *Toj/Taa/Toa kje dopira/dopre* | They will touch - Тие ќе допираат/допрат *Tie kje dopiraat/doprat* |

| **used to + infinitive or would + infinitive** | | |
|---|---|---|
| *Person* | *Singular* | *Plural* |
| 1st person | I would touch-<br>Јас ќе д**о**пирав/д**о**прев<br>*Jas kje d**o**pirav/d**o**prev* | We would touch -<br>Ние ќе доп**и**равме/д**о**превме<br>*Nie kje dop**i**ravme/d**o**prevme* |
| 2nd person | You would touch -<br>Ти ќе доп**и**раше/д**о**преше<br>*Ti kje dop**i**rashe/d**o**preshe* | You would touch -<br>Вие ќе доп**и**равте/д**о**превте<br>*Vie kje dop**i**ravte/d**o**prevte* |
| 3rd person | He/She/It would touch-<br>Тој/Таа/Тоа ќе<br>доп**и**раше/д**о**преше<br>*Toj/Taa/Toa*<br>*dop**i**rashe/d**o**preshe* | They would touch -<br>Тие ќе доп**и**раа/д**о**преа<br>*Tie kje d**o**piraa/d**o**prea* |

| **Personal endings for future perfect-in-the-past tense** | | |
|---|---|---|
| *Person* | *Singular* | *Plural* |
| 1st person | I would have touched-<br>Јас ќе сум д**о**пирал/д**о**прел(а)<br>*Jas kje sum d**o**piral/d**o**prel(a)* | We would have touched -<br>Ние ќе сме доп**и**рале/д**о**преле<br>*Nie* kje сме dop**i**rale/d**o**prele |
| 2nd person | You would have touched -<br>Ти ќе си д**о**пирал/д**о**прел(а)<br>*Ti kje si d**o**piral/d**o**prel(a)* | You would have touched -<br>Вие ќе сте доп**и**рале/д**о**преле<br>*Vie kje ste* dop**i**rale/d**o**prele |
| 3rd person | He/She/It would have -touched<br>Тој/Таа/Тоа ќе<br>д**о**пирал/д**о**прел(а)(о)<br>*Toj/Taa/Toa kje*<br>*d**o**piral/d**o**prel(a)(o)* | They would have touched-<br>Тие ќе доп**и**рале/д**о**преле<br>*Tie kje* dop**i**rale/d**o**prele |

***To travel – Патува/Пропатува***

| | | |
|---|---|---|
| *Infinitive* | To travel | П**а**тува<br>P**a**tuva |

| | **Present Simple Tense** | |
|---|---|---|
| *Person* | *Singular* | *Plural* |
| 1st person | I travel -<br>Јас п**а**тувам<br>*Jas p**a**tuvam* | We travel-<br>Ние пат**у**ваме<br>*Nie pat**u**vame* |
| 2nd person | You travel -<br>Ти п**а**туваш<br>*Ti p**a**tuvash* | You travel -<br>Вие пат**у**вате<br>*Vie pat**u**vate* |
| 3rd person | He/She/It travels -<br>Тој/Таа/Тоа п**а**тува<br>*Toj/Taa/Toa p**a**tuva* | They travel-<br>Тие пат**у**ваат<br>*Tie pat**u**vaat* |

| | **Past Simple Tense** | |
|---|---|---|
| *Person* | *Singular* | *Plural* |
| 1st person | I traveled-<br>Јас проп**а**тував<br>*Jas prop**a**tuvav* | We traveled -<br>Ние пропат**у**вавме<br>*Nie propat**u**vavme* |
| 2nd person | You traveled -<br>Ти проп**а**тува<br>*Ti prop**a**tuva* | You traveled -<br>Вие пропат**у**вавте<br>*Vie propat**u**vavte* |
| 3rd person | He/She/It traveled -<br>Тој/Таа/Тоа проп**а**тува<br>*Toj/Taa/Toa prop**a**tuva* | They traveled-<br>Тие пропат**у**ва<br>*Tie propat**u**va* |

| | **Past Continuous Tense** | |
|---|---|---|
| *Person* | *Singular* | *Plural* |
| 1st person | I was traveling-<br>Јас п**а**тував<br>*Jas p**a**tuvav* | We were traveling-<br>Ние пат**у**вавме<br>*Nie pat**u**vavme* |
| 2nd person | You were traveling-<br>Ти пат**у**ваше<br>*Ti pat**u**vashe* | You were traveling-<br>Вие пат**у**вавте<br>*Vie pat**u**vavte* |
| 3rd person | He/She/It was traveling-<br>Тој/Таа/Тоа пат**у**ваше<br>*Toj/Taa/Toa pat**u**vashe* | They were traveling-<br>Тие пат**у**ваа<br>*Tie pat**u**vaa* |

| | **Present Perfect Simple Tense** | |
|---|---|---|
| *Person* | *Singular* | *Plural* |
| 1st person | I have traveled -<br>Јас сум пропатувал(а)<br>*Jas su propatuval(a)* | We have traveled -<br>Ние сме пропат**у**вале<br>*Ne sme propat**u**vale* |

| | | |
|---|---|---|
| 2nd person | You have traveled -<br>Ти си проп**а**тувал(а)<br>*Ti si prop**a**tuval(a)* | You have traveled -<br>Вие сте пропат**у**вале<br>*Vie ste propat**u**vale* |
| 3rd person | He/She/It has traveled -<br>Тој/Таа/Тоа проп**а**тувал(а)(о)<br>*Toj/Taa/Toa prop**a**tuval(a)(o)* | They have traveled -<br>Тиепропат**у**вале<br>*Tie propat**u**vale* |

| **Present Perfect Continuous Tense** | | |
|---|---|---|
| *Person* | *Singular* | *Plural* |
| 1st person | I have been traveling -<br>Јас сум п**а**тувал(а)<br>*Jas sum p**a**tuval(a)* | We have been traveling -<br>Ние сме пат**у**вале<br>*Nie sme pat**u**vale* |
| 2nd person | You have been traveling -<br>Ти си п**а**тувал(а)<br>*Ti si p**a**tuval(a)* | You have been traveling -<br>Вие сте пат**у**вале<br>*Vie ste pat**u**vale* |
| 3rd person | He/She/It has been travelling -<br>Тој/Таа/Тоа п**а**тувал(а)(о)<br>*Toj/Taa/Toa p**a**tuval(a)(o)* | They have been traveling -<br>Тие пат**у**вале<br>*Tie pat**u**vale* |

| **Past Perfect Simple Tense** | | |
|---|---|---|
| *Person* | *Singular* | *Plural* |
| 1st person | I had traveled-<br>Јас бев проп**а**тувал(а)<br>*Jas bev prop**a**tuval(a)* | We had traveled-<br>Ние бевме пропат**у**вале<br>*Nie sme propat**u**vale* |
| 2nd person | You had traveled-<br>Ти беше проп**а**тувал (а)<br>*I beshe prop**a**tuval(a)* | You had traveled-<br>Вие бевте пропат**у**вале<br>*Vie ste propat**u**vale* |
| 3rd person | He/She/It had traveled-<br>Тој/Таа/Тоа беше<br>проп**а**тувал(а)(о)<br>*Toj/Taa/Toa prop**a**tuval(a)(o)* | They had traveled-<br>Тие беа пропат**у**вале<br>*Tie bea propat**u**vale* |

| **Future Simple Tense** | | |
|---|---|---|
| *Person* | *Singular* | *Plural* |
| 1st person | I will travel-<br>Јас ќе п**а**тувам/проп**а**тувам<br>*Jas kje p**a**tuvam/prop**a**tuvam* | We will travel-<br>Ние ќе пат**у**ваме/пропат**у**ваме<br>*Nie kje pat**u**vame/propat**u**vame* |
| 2nd person | You will travel-<br>Ти ќе п**а**туваш/проп**а**туваш<br>*Ti kje p**a**tuvash/prop**a**tuvash* | You will travel-<br>Вие ќе пат**у**вате/пропат**у**вате<br>*Vie kje pat**u**vate/propat**u**vate* |
| 3rd person | He/She/It will travel-<br>Тој/Таа/Тоа ќе<br>п**а**тува/проп**а**тува<br>*Toj/Taa/Toa kje*<br>*p**a**tuvash/prop**a**rtuva* | They will travel-<br>Тие ќе пат**у**ваат/пропат**у**ваат<br>*Tie kje pat**u**vaat/propat**u**vaat* |

| used to + infinitive or would + infinitive | | |
|---|---|---|
| *Person* | *Singular* | *Plural* |
| 1st person | I would travel -<br>Јас ќе п**а**тував/проп**а**тував<br>*Jas kje p**a**tuvav/prop**a**tuvav* | We would travel -<br>Ние ќе<br>пат**у**вавме/пропат**у**вавме<br>*Nie kje*<br>*pat**u**vavme/propat**u**vavme* |
| 2nd person | You would travel -<br>Ти ќе п**а**туваше/пропат**у**ваше<br>*Ti kje p**a**tuvashe/propat**u**vashe* | You would travel-<br>Вие ќе пат**у**вате/пропат**у**вавме<br>*Vie kje pat**u**vavte/propat**u**vavme* |
| 3rd person | He/She/It would travel -<br>Тој/Таа/Тоа пат**у**ваше/<br>пропат**у**ваше<br>*Toj/Taa/Toa kje*<br>*pat**u**vashe/propat**u**vashe* | They would travel -<br>Тие ќе пат**у**ваа/пропат**у**ваа<br>*Tie kje pat**u**vaa/propat**u**vaa* |

| Personal endings for future perfect-in-the-past tense | | |
|---|---|---|
| *Person* | *Singular* | *Plural* |
| 1st person | I would have traveled -<br>Јас ќе сум<br>п**а**тувал/проп**а**тувал(а)<br>*Jas kje sum*<br>*p**a**tuval/prop**a**tuval(a)* | We would have traveled -<br>Ние ќе сме пат**у**вале/<br>пропат**у**вале<br>*Nie kje sme*<br>*pat**u**vale/propat**u**vale* |
| 2nd person | You would have traveled -<br>Ти ќе си п**а**тувал/проп**а**тувал(а)<br>*Ti kje si p**a**tuval/prop**a**tuval(a)* | You would have traveled -<br>Вие ќе сте пат**у**вале/<br>пропат**у**вале<br>*Vie kje ste pat**u**vale/propat**u**vale* |
| 3rd person | He/She/It would have -traveled<br>Тој/Таа/Тоа ќе<br>п**а**тувал/проп**а**тувал(а)(о)<br>*Toj/Taa/Toa kje*<br>*p**a**tuval/prop**a**tuval(a)(o)* | They would have traveled -<br>Тие ќе пат**у**вале/пропат**у**вале<br>*Tie kje pat**u**vale/propat**u**vale* |

### *To understand – Разбира/Разбра*

| | | |
|---|---|---|
| *Infinitive* | To understand | Р**а**збира<br>R**a**zbira |

| Present Simple Tense | | |
|---|---|---|
| *Person* | *Singular* | *Plural* |
| 1st person | I understand -<br>Јас р**а**збирам<br>*Jas r**a**zbiram* | We understand -<br>Ние разб**и**раме<br>*Nie raz**i**rame* |
| 2nd person | You understand -<br>Ти р**а**збираш<br>*Ti r**a**zbirash* | You understand -<br>Вие разб**и**рате<br>*Vie raz**i**rate* |
| 3rd person | He/She/It understand -<br>Тој/Таа/Тоа р**а**збира<br>*Toj/Taa/Toa r**a**zbira* | They understand -<br>Тие разб**и**раат<br>*Tie razb**i**raat* |

| Past Simple Tense | | |
|---|---|---|
| *Person* | *Singular* | *Plural* |
| 1st person | I understood -<br>Јас р**а**збрав<br>*Jas r**a**zbrav* | We understood -<br>Ние р**а**збравме<br>*Nie r**a**zbirame* |
| 2nd person | You understood -<br>Ти р**а**збра<br>*Ti r**a**zbra* | You understood -<br>Вие р**а**збравте<br>*Vie r**a**zbirate* |
| 3rd person | He/She/It understood -<br>Тој/Таа/Тоа р**а**збра<br>*Toj/Taa/Toa r**a**zbra* | They understood -<br>Тие р**а**збраа<br>*Tie r**a**zbraa* |

| Past Continuous Tense | | |
|---|---|---|
| *Person* | *Singular* | *Plural* |
| 1st person | I was understanding -<br>Јас р**а**збирав<br>*Jas r**a**zbirav* | We were understanding -<br>Ние разб**и**равме<br>*Nie razb**i**ravme* |
| 2nd person | You were understanding -<br>Ти разб**и**раше<br>*Ti razb**i**rashe* | You were understanding -<br>Вие разб**и**равте<br>*Vie razb**i**ravte* |
| 3rd person | He/She/It was understanding -<br>Тој/Таа/Тоа разб**и**раше<br>*Toj/Taa/Toa razb**i**rashe* | They were understanding -<br>Тие разб**и**раа<br>*Tie razb**i**raa* |

| Present Perfect Simple Tense | | |
|---|---|---|
| *Person* | *Singular* | *Plural* |
| 1st person | I have understood -<br>Јас сум р**а**збрал(а)<br>*Jas sum r**a**zbral(a)* | We have understood -<br>Ние сме р**а**збрале<br>*Nie sme r**a**zbrale* |
| 2nd person | You have understood -<br>Ти си р**а**збрал(а)<br>*Ti si r**a**zbral(a)* | You have understood -<br>Вие сте р**а**збрале<br>*Vie ste r**a**zbrale* |

| | | |
|---|---|---|
| 3rd person | He/She/It has understood - Тој/Таа/Тоа разбрал(а)(о) *Toj/Taa/Toa razbral(a)(o)* | They have understood - Тие разбрале *Tie razbrale* |

| Present Perfect Continuous Tense | | |
|---|---|---|
| *Person* | *Singular* | *Plural* |
| 1st person | I have been understanding - Јас сум разбирал(а) *Jas sum razbiral(a)* | We have been standing - Ние сме разбирале *Nie sme razbirale* |
| 2nd person | You have been understanding Ти си разбирал(а) *Ti si razbiral(a)* | You have been understanding Вие сте разбирале *Vie ste razbirale* |
| 3rd person | He/She/It has been understanding- Тој/Таа/Тоа разбирал(а)(о) *Toj/Taa/Toa razbiral(a)(o)* | They have been understanding - Тие разбирале *Tie razbirale* |

| Past Perfect Simple Tense | | |
|---|---|---|
| *Person* | *Singular* | *Plural* |
| 1st person | I had understood - Јас бев разбрал(а) *Jas bev razbral(a)* | We had understood- Ние бевме разбрале *Nie bevme razbrale* |
| 2nd person | You had understood - Ти беше разбрал(а) *Ti beshe razbral(a)* | You had understood - Вие бевте разбрале *Vie bevte razbrale* |
| 3rd person | He/She/It had understood - Тој/Таа/Тоа беше разбрал(а)(о) *Toj/Taa/Toa razbral(a)(o)* | They had understood - Тие беа разбрале *Tie bea razbrale* |

| Future Simple Tense | | |
|---|---|---|
| *Person* | *Singular* | *Plural* |
| 1st person | I will understand - Јас ќе разбирам/разберам *Jas kje razbiram/razberam* | We will understand - Ние ќе разбираме/разбереме *Nie kje razbirame/razbereme* |
| 2nd person | You will understand - Ти ќе разбираш/разбереш *Ti kje razbirash/razberesh* | You will understand - Вие ќе разбирате/разберете *Vie kje razbirate/razberete* |
| 3rd person | He/She/It will understand - Тој/Таа/Тоа ќе разбира/разбере *Toj/Taa/Toa kje razbira/razbere* | They will understand- Тие ќе разбираат/разберат *Tie kje razbiraat/razberat* |

| used to + infinitive or would + infinitive | | |
|---|---|---|
| *Person* | *Singular* | *Plural* |
| 1st person | I would understand- Јас ќе разбирав/разбрав *Jas kje razbirav/razbrav* | We would understand - Ние ќе разбиравме/разбравме Nie kje razbiravme/razbravme |

| | | |
|---|---|---|
| 2nd person | You would understand -<br>Ти ќе разб**и**раше/разб**е**реше<br>*Ti kje razb**i**rashe/razb**e**reshe* | You would understand -<br>Вие ќе разб**и**равте/р**а**збравте<br>*Vie kje razb**i**ravte/r**a**zbravte* |
| 3rd person | He/She/It would understand -<br>Тој/Таа/Тоа ќе<br>разб**и**раше/разб**е**реше<br>*Toj/Taa/Toa kje*<br>*razb**i**rashe/razb**e**reshe* | They would understand -<br>Тие ќе разб**и**раа/р**а**збраа<br>*Tie kje razb**i**raa/r**a**zbraa* |

| **Personal endings for future perfect-in-the-past tense** | | |
|---|---|---|
| *Person* | *Singular* | *Plural* |
| 1st person | I would haveunderstood -<br>Јас ќе сум р**а**збирал/р**а**збрал(а)<br>*Jas kje sum r**a**zbiral/r**a**zbral(a)* | We would have understood-<br>Ние ќе сме<br>разб**и**рале/р**а**збрале<br>*Nie kje sme razb**i**rale/r**a**zbrale* |
| 2nd person | You would have understood -<br>Ти ќе си р**а**збирал/р**а**збрал(а)<br>*Ti kje si r**a**zbiral/r**a**zbral(a)* | You would have understood -<br>Вие ќе сте разб**и**рале/р**а**збрале<br>*Vie kje ste razb**i**rale/r**a**zbrale* |
| 3rd person | He/She/It would haveunderstood<br>-<br>Тој/Таа/Тоа ќе<br>р**а**збирал/р**а**збрал(а)(о)<br>*Toj/Taa/Toa kje*<br>*r**a**zbiral/r**a**zbral(a)(o)* | They would have understood -<br>Тие ќе разб**и**рале/р**а**збрале<br>*Tie kje razb**i**rale/r**a**zbrale* |

**To use – Користи/Искористи**

| | | |
|---|---|---|
| *Infinitive* | To use | Користи<br>Koristi |

| Present Simple Tense | | |
|---|---|---|
| *Person* | *Singular* | *Plural* |
| 1st person | I use -<br>Јас користам<br>*Jas koristam* | We use -<br>Ние користиме<br>*Nie koristime* |
| 2nd person | You use -<br>Ти користиш<br>*Ti koristish* | You use-<br>Вие користите<br>*Vie koristite* |
| 3rd person | He/She/It uses -<br>Тој/Таа/Тоа користи<br>*Toj/Taa/Toa koristi* | They use -<br>Тие користат<br>*Tie koristat* |

| Past Simple Tense | | |
|---|---|---|
| *Person* | *Singular* | *Plural* |
| 1st person | I used-<br>Јас искористив<br>*Jas iskoristiv* | We used-<br>Ние искористивме<br>*Nie iskoristivme* |
| 2nd person | You used -<br>Ти искористи<br>*Ti iskoristi* | You used-<br>Вие искористивте<br>*Vie iskoristivte* |
| 3rd person | He/She/It used-<br>Тој/Таа/Тоа искористи<br>*Toj/Taa/Toa iskoristi* | They used -<br>Тие искористија<br>*Tie iskoristija* |

| Past Continuous Tense | | |
|---|---|---|
| *Person* | *Singular* | *Plural* |
| 1st person | I was using -<br>Јас користев<br>*Jas koristev* | We were using -<br>Ние користевме<br>*Nie koristevme* |
| 2nd person | You were using -<br>Ти користише<br>*Ti koristeshe* | You were using -<br>Вие користевте<br>*Vi koristevte* |
| 3rd person | He/She/It was using -<br>Тој/Таа/Тоа користеше<br>*Toj/Taa/Toa koristeshe* | They were using -<br>Тие користеа<br>*Tie koristea* |

| Present Perfect Simple Tense | | |
|---|---|---|
| *Person* | *Singular* | *Plural* |
| 1st person | I have used -<br>Јас сум искористил(а)<br>*Jas sum iskoristil(a)* | We have used -<br>Ние сме искористиле<br>*Nie sme iskoristile* |
| 2nd person | You have used -<br>Ти си искористил(а)<br>*Ti si iskoristil(a)* | You have used -<br>Вие сте искористиле<br>*Vie ste iskoristile* |

| | | |
|---|---|---|
| 3rd person | He/She/It has used -<br>Тој/Таа/Тоа искористил(а)(о)<br>*Toj/Taa/Toa iskoristil(a)(o)* | They have used -<br>Тие искористиле<br>*Tie iskoristile* |

| **Present Perfect Continuous Tense** | | |
|---|---|---|
| *Person* | *Singular* | *Plural* |
| 1st person | I have been using -<br>Јас сум користел(а)<br>*Jas sum koristel(a)* | We have been using-<br>Ние сме користеле<br>*Nie sme koristele* |
| 2nd person | You have been using -<br>Ти си користел(а)<br>*Ti si koristel(a)* | You have been using-<br>Вие сте користеле<br>*Vie ste koristele* |
| 3rd person | He/She/It has been using -<br>Тој/Таа/Тоа користел(а)(о)<br>*Toj/Taa/Toa koristel(a)(o)* | They have been using-<br>Тие користеле<br>*Tie koristele* |

| **Past Perfect Simple Tense** | | |
|---|---|---|
| *Person* | *Singular* | *Plural* |
| 1st person | I had used-<br>Јас бев искористил(а)<br>*Jas bev iskoristil(a)* | We had used -<br>Ние бевме искористиле<br>*Nie sme iskoristile* |
| 2nd person | You had used -<br>Ти беше искористил(а)<br>*Ti beshe iskoristil(a)* | You had used -<br>Вие бевте искористиле<br>*Vie bevte iskoristile* |
| 3rd person | He/She/It had used-<br>Тој/Таа/Тоа беше<br>искористил(а)(о)<br>*Toj/Taa/Toa beshe*<br>iskoristil(a)(o) | They had used-<br>Тие беа искористиле<br>*Tie bea iskoristile* |

| **Future Simple Tense** | | |
|---|---|---|
| *Person* | *Singular* | *Plural* |
| 1st person | I will use-<br>Јас ќе користам/искористам<br>*Jas kje koristam/iskoristam* | We will use -<br>Ние ќе користиме/искористиме<br>*Nie kje koristime/iskoristime* |
| 2nd person | You will use -<br>Ти ќе користиш/искористиш<br>*Ti kje koristish/iskoristish* | You will use -<br>Вие ќе користите/искористите<br>*Vie kje koristi*te/iskoristite* |
| 3rd person | He/She/It will use -<br>Тој/Таа/Тоа користи/искористи<br>*Toj/Taa/Toa kje koristi/iskoristi* | They will use -<br>Тие ќе користат/искористат<br>*Tie kje koristat/iskoristat* |

| **used to + infinitive or would + infinitive** | | |
|---|---|---|
| *Person* | *Singular* | *Plural* |
| 1st person | I would use -<br>Јас ќе користев/искористев<br>*Jas kje koristev/iskoristev* | We would use -<br>Ние ќе<br>користевме/искористевме<br>*Nie kje koristevme/iskoristevme* |

| | | |
|---|---|---|
| 2nd person | You would use -<br>Ти ќе користеше/искористеше<br>*Ti kje koristeshe/iskoristeshe* | You would use -<br>Вие ќе<br>користевте/искористевте<br>*Vie kje koristevte/iskoristevte* |
| 3rd person | He/She/It would use -<br>Тој/Таа/Тоа ќе<br>користеше/искористеше<br>*Toj/Taa/Toa kje*<br>*koristeshe/iskoristeshe* | They would use -<br>Тие ќе користеа/искористеа<br>*Tie kje koristea/iskoristea* |

| **Personal endings for future perfect-in-the-past tense** | | |
|---|---|---|
| *Person* | *Singular* | *Plural* |
| 1st person | I would have used -<br>Јас ќе сум<br>користел/искористел(а)<br>*Jas kje sum koristel/iskoristel(a)* | We would have used -<br>Ние ќе сме<br>користеле/искористеле<br>*Nie kje sme koristele/iskoristele* |
| 2nd person | You would have used -<br>Ти ќе си<br>користел/искористел(а)<br>*Ti kje si koristel/iskoristel(a)* | You would have used -<br>Вие ќе сте<br>користеле/искористеле<br>*Vie kje ste koristele/iskoristele* |
| 3rd person | He/She/It would have used -<br>Тој/Таа/Тоа ќе<br>користел/искористел(а)(о)<br>*Toj/Taa/Toa kje*<br>*koristel/iskoristel(a)(o)* | They would have used -<br>Тие ќе користеле/искористеле<br>*Tie kje koristele/iskoristele* |

**_To wait – Чека/Дочека_**

| | | |
|---|---|---|
| *Infinitive* | To wait | Чека<br>Cheka |

| Present Simple Tense | | |
|---|---|---|
| *Person* | *Singular* | *Plural* |
| 1st person | I wait-<br>Јас чекам<br>*Jas chekam* | We wait-<br>Ние чекаме<br>*Nie chekame* |
| 2nd person | You wait-<br>Ти чекаш<br>*Ti chekash* | You wait-<br>Вие чекате<br>*Vie chekate* |
| 3rd person | He/She/It waites-<br>Тој/Таа/Тоа чека<br>*Toj/Taa/Toa cheka* | They wait-<br>Тие чекаат<br>*Tie chekaat* |

| Past Simple Tense | | |
|---|---|---|
| *Person* | *Singular* | *Plural* |
| 1st person | I waited -<br>Јас дочекав<br>*Jas dochekav* | We waited -<br>Ние дочекавме<br>*Nie dochekavme* |
| 2nd person | You waited -<br>Ти дочека<br>*Ti docheka* | You waited -<br>Вие дочекавте<br>*Vie dochekavte* |
| 3rd person | He/She/It waited -<br>Тој/Таа/Тоа дочека<br>*Toj/Taa/Toa docheka* | They waited -<br>Тие дочекаа<br>*Tie dochekaa* |

| Past Continuous Tense | | |
|---|---|---|
| *Person* | *Singular* | *Plural* |
| 1st person | I was waiting -<br>Јас чекав<br>*Jas chekav* | We were waiting -<br>Ние чекавме<br>*Nie chekavme* |
| 2nd person | You were waiting -<br>Ти чекаше<br>*Ti chekashe* | You were waiting -<br>Вие чекавте<br>*Vie chekavte* |
| 3rd person | He/She/It was waiting -<br>Тој/Таа/Тоа чекаше<br>*Toj/Taa/Toa chekashe* | They were waiting -<br>Тие чекаа<br>*Tie chekaa* |

| Present Perfect Simple Tense | | |
|---|---|---|
| *Person* | *Singular* | *Plural* |
| 1st person | I have waited -<br>Јас сум дочекал(а)<br>*Jas sum dochekal(a)* | We have waited -<br>Ние сме дочекале<br>*Nie sme dochekale* |

| | | |
|---|---|---|
| 2nd person | You have waited -<br>Ти си д**о**чекал(а)<br>*Ti si d**o**chekal(a)* | You have waited -<br>Вие сте доч**е**кале<br>*Vie stw doch**e**kale* |
| 3rd person | He/She/It has waited -<br>Тој/Таа/Тоа д**о**чекал(а)(о)<br>*Toj/Taa/Toa d**o**chekal(a)(o)* | They have waited -<br>Тие доч**е**кале<br>*Tie doch**e**kale* |

| **Present Perfect Continuous Tense** | | |
|---|---|---|
| *Person* | *Singular* | *Plural* |
| 1st person | I have been waiting -<br>Јас сум ч**е**кал(а)<br>*Jas sum ch**e**kal(a)* | We have been waiting -<br>Ние сме ч**е**кале<br>*Nie sme ch**e**kale* |
| 2nd person | You have been waiting -<br>Ти си ч**е**кал(а)<br>*Ti si ch**e**kal(a)* | You have been waiting -<br>Вие сте ч**е**кале<br>*Vie ste ch**e**kale* |
| 3rd person | He/She/It has been waiting -<br>Тој/Таа/Тоа ч**е**кал(а)(о)<br>*Toj/Taa/Toa ch**e**kal(a)(o)* | They have been waiting -<br>Тие ч**е**кале<br>*Tie ch**e**kale* |

| **Past Perfect Simple Tense** | | |
|---|---|---|
| *Person* | *Singular* | *Plural* |
| 1st person | I had waited-<br>Јас бев д**о**чекал(а)<br>*Jas bev d**o**chekal(a)* | We had waited-<br>Ние бевме доч**е**кале<br>*Nie bevme doch**e**kale* |
| 2nd person | You had waited-<br>Ти беше д**о**чекал(а)<br>*Ti beshe d**o**chekal(a)* | You had waited-<br>Вие бевте доч**е**кале<br>*Vie bevte doch**e**kale* |
| 3rd person | He/She/It had waited-<br>Тој/Таа/Тоа беше<br>д**о**чекал(а)(о)<br>*Toj/Taa/Toa beshe*<br>*d**o**chekal(a)(o)* | They had waited-<br>Тие беа доч**е**кале<br>*Tie bea doch**e**kale* |

| **Future Simple Tense** | | |
|---|---|---|
| *Person* | *Singular* | *Plural* |
| 1st person | I will wai t-<br>Јас ќе ч**е**кам/д**о**чекам<br>*Jas kje ch**e**kam/d**o**chekam* | We will wait -<br>Ние ќе ч**е**каме/доч**е**каме<br>*Nie kje ch**e**kame/doch**e**kame* |
| 2nd person | You will wait -<br>Ти ќе ч**е**каш/д**о**чекаш<br>*Ti kje ch**e**kash/d**o**chekash* | You will wait -<br>Вие ќе ч**е**кате/доч**е**кате<br>*Vie kje ch**e**kate/doch**e**kate* |
| 3rd person | He/She/It will wait -<br>Тој/Таа/Тоа ќе ч**е**ка/д**о**чека<br>*Toj/Taa/Toa kje ch**e**ka/d**o**cheka* | They will wait -<br>Тие ќе ч**е**каат/доч**е**каат<br>*Tie kje ch**e**kaat/doch**e**kaat* |

| **used to + infinitive or would + infinitive** | | |
|---|---|---|
| *Person* | *Singular* | *Plural* |
| 1st person | I would wait -<br>Јас ќе чекав/дочекав<br>*Jas kje chekav/dochekav* | We would wait -<br>Ние ќе чекавме/дочекавме<br>*Nie kje chekavme/dochekavme* |
| 2nd person | You would wait -<br>Ти ќе чекаше/дочекаше<br>*Ti kje chekashe/dochekashe* | You would wait -<br>Вие ќе чекавте/дочекавте<br>*Vie kje chekavte/dochekavte* |
| 3rd person | He/She/It would wait -<br>Тој/Таа/Тоа ќе чекаше/дочекаше<br>*Toj/Taa/Toa chekashe/dochekashe* | They would wait -<br>Тие ќе чекаа/дочекаа<br>*Tie kje chekaa/dochekaa* |

| **Personal endings for future perfect-in-the-past tense** | | |
|---|---|---|
| *Person* | *Singular* | *Plural* |
| 1st person | I would have waited-<br>Јас ќе сум чекал/дочекал(а)<br>*Jas kje sum chekal/dochekal(a)* | We would have waited-<br>Ние ќе сме чекале/дочекале<br>*Nie kje sme chekale/dochekale* |
| 2nd person | You would have waited-<br>Ти ќе си чекал/дочекал(а)<br>*Ti kje si chekal/dochekal(a)* | You would have waited-<br>Вие ќе сте чекале/дочекале<br>*Vie kje ste chekale/dochekale* |
| 3rd person | He/She/It would have waited-<br>Тој/Таа/Тоа ќе чекал/дочекал(а)(о)<br>*Toj/Taa/Toa kje chekal/dochekal(a)(o)* | They would have waited-<br>Тие ќе чекале/дочекале<br>*Tie kje chekale/dochekale* |

***To walk – Оди/Изоди***

| | | |
|---|---|---|
| *Infinitive* | To walk | **О**ди<br>**O**di |

| Present Simple Tense | | |
|---|---|---|
| *Person* | *Singular* | *Plural* |
| 1st person | I walk -<br>Јас **од**ам<br>*Jas **od**am* | We walk -<br>Ние **од**име<br>*Nie **od**ime* |
| 2nd person | You walk -<br>Ти **од**иш<br>*Ti **od**ish* | You walk -<br>Вие **од**ите<br>*Vie **od**ite* |
| 3rd person | He/She/It walks -<br>Тој/Таа/Тоа **оди**<br>*Toj/Taa/Toa **o**di* | They walk -<br>Тие **од**ат<br>*Tie **od**at* |

| Past Simple Tense | | |
|---|---|---|
| *Person* | *Singular* | *Plural* |
| 1st person | I walked -<br>Јас **из**одив<br>*Jas **iz**odiv* | We walked -<br>Ние из**од**ивме<br>*Nie iz**od**ivme* |
| 2nd person | You walked -<br>Ти **из**оди<br>*Ti **iz**odi* | You walked -<br>Вие из**од**ивте<br>*Vie iz**od**ivte* |
| 3rd person | He/She/It walked -<br>Тој/Таа/Тоа **из**оди<br>*Toj/Taa/Toa **iz**odi* | They walked -<br>Тие из**од**еа<br>*Tie iz**od**ea* |

| Past Continuous Tense | | |
|---|---|---|
| *Person* | *Singular* | *Plural* |
| 1st person | I was walking -<br>Јас **од**ев<br>*Jas **od**ev* | We were walking -<br>Ние **од**евме<br>*Nie **od**evme* |
| 2nd person | You were walking -<br>Ти **од**еше<br>*Ti **o**deshe* | You were walking -<br>Вие **од**евте<br>*Vie **od**evte* |
| 3rd person | He/She/It was walking -<br>Тој/Таа/Тоа **од**еше<br>*Toj/Taa/Toa **o**deshe* | They were walking -<br>Тие **од**еа<br>*Tie **o**dea* |

| Present Perfect Simple Tense | | |
|---|---|---|
| *Person* | *Singular* | *Plural* |
| 1st person | I have walked -<br>Јас сум **из**одил(а)<br>*Jas sum **iz**odil(a)* | We have walked -<br>Ние сме из**од**иле<br>*Nie sme iz**od**ile* |

| | | |
|---|---|---|
| 2nd person | You have walked -<br>Ти си **и**зодил(а)<br>*Ti si **i**zodil(a)* | You have walked -<br>Вие сте из**о**диле<br>*Vie ste iz**o**dile* |
| 3rd person | He/She/It has walked -<br>Тој/Таа/Тоа **и**зодил(а)(о)<br>*Toj/Taa/Toa **i**zodil(a)(o)* | They have walked -<br>Тие из**о**диле<br>*Tie iz**o**dile* |

| **Present Perfect Continuous Tense** | | |
|---|---|---|
| *Person* | *Singular* | *Plural* |
| 1st person | I have been walking -<br>Јас сум **о**дел(а)<br>*Jas sum **o**del(a)* | We have been walking -<br>Ние сме **о**деле<br>*Nie sme **o**dele* |
| 2nd person | You have been walking -<br>Ти си **о**дел(а)<br>*Ti si **o**del(a)* | You have been walking -<br>Вие сте **о**деле<br>*Vie ste **o**dele* |
| 3rd person | He/She/It has been walking -<br>Тој/Таа/Тоа **о**дел(а)(о)<br>*Toj/Taa/Toa **o**del(a)(o)* | They have been walking -<br>Тие **о**деле<br>*Tie **o**dele* |

| **Past Perfect Simple Tense** | | |
|---|---|---|
| *Person* | *Singular* | *Plural* |
| 1st person | I had walked -<br>Јас бев **и**зодел(а)<br>*Jas bev **i**zodil(a)* | We had walked -<br>Ние бевме **и**зоделе<br>*Nie bevme **i**zodile* |
| 2nd person | You had walked -<br>Ти беше **и**зодел(а)<br>*Ti beshe **i**zodil(a)* | You had walked -<br>Вие бевте **и**зоделе<br>*Vie bevte **i**zodile* |
| 3rd person | He/She/It had walked -<br>Тој/Таа/Тоа беше **и**зодел(а)(о)<br>*Toj/Taa/Toa beshe **i**zodil(a)(o)* | They had walked -<br>Тие беа **и**зоделе<br>*Tie bea **i**zodile* |

| **Future Simple Tense** | | |
|---|---|---|
| *Person* | *Singular* | *Plural* |
| 1st person | I will walk -<br>Јас ќе **о**дам/**и**зодам<br>*Jas kje **o**dam/**i**zodam* | We will walk -<br>Ние ќе **о**диме/из**о**диме<br>*Nie kje **o**dime/iz**o**dime* |
| 2nd person | You will walk -<br>Ти ќе **о**диш/**и**зодиш<br>*Ti kje **o**dish/**i**zodish* | You will walk -<br>Вие ќе **о**дите/из**о**дите<br>*Vie kje **o**dite/iz**o**dite* |
| 3rd person | He/She/It will walk -<br>Тој/Таа/Тоа ќе **о**ди/**и**зоди<br>*Toj/Taa/Toa kje **o**di/**i**zodi* | They will walk -<br>Тие ќе **о**дат/**и**зодат<br>*Tie kje **o**dat/**i**zodat* |

| **used to + infinitive or would + infinitive** | | |
|---|---|---|
| *Person* | *Singular* | *Plural* |
| 1st person | I would walk -<br>Јас ќе **о**дев/**и**зодев<br>*Jas kje **o**dev/**i**zodev* | We would walk -<br>Ние ќе **о**девме/из**о**девме<br>*Nie kje **o**devme/iz**o**devme* |

| | | |
|---|---|---|
| 2nd person | You would walk -<br>Ти ќе **о**деше/из**о**деше<br>*Ti kje* ***o****deshe/iz****o****deshe* | You would walk -<br>Вие ќе **о**девте/из**о**девте<br>*Vie kje* ***o****devte/iz****o****devte* |
| 3rd person | He/She/It would walk -<br>Toj/Taa/Toa ќе **о**деше/из**о**деше<br>*Toj/Taa/Toa kje* ***o****deshe/iz****o****deshe* | They would walk -<br>Тие ќе **о**деа/из**о**деа<br>*Tie kje* ***o****dea/iz****o****dea* |

| **Personal endings for future perfect-in-the-past tense** | | |
|---|---|---|
| *Person* | *Singular* | *Plural* |
| 1st person | I would have walked -<br>Јас ќе сум **о**дел/из**о**дел(а)<br>*Jas kje sum* ***o****del/iz****o****del(a)* | We would have walked -<br>Ние ќе сме **о**деле/из**о**деле<br>*Nie kje sme* ***o****dele/iz****o****dele* |
| 2nd person | You would have walked -<br>Ти ќе си **о**дел/из**о**дел(а)<br>*Ti kje si* ***o****del/iz****o****del(a)* | You would have walked -<br>Вие ќе сте **о**деле/из**о**деле<br>*Vie kje ste* ***o****dele/iz****o****dele* |
| 3rd person | He/She/It would have walked -<br>Toj/Taa/Toa ќе<br>**о**дел/из**о**дел(а)(о)<br>*Toj/Taa/Toa kje* ***o****del/iz****o****del(a)(o)* | They would have walked -<br>Тие ќе **о**деле/из**о**деле<br>*Tie kje* ***o****dele/iz****o****dele* |

***To want – Сака/Посака***

| | | |
|---|---|---|
| *Infinitive* | To want | С**а**ка<br>S**a**ka |

| **Present Simple Tense** | | |
|---|---|---|
| *Person* | *Singular* | *Plural* |
| 1st person | I want -<br>Јас с**а**кам<br>*Jas s**a**kam* | We want -<br>Ние с**а**каме<br>*Nie s**a**kame* |
| 2nd person | You want -<br>Ти с**а**каш<br>*Ti s**a**kash* | You want -<br>Вие с**а**кате<br>*Vie s**a**kate* |
| 3rd person | He/She/It wants -<br>Тој/Таа/Тоасака<br>*Toj/Taa/Toa s**a**ka* | They want -<br>Тие с**а**каат<br>*Tie s**a**kaat* |

| **Past Simple Tense** | | |
|---|---|---|
| *Person* | *Singular* | *Plural* |
| 1st person | I wanted-<br>Јас п**о**сакав<br>*Jas p**o**sakav* | We wanted -<br>Ние пос**а**кавме<br>*Nie pos**a**kavme* |
| 2nd person | You wanted -<br>Тип**о**сака<br>*Ti p**o**saka* | You wanted-<br>Вие пос**а**кавте<br>*Vie pos**a**kavte* |
| 3rd person | He/She/It wanted -<br>Тој/Таа/Тоа п**о**сака<br>*Toj/Taa/Toa p**o**saka* | They wanted-<br>Тие пос**а**каа<br>*Tie pos**a**kaa* |

| **Past Continuous Tense** | | |
|---|---|---|
| *Person* | *Singular* | *Plural* |
| 1st person | I was wanting-<br>Јас с**а**кав<br>*Jas s**a**kav* | We were wanting-<br>Ние с**а**кавме<br>*Nie s**a**kavme* |
| 2nd person | You were wanting-<br>Ти с**а**каше<br>*Ti s**a**kashe* | You were wanting-<br>Вие с**а**кавте<br>*Vie s**a**kavte* |
| 3rd person | He/She/It was wanting-<br>Тој/Таа/Тоа с**а**каше<br>*Toj/Taa/Toa s**a**kashe* | They were wanting-<br>Тие с**а**каа<br>*Tie s**a**kaa* |

| **Present Perfect Simple Tense** | | |
|---|---|---|
| *Person* | *Singular* | *Plural* |
| 1st person | I have wanted -<br>Јас сум п**о**сакал(а)<br>*Jas sum p**o**sakal(a)* | We have wanted -<br>Ние сме пос**а**кале<br>*Nie sme pos**a**kale* |

| | | |
|---|---|---|
| 2nd person | You have wanted-<br>Ти си п**о**сакал(а)<br>*Ti si p**o**sakal(a)* | You have wanted -<br>Вие сте пос**а**кале<br>*Vie ste pos**a**kale* |
| 3rd person | He/She/It has wanted -<br>Тој/Таа/Тоа п**о**сакал(а)(о)<br>*Toj/Taa/Toa p**o**sakal(a)(o)* | They have wanted -<br>Тие пос**а**кале<br>*Tie pos**a**kale* |

| **Present Perfect Continuous Tense** | | |
|---|---|---|
| *Person* | *Singular* | *Plural* |
| 1st person | I have been wanting-<br>Јас сум с**а**кал(а)<br>*Jas sum s**a**kal(a)* | We have been wanting-<br>Ние сме с**а**кале<br>*Nie sme s**a**kale* |
| 2nd person | You have been wanting-<br>Ти си с**а**кал(а)<br>*Ti si s**a**kal(a)* | You have been wanting-<br>Вие сте с**а**кале<br>*Vie ste s**a**kale* |
| 3rd person | He/She/It has been wanting-<br>Тој/Таа/Тоа с**а**кал(а)(о)<br>*Toj/Taa/Toa s**a**kal(a)(o)* | They have been wanting-<br>Тие с**а**кале<br>*Tie s**a**kale* |

| **Past Perfect Simple Tense** | | |
|---|---|---|
| *Person* | *Singular* | *Plural* |
| 1st person | I had wanted-<br>Јас бев п**о**сакал(а)<br>*Jas bev p**o**sakal(a)* | We had wanted -<br>Ние бевме<br>пос**а**кале<br>*Nie bevme pos**a**kale* |
| 2nd person | You had wanted -<br>Ти беше п**о**сакал(а)<br>*Ti beshe p**o**sakal(a)* | You had wanted -<br>Вие бевте пос**а**кале<br>*Vie bevte pos**a**kale* |
| 3rd person | He/She/It had wanted-<br>Тој/Таа/Тоа беше<br>пос**а**кал(а)(о)<br>*Toj/Taa/Toa p**o**sakal(a)(o)* | They had wanted -<br>Тие беа пос**а**кале<br>*Tie bea pos**a**kale* |

| **Future Simple Tense** | | |
|---|---|---|
| *Person* | *Singular* | *Plural* |
| 1st person | I will want-<br>Јас ќе с**а**кам/п**о**сакам<br>*Jas kje s**a**kam/p**o**sakam* | We will want -<br>Ние ќе с**а**каме/пос**а**каме<br>*Nie kje s**a**kame/pos**a**kame* |
| 2nd person | You will want -<br>Ти ќе с**а**каш/п**о**сакаш<br>*Ti kje s**a**kash/p**o**sakash* | You will want -<br>*Вие ќе с**а**каме/пос**а**каме*<br>Vie kje s**a**kate/pos**a**kate |
| 3rd person | He/She/It will want -<br>Тој/Таа/Тоа Ќе с**а**ка/п**о**сака<br>*Toj/Taa/Toa kje s**a**ka/p**o**saka* | They will want -<br>Тие ќе с**а**каат/пос**а**каат<br>*Tie kje s**a**kaat/pos**a**kaat* |

| used to + infinitive or would + infinitive | | |
|---|---|---|
| *Person* | *Singular* | *Plural* |
| 1st person | I would want -<br>Јас ќе сакав/посакав<br>*Jas kje sakav/posakav* | We would want -<br>Ние ќе сакавме/посакавме<br>*Nie kje sakavme/posakavme* |
| 2nd person | You would want -<br>Ти ќе сакаше/посакаше<br>*Ti kje sakashe/posakashe* | You would want -<br>Вие ќе сакавте/посакавте<br>*Vie kje sakavte/posakavte* |
| 3rd person | He/She/It would want-<br>Тој/Таа/Тоа ќе<br>сакаше/посакаше<br>Toj/Taa/Toa kje<br>*sakashe/posakashe* | They would want-<br>Тие ќе сакаа/посакаа<br>*Tie kje sakaa/posakaa* |

| Personal endings for future perfect-in-the-past tense | | |
|---|---|---|
| *Person* | *Singular* | *Plural* |
| 1st person | I would have wanted-<br>Јас ќе сум сакал/посакал(а)<br>*Jas kje sum sakal/posakal(a)* | We would have wanted -<br>Ние ќе сме сакале/посакале<br>*Nie kje sme sakale/posakale* |
| 2nd person | You would have wanted -<br>Ти ќе си сакал/посакал(а)<br>*Ti kje si sakal/posakal(a)* | You would have wanted -<br>Вие ќе сте сакале/посакале<br>*Vie kje ste sakale/posakale* |
| 3rd person | He/She/It would have wanted<br>Тој/Таа/Тоа Тоа ќе<br>сакал/посакал(а)(о)<br>*Toj/Taa/Toa kje*<br>*sakal/posakal(a)(o)* | They would have wanted-<br>- Тие ќе сакале/посакале<br>*Tie kje sakale/posakale* |

***To watch – Гледа/Догледа***

| | | |
|---|---|---|
| *Infinitive* | To watch | Гледа<br>Gleda |

| Present Simple Tense | | |
|---|---|---|
| *Person* | *Singular* | *Plural* |
| 1st person | I watch-<br>Јас гледам<br>*Jas gledam* | We watch -<br>Ние гледаме<br>*Nie gledame* |
| 2nd person | You watch -<br>Ти гледаш<br>*Ti gledash* | You watch -<br>Вие гледате<br>*Vie gledate* |
| 3rd person | He/She/It watches -<br>Тој/Таа/Тоа гледа<br>*Toj/Taa/Toa gleda* | They watch -<br>Тие гледаат<br>*Tie gledat* |

| Past Simple Tense | | |
|---|---|---|
| *Person* | *Singular* | *Plural* |
| 1st person | I watched -<br>Јас догледав<br>*Jas dogledav* | We watched -<br>Ние догледавме<br>*Nie dogledavme* |
| 2nd person | You watched -<br>Ти догледа<br>*Ti dogleda* | You watched -<br>Вие догледавте<br>*Vie dogledavte* |
| 3rd person | He/She/It watched -<br>Тој/Таа/Тоа догледа<br>*Toj/Taa/Toa dogleda* | They watched -<br>Тие догледаа<br>*Tie dogledaa* |

| Past Continuous Tense | | |
|---|---|---|
| *Person* | *Singular* | *Plural* |
| 1st person | I was watching -<br>Јас гледав<br>*Jas gledav* | We were watching -<br>Ние гледавме<br>Nie gledavme |
| 2nd person | You were watching -<br>Ти гледаше<br>*Ti gledashe* | You were watching -<br>Вие гледавте<br>*Vie gledavte* |
| 3rd person | He/She/It was watching -<br>Тој/Таа/Тоа гледаше<br>*Toj/Taa/Toa gledashe* | They were watching -<br>Тие гледаа<br>*Tie gledaa* |

| Present Perfect Simple Tense | | |
|---|---|---|
| *Person* | *Singular* | *Plural* |
| 1st person | I have watched -<br>Јас сум догледал(а)<br>*Jas sumzdogledal(a)* | We have watched -<br>Ние сме догледале<br>*Nie sme dogledale* |

| | | |
|---|---|---|
| 2nd person | You have watched -<br>Ти си д**о**гледал(а)<br>*Ti sid**o**gledal(a)* | You have watched -<br>Вие сте догл**е**дале<br>*Vie ste dogl**e**dale* |
| 3rd person | He/She/It has watched -<br>Тој/Таа/Тоа д**о**гледал(а)(о)<br>*Toj/Taa/Toa d**o**gledal(a)(o)* | They have watched -<br>Тие догл**е**дале<br>*Tie dogl**e**dale* |

| **Present Perfect Continuous Tense** | | |
|---|---|---|
| *Person* | *Singular* | *Plural* |
| 1st person | I have been watching -<br>Јас сум гл**е**дал(а)<br>*Jas sum gl**e**dal(a)* | We have been watching -<br>Ние сме гл**е**дале<br>*Nie sme gl**e**dale* |
| 2nd person | You have been watching -<br>Ти си гл**е**дал(а)<br>*Ti si gl**e**dal(a)* | You have been watching -<br>Вие сте гл**е**дале<br>*Vie ste gl**e**dale* |
| 3rd person | He/She/It has been watching -<br>Тој/Таа/Тоа гл**е**дал(а)(о)<br>*Toj/Taa/Toa gl**e**dal(a)(o)* | They have been watching -<br>Тие гл**е**дале<br>*Tie gl**e**dale* |

| **Past Perfect Simple Tense** | | |
|---|---|---|
| *Person* | *Singular* | *Plural* |
| 1st person | I had watched -<br>Јас бев д**о**гледал(а)<br>*Jas bev d**o**gledal(a)* | We had watched -<br>Ние бевме догл**е**дале<br>*Nie bevme dogl**e**dale* |
| 2nd person | You had watched -<br>Ти беше д**о**гледал(а)<br>*Ti beshe d**o**gledal(a)* | You had watched -<br>Вие бевте догл**е**дале<br>*Vie bevte dogl**e**dale* |
| 3rd person | He/She/It had watched -<br>Тој/Таа/Тоа д**о**гледал(а)(о)<br>*Toj/Taa/Toa beshe d**o**gledal(a)(o)* | They had watched -<br>Тие беа догл**е**дале<br>*Tie bea dogl**e**dale* |

| **Future Simple Tense** | | |
|---|---|---|
| *Person* | *Singular* | *Plural* |
| 1st person | I will watch -<br>Јас ќе гл**е**дам/зд**о**гледам<br>*Jas kje gl**e**dam/zd**o**gledam* | We will watch -<br>Ние ќе гл**е**даме/здогл**е**даме<br>*Nie kje gl**e**dame/zdogl**e**dame* |
| 2nd person | You will watch -<br>Ти ќе гл**е**даш/зд**о**гледаш<br>*Ti kje gl**e**dash/zd**o**gledash* | You will watch -<br>Вие ќе гл**е**дате/здогл**е**дате<br>*Vie kje gl**e**date/zd**o**gledate* |
| 3rd person | He/She/It will watch -<br>Тој/Таа/Тоа ќе гл**е**да/зд**о**гледа<br>*Toj/Taa/Toa kje gl**e**da/zd**o**gleda* | They will watch -<br>Тие ќе гл**е**даат/здогл**е**даат<br>*Tie kje gl**e**daat/zdogl**e**daat* |

| used to + infinitive or would + infinitive | | |
|---|---|---|
| *Person* | *Singular* | *Plural* |
| 1st person | I would watch - Јас ќе гл**е**дав/д**о**гледав *Jas kje gl**e**dav/d**o**gledav* | We would watch - Ние ќе гл**е**давме/догл**е**давме *Toj/Taa/Toa kje gl**e**dashe/dogl**e**dashe* |
| 2nd person | You would watch - Ти ќе гл**е**даше/догл**е**даше *Ti kje gl**e**dashe/dogl**e**dashe* | You would watch - Вие ќе гл**е**давте/догл**е**давте *Vie kje gl**e**davte/dogl**e**davte* |
| 3rd person | He/She/It would watch - Тој/Таа/Тоа глед**а**ше/догл**е**даше *Toj/Taa/Toa kje gl**e**dashe/dogl**e**dashe* | They would watch - Тие ќе гл**е**даа/догл**е**даа *Tie kje gl**e**daa/dogl**e**daa* |

| Personal endings for future perfect-in-the-past tense | | |
|---|---|---|
| *Person* | *Singular* | *Plural* |
| 1st person | I would have watched - Јас ќе сум гл**е**дал/д**о**гледал(а) *Jas kje sum gl**e**dal/d**o**gledal(a)* | We would have watched - Ние ќе сме гл**е**дале/догл**е**дале *Nie kje sme gl**e**dale/dogl**e**dale* |
| 2nd person | You would have watched - Ти ќе си гл**е**дал/д**о**гледал(а) *Ti kje si gl**e**dal/d**o**gledal(a* | You would have watched - Вие ќе сте гл**е**дале/догл**е**дале *Vie kje ste gl**e**dale/dogl**e**dale* |
| 3rd person | He/She/It would have watched Тој/Таа/Тоа ќе гл**е**дал/д**о**гледал(а)(о) *Toj/Taa/Toa kje gl**e**dal/dogl**e**dal(a)(o)* | They would have watched - Тие ќе гл**е**дале/догл**е**дале *Tie kje gl**e**dale/dogl**e**dale* |

### *To win – Победува/Победи*

| | | |
|---|---|---|
| *Infinitive* | To win | Поб**е**дува<br>Pob**e**duva |

| Present Simple Tense | | |
|---|---|---|
| *Person* | *Singular* | *Plural* |
| 1st person | I win-<br>Јас поб**е**дувам<br>*Jas pob**e**duvam* | We win-<br>Ние победу**в**аме<br>*Nie pobed**u**vame* |
| 2nd person | You win-<br>Ти поб**е**дуваш<br>*Ti pob**e**duvash* | You win-<br>Вие побед**у**вате<br>*Vie pobed**u**vate* |
| 3rd person | He/She/It wins-<br>Тој/Таа/Тоа поб**е**дува<br>*Toj/Taa/Toa pob**e**duva* | They win-<br>Тие побед**у**ваат<br>*Tie pobed**u**vaat* |

| Past Simple Tense | | |
|---|---|---|
| *Person* | *Singular* | *Plural* |
| 1st person | I won-<br>Јас п**о**бедив<br>*Jas p**o**bediv* | We won-<br>Ние поб**е**дивме<br>*Nie pob**e**divme* |
| 2nd person | You won-<br>Ти п**о**деди<br>*Ti p**o**bedi* | You won-<br>Вие поб**е**дивте<br>*Vie pob**e**divte* |
| 3rd person | He/She/It won-<br>Тој/Таа/Тоа п**о**беди<br>*Toj/Taa/Toa p**o**bedi* | They won-<br>Тие поб**е**дија<br>*Tie pob**e**dija* |

| Past Continuous Tense | | |
|---|---|---|
| *Person* | *Singular* | *Plural* |
| 1st person | I was winning-<br>Јас поб**е**дував<br>*Jas pob**e**duvav* | We were winning-<br>Ние побед**у**вавме<br>*Nie pobed**u**vavme* |
| 2nd person | You were winning-<br>*Ти побед**у**ваше*<br>Ti pobed**u**vashe | You were winning-<br>Вие побед**у**вавте<br>*Vie poed**u**vavte* |
| 3rd person | He/She/It was winning-<br>Тој/Таа/Тоа побед**у**ваше<br>*Toj/Taa/Toa pobed**u**vashe* | They were winning-<br>Тие побед**у**ваа<br>*Tie pobed**u**vaa* |

| Present Perfect Simple Tense | | |
|---|---|---|
| *Person* | *Singular* | *Plural* |
| 1st person | I have won-<br>Јас сум п**о**бедил(а)<br>*Jas sum p**o**bedil(a)* | We have won-<br>Ние сме поб**е**диле<br>*Nie sme pob**e**dile* |

| | | |
|---|---|---|
| 2nd person | You have won-<br>Ти си п**о**бедил(а)<br>*Ti si p**o**bedil(a)* | You have won-<br>Вие сте поб**е**диле<br>*Vie ste pob**e**dile* |
| 3rd person | He/She/It has won-<br>Тој/Таа/Тоа п**о**бедил(а)(о)<br>*Toj/Taa/Toa p**o**bedil(a)(o)* | They have won-<br>Тие поб**е**диле<br>*Tie pob**e**dile* |

| **Present Perfect Continuous Tense** | | |
|---|---|---|
| *Person* | *Singular* | *Plural* |
| 1st person | I have been winning-<br>Јас сум поб**е**дувал(а)<br>*Jas sum pob**e**duval(a)* | We have been winning-<br>Ние сме побед**у**вале<br>*Nie sme pobed**u**vale* |
| 2nd person | You have been winning-<br>Ти си поб**е**дувал(а)<br>*Ti si pob**e**duval(a)* | You have been winning-<br>Вие сте побед**у**вале<br>*Vie ste pobed**u**vale* |
| 3rd person | He/She/It has been winning-<br>Тој/Таа/Тоа поб**е**дувал(а)(о)<br>*Toj/Taa/Toa pob**e**duval(a)(o)* | They have been winning-<br>Тие побед**у**вале<br>*Tie pobed**u**vale* |

| **Past Perfect Simple Tense** | | |
|---|---|---|
| *Person* | *Singular* | *Plural* |
| 1st person | I had won-<br>Јас бев п**о**бедил(а)<br>*Jas bev p**o**bedil(a)* | We had won -<br>Ние бевме поб**е**диле<br>*Nie bevme pob**e**dile* |
| 2nd person | You had won-<br>Ти беше п**о**бедил(а)<br>*Ti beshe p**o**bedil(a)* | You had won -<br>Вие бевте поб**е**диле<br>*Vie bevte pob**e**dile* |
| 3rd person | He/She/It had won-<br>Тој/Таа/Тоа беше<br>п**о**бедил(а)(о)<br>*Toj/Taa/Toa beshe p**o**bedil(a)(o)* | They had won -<br>Тие беа поб**е**диле<br>*Tie bea pob**e**dile* |

| **Future Simple Tense** | | |
|---|---|---|
| *Person* | *Singular* | *Plural* |
| 1st person | I will win -<br>Јас ќе поб**е**дувам/п**о**бедам<br>*Jas kje pob**e**duvam/p**o**bedam* | We will win -<br>Ние ќе побед**у**ваме/поб**е**диме<br>*Nie kje pobed**u**vame/pob**e**dime* |
| 2nd person | You will win -<br>Ти ќе поб**е**дуваш/п**о**бедиш<br>*Ti kje pob**e**duvash/p**o**bedish* | You will win -<br>Вие побед**у**вате/поб**е**дите<br>*Vie kje pobed**u**vate/pob**e**dite* |
| 3rd person | He/She/It will win -<br>Тој/Таа/Тоа ќе<br>поб**е**дува/п**о**беди<br>*Toj/Taa/Toa kje*<br>*pob**e**duva/p**o**bedi* | They will win -<br>Тие ќе побед**у**ваат/п**о**бедат<br>*Tie kje pobed**u**vaat/p**o**bedat* |

| **used to + infinitive or would + infinitive** | | |
|---|---|---|
| *Person* | *Singular* | *Plural* |
| 1st person | I would win -<br>Јас ќе поб**е**дував/п**о**бедев<br>*Jas kje **pobeduvav**/p**o**bedev* | We would win -<br>Ние ќе<br>побед**у**вавме/поб**е**девме<br>*Nie kje pobed**u**vame/pob**e**dime* |
| 2nd person | You would win -<br>Ти ќе побед**у**ваше/поб**е**деше<br>*Ti kje pobed**u**vashe/pob**e**deshe* | You would win -<br>Вие ќе побед**у**вавте/поб**е**девте<br>*Vie kje pobes**u**vate/pob**e**dete* |
| 3rd person | He/She/It would win -<br>Тој/Таа/Тоа ќе<br>побед**у**ваше/поб**е**деше<br>*Toj/Taa/Toa kje<br>pobed**u**vashe/pob**e**deshe* | They would win -<br>Тие ќе побед**у**ваа/поб**е**деа<br>*Tie kje pobed**u**vaa/pob**e**dea* |

| **Personal endings for future perfect-in-the-past tense** | | |
|---|---|---|
| *Person* | *Singular* | *Plural* |
| 1st person | I would have won -<br>Јас ќе сум<br>поб**е**дувал/п**о**бедил(а)<br>*Jas kje sum<br>pob**e**duval/p**o**bedil(a)* | We would have won-<br>Ние ќе сме<br>побед**у**вале/поб**е**диле<br>*Nie kje sme pobed**u**vale/pob**e**dile* |
| 2nd person | You would have won -<br>Ти ќе си поб**е**дувал/п**о**бедил(а)<br>*Ti kje si pob**e**duval/p**o**bedil(a)* | You would have won-<br>Вие ќе сте<br>побед**у**вале/поб**е**диле<br>*Vie kje ste pobeduvale/pob**e**dile* |
| 3rd person | He/She/It would have won -<br>Тој/Таа/Тоа ќе<br>поб**е**дувал/п**о**бедил(а)(о)<br>*Toj/Taa/Toa kje<br>pob**e**duval/p**o**bedil(a) (o)* | They would have won-<br>Тие ќе побед**у**вале/поб**е**диле<br>*Tie kje pobed**u**vale/pob**e**dile* |

### *To work – Работи/Изработи*

| | | |
|---|---|---|
| *Infinitive* | To work | Р**а**боти<br>R**a**boti |

| Present Simple Tense | | |
|---|---|---|
| *Person* | *Singular* | *Plural* |
| 1st person | I work-<br>Јас р**а**ботам<br>*Jas r**a**botam* | We work-<br>Ние раб**о**тиме<br>*Nie rab**o**time* |
| 2nd person | You work-<br>Ти р**а**ботиш<br>*Ti r**a**botish* | You work-<br>Вие раб**о**тите<br>*Vie rab**o**tite* |
| 3rd person | He/She/It works-<br>Тој/Таа/Тоа р**а**боти<br>*Toj/Taa/Toa r**a**boti* | They work-<br>Тие р**а**ботат<br>*Tie r**a**botat* |

| Past Simple Tense | | |
|---|---|---|
| *Person* | *Singular* | *Plural* |
| 1st person | I worked-<br>Јас изр**а**ботив<br>*Jas izr**a**botiv* | We worked-<br>Ние израб**о**тивме<br>*Nie izrab**o**tivme* |
| 2nd person | You worked-<br>Ти изр**а**боти<br>*Ti izr**a**boti* | You worked-<br>Вие израб**о**тивте<br>*Vie izrab**o**tivte* |
| 3rd person | He/She/It worked-<br>Тој/Таа/Тоа изр**а**боти<br>*Toj/Taa/Toa izr**a**boti* | They worked-<br>Тие израб**о**тија<br>*Tie izrab**o**tija* |

| Past Continuous Tense | | |
|---|---|---|
| *Person* | *Singular* | *Plural* |
| 1st person | I was working-<br>Јас р**а**ботев<br>*Jas r**a**botev* | We were working-<br>Ние раб**о**тевме<br>*Nie rab**o**tevme* |
| 2nd person | You were working-<br>Ти раб**о**теше<br>*Ti rab**o**teshe* | You were working-<br>Вие раб**о**тевте<br>*Vie rab**o**tevte* |
| 3rd person | He/She/It was working-<br>Тој/Таа/Тоа раб**о**теше<br>*Toj/Taa/Toa rab**o**teshe* | They were working-<br>Тие р**а**ботеја<br>*Tie r**a**boteja* |

| Present Perfect Simple Tense | | |
|---|---|---|
| *Person* | *Singular* | *Plural* |
| 1st person | I have worked -<br>Јас сум изр**а**ботил(а)<br>Jas sum izr**a**botil(a) | We have worked -<br>Ние сме изр**а**ботиле<br>Nie sme izr**a**botile |

| | | |
|---|---|---|
| 2nd person | You have worked -<br>Ти си изработил(а)<br>Ti si izrabotil(a) | You have worked -<br>Вие сте изработиле<br>Vie ste izrabotile |
| 3rd person | He/She/It has worked -<br>Тој/Таа/Тоа изработил(а)(о)<br>Toj/Taa/Toa izrabotil(a)(o) | They have worked -<br>Тие изработиле<br>Tie izrabotile |

| **Present Perfect Continuous Tense** | | |
|---|---|---|
| *Person* | *Singular* | *Plural* |
| 1st person | I have been working -<br>Јас сум работел(а)<br>*Jas sum rabotel(a)* | We have been working -<br>Ние сме работеле<br>*Nie sme rabotele* |
| 2nd person | You have been working -<br>Ти си работел(а)<br>*Ti si rabotel(a)* | You have been working -<br>Вие сте работеле<br>*Vie ste rabotele* |
| 3rd person | He/She/It has been working -<br>Тој/Таа/Тоа работел(а)(о)<br>*Toj/Taa/Toa rabotel(a)(o)* | They have been standing -<br>Тие работеле<br>*Tie rabotele* |

| **Past Perfect Simple Tense** | | |
|---|---|---|
| *Person* | *Singular* | *Plural* |
| 1st person | I had worked -<br>Јас бев изработил(а)<br>*Jas bev izrabotil(a)* | We had worked -<br>Ние бевме изработиле<br>*Nie bevme izrabotile* |
| 2nd person | You had worked -<br>Ти беше изработил(а)<br>*Ti beshe izrabotil(a)* | You had worked -<br>Вие бевте изработиле<br>*Vie bevte izrabotile* |
| 3rd person | He/She/It had worked -<br>Тој/Таа/Тоа беше изработил(а)(о)<br>*Toj/Taa/Toa beshe izraboteil(a)(o)* | They had worked -<br>Тие беа изработиле<br>*Tie bea izrabotile* |

| **Future Simple Tense** | | |
|---|---|---|
| *Person* | *Singular* | *Plural* |
| 1st person | I will work -<br>Јас ќе работам/изработам<br>*Jas kje rabotam/izrabotam* | We will work -<br>Ние ќе работиме/изработиме<br>*Nie kje rabotime/izrabotime* |
| 2nd person | You will work -<br>Ти ќе работиш/изработиш<br>*Ti kje rabotish/izrabotish* | You will work -<br>Вие ќе работите/изработите<br>*Vie kje rabotite/izrabotite* |
| 3rd person | He/She/It will work -<br>Тој/Таа/Тоа ќе работи/изработи<br>*Toj/Taa/Toa kje raboti/izraboti* | They will work -<br>Тие ќе работат/изработат<br>*Tie kje rabotat/izrabotat* |

| **used to + infinitive or would + infinitive** | | |
|---|---|---|
| *Person* | *Singular* | *Plural* |
| 1st person | I would work -<br>Јас ќе работев/изработев<br>*Jas kje rabotev/izrabotev* | We would work -<br>Ние ќе работевме/изработевме<br>Nie kje *rabotevme/izrabotevme* |
| 2nd person | You would work-<br>Ти ќе работеше/изработеше<br>*Ti kje raboteshe/izraboteshe* | You would work-<br>Вие ќе работевте/изработевте<br>*Vie kje rabotevte/izrabotevte* |
| 3rd person | He/She/It would work-<br>Тој/Таа/Тоа ќе работеше/изработеше<br>*Toj/Taa/Toa kje raboteshe/izraboteshe* | They would work-<br>Тие ќе работеа/изработеа<br>*Tie kje rabotea/izrabotea* |

| **Personal endings for future perfect-in-the-past tense** | | |
|---|---|---|
| *Person* | *Singular* | *Plural* |
| 1st person | I would have worked-<br>Јас ќе сум работел/изработил(а)<br>*Jas kje sum rabotel/izrabotil(a)* | We would have worked -<br>Ние ќе сме работеле/изработиле<br>*Nie kje sme rabotele/izrabotile* |
| 2nd person | You would have worked-<br>Ти ќе си работел/изработил(а)<br>*Ti kje si rabotel/izrabotil(a)* | You would have worked -<br>Вие ќе сте работеле/изработиле<br>*Vie kje ste rabotele/izrabotile* |
| 3rd person | He/She/It would have worked<br>Тој/Таа/Тоа ќе работел/изработил(а)(о)<br>*Toj/Taa/Toa kje rabotel/izrabotil(a)(o)* | They would have worked -<br>Тие ќе работеле/изработиле<br>*Tie kje rabotele/izrabotile* |

**To write – Пишува/Напиша**

| | | |
|---|---|---|
| *Infinitive* | To write | П**и**шува<br>P**i**shuva |

| Present Simple Tense | | |
|---|---|---|
| *Person* | *Singular* | *Plural* |
| 1st person | I write -<br>Јас п**и**шувам<br>Jas p**i**shuvam | We write -<br>Ние пиш**у**ваме<br>Nie pish**u**vame |
| 2nd person | You write -<br>Ти п**и**шуваш<br>Ti p**i**shuvash | You write -<br>Вие пиш**у**вате<br>Vie pish**u**vate |
| 3rd person | He/She/It writes -<br>Тој/Таа/Тоа п**и**шува<br>Toj/Taa/Toa p**i**shuva | They write -<br>Тие пиш**у**ваат<br>Tie pish**u**vaat |

| Past Simple Tense | | |
|---|---|---|
| *Person* | *Singular* | *Plural* |
| 1st person | I wrote -<br>Јас н**а**пишав<br>Jas n**a**pishav | We wrote -<br>Ние нап**и**шавме<br>Nie nap**i**shavme |
| 2nd person | You wrote -<br>Ти н**а**пиша<br>Ti n**a**pisha | You wrote -<br>Вие нап**и**шавте<br>Vie nap**i**shavte |
| 3rd person | He/She/It wrote -<br>Тој/Таа/Тоа н**а**пиша<br>Toj/Taa/Toa n**a**pisha | They wrote -<br>Тие нап**и**шаа<br>Tie nap**i**shaa |

| Past Continuous Tense | | |
|---|---|---|
| *Person* | *Singular* | *Plural* |
| 1st person | I was writing -<br>Јас п**и**шував<br>Jas p**i**shuvav | We were writing -<br>Ние пиш**у**вавме<br>Nie pish**u**vavme |
| 2nd person | You were writing -<br>Ти пиш**у**ваше<br>Ti pish**u**vashe | You were writing -<br>Вие пиш**у**вавте<br>Vie pish**u**vavte |
| 3rd person | He/She/It was writing -<br>Тој/Таа/Тоа пиш**у**ваше<br>Toj/Taa/Toa pish**u**vashe | They were writing -<br>Тие пиш**у**ваа<br>Tie pish**u**vaa |

| Present Perfect Simple Tense | | |
|---|---|---|
| *Person* | *Singular* | *Plural* |
| 1st person | I have written -<br>Јас сум н**а**пишал(а)<br>Jas sum n**a**pishal(a) | We have written -<br>Ние сме нап**и**шале<br>Nie sme nap**i**shale |
| 2nd person | You have written -<br>Ти си н**а**пишал(а)<br>Ti si n**a**pishal(a) | You have written -<br>Вие сте нап**и**шале<br>Vie ste nap**i**shale |

| | | |
|---|---|---|
| 3rd person | He/She/It has written -<br>Toj/Taa/Toa **на**пишал(а)(о)<br>Toj/Taa/Toa **na**pishal(a)(o) | They have written -<br>Тие нап**и**шале<br>Tie nap**i**shale |

| Present Perfect Continuous Tense | | |
|---|---|---|
| *Person* | *Singular* | *Plural* |
| 1st person | I have been writing -<br>Јас сум **пи**шувал(а)<br>Jas sum **pi**shuval(a) | We have been writing -<br>Ние сме пиш**у**вале<br>Nie sme pish**u**vale |
| 2nd person | You have been writing -<br>Ти си **пи**шувал(а)<br>Ti si **pi**shuval(a) | You have been writing -<br>Вие сте пиш**у**вале<br>Vie ste pish**u**vale |
| 3rd person | He/She/It has been writing -<br>Toj/Taa/Toa **пи**шувал(а)(о)<br>Toj/Taa/Toa **pi**shuval(a)(o) | They have been writing -<br>Тие пиш**у**вале<br>Tie pish**u**vale |

| Past Perfect Simple Tense | | |
|---|---|---|
| *Person* | *Singular* | *Plural* |
| 1st person | I had written -<br>Јас бев **на**пишал(а)<br>Jas bev **na**pishal(a) | We had written -<br>Ние бевме нап**и**шале<br>Nie bevme nap**i**shale |
| 2nd person | You had written -<br>Ти беше **на**пишал(а)<br>Ti beshe **na**pishal(a) | You had written -<br>Вие бевте нап**и**шале<br>Vie bevte nap**i**shale |
| 3rd person | He/She/It had written -<br>Toj/Taa/Toa беше<br>**на**пишал(а)(о)<br>Toj/Taa/Toa beshe **na**pishal(a)(o) | They had written -<br>Тие беа нап**и**шале<br>Tie bea nap**i**shale |

| Future Simple Tense | | |
|---|---|---|
| *Person* | *Singular* | *Plural* |
| 1st person | I will write -<br>Јас ќе **пи**шувам/**на**пишам<br>Jas kje **pi**shuvam/**na**pisham | We will write -<br>Ние ќе пиш**у**ваме/нап**и**шеме<br>Nie kje pish**u**vame/nap**i**sheme |
| 2nd person | You will write -<br>Ти ќе **пи**шуваш/**на**пишеш<br>Ti kje **pi**shuvash/**na**pishesh | You will write -<br>Вие ќе пиш**у**вате/нап**и**шете<br>Vie kje pish**u**vate/nap**i**shete |
| 3rd person | He/She/It will write -<br>Toj/Taa/Toa ќе **пи**шува/**на**пише<br>Toj/Taa/Toa kje **pi**shuva/**na**pishe | They will write -<br>Тие ќе пиш**у**ваат/**на**пишат<br>Tie kje pish**u**vaat/**na**pishat |

| used to + infinitive or would + infinitive | | |
|---|---|---|
| *Person* | *Singular* | *Plural* |
| 1st person | I would write -<br>Јас ќе **пи**шував/**на**пишев<br>Jas kje **pi**shuvav/**na**pishev | We would write -<br>Ние ќе пиш**у**вавме/нап**и**шевме<br>Nie kje pish**u**vavme/nap**i**shevme |

| | | |
|---|---|---|
| 2nd person | You would write -<br>Ти ќе пиш**у**ваше/нап**и**шеше<br>Ti kje pish**u**vashe/nap**i**sheshe | You would write -<br>Вие ќе пиш**у**вавте/нап**и**шевте<br>Vie kje pish**u**vavte/nap**i**shevte |
| 3rd person | He/She/It would write -<br>Тој/Таа/Тоа ќе<br>пиш**у**ваше/нап**и**шеше<br>Toj/Taa/Toa kje<br>pish**u**vashe/nap**i**sheshe | They would write -<br>Тие ќе пиш**у**ваа/нап**и**шеа<br>Tie kje pish**u**vaa/nap**i**shea |

| **Personal endings for future perfect-in-the-past tense** | | |
|---|---|---|
| *Person* | *Singular* | *Plural* |
| 1st person | I would have written -<br>Јас ќе сум п**и**шувал/н**а**пишал(а)<br>Jas kje sum p**i**shuval/n**a**pishal(a) | We would have written -<br>Ние ќе сме<br>пиш**у**вале/нап**и**шеле<br>Nie kje sme pish**u**vale/nap**i**shele |
| 2nd person | You would have written -<br>Ти ќе си п**и**шувал/н**а**пишал(а)<br>Jas kje sum p**i**shuval/n**a**pishal(a) | You would have written -<br>Вие ќе сте пиш**у**вале/нап**и**шеле<br>Vie kje ste pish**u**vale/nap**i**shele |
| 3rd person | He/She/It would have written -<br>Тој/Таа/Тоа ќе<br>п**и**шувал/н**а**пишал(а)(о)<br>Toj/Taa/Toa kje<br>p**i**shuval/n**a**pishal(a)(o) | They would have written -<br>Тие ќе пиш**у**вале/нап**и**шеле<br>Tie kje pish**u**vale/nap**i**shele |

www.ingramcontent.com/pod-product-compliance
Lightning Source LLC
Chambersburg PA
CBHW081226090426
42738CB00016B/3204
* 9 7 8 1 6 1 9 4 9 4 4 0 4 *